PROTEST AND POWER

PROTEST AND POWER

The Battle for the Labour Party

DAVID KOGAN

BLOOMSBURY READER
LONDON · OXFORD · NEW YORK · NEW DELHI · SYDNEY

BLOOMSBURY READER
Bloomsbury Publishing Plc
50 Bedford Square, London, WC1B 3DP, UK

BLOOMSBURY, BLOOMSBURY READER and the Diana logo are trademarks of
Bloomsbury Publishing Plc

First published in Great Britain in 2019 by Bloomsbury Reader
This edition published 2019

A catalogue record for this book is available from the British Library

Library of Congress Cataloguing-in-Publication data has been applied for

ISBN: HB: 978-1-4482-1728-1; eBook: 978-1-4482-1729-8

2 4 6 8 10 9 7 5 3 1

Typeset by Deanta Global Publishing Services, Chennai, India
Printed by CPI Group (UK) Ltd, Croydon, CR0 4YY

To find out more about our authors and books visit www.bloomsbury.com
and sign up for our newsletters

To my father Philip and my uncle Maurice, without whom neither book would have been written

Contents

Preface

In May 2015, Ed Miliband became the latest in a long line of Labour party leaders to lose a general election. Since 1945 only Clement Atlee, Harold Wilson and Tony Blair have won power from a sitting Conservative government and of the ten general elections since 1979, Labour has won only three, all under Blair. This record of failure, if applied to any other walk of life, would raise the fundamental question of why continue to fight a losing battle? For Labour, it asks whether it is a party of protest – designed to be only a voice from opposition, commenting on the flaws and falsities of Conservative policy – or a party of power?

I watched the 2015 general election results with two representatives of the Labour movement who exemplified the fractured history of the party; Jon Lansman, who had been a young activist and acolyte of Tony Benn in the brief period of New Left supremacy between 1978 and 1982, and David Triesman, who had been a trade unionist and then general secretary of the Labour party under Tony Blair. Both were committed Labour members, both lifelong anti-Tories, both tired of another Labour defeat and both completely at odds with one another about the past and future of the Labour party. Three months later, to the utter surprise of all three of us, Jon Lansman spearheaded the resurgence of the left with the election to the leadership of another Bennite veteran, Jeremy Corbyn, who in 2017 became the latest Labour party leader to lose a general election.

If the Conservative party is a modern version of the Borgias – far more powerful when united and vicious when not – then

Labour is *Game of Thrones*, with kingdoms constantly fighting it out for different moments of supremacy, to the greater cost of the throne. Different factions have held power within the Labour party at different times with the fundamental struggle always being between those wishing to take a reformist approach to the social and economic institutions of Britain and those who take a much more radical view of managing the economy and using the State to introduce change. These competing groups have seen Labour's pendulum swing from the centrist governments of the 1960s and 1970s, to the first manifestation of the New Left between 1978 and 1982, and back to the centre under New Labour in the 1990s. New Labour had thirteen years in government until 2010 when it was repudiated, first by the country and then by the party. In 2015 the left rose again, reincarnated by the veterans of the 1980s who used the new, powerful engine of social media to elect Jeremy Corbyn as leader. The left had won an unexpected second chance four decades after its last resurgence. This evolution has also been marked by the evolution of its own name. I've called it the 'New Left' in the 1970s to reflect its rise to prominence. After Tony Benn's run for the deputy leadership in 1981, this group started to refer to itself as the 'Bennite left'. Once it was cast into the wilderness in the 1980s, it became common usage to simply call it the 'left' and so it has remained until today.

This book seeks to chronicle the history of the Labour party since the late 1970s. It is both an account of high political drama and a cautionary tale. Labour today is a party of over 500,000 members; transformed since Corbyn's election, with 350,000 new members joining since 2015. The belief is that this huge growth in membership, driven by frustration with traditional Labour politics, means the party bears no resemblance to its 1979 incarnation; that its history is of no value in assessing its prospects in the future, and that everything is new. The opposite is true. The current leadership of the Labour party learned its politics in the 1970s and 1980s. In today's era of austerity, rage, social media, poverty and a Conservative government of moderate achievement, the left could realise its potential for victory and radical change. If it does, the veterans of those earlier campaigns will be in government.

In 1973, this all seemed impossible. The New Left's long march may have started as a general protest against the Labour leadership, but it led to the realisation that power could be won *boringly* by using the arcane nature of the Labour party rulebook to force a radical new idea; that policy could be made not just by the parliamentary leadership, but by its activist membership through what it termed 'Labour party democracy'. The rise of the New Left was founded on an attack on the previous eighty years of deference paid to the leadership of the party. It fought to ensure that the traditional bastions of authority – writing the manifesto, securing the election of members of parliament and the selection of the leader – should all be driven by the membership of the party outside parliament.

This was not just political theory, it was about power. It was rooted in the view that the more power was held by activist grassroots, the more the Labour party would move to the left. The more power could be devolved, the more the left could influence events. Why were these objectives so important and why have they lasted so long? In its search for power the left could not depend on the party leadership to support it. The plan had always been to take power from within the party structure and use it to drive policy, usually against the party leader's wishes. Only twice did the left think it might win: in 1981 when Tony Benn ran for the deputy leadership, and again in 2015 with Jeremy Corbyn's election as leader.

The lessons of 1978 to 1982 were never forgotten, but the opportunity to benefit from them only arose in 2014. Since then, the Labour party has changed and a new generation has taken the left to new heights that were unimaginable even in 2014, but nothing in Labour can ever be taken for granted. Tony Benn, Neil Kinnock, Tony Blair, Gordon Brown and Ed Miliband can all attest to that. This is a political party that may see power again, with a most unlikely group of activists from the 1970s becoming the fourth generation to win power since 1945. If so, the forty-year battle for the Labour party will have been won conclusively, and protest turned into power.

1981 INTERVIEWEES

Vladimir Derer, Roy Grantham, Andy Harris, Roy Hattersley, Jon Lansman, Ken Livingstone, Claer Lloyd-Jones, Frances Morrell, Chris Mullin, Giles Radice, Bill Rodgers, Laurie Sapper, Nigel Stanley, Shirley Williams, Nigel Williamson, Audrey Wise and Valerie Wise.

2018 INTERVIEWEES

The 2018 interview list is identified by the year they joined the Labour party. All interviews in the sections after 1982 were undertaken by me from June to December 2018.

Interviewee	Joined the Labour party
Neil Kinnock	1957
David Triesman	1963
Peter Mandelson	1969
Ray Collins	1970
John McDonnell	1972
Jon Lansman	1974
Tony Blair	1975
Paul Kenny	1975
Michael Cashman	1975
Alastair Campbell	1980
Pat McFadden	1984
Andy Burnham	1985
Manuel Cortes	1985
Stephen Kinnock	1985
Ed Miliband	1987
Lucy Powell	1989

Interviewee	Joined the Labour party
Anna Yearley	1993
Patrick Loughran	1993
Stewart Wood	1994
Jonathan Ashcroft	1994
Spencer Livermore	1994
Byron Taylor	1994
Eloise Todd	1995
Simon Fletcher	1997
Luciana Berger	2001
Emilie Oldknow	2001
Richard Angell	2002
Anneliese Midgley	2004
Ayesha Hazarika	2005
Max Lansman	2009
Rebecca Long-Bailey	2010
Max Shanly	2010
Michael Chessum	2012
Beth Foster-Ogg	2014
Laura Parker	2010 and 2015
Emma Rees	2015
Adam Klug	2015
Harry Hayball	2015
Rachel Godfrey Wood	2015
Zoe Williams	1988 and 2015

Abbreviations

AEIP	Another Europe is Possible
AGM	Annual General Meeting
AUEW	Amalgamated Engineering Union
AWL	Alliance for Workers' Liberty
BAME	Black, Asian and Minority Ethnic
BBC	British Broadcasting Corporation
BDS	Boycott, Divestment and Sanctions
CBI	Confederation of British Industry
CLP	Constituency Labour Party
CLV	Campaign for Labour Victory
CLPD	Campaign for Labour Party Democracy
DUP	Democratic Unionist Party
EEA	Europe Economic Area
EEC	European Economic Community
ERG	European Research Group
ERM	European Exchange Rate Mechanism
EU	European Union

FFS	For Our Future's Sake
GDP	Gross Domestic Product
GLA	Greater London Authority
GLC	Greater London Council
GMB	British Trade Union (originally General Municipal Boilermakers)
GRA	Grassroots Alliance
IHRA	International Holocaust Remembrance Alliance
ISIS	Islamic State of Iraq and the Levant
JLM	Jewish Labour Movement
LBC	London Broadcasting Company
LGBT	Lesbian, Gay, Bisexual, and Transgender
LOTO	Leader of the Opposition's Office
LPYS	Labour Party Young Socialists
MEP	Member of the European Parliament
MP	Member of Parliament
NACODS	National Association of Colliery Overmen, Deputies and Shotfirers
NAO	National Audit Office
NATO	North Atlantic Treaty Organization
NCC	National Constitutional Committee
NEC	National Executive Committee
NGO	Non-Governmental Organisation
NHS	National Health Service
NPF	National Policy Forum
NUM	National Union of Mineworkers

NUPE	National Union of Public Employees
OFCOM	Office of Communications
OFOC	Our Future Our Choice
OMOV	One Member One Vote
PFIs	Private Finance Initiatives
PFLP	Popular Front for the Liberation of Palestine
PLO	Palestine Liberation Organisation
PLP	Parliamentary Labour party
PMQs	Prime Minister's Questions
PPS	Private Parliamentary Secretaries
RFMC	Rank and File Mobilising Committee
SCA	Shadow Communications Agency
SDP	Social Democratic Party
SNP	Scottish National Party
TGWU	Transport and General Workers' Union
TSSA	Transport Salaried Staffs' Association
TUC	Trades Union Congress
TULO	Trade Unions and Labour Party Liaison Organisation
TWT	The World Transformed
UKIP	UK Independence Party
UN	United Nations
USDAW	Union of Shop, Distributive and Allied Workers
VAT	Value Added Tax
WA	Withdrawal Agreement
WMD	Weapons of Mass Destruction

PART ONE

Protest:
The Rise and Fall of the New Left

'We won against the National Executive Committee, the Transport and General Workers' Union, the parliamentary party and Michael Foot. We won against all the establishment figures'
Jon Lansman, 1981

I

Vladimir's Plan

The rise of Labour's New Left in the 1970s was a reflection of an era of economic upheaval and industrial unrest that drove seismic change in British politics. The decade began and ended with Conservative victories: in June 1970 when Edward Heath beat Harold Wilson's Labour government and in May 1979 when Margaret Thatcher pushed Labour into eighteen years of opposition. In the nine years between there was political turmoil affecting both major parties. Heath was elected on the basis of two controversial policies: to restrict the trade unions' power to strike and to get the UK into the European Economic Community (EEC). In 1971, following 11 million working days lost to strikes in 1970 and 13.5 million in 1971, he passed the Industrial Relations Act that sought to control union power through the courts. The same year, he sought to take the United Kingdom into the EEC causing then, as now, divisions in both major political parties. Labour's official position was to oppose entry but Roy Jenkins, its deputy leader, led sixty-nine Labour MPs into voting with the Conservatives to pass the bill. This was the first big split within Labour that would set the tone of internal conflict for the next decade.

Edward Heath's government existed for four years in a state of perpetual crisis. It faced two crippling strikes by the National Union of Mineworkers, first in 1972 and then again in late 1973, when a combination of the miners striking for a 40 per cent wage increase and a quadrupling of the price of oil after the Arab-Israel Yom Kippur War led to power cuts, a three-day working week and the declaration of a state of emergency. Heath called a general election in February 1974 in which he was defeated and Harold Wilson was returned as leader of a minority government and then re-elected in October with a tiny parliamentary majority of three seats over all other parties. In February 1975 Heath lost the leadership of his party to Margaret Thatcher, an insurgent from the Conservative's right wing who would be leader of the opposition for the next four years. In June Wilson called a referendum, Britain's first, on membership of the EEC. Roy Jenkins once again worked with the Conservative and Liberals to support the motion to remain but was opposed by two other Labour cabinet ministers, Tony Benn and Michael Foot, whose argument was that the EEC was primarily a mechanism to protect capitalism and gave Europe too much control over the British economy. This established the case against the EEC (and the EU) that has remained in some parts of the left ever since. Although out of office and replaced by Thatcher, Edward Heath saw his European dream fulfilled.

The referendum over Europe exposed fault lines within Labour that were to last through successive generations over the next forty years. On one wing of the party was the group led by Roy Jenkins, which was pro-European, socially liberal and globalist. He and his allies, David Owen, Shirley Williams and Bill Rodgers, took positions that would increasingly alienate them from the Labour party as the 1970s continued. They were the original 'big tent' at the centre of British politics, prepared to work with members of other parties when necessary. In 1981 they would run out of patience with Labour and leave to set up their own party, the Social Democratic Party (SDP).

Within the parliamentary Labour party (PLP) there was a second group that had been the core of Labour's government in the 1960s, comprised of James Callaghan, Denis Healey and Tony Crosland, together with the younger, up-and-coming generation in the 1970s of Roy Hattersley and John Smith. They were also pro-European, pro-NATO and pro-US, believers in traditional Labour social and economic values and solidly of the Labour movement. To their left was the Tribune group led in the 1960s by Michael Foot, Barbara Castle and Ian Mikardo, later joined by Neil Kinnock in the 1970s. Named after the *Tribune* newspaper, this group was closely aligned with the Campaign for Nuclear Disarmament and believed in redistributive economics driven by taxation and public spending. It operated as a rebellious group within the mainstream of Labour politics in parliament. In the 1960s Foot had refused a ministerial job under Harold Wilson, preferring to be the leader of the left from the backbenches. Neil Kinnock also refused a ministerial job under James Callaghan in the 1970s over Welsh devolution and public expenditure cuts.

The Tribune Group was radical, non-Marxist, but balanced between the centre and the New Left that emerged from 1970 with a more aggressive view of economic and industrial policy. Its public face was Tony Benn, who had moved from being a centrist, technophilic cabinet minister in the 1960s to being much more radical after Labour lost power in 1970. The New Left believed in widespread nationalisation, was anti-EEC, pro-trade union and workers' power, and advocated a 'new economic deal' with far more state control of the economy. Its power base was also different, rooted less in parliament than in the Labour party's constituency parties (CLPs), those groups of activists who ran local organisations devoted to electing local councillors and MPs and supported the party at general elections. The CLPs were both the bedrock of the party and mostly ignored by it. As foot soldiers of the Labour movement they had the right to elect representatives to the party's ruling body, The National Executive Committee (NEC), including representatives of the trade unions (the industrial wing of the movement), and leading members of the shadow cabinet. As the CLPs became more radicalised, they elected MPs such as Tony Benn and Eric Heffer to the constituency section of the NEC to represent politics that challenged the Labour leadership, despite the fact that Benn himself was a both a shadow cabinet and cabinet member in the 1970s.

Planning for a general election in 1973, the NEC launched a new industrial policy document: *Labour's Programme for Britain*, which included the proposal that a newly-elected Labour government would take stakes or fully nationalise the twenty-five leading manufacturing companies. Harold Wilson, whilst accepting some parts of the plan, publicly repudiated it as too extreme and would not commit a future Labour government to implementing it. One small group of activists thought that this decision should be challenged. The power of the party leader to amend policy from the ruling body of the party was accepted as normal behaviour at the time, but to Vladimir Derer, it was both undemocratic and a call for the left to organise. He and his wife Vera launched the Campaign for Labour Party Democracy (CLPD) from their house in 11 Park Drive, Golders Green, north London. An unlikely centre of radicalism, even in 1973.

Vladimir Derer had arrived in Britain as a Czech refugee in 1939 and, although a committed party activist, was unknown outside a small group of people within the party – but he knew how to organise. He was a genial father figure to the young activists who visited Park Drive looking for a cause. From 2015, Jon Lansman would play a similar (if less genial) role when setting up Momentum with another group of young activists. Vladimir Derer died in 2014, just before the election of a CLPD supporter, Jeremy Corbyn, to the leadership of the party. He had spent nearly fifty years working towards that moment. In Derer's own words at the time:

> In 1973 there was a demand for twenty-five companies to be taken into public ownership. When this was published in June 1973 Wilson said we can't do anything about it and unilaterally dismissed it . . . That produced a certain amount of resentment, fairly wide resentment, and that was when a number of us came together.

His unique contribution over the next ten years was to bring discipline and focus into the campaigns of the New Left. He realised that by using the internal processes of the Labour party, the New Left could win where years of arguing about the minutiae of state ownership and defence policy had failed. To achieve any of this would require power transferring from the leadership to the membership who would, in theory, elect better leaders and create new policy. This fit the mood of the times perfectly, as it fed on the rising level of division within the Labour movement as it faced severe economic challenges in government from February 1974. Harold Wilson initially allowed public spending to rise by a staggering 35 per cent in 1974-75 and a further 25 per cent the following year. Inflation rose to 25 per cent in 1975. In 1976 he resigned, and James Callaghan was elected by the PLP as leader and prime minister, with Michael Foot elected as his deputy. Denis Healey, the chancellor of the exchequer, imposed a cap on wage increases at £6 an hour. As Britain sweltered in the long, hot summer of 1976, the country was hit by repeated strikes and the National Union of Seamen declared a national strike against the £6 wage policy as the pound collapsed. By now, high street lending rates were at 16.5 per cent and mortgage rates at 12.5 per cent. Unemployment rose to 2 million.

At the Labour party conference in Blackpool in September 1976, Healey was allotted five minutes to defend his economic policy. The conference was set on the economic programme defined by Benn and the NEC, and voted through resolutions demanding a siege economy and nationalisation of key companies, including all four major banks. Healey instead announced that there would be cuts in public expenditure and a continuation of the £6 pay policy. He was loudly booed. Healey then approached the International Monetary Fund for a bailout package that would mean further cuts in public expenditure. This produced a three-way split in the Labour cabinet. Tony Benn advocated a siege economy; Tony Crosland argued for a full Keynesian economic policy of expenditure and reinvestment and challenged the Treasury's borrowing forecasts; Denis Healey advocated cuts to protect both market confidence and the pound.

By December Healey, with Callaghan's backing, had won. In a mini-budget on 15 December he announced cuts of £1 billion in 1977-78 and £1.5 billion in 1978-79. Afterwards it was discovered that the Treasury had got its sums wrong (Tony Crosland was right). Its forecasts assumed the need to borrow £11 billion, but never more than £8.5 billion was needed. This mistake and the actions it precipitated were to haunt the Labour party's reputation for economic competence for the next twenty years. The actions of the Labour government may have stopped economic collapse, but to constituency and trade union activists it was a repudiation of the socialist path.

Chris Mullin, a CLPD activist and journalist, later an editor of *Tribune* and even later a Labour MP and minister under Tony Blair, maintained there was:

> . . . a huge wave of disillusion and a haemorrhage of members out of the movement at the end of the 1960s. [The left] had hoped that the new policies upon which some of them had been working would be accepted when Harold Wilson returned to power in 1974. By early 1974 or 1975 it was quite clear that the same people who had led us to ruin between 1966 and 1970 were now about to behave in precisely the same way.

For the fledgling CLPD it was fertile ground. Although its initial aim focused solely on getting the election manifesto to reflect Labour party conference decisions, it moved to launch other campaigns to transfer power to the membership, including mandatory reselection and changing the election of the party leader. Mandatory reselection would make it obligatory for a CLP to judge its MP once in every parliament and gave the CLP the power to replace the MP with a different candidate. It was much more dramatic to remove MPs from power than to argue over the manifesto, and as two MPs – Dick Taverne in Lincoln and Reg Prentice in Newham North East – were in conflict with their constituency parties, CLPD focused campaigns around them.

Derer now had a tiny group of activists surrounding him. They were Victor Schonfield, Francis Prideaux, Pete Willsman, Andy Harris and his flatmate Jon Lansman, then a 25-year-old Cambridge graduate and semi-employed van driver. They did the routine work of keeping the machine running by lobbying individual delegates at party and union conferences and helping to produce CLPD leaflets. The group learned how to draft conference resolutions, lobby sympathetic MPs and trade union officials and galvanise support in CLPs. Willsman and Lansman were to become fixtures on the Labour left for the next forty years.

Jon Lansman is a recurring figure throughout this narrative. From joining CLPD whilst living on benefits as an unemployed graduate, he was to become one of the very few figures who would represent the continuity of the left in the Labour party. In the late 1970s he was forceful, articulate and unusually tactical, as he learned from Derer and the others how to mobilise support among CLPs, trade unionists and MPs who might not want to take him seriously. By the 1980s, he was the figure most closely identified with Tony Benn. From then, as with others such as Jeremy Corbyn and John McDonnell, he entered the wilderness years with no expectation of success. Why did he spend his life doing this? As Lansman said in 2018, he joined the Labour party rather than any other party because 'I was never a Trotskyist. I wanted to change the world. That's what drew me to the Labour party. I know it sounds corny.'

In the late 1970s it looked like CLPD had a chance. The group punched far above its weight, as no one before had used the power of lobbying and the archaic rules of the Labour party to drive such a focused agenda. Derer realised that if you could get the constituency parties to submit conference resolutions, friendly trade unions to use their block votes to pass them, and have your representatives on the NEC take a lead, you could change anything.

He drafted many conference resolutions designed for maximum impact and circulated them in the CLPD *Newsletter*. The tactic worked because:

> What was novel was circulating the resolution massively. We sent out to each constituency some twenty, twenty-five, thirty copies of *the Newsletter* asking the secretary to pass it on for discussion in the wards, and that's how we got on.

With the help of this guidance, twelve constituencies submitted resolutions on mandatory reselection in 1975, forty-five in 1976, seventy-nine in 1977 and sixty-seven in 1978.

After losing the battle against the IMF bailout package in cabinet in 1976, Tony Benn could depend on the NEC to push the New Left's agenda, but the only way to win votes was by winning trade union support. The union general secretaries, their use of the block vote to support the leadership and their fundamental conservatism had been a barrier to the left for years. If union power could be used to support campaigns for party democracy then CLPD stood a chance. There were dozens of small unions, each of whom had branches that could support a new campaign. In 1974, CLPD had no affiliated trade union branches. By 1977, thirty-nine branches were affiliated and by 1980, there were 161. Such varied unions as ACTT (the television technicians), ASTMS (the technical and managerial staff union). NATSOPA (the print union), The Amalgamated Society of Boilermakers, FTAT (the Furniture, Timber and Allied Trades Union) and the NGA (the National Graphical Association) all supported CLPD. None of these exist today in the era of mergers and super unions.

As its support slowly grew, so CLPD started to push its wider agenda. Mandatory reselection was raised for the first time at the 1974 Labour party conference, winning 2 million votes but failing overall, and under Labour rules the measure could not be reintroduced for three years. This attempt created the first split with the Tribune group of MPs, who regarded it as an attack on them as much as on the centre and right of the party. The Tribunite left saw CLPD first as an irritant and then as a threat, but its main differences were stylistic and ideological. Jon Lansman:

> The Tribune rally is in a big hall, you have people on the platform, you have long speeches. It is all very theatrical and all you have is names preaching at or to the masses. What the New Left is doing is actually ensuring that those policies are carried out. We are not just geared to preaching. It's all about being effective.

This clash of styles and ideologies between the centre-left in parliament and the New Left would become critical in the 1980s. In 1977 and 1978, the skirmishes between them were about very specific CLPD campaigns to challenge the leadership. Having obtained seventy-nine resolutions calling for mandatory reselection in 1977, CLPD pressured the NEC to look at a new campaign. The cabinet splits in 1976 had raised the issue of how to elect the leader of the party by means other than by MPs alone. Mandatory reselection and election of the leader were put on the agenda of the 1978 conference.

The challenge posed by CLPD had not gone unnoticed. In 1978 it faced the first big reaction from the leadership and trade union barons. Conference first voted to retain the PLP's right to elect the leader by a majority of nearly 4.5 million votes to one million; the combination of the PLP and trade union leadership was enough to push away the challenge. Labour was still in government, James Callaghan was still prime minister and there would be an election if not in 1978, then in 1979. Conference was not going to rock the boat.

On mandatory reselection, CLPD's motion had proposed that within the lifetime of any parliament, all MPs were to face reselection. It appeared that CLPD had the votes in the bag but for a late move by the engineering union (AUEW) in which it 'lost' one million votes. Not for the first or last time, the union block vote had been wielded to block change. There was outrage from the constituency delegates but the unions were not going to budge. They voted for what became known as the 'Mikardo Compromise'.

Only if a vote of no confidence was passed on a sitting member could a constituency party proceed to deselect and to consider other candidates. This would substantially reduce the likelihood of an MP being deselected. These defeats carried serious lessons for CLPD and for the future tactics of the New Left: don't accept victory in principle; secure it in practice. Don't depend on unions unless you get strong mandates *within* them. Focus on the winnable position. Don't depend on the Tribunites.

In 1979, the battles would have to be fought all over again but before the next conference, Labour's world fell apart and all the rules of engagement were rewritten.

2

The Years that Changed Everything

In September 1978, James Callaghan teased the Labour movement with a possible general election and then failed to call it. The public sector trade unions declared a series of strikes against Callaghan's pay cap in what was known as 'the winter of discontent' and in May 1979, Margaret Thatcher's Conservative party was elected to power.

The Callaghan government was exhausted, out of ideas and open to attack from both flanks. Labour had been the party of government for eleven of the previous fifteen years. Margaret Thatcher was seen as an unlikely choice for prime minster as her monetarist agenda was not only at odds with the prevailing political orthodoxy of both parties, it was thought to be unworkable. This was one of the moments that political orthodoxy failed to recognise the electorate's desire for change. The parallels with Gordon Brown thirty years later were strikingly similar when, after ten years as chancellor, he acceded to the top job, failed to call an election in 2007 and, after an economic crash, fell from grace, exhausted, after only three years in power.

No sooner had Callaghan lost office in May 1979 than the battle for the 1979 conference was set. For the first time in its history, CLPD was confident that all three of its constitutional campaigns: the election of the party leader, control over the manifesto, and the reselection of MPs, could be fought and won at conference as delegates maintained that the policies – the wage freeze in particular – were responsible for the electoral defeat, and that the Callaghan government had betrayed the movement.

In the ensuing years of conference micro-management, it is difficult to recall the frenzy and drama of conferences that were not foregone conclusions. The smoke-filled rooms, long nights of drinking and general mayhem of the period are no more. On arrival at conference, delegates and visitors were bombarded with pieces of paper and approached by groups of contending lobbyists seeking to make their case. The Labour leadership was under constant attack. Leaders of the party who only a few months before had been cabinet ministers were accused of betraying the principles of the movement. The demonisation of the 1970s Labour government and of the New Labour government after it fell from power in 2010 is much alike. In 1979 and again in 2010, the New Left had to justify a new path by establishing a rhetoric of failure and lost opportunity. This also fuelled the need for constitutional change in 1979.

The 1979 conference opened by addressing control of the manifesto. For the first time, it was to consider the transfer of control over the party manifesto from the leader of the party to the NEC. Although the resolution passed by 800,000 votes, the NEC debated the issue and decided, by one vote, that it would defer the final decision to 1980. By all accounts, the key vote was cast by the Tribunite Neil Kinnock. Jon Lansman:

> Possibly only one of the crucial votes, but certainly one of those in favour of withdrawing, was that of Neil Kinnock. In many ways, Neil Kinnock can be held responsible for the fact that the NEC does not have ultimate control for drafting the manifesto: that is a significant crime.

This wouldn't be the last time the two would be in conflict. It further exacerbated the split between the Tribunite left and the New Left.

Conference then focused on how the leader should be appointed. Taking the unique power to select the leader from the PLP to the membership was at the heart of the CLPD agenda. It originally proposed that conference should elect the leader, but now made the tactical decision to support an electoral college with three components; the PLP, the CLPs and the unions. Jon Lansman:

> We changed our position from election of leader by conference to that of the electoral college because the former was unwinnable. Our decision on the electoral college was entirely tactical. we had to take into account the views of the trade unions.

Thus, the concept of the electoral college was born. A purely tactical move designed to gain maximum support. Like the manifesto, this was deferred to the 1980 conference. Two deferred, one to go and in this case, victory. After the chaos the previous year, the NEC returned to mandatory reselection. This time, no votes were lost. The resolution was carried by four million votes to three million. After a campaign lasting six years CLPD had triumphed. As Vladimir Derer reported to the 1980 AGM (Annual General Meeting) of CLPD:

> For CLPD, 1979 was a breakthrough year. After years of intensive campaigning on the reselection issue, the constitutional amendments sponsored by CLPD and submitted in 1979 by twenty CLPs were finally approved by annual conference.

If nothing else, CLPD had proved that its tactics could win. This wasn't just down to Vladimir Derer's drafting, or CLPD's lobbying and pressure. It was also due to the failure of others to respond to the CLPD threat. The right of the Labour party was divided and uncertain.

The centre-left and centre-right in the PLP had never been able to agree on tactics or a unified position. They were split on whether to fight against the New Left or quit Labour and start a new party. Of course, the problem was that the fight was not really in the PLP. The battlefield had been moved to the constituencies by CLPD and the trade union branches where the traditional right had no organisation. One group set up to fight the left was the Campaign for Labour Victory (CLV) but its potential to challenge was never fully utilised. As Roy Hattersley, a moderate former cabinet member and soon to be deputy leader of the party, put it:

> The Campaign for Labour Victory was disastrous and an awfully elitist organisation. It sent out messages to its few contacts saying what its policy was. [Its] failure was threefold: it was London-based, a leadership organisation, had the Common Market obsession and also had a lot of personality problems.

In parliament, leading members of the Labour frontbench were also divided in considering whether to fight or to leave to set up a new party. The first signs of a split had been over membership of the common market, but the attacks on the primacy of the PLP now took centre stage. The centre-right was completely divided as to how to counter it. There was no unified leadership or tactical organisation, but CLPD was winning the argument and something had to be done. The NEC decided on a time-honoured tactic to address the issue; it established a Commission of Enquiry under union leader David Basnett, to determine what to do on the constitutional issues facing the conference in 1980. Both the left and right lobbied it intensively, knowing it could swing future decisions either way.

One tactic was to accuse CLPD of being a Trotskyist organisation devoted to destroying the Labour party. This didn't work since Derer, Lansman and the CLPD campaigners were not Trotskyists, they were all were long-standing members of Labour left. It was a blanket accusation that carried little potency while real Trotskyist groups, such as the Militant Tendency, were not involved in CLPD's campaigns. As Derer was drafting carefully worded and pragmatic motions aimed at gathering the widest possible support, leaders of Militant submitted far more radical proposals that few supported, but which reinforced its own image. Militant was an openly Trotskyist organisation devoted to joining the Labour party as a vehicle for its strategy of permanent class war. It was infamous for never working within other organisations and for being totally devoted to its own closed agenda.

CLPD now made a major tactical decision, recognising that it could not do all this on its own. The normal faction fighting on the left needed to be put aside to broaden its range of operations, so it formed an alliance with other groups in a new organisation – the Rank and File Mobilising Committee (RFMC) to fight for the constitutional changes. It took the decision to include the Militant Tendency and the Labour Party Young Socialists (LPYS), a group dominated by Militant. By allying with Militant, CLPD was taking a risk. Roy Hattersley pointed to this at the time, identifying CLPD and RFMC as the true enemy.

The problem is not Militant, about whom we always talk, because Militant is so easily identifiable and so unpleasant that most people are prepared to squash it. The problem is those organisations which talk in the language of democratic socialism.

When the Commission of Inquiry reported its findings in June, it recommended both the mandatory reselection of MPs and the creation of an electoral college. For the first time, MPs would not be the only group voting for the party leader. It stunned James Callaghan and the Labour right. The Commission tried to mitigate its ruling by proposing MPs would have the largest proportion of the College: 50 per cent for MPs, 25 per cent for trade unions, 20 per cent for constituency parties and 5 per cent for socialist societies. This still was a huge win for CLPD. The principle of the electoral college was now affirmed. The Commission of Inquiry also considered the manifesto and recommended that it should not be written by the party leader but drafted by the NEC and endorsed by the electoral college. An idea that had not been advocated by either the left or right of the party.

There were now only a few months to lobby support for the shape
of the electoral college before the 1980 conference in Blackpool.
It was unclear whether the power of MPs within the electoral
college would be upheld or whether something could be created
that gave the natural supporters of the New Left – constituencies
and unions branches – the majority of the votes. Everything would
depend on mobilising CLP and union branches to support one
clear, unified position.

At the same time, the right of the party was beginning to make
its own plans. Roy Jenkins had left Britain to become the president
of the European commission in 1977 but the frustration with
losing power in 1979 and being challenged from the New Left
was exasperating his remaining allies in the shadow cabinet. On
1 August 1980, the three former senior cabinet ministers, David
Owen, Shirley Williams and William Rodgers, published a letter
in the *Guardian* declaring their belief in policies almost wholly
contradictory to the general trend of constituency opinion. This
3000-word statement suggested that a new party might have to
emerge. However, the centre and right were divided between those
led by the 'Gang of Three', as Owen, Williams and Rodgers became
known, who believed the party had changed forever and that it was
better to consider quitting Labour, and those who were prepared to
fight it out at conference.

The 1980 Blackpool conference dominated Labour politicians'
thinking for future generations. For the left, it was a highpoint
of victory not to be repeated until 2015. For future Labour
leaderships, it was a textbook example of everything to be avoided.
The unpredictability of events in the hothouse environment of a
conference has rarely been repeated, as different generations of
leadership remembered the loss of control and sought to avoid it.

The Labour leader, James Callaghan, reacted to what he perceived
to be the mood of the conference with a hint of defiance. He talked
about the disaster of the new Thatcherite government, the global
economic climate and the internal fight over the constitutional
issues. The one issue he identified was control of the manifesto;

exactly the issue that had led to the creation of CLPD seven years earlier.

> As for the PLP, the one thing to which it is bound under the constitution is the election manifesto because the parliamentary party has to carry it out . . . and why the National Executive (and I say it in all good comradeship) are wrong to try to assume sole responsibility for the preparation of the manifesto.

In contrast, Tony Benn gave a speech in which he put forward the notion that one thousand Labour peers would be created to abolish the Lords and its apparent veto right to stop a future Labour government carrying out its programme. In his diary, he predicted that Callaghan would go as leader in the next few weeks.

At conference, frenetic lobbying took place both in public and in private. First up was mandatory reselection, which was challenged again but approved. CLPD's victory from 1979 was allowed to stand. The NEC amendment to the party constitution, which would have given it the power to draft the manifesto, was lost again by the narrow margin of 117,000 votes. Callaghan's speech had worked. It was one victory and one defeat. Next, conference came to consider the procedures for electing the party leadership. The motion for establishing an electoral college was carried by a tiny margin of 98,000 votes. The principle for an electoral college was finally agreed. Tony Benn described it as 'a most thrilling day'.

Conference then proceeded to vote down, with virtually no debate, two possible versions of the electoral college. The first would have given the trade unions 50 per cent of the vote with the PLP and the constituencies 25 per cent each. The second would have given each group an equal third of the votes; 33 per cent each. Conference adjourned and agreed to resume the vote the following afternoon. During this lull in the public action, the private lobbying became frenzied, and the impact of CLPD became a critical factor.

At 6 p.m. that Wednesday night, an NEC meeting told its officers to return with a new set of proposals to be put to conference on

Thursday afternoon. At 11 p.m. a caucus meeting of left supporters on the NEC, including Tony Benn and Dennis Skinner, opted for 40 per cent of the vote for the parliamentary party, adjourned and set off to get some sleep before the 8 a.m. meeting of the NEC the next day. A group of CLPD activists including Jon Lansman and Frances Morrell were not happy.

> We had all gone from the conference to the Imperial which was at the other end of Blackpool and we hung around the bar all evening. We decided that the best thing to do was to go for a compromise, 40 per cent for the trade unions. However, the left caucus that night decided that they would go for 40 per cent for the PLP. A lot of us thought that was absolutely crazy. In particular, there were four people . . . [who] thought the NEC left had completely lost its nerve and given up far too much to the PLP.

Frances Morrell visited Tony Benn at 1.45 a.m. who was, as he reported in his diary, in his underwear in his hotel room. She asked Benn to support the proposal of an electoral college in which the trade unions held 40 per cent of the votes and to help overturn the caucus decision. He commented that 'I suppose you are right, but isn't it late now?' Undeterred, the four activists agreed to lobby the rest. They were only able to find Jo Richardson, and so abandoned the search until the following morning. They were up at 7.00 a.m. and back at the Imperial Hotel. Jon Lansman was supposed to be 'gunning for Dennis Skinner' who refused on principle to stay at the Imperial, preferring a boarding house nearby. Lansman takes up the story:

> I went out to the toilets and found Dennis Skinner, having just washed his face, combing his hair in front of the mirror. I started talking to him. All of a sudden in walks Chris Mullin doing precisely the same thing, completely independently on his own initiative. And we managed to persuade Dennis Skinner, whose attitude was, well I'd certainly go along with you. We spoke to

all the left NEC members and persuaded them that that the proposal was what they were going to go for and put to the conference. The NEC then proposed what we had suggested to them, namely forty/thirty/thirty. So we got what we wanted on that day.

Benn's description of the same event:

The National Executive met at eight and it was clear that Frances, Vladimir, Jon Lansman, Victor Schonfield and Francis Prideaux had bullied members of the executive into agreeing the new CLPD alternative. We kicked this around for a bit and eventually it was carried thirteen to seven which was excellent.

In a turnaround that could never happen after the 1980s, when far greater control was exerted on party conferences, a group of virtually unknown activists persuaded the NEC to adopt a particular solution that no one had supported the previous day. It reversed the idea that MPs would be the largest group voting for a leader and future prime minister if Labour was to be elected in the future. What made this even more unlikely was that the right on the NEC could have prevented forty/thirty/thirty but failed to act against it. Shirley Williams accounted for this in 1981 after she had left the Labour party to create the SDP. The right of the NEC had been outgunned for the last three years because its power base had always rested on union representatives countering the New Left.

. . . we were hampered by the fact that we still often had to spend hours on the phone rather than in meetings and very often we had to explain to people who themselves were to some extent bound by decisions made by their unions — not left-wing decisions, but decisions made in ignorance of what was the latest move. They were much slower in moving.

On this particular day it was too late and the fight was going out of them.

There was an early morning breakfast meeting and two or three people were missing . . . There were mixed feelings on the right: there were those of us who felt we had to fight it and there were those who felt it was so dreadful at the conference and therefore took the view that it was better to let the worst outcome go forward because it couldn't be carried as it reduced the PLP to a ludicrous situation. People like me, although we voted against it, had lost all interest because I wasn't interested in what happened to the electoral college. As far as I was concerned the whole principle was wrong so we didn't fight on that one. We didn't organise very much. Our view was that they had made their bed, now they can get out of it.

Jim Callaghan stated that if this were implemented he would resign and recommend to the PLP that it elect a leader under the old rules. A crisis was building.

That afternoon, conference met again. The NEC put forward a resolution proposing the forty/thirty/thirty proposal, but unexpected opposition arose from some of the trade union leaders who maintained that they had not had time to consult their members and successfully proposed a resolution postponing the decision for three months. The issue was deferred until a special conference at Wembley in January 1981.

In contrast to the optimism and coherence of the left, the right wing retired from Blackpool in disarray. It had failed to stem the left-wing campaign on all but control over the manifesto, and had no clear or concerted policies on the other key issues concerning the party constitution. As Roy Hattersley put it at the time:

For some reason I can't explain . . . my half of the party is always in a mood to accept defeats . . . and to lie down under them.

Hattersley and those with whom he worked within the PLP, remained opposed to the concept of an electoral college. They therefore took a leaf out of CLPD's book and provided a model constitutional amendment, providing for the party leader to be elected by secret postal ballot of all party members. The election would take place on an electoral roll of party members of at least one year's standing. Significantly, nominations would be restricted to Labour MPs who could secure the support of 10 per cent of the PLP for their nomination. There would be, in effect, a prior electoral screening by the PLP for the leadership.

To anyone who watched the leadership election rules created under the Collins Report in 2014, this document written thirty-four years earlier is almost exactly the proposal that eventually led to the election of Jeremy Corbyn in 2015. The right's long-term support for one member one vote (OMOV) was going to be a recurring theme for the next forty years. Those members of the right who did accept the principle of the electoral college were divided about the proportions that should be adopted. The engineering union, AUEW, under Terry Duffy wanted the PLP to have an absolute majority, not less than 51 per cent, of the electoral college votes. This principle of 51 per cent was not to be deviated from under any circumstances. Others, such as David Basnett proposed 50 per cent. For CLPD, the key issues were to get forty/thirty/thirty, but also to make sure that the voting for leader and deputy leader would be annual and transparent. As Vladimir Derer explained:

> We said to the NEC, through our sympathisers, we obviously want you to go for our proportions, but we have a difficult conference coming up. We want the procedures to be right. Two key points were incorporated: annual election and recorded voting. Absolutely fundamentally important.

The NEC rejected CLPD's suggestion that it should support forty/thirty/thirty and recommended that votes in the college should be divided equally between trade unions, CLPs and the PLP thirty-three/thirty-three/thirty-three per cent each.

With three months to the special conference at Wembley, the campaign began in earnest to encourage a trade union to support CLPD's position and swing as much support behind it to become the favoured option of the left. The RFMC decided to fight for this rather than support the NEC's recommendation of 33/33/33. Finally, the Union of Shop, Distributive and Allied Workers (USDAW) agreed to put forward a motion for forty/thirty/thirty. Then it all got thrown into the air. Jim Callaghan carried out his threat to resign as party leader. No electoral college had yet been agreed, so the old method of election by the PLP still stood. This was clearly a device to get Denis Healey elected leader prior to the electoral college being established. Should Tony Benn, who like Healey had stood in the previous leadership election in 1976, stand in this 'illegitimate' election three months before the establishment of a new method for which he and the left had fought so hard? The Tribunite deputy leader, Michael Foot, had yet to express any interest in fighting the election. Healey would be a formidable opponent who could unite the unions and the main body of the parliamentary party against the left. There needed to be a strong candidate to oppose him.

Two days after Callaghan's resignation, a meeting was held in Tony Benn's house attended by Vladimir Derer, Victor Schonfield, Stuart Holland, Audrey Wise, Ken Coates, Jo Richardson, Norman Atkinson, Chris Mullin, Reg Race, Frances Morrell, Benn's two sons and Martin Flannery. Nine of them spoke against him standing and two in favour. Benn wanted to stand, but eventually deferred to the majority view. It was agreed that they would settle for Foot as the candidate who would give them the least trouble and stand the most chance of beating Healey. However, the decision by the PLP to appoint a leader and not a caretaker meant that the legitimacy of the decision had to be challenged. CLPD proclaimed in a leaflet in October that:

> The shadow cabinet has thrown down the gauntlet. They are banking on the hope that the Labour movement will not have time to challenge the hurried election they are arranging in defiance of conference decisions. Afterwards, when they have installed their nominee, they will demand for the sake of 'unity' that no one should challenge him even though he was installed

by a coup . . . The claim by some MPs that they have to have an
election is a fake.

In 1980, Michael Foot was the 67-year-old lion of the Tribune
left who had been an outstanding backbencher, a former editor
of the *Tribune* newspaper and a cabinet minister under Wilson
in 1974 and then Callaghan in 1976. He decided to stand as the
one candidate who might beat Healey. Some MPs were pressed
by their constituency Labour parties to support him. Many MPs
from the centre and some on the right were prepared to support
him because they feared that Healey would further divide the
party. Some supported Foot to make things worse before setting
up the SDP. Indeed, four defecting MPs later admitted they voted
for Foot as a deliberate act of sabotage. Either way, this support
was sufficient for Foot to win the final ballot by ten votes. The
precedent was set for a leader elected by different factions without
necessarily commanding overall support of the party he was
leading. This was seen again in 2010 with Ed Miliband's election
as leader. In both cases, it was the left finding a candidate in order
to stop someone else gaining power. Healey was elected unopposed
as deputy leader.

With Foot installed as leader, left and right began to prepare for
the anticipated struggle at the conference on the electoral college.
It was widely expected that David Owen, William Rodgers and
Shirley Williams would soon leave the party. This was compounded
by the right lacking an effective organisation. Its leading members
failed to counter-attack or to unify around a single set of proposals.
As the Wembley conference approached, intensive lobbying from
CLPD and the other left groups resulted in a clear split between
their position and that of the NEC. CLPD's figures showed that
its formula of forty/thirty/thirty was supported by just under one
million potential voters, whereas the NEC's proposal had the
support of more than 2 million.

On the other side of the political divide, the Campaign for
Labour Victory and right-wing Labour MPs were far less active
and relatively muted. The CLV put out a special conference edition

of its newspaper, *Labour Victory*, that outlined the arguments for one member one vote, but it did not give a detailed analysis of conference strategy, provide model resolutions or even indicate that it was preparing to fight changes with which it clearly disagreed. This edition of *Labour Victory* gave the reader the impression that the CLV and leading figures in it such as David Owen, who wrote an article in the journal, had almost given up the fight.

On the first vote at conference there was an overwhelming majority for the electoral college, with six million votes. The proposed postal ballot of all members received just over 400,000 votes. The right-wing was thus demolished on this issue. The electoral college was set in stone.

Conference then moved to discussion of its composition. This unleashed a series of proposals from different factions. The two from the left were either USDAW's forty/thirty/thirty or the NEC's thirty-three/thirty-three/thirty-three. Both of these removed the parliamentary party from having the biggest say in choosing the leader. The alternative proposal from the centre was for MPs to have 50 per cent and 25 per cent would go to trade unions and CLPs each. The last proposal from the right was from the AUEW and it was that MPs should have 75 per cent, trade unions and CLPs 10 per cent each, and socialist societies 5 per cent. Crucially its president, Terry Duffy, made it clear that if this failed his union would not support any motion giving MPs less than 51 per cent. It was going to be very tight.

The results of the first ballot created havoc. The NEC amendment and the left's proposal both received exactly the same vote, 1,763,000, and were tied behind Basnett's proposal of 50 per cent for the PLP. The AUEW proposal had little support. Basnett's proposal still led the second vote with 2,685,000 votes or 42 per cent of the total conference vote. After intense lobbying the proposal favoured by the New Left received nearly 29 per cent of the vote – a mere 50,000 votes ahead of the NEC's proposal on 28 per cent. The NEC proposal fell, leaving the issue to be decided between explicitly left and right-wing proposals. In the third vote, the AUEW's decision caused the right to lose. It refused to support the Basnett solution because it was not prepared to support any motion giving less than 51 per cent to the PLP. It was only this abstention that allowed the left to win as it had failed to swing all of those who had previously supported the NEC to support it. It was the most unlikely victory based on a series of bad tactical decisions and lack of comprehension of the right. No one had expected it to happen. Jon Lansman:

> The left won against the National Executive Committee, the Transport and General Workers' Union, the parliamentary party and Michael Foot. We won against all the establishment figures. The only reason we won was because the AUEW did not vote against us.

As Wembley reached a crescendo Michael Foot expressed his dismay:

> I cannot pretend to you that absolutely all the results this afternoon were the ones I wanted. I believe that very often the rights and duties and the performance of the parliamentary Labour party are quite improperly derided in our movement.

Tony Benn recorded in his diary that night Saturday, 24 January 1981:

> It was an absolutely astonishing result . . . the product of ten years of work . . . We have lost the manifesto fight, but we have won the battles over the leadership election and mandatory reselection and this has been a historic, an enormous change, because the PLP, which has been the great centre of power in British politics, has had to yield to the movement that put Members there.

The conference closed with 'The Red Flag' and three cheers for international socialism. The historic significance of the Blackpool and Wembley conferences was enormous. From 1981, the unique power of MPs to select their leader was removed. As remarkable was that the electoral college lasted until 2015. No one would have predicted that in 1981. In eight years, CLPD had succeeded in getting mandatory reselection and a new method of electing the leader. It used techniques of composite motions, conference lobbying, tactical skill and its own total commitment by a few activists. It appeared that the New Left could do anything. The Labour party had swung in a completely new direction.

Yet it could just as easily not have happened, and these victories disguised some serious problems. If the right had been more organised, it could have blocked the changes at a number of crucial moments. The division on the moderate and right wings between those who wanted to leave the party and those who were prepared to stay and fight the constitutional changes caused a lack of tactical awareness. At the same time, despite its power in the CLPs and membership, the New Left had only won by exerting its *influence* rather than power. Whoever controlled the leadership and the structures of the party would always win in the end. The left had one last big campaign to go, but its opponents were also realising that a fight was on. The next two years were to take the battle to a new level but contained the seeds of its downward slide. The only way to lock in changes for the long term was to try to control the party through the NEC, the leadership and the conference. This was the battle ahead and now both sides knew it.

3

The High-Water Mark: The Benn Campaign and its Aftermath

The 1981 Wembley conference may have made historic changes to the constitution of the Labour party, but it also helped to precipitate a new party. The day after the conference, the Gang of Three, augmented to four by Roy Jenkins, met at David Owen's house in Limehouse, London. They declared their intention to leave the Labour party and set up a Council for Social Democracy that two months later would become the Social Democratic Party. Labour MPs began to defect to it.

Of those centrist MPs who remained in the party, no one had expected the Wembley conference to decide on proportions of forty/thirty/thirty. One hundred and fifty MPs signed a statement in the following week opposing the conference decision. As a result of this initiative, the Labour Solidarity campaign was born. Roy Hattersley:

> We know what we are fighting in 1982, '83 and '84 as our opponents knew in 1972, '73, and '74 . . . the people who set (Solidarity) up in parliament were doing their best to push it out into the constituencies and going around begging the constituencies to set up organisations and contacts.

In fact, Solidarity was less successful in building up support in the constituencies than with the trade union leaders. Over the next eighteen months, this became the critical tactic to halt the advance of the New Left. Attention started to switch from constitutional change to a much more direct fight over the deputy leadership. This role was then, and always has been, one of almost total inconsequence. After their election, deputy leaders serve at the behest and pleasure of the leader in whatever role is deemed relevant. It would be a good pub quiz test for Labour activists to name every deputy leader of the party since 1945. Very few step up to being leader (Michael Foot is the last one to have done so on a permanent basis) and they vary enormously in terms of influence.

So why, in 1981, did this become the most hotly contested election until the leadership election in 2010? Denis Healey had become deputy to Foot under PLP rules in 1980, but the creation of the electoral college and the annual re-election rule allowed a shot for the left at the 1981 conference. It was not worth challenging Foot, but Healey was fair game and there was a strategic reason to mount any sort of challenge, as Lansman explained:

> There was a general feeling that Healey should not go unchallenged because he had been elected unopposed the previous November. There was a widespread feeling in CLPD circles that one of the most important things was for the electoral college to be used. Immediately after Wembley, which we were bloody lucky to have won, we had a big job to do to actually save the decision. One of the best ways was to test [the electoral college] because we completely shifted the front that we were fighting on. The right would be far more interested in stopping Benn than changing the proportions in a college. It is a big job to get people interested in constitutional changes; it is a much bigger job for the right than for the left because the right doesn't have activists on the ground, they don't have active support.

This was an early sign of the tactical thinking applied to preserve one area of the left's victory. It was also the same logic used to try and put up left candidates in what appeared to be hopeless causes in 2007, 2010 and 2015 – to activate the base and show impact. Winning was a secondary, unlikely consideration.

Throughout the weeks that followed the special conference, repeated attempts were made by Michael Foot and the trade unions' leadership to stop Benn from running against Healey. During Benn's campaign, Foot publicly urged him not to stand or, if he must contest an election, to stand against Foot himself for the leadership. Benn refused to do this on the grounds that he did not oppose Michael Foot as leader; it was Denis Healey and his views that Benn wished to oppose. For Foot, the impact of the Social Democrats was beginning to be felt in opinion polls at a time when the Thatcher government was also failing.

Polling data on 24 January 1981, the day of the special conference, showed Labour to be 10 per cent ahead of the Conservatives at 45 per cent to 35 per cent. The SDP were on 17 per cent. By July the Liberals and SDP had created an Alliance that was neck and neck with both other parties. The external threat was real but when Benn held a meeting at his house on Sunday 29 March with the core group of the New Left, it was a unanimous decision for him to stand as deputy leader. The following day, 1 April, he told Foot and then publicly announced his candidacy.

Denis Healey had, up to this point, kept out of the fray. After the 1980 conference, at which the electoral college was accepted in principle, he refused to join the Gang of Three. He was a politician of the old school who preferred dining with trade union general secretaries and other leading figures in the Labour movement, in the hope that they would control the votes of their members. However, he was also a lifelong member of the Labour party and was prepared to accept being deputy to Foot rather than defecting to the SDP. Solidarity now became an election machine for Healey and in one sense, the right had fallen for the left's ploy. By concentrating all of its resources on getting Denis Healey elected rather than challenging the composition of the electoral college, the right accepted the existence and legitimacy of the electoral college. There was one other candidate for the deputy leadership from the

Tribune wing – John Silkin – who was not expected to win but could, in an electoral college, take votes from the front runners and see those votes either redistributed or withheld to influence the final outcome.

The RFMC became the prime agency of Benn's campaign. Immediately after Wembley, Jon Lansman wrote 'The Future of the Rank and File Mobilising Committee' describing its achievements in coordinating efforts between the different groups by demonstrating 'the potential strength of left unity in the face of concerted right opposition', and by serving as a forum of discussion between the left groups which otherwise would not have taken place. The emphasis placed by the RFMC on activity at trade union conferences was a new feature of the Benn election campaign. For the first time, senior politicians were rushing to small seaside towns in an effort to convert the vital few thousand votes of each of the minor unions into a substantial proportion of the electoral college. The campaign was one of trade union politicisation. It also reached out to other organisations outside the Labour party such as CND. By the end of it, even Denis Healey was trying to emulate this new presidential election style. Benn forced Healey to define his own political position, which in turn allowed him to argue that Healey's political convictions were out of line with stated conference policy.

Numerous meetings were held throughout the country, even when Benn was ill and absent having been diagnosed with the debilitating Guillain-Barré Syndrome in June. Despite this, he returned to full campaigning in September 1981 with nineteen speaking engagements including six radio and television broadcasts, from 3 to 26 September. The electoral college had forced campaigning into the open with such slim margins of victory that every vote counted. This campaign became the model for all successive leadership and deputy election campaigns. It also marked the final split between the Tribune left and the Bennite left (as it had become known), when Benn had refused to tell the Tribune Group in advance of his decision to stand. John Silkin stood as a Tribune candidate against him.

It was now that Neil Kinnock came to the fore. He had been elected MP in 1970 as a 28-year-old from South Wales firmly in the tradition of the mining communities of the area. In the eleven years he had spent in parliament he had won a reputation as an energetic, if prolix, speaker and leader of the Tribune Group under his mentor, Michael Foot. Unlike Tony Benn, Kinnock had refused to join the Callaghan government and campaigned against its cuts to public spending. After the 1979 general election he finally agreed to be on the frontbench as shadow education spokesman and was a clear potential candidate for the leadership of the party if Foot was to go. Once John Silkin announced his candidature for deputy leader, Kinnock led a group of MPs who decided, after voting for Silkin on the first ballot, that on a second vote they would abstain rather than vote for Benn. CLPD victories over mandatory reselection, its combination with Militant within the RFMC, the aggressive style of campaigning for Benn and Kinnock's support for Foot had all come to a head.

Whilst Benn's candidature had the support of 83 per cent of the CLPs and had footholds in the trade union movement, his tactics were based increasingly on attendance of mass meetings and exposure to publicity. However, the nature of the electoral college meant that tactical voting was important and could change a result on successive ballots. The media was also seen as being a vital component to influencing uncommitted delegates and its impact was seen in an attack on Jon Lansman a week before the election. Although he was an active member of CLPD and the RMFC, Lansman was scarcely known outside these groups. He suddenly shot to prominence on the Sunday before the deputy leadership election when Denis Healey wrongly identified him as the man who had orchestrated heckling at two Labour party meetings in September, in Cardiff and Birmingham. By this stage in the campaign, Healey and Benn were running neck and neck. Healey clearly believed that by naming a prominent member of the Benn campaign he would discredit both Benn and his supporters. In fact, Lansman was on holiday in Spain at the time of the Cardiff meeting and was travelling to Aberystwyth during the Birmingham meeting. For the following two days he was followed and questioned by reporters and, when his denial was publicised, it became clear that Healey had made a mistake. It changed the tone of the last week.

The Healey campaign alleged that Benn supporters were undemocratic and thuggish. The Benn campaign retorted that Healey was running a smear campaign based on incorrect evidence. Solidarity was beginning to meet with success by some general secretaries using their power to organise block votes behind Healey. Both sides, in entirely different ways, were beginning to feel their strength. The politicisation of the unions and the stimulation of CLP activity had awakened politicisation on the right.

The opening evening of the Brighton conference presented the sight of Labour's first electoral college sitting down to vote. It did so in a packed conference hall and in the view of a large television audience. For the first time in the party's history, Labour MPs were drawn out of the Palace of Westminster to participate in the election of a deputy party leader. MPs occupied a central block of the conference hall. In the front of the hall there were the trade unions, governing 40 per cent of the votes, and the constituency Labour parties holding 30 per cent of the vote. The press had made an obsessive analysis of the prospects of the three candidates. Particular attention had been paid to the trade unions on how delegates should cast their votes. The Transport and General Workers' Union (TGWU) provided the clearest example of the vagaries of union procedure. Whilst a majority of regions voted for Healey, the union's Executive Committee decided to recommend a vote for Tony Benn on the grounds that a majority of the largest regions had expressed a preference for him. Despite this recommendation, the union's delegation at conference decided to vote for John Silkin in the first ballot and then, after a second consultation among themselves, opted for Tony Benn. The National Union of Public Employees (NUPE) had, by contrast, consulted its members individually and had committed itself to Healey. At the start of the conference, it seemed that Healey would win because of the NUPE decision. This was despite its London organiser, Jeremy Corbyn, being a campaigner for Benn.

The right had been invigorated by a meeting of Solidarity which took place at lunchtime on the day of the conference. At this, James Callaghan had angrily rebutted the charge that he and his colleagues had betrayed socialist principles while in office. He also made a direct attack on Tony Benn.

> This falsehood, this allegation that we have been treacherous to the party betraying a whole lifetime of work and service . . . as far as I am concerned my colleagues are entitled to resent that he should have built his campaign on this implication.

A warning was issued by Benn's supporters in a letter to MPs before the vote:

> Abstain if you will, but do not expect the no doubt sophisticated reasons for doing so to be understood. That is asking too much.

It was a clear threat that those who did not vote for Benn on the second ballot might not be reselected. Neil Kinnock, because he did not vote for Benn and abstained in the second ballot, was himself to be treated to cries of 'Judas!' when he appeared at the Tribune meeting at conference. In fact, he nearly went the other way. Reflecting on this in 2018 he said:

> For some minutes, sitting there on the platform waiting for the result of the deputy leadership campaign I thought 'you bloody fool, why didn't you vote for Healey'.

After the preliminary skirmishes, many of which were broadcast live on television, conference proceeded to the first ballot. In this, Denis Healey won the largest vote of 45 per cent, Benn came second with 36 per cent and Silkin received 18 per cent. Silkin was thus eliminated and conference had a second ballot which resulted in a wafer-thin majority of 50.4 per cent for Healey to Benn's 49.5 per cent. The TGWU had voted for Silkin in the first ballot, but then swung to support Benn in the second, a decision which only became apparent at the last minute, making the result so close. As everyone in the hall began to realise that Healey had won, there was pandemonium. This was a huge moment with implications that went far beyond the election of an irrelevant job title.

From the perspective of the right and moderates within the PLP and the union leadership it showed that, for the first time since the mid-1970s, the onward march of the left could be halted. Despite losing MPs to the SDP, those who had remained and were led by Denis Healey and Roy Hattersley now had a platform. From the perspective of the Tribune left and particularly Neil Kinnock, it was a clear indication that their future lay in working against the Bennite left. For the Bennite left, it appeared to be a victory even though it was an actual defeat. It seemed that Benn had not just nearly won, he had prepared the basis for a future campaign to be leader when Foot retired. The electoral college had been tested and secured. But as Jon Lansman recalled in 2018:

> As we walked out of the count, Chris Mullin and I walked down the steps and he said 'You know, I think we will look back on this as our finest hour. It's going to be downhill all the way.'

After the election, the conference was marked by vehement contributions from the CLPs. Some activists denounced MPs and the traditional leadership. On almost all issues, conference voted solidly with the left. The remaining constitutional issue to be decided was that of responsibility for the manifesto. On the first vote, conference decided by a slender majority that the NEC should have control, and thus reversed previous decisions on the subject. Michael Foot then persuaded conference to rebut its own resolution by failing to incorporate it into constitutional wording. Yet again it failed.

Although Denis Healey had only won by a whisker, the right was triumphant when it came to NEC elections. Five right-wingers replaced five left-wingers and Eric Varley, a right-wing frontbencher, replaced Norman Atkinson as treasurer. The NEC was now evenly balanced. The ambiguous figure of Michael Foot was there to defend the rights of MPs whilst making no effective stand against radical changes in constitutional arrangements or against left-wing policies. The conclusion of the 1981 conference was that there was all to play for. In the end, Chris Mullin was right. Benn's defeat by Healey was a high watermark for the left.

While Labour focused on its internal battles, the new SDP enjoyed a huge fillip. The Conservative government was split over Margaret Thatcher's new monetarist economic policies and the traditional 'wets' of one-nation Conservatism. It was not a foregone conclusion in 1981 that she would remain in office. The opportunity to challenge Thatcher was there but the political map was now confused with a divided Labour party, a new centre party with dynamic leadership, and a weakened government. From this period until the Falklands war in early 1982, polling showed Labour and Conservatives remained around 30 per cent whilst the SDP was around 40 per cent rising to over 50 per cent on 14 December.

In 1975, a young lawyer had joined the Labour party and was to have a big impact on it for the next four decades. Tony Blair was a parliamentary candidate in 1982. His view in 2018 was that Healey's win was the decisive moment in the battle for the Labour party:

> It was clear that there was a systematic attempt to take over the Labour party. Tony Benn had really reached out to the far-left, to the left that had either been completely marginalised or were excluded from the Labour party over its history and that had links much more with Trotskyism than communism, kind of the Marxist part of the left. There was a sustained assault to take the Labour party over and it would probably have succeeded had he won the deputy leadership from Denis Healey, but he didn't.
>
> Really from that moment on, I think it was a matter of time before the party was recaptured for more mainstream politics, but it was an ugly time and the trouble with people from that tradition of the left is that they combine a huge degree of commitment with intolerance and misunderstanding about the

nature of people and their relation to politics. It's a pretty deadly combination electorally and it creates a very harsh climate in which to conduct politics. So people were leaving the Labour party and the SDP was created. But I think for a lot of the young ones in the Labour party at the time, we could see the way it was going to be taken back.

The question was, who was to lead the response against the left, and how was it going to happen?

4

The Reaction and the Response

Until 1981, the New Left had taken the initiative but now that its main constitutional objectives had been achieved, it fell back on the defensive. Should it encourage Tony Benn to run again for the deputy leadership in 1982? Should it continue to press for conference control over the manifesto? Or was it time to reduce the conflict in an effort to secure Labour victory in the polls? If Labour were to be defeated, the left might be blamed and perhaps forced back into irrelevance.

These questions were precipitated by the internal problems of the RFMC immediately after the Brighton conference. It had always been a tactical alliance comprising disparate groups, and the ties between them had weakened once its five constitutional aims had been achieved. When the Benn campaign ended, the RFMC fragmented. By the end of 1981, Vladimir Derer decided it was time 'to suggest that the left lies low' or 'treads water' for a year or two, until after the next election. Previously Derer's CLPD had been able to conduct meetings concerned with mainly technical and tactical issues, but now the more radical members of CLPD wanted Tony Benn to run again for the deputy leadership, or even the leadership. Derer and other leading CLPD members argued that this would be seen as 'tactical confrontation'. They saw the next essential step as winning back more seats on the NEC and thought this could be best achieved through the creation of discreet alliances, particularly with the trade unions, which would involve adopting a low profile.

Meanwhile, the NEC elections of 1981 reinforced the trade unions' determination to intervene more actively in the party. There was a fragile balance of power on the NEC with Foot's hold over the balance of votes that enabled him to contain Benn. It became all the more important for Benn to re-establish his position in the party at large by winning a place in the shadow cabinet. He failed to do so and thereby deprived the left of its most visible public rallying point. A steady trickle of defections to the SDP continued and the by-election victories of Liberal Bill Pitt in Croydon North and the SDP's Shirley Williams in Crosby spurred the NEC to action. Its nervousness was increased by the controversy caused by the nomination of Peter Tatchell as Labour candidate for Bermondsey.

Bermondsey was a traditional Labour stronghold, with a largely working-class membership. The sitting member, Robert Mellish, was a right-wing Roman Catholic member who had been minister of state for housing and chief whip. Peter Tatchell was a 29-year-old Australian social worker who became a famous campaigner for gay rights. On the announcement of this decision, Mellish declared his intention of immediately resigning his seat and fighting the ensuing by-election, unless the constituency reversed its decision. The NEC voted fifteen to fourteen to refuse Tatchell's candidature and by a vote of nineteen to ten endorsed an inquiry into Militant.

At national level, it was recognised that the party had to reconcile and on 5 and 6 January 1982, a meeting was held at Bishops Stortford at which the NEC and the trade unions declared 'peace has broken out'. All the groups represented at Bishops Stortford came away feeling they had gained something. Moderate and right-wing trade union leaders were relieved that the right and left seemed able to discuss common causes and present at least an appearance of unity. The right believed that Tony Benn would not contest the deputy leadership again and accepted Michael Foot's request that there should be no 'witch hunt' against all the groups on the Labour left. That said, its intention was to exclude Militant from the party. The left, however, had good cause to feel relieved at the outcome of Bishops Stortford. Not a single constitutional change had been dropped. The party still had its electoral college and mandatory reselection of MPs. No specific move against Militant or against the Tatchell candidature had been made, and expulsions seemed a long way off. From all sides, fudging the issues was the agreed order of the day to achieve some semblance of peace.

The following Saturday, Tony Benn had a meeting at his home at which the cream of the New Left gathered, including Vladimir Derer, Jon Lansman, Chris Mullin, Ken Livingstone, Michael Meacher and Tony Banks. After presenting a paper from Chris Mullin, 'The Basis for a Truce', it was agreed. That lasted a week. On 11 January 1982, the organisation subcommittee of the NEC quashed the candidatures of two left activists, Pat Wall of Militant and Bob Clay, and ordered their constituencies in Bradford and Sunderland to restart the selection procedures. This emphasised that the apparent reconciliation at Bishops Stortford was tenuous, and that potentially damaging conflicts remained.

The issue that united all the trade unions was the overwhelming desire to secure the defeat of the Conservative government. The party had lost one in five of its individual members between 1980 and 1981 (71,000 out of a total of 348,156, according to the 1982 NEC Annual Report). A continuing Conservative government or an SDP alternative could change the basis on which workers belonging to an affiliated trade union automatically paid a levy to the Labour party. The SDP was committed to attacking the levy. The unions were losing large numbers of members as unemployment grew and the party was already in severe financial difficulties. It needed £3 million to fight the next general election. Only the trade unions could produce such a sum and they made it clear that they would only provide it if the party put its own house in order. The St Ermin's Group was the name of right-wing trade union leaders who met at that hotel to plot how they could achieve their objectives. Since 1980, it worked to gain control of the NEC by securing the transfer from left to right of five seats on the NEC in 1981. As the left became more divided and lost its focus, so the right became more organised.

In the world outside the Labour party, the political map was being redrawn. Throughout her political career, Margaret Thatcher had been fortunate in her opponents and had the courage to take them on, as Edward Heath and James Callaghan had experienced. However from 1979, as Labour was going through its internal fights, the Conservative government had an equally torrid time. All the economic indicators were terrible. There was a recession, unemployment rose to 3 million, consumer confidence crashed as value added tax (VAT) increased to 17.5 per cent and gross domestic product (GDP) shrank by 2.2 per cent. In 1981 riots took place in Brixton in London and Toxteth in Liverpool. It was incredibly grim. By December that year, the Conservatives were languishing below 30 per cent in every opinion poll. Margaret Thatcher was highly vulnerable to an internal challenge from her party.

Then General Galtieri, the Argentine president, invaded the Falkland Islands – a British Overseas Territory some 400 miles off the south-eastern tip of Argentina. Argentina had been under military dictatorship for some years and its economy was collapsing. On 2 April 1982, it decided to raise patriotic sentiment by invading on the basis of restoring the islands' sovereignty to Argentina. Thatcher took the decision to send a British task force to recapture the islands. This was courageous as many military observers believed it was impossible to defeat an enemy so far from Britain. It was a bloody ten-week war with the British public given only part of the story of the brutality of both sides. The Argentinian and British navies both suffered dramatic losses with the sinking of the vessels *ARA General Belgrano* and *HMS Sheffield*.

Britain regained control of the islands and with this victory, Margaret Thatcher became Britannia – at least, as far as the Conservative press was concerned. The impact was immediate. By 30 April 1982, four weeks after the declaration of war, the Conservatives had risen to 43 per cent in the polls and by May 1982, 50 per cent.

As the Falklands war raged on, Labour's focus stayed on Militant and its growing power within the party. It had a fighting fund of £103,000, a headquarters staff of thirty people in London and thirty-four more staff in the regions. Its membership had risen from 1,800 in 1979, to 3,500 in 1982. The NEC considered a report proposing a series of rules that would effectively eliminate Militant, and at the NEC meeting of 23 June 1982, adopted a resolution moved by Michael Foot to implement the recommendations of the report immediately. Groups permitted to operate within the party would be registered. The NEC would decide which groups were acceptable and groups found to be in breach of the rules were to be given three months to make themselves acceptable. Individuals and groups breaking the rules would be liable to party discipline, including expulsion. Militant would not be eligible for registration. The NEC allowed Tatchell's nomination to stand in Bermondsey and, at the beginning of August, Mellish left the Labour party. Emphasis on the Tatchell affair was reduced as the Militant inquiry became more important.

CLPD set about tackling the matter in its usual way. It circulated a model amendment to resolutions on the Labour party's conference agenda which would delay any decision on Militant for at least another twelve months. The amendment was agreed by twelve votes to eleven at a heated CLPD executive meeting. The controversy was deeply divisive. Derer was unhappy that the only model resolution the CLPD had to offer that year had been passed by so narrow a margin, serving as another example of the conflicts within the organisation which he had founded.

The atmosphere of the 1982 Blackpool conference reflected changes in expectations and power that had occurred since the Brighton conference of 1981. In the previous three conferences, the left and their allies had taken the initiative and the leadership, and the right wing of the party had been in disarray. By 1982, however, the right had recovered and was looking forward to establishing the register, outlawing Militant and securing a working majority on the NEC. A good deal of lobbying occurred before the conference began and all but seven unions had declared their intention to vote in favour of the register. The NEC resolution was carried by 5,173,000 votes to 1,565,000 votes. About two-thirds of the constituencies voted against the register, but the great majority of trade union block votes backed.

The focus of attention now shifted to the NEC elections. The right won victory after victory in every section of the NEC. A right-wing majority now replaced the previous balance in which Foot and his allies occupied the centre. The NEC would now reduce the influence of the left on its committees and pursue the eradication of Militant. However, the conference did vote for left-wing positions on virtually every major issue of policy: unilateral nuclear disarmament, the decision that future Labour governments and conferences should not even consider an incomes policy, and withdrawal from the common market were all contained in the 1982 party programme for inclusion in a manifesto.

The left reappraised its position. Within parliament, more than twenty left-wing Labour MPs decided to split from the Tribune Group and form a new group, the Socialist Campaign Group.

> The parliamentary Tribune group performs no useful function. It is a talking shop, and an exclusively parliamentary one at that. Its membership is disparate: some MPs are members because they consider themselves on the left; some are members because their constituency parties expect it of them; some are members for no apparent reason at all.

The Campaign Group, as it became more commonly known, remained the key bastion of the left for the next thirty-five years – at times the only bastion of the left. CLPD's leadership now believed that it should register to counteract any risk of expulsion. It was not prepared to risk its position by defending Militant from further inquiry and probable expulsion. The New Left alliance was dead.

The right continued to assert its new power. On 27 October it voted every left representative off the key committees. Tony Benn was forced off the TUC-Labour party liaison committee, the key economic policy committee that was central in the formulation of general policy for the election manifesto. The changes were carried by fourteen votes to twelve with three abstentions. The tone was set for every successive generation in which the dominant group within the Labour party took total control of the NEC. New Labour and the left were to do so in their periods of power. The losers always complain it would not happen if they were in control, and power always goes to the victors.

1983 was a general election year and the Conservatives still enjoyed a Falklands bounce at 44 per cent, with Labour at 35 per cent in the polls. The SDP had begun to decline and remained around 20 per cent for the early part of the year. In February, a much bigger fight occurred between Labour and the Liberal party in the Bermondsey by-election. The day before the by-election the NEC finally expelled five members of the Militant editorial board.

24 February 1983 saw one of the nastiest and most dramatic by-elections of any era. The Liberal party had always been seen as the nice party of politics but, in fact, it had a very tough organisational spine. Its candidate, Simon Hughes, was a 32-year-old barrister who was selected to fight Peter Tatchell. The campaign was overtly homophobic. 'It is a straight choice' for Bermondsey as the Liberal leaflet put it. The *News of the World* published a retouched photo showing Tatchell with plucked eyebrows, lipstick and eyeliner. He was accused of being a member of Militant, which he was not. Simon Hughes won the seat with 57 per cent of the vote and kept it until 2015, but even he admitted thirty years later that the campaign had gone too far. By then he also confirmed that he was a bisexual after being outed by the *Sun* in 2006.

A Labour majority of 11,000 had been converted into a Liberal majority of 10,000. This could be written off as an aberration, but the signs were not good for Labour in an election year. A victory in a subsequent by-election in Darlington in March calmed the nerves, although it was only held for three months as Labour lost it in the general election in June. In the run-up to the election, the boundary commission had rewritten the size and distribution of parliamentary seats. This had a huge impact on Bristol South West which was abolished under the changes. Its MP, Tony Benn, had the difficult choice of getting another safe seat elsewhere or staying in Bristol. He opted to fight a highly marginal new seat, Bristol East, rather than fight the safe seat of Livingston in Glasgow. It was a brave decision and he knew how risky it was.

In twelve months, the left had lost its majority in the NEC, lost its purpose as the debates over the constitution petered out, lost Bermondsey, seen the establishment of the register and now saw its leader under threat. And then Margaret Thatcher called a general election.

PART TWO

The Counter-Revolution

'The contest in the Labour party was between those people
who put a premium on getting power
in the Labour party and those on getting power *for*
the Labour party'
Neil Kinnock, 2018

5

The Dream Team

For those who like their politics raw, the 1983 general election is a collector's item. Labour's campaign plummeted to depths of ridicule and chaos. The manifesto was thirty-nine pages of every commitment from the 1982 conference and included unilateral nuclear disarmament, withdrawal from the EEC, abolition of the House of Lords, renationalisation of a number of large corporations and taxation hikes. It was famously described by Labour frontbencher Gerald Kaufman as the longest suicide note in history. It did not command support from the Labour frontbench, who ignored it on the campaign trail. The campaign was mounted against a resurgent Conservative party and the SDP-Liberal Alliance, which split the anti-Tory vote and further killed any hope of victory.

In the final result, the Conservatives had 397 seats to Labour's 209 and the SDP-Liberal Alliance's twenty-three. Labour's share of the vote had dropped to 27 per cent but narrowly ahead of the SDP-Liberal Alliance's 25 per cent, a margin of 700,000 votes. This was way behind the Conservative's 42 per cent. It was the worst result for Labour since 1935 and there has not been as bad a result since. The reactions were immediate. Denis Healey attacked the SDP as a 'party of renegades that played into the hands of the Tories'. Two of the SDP's founders, Shirley Williams and Bill Rodgers, lost their seats, as did numerous Labour MPs including

Tony Benn, who lost Bristol East. This was the final shattering blow to the left after a dismal year. It was clear Michael Foot would have to stand down and a leadership election be called without a clear leader of the New Left.

The incoming list of Labour MPs was, however, to provide an introduction to the politics of the next thirty-five years. A combination of retirements and the loss of sixty seats meant that the new PLP had a wave of fresh faces. On the left they included Tony Banks and Jeremy Corbyn along with Terry Fields and Dave Nellist, (the latter were two members of the Militant Tendency and both subsequently expelled in 1991). They were joined as new MPs by Tony Blair and Gordon Brown. This election had produced three future Labour leaders, of whom two became prime minister and one a three-time general election winner. Not bad for a crushing defeat. The Labour whips, who allocated office space for new MPs, must have been looking for ways to cheer up. Tony Blair, as a new MP, was put in a small office with the Militant Dave Nellist. Speaking in 2018, he recalled sharing the office:

> . . . for a period of months until I finally got together with Gordon and managed to get it changed. I think this was a deliberate piece of humour on the part of the whips because in those days, office space was allocated on a sort of Mafia-like basis and unless you paid court to the right people, they punished you for it. But I'm sure it was as big a punishment for Dave Nellist as it was for me, but it was a very odd pairing, obviously. But that was the Labour party at the time.
>
> The important thing to realise is that I first came across Michael Foot, not in the Beaconsfield by-election, but when he consulted me and Derry Irvine with Denis Healey on the expulsion of Militant from the Labour party. I was the Labour party's lawyer in the case expelling Militant because when Militant took a legal action against the Labour party, we defended it and saw them off.

Unfortunately, history does not record the Blair-Nellist chats over morning coffee. It was obvious that Michael Foot would stand down and that Neil Kinnock would run from the centre-left with Roy Hattersley from the centre-right. This new generation of Labour leaders would have a clear run against one another because the New Left, without Tony Benn, had no viable candidate. On Sunday 12 June 1983, they all gathered at Chris Mullin's small flat in Brixton. The meeting included CLPD stalwarts, the newly-elected MPs Banks and Corbyn, and a few older MPs – Michael Meacher and Jo Richardson as well as Ken Livingstone, the leader of the GLC, with NUPE's Tom Sawyer of the NEC and Tony Benn. It was a crucial moment. The lack of credible winning candidates for the top jobs was a problem that would haunt the left again and again and, in 1983, the best chance seemed to have gone forever. Benn had got within one per cent of beating Healey only eighteen months earlier, but now who could they run? Jeremy Corbyn, as recorded in Tony Benn's diaries, said:

> Kinnock lost the deputy leadership for Tony in 1981 deliberately and specifically and he was busy preparing himself for the leadership campaign during the general election. There must be a left candidate.

Would Tony Benn have beaten Neil Kinnock in 1983? Jon Lansman, speaking in 2018, thought so:

> [Victory] was ripped away from us primarily because we fairly quickly lost control of the NEC and because Benn was out of parliament at the leadership election.

If Benn had won a parliamentary seat in 1983 he:

> . . . would have been in the leadership election and I think he would have squeezed Kinnock out. We might even had Healey

standing against Benn, as Benn and Healey were still the real leaders of the right and left. In that contest we probably still would have won because we had the membership and some of the MPs on our side.

Within two weeks of the 1983 general election, Tony Benn made the claim that it was 'the first time since 1945 a political party with an openly socialist policy has received the support of eight and a half million votes.' This was an incredible statement given that Labour's vote was the lowest in any election since 1935. In 2018 Neil Kinnock commented:

> Benn took comfort that even though we had been absolutely hammered, 'Nine million people voted for socialism'. I wish he could have run. I would have beaten him then. Partly because of the experience the movement had had when he ran for the deputy leadership, partly because by 1983 the trade union leadership was even more resolute in its mainstream commitment. In their view, Tony Benn had no public credibility. That certainly applied to the parliamentary party where I would have had a huge majority. In the constituencies, he would have got a large vote but I'm not sure he would have done better than I did because by 1983 and in the wake of the general election campaign I had gigantic support.

Eventually, the left nominated Eric Heffer for the leadership, who received 6 per cent of the vote, and Michael Meacher for the deputy leadership, who managed 28 per cent. Neil Kinnock won every section of the electoral college with 73 per cent of the vote overall. Roy Hattersley became his deputy. This 'dream team' worked in tandem until 1992 and laid the foundation for wide scale changes within the Labour party. The centre-left and centre-right had come together to take back control.

Kinnock was the key figure in the transformation of the Labour party in the 1980s and early 1990s. Even then, he was like a politician of a slightly earlier age. His speeches owed more to the 1960s and

1970s for their length and personality than to the style that would come in under Blair and Brown. His television appearances in 1983 and 1984 were not those of a polished TV performer. He never seemed truly comfortable against Margaret Thatcher. However, it was always a mistake to underestimate him because, although he could appear uncertain in the early stages, his grip in key moments was considerable. In his first three years as leader he had to deal with the miners' strike, the abolition of the Greater London Council, Militant in Liverpool and a rampant Conservative government. By the end of this period, he had secured an internal victory against his enemies of the left and brought Labour back from the cataclysm of 1983. For the New Left, Kinnock was hard to confront and harder to defeat. He had a new young staff including Charles Clarke as his chief-of-staff and Patricia Hewitt as press secretary who, with new MPs elected in 1979 and 1983 including Brown and Blair, made a formidable team.

Despite this influx of talent, the years between 1983 and 1986 were tough. Margaret Thatcher had won a huge parliamentary majority and her victory established her dominance without restraint. There were scores to be settled and political battles to be fought afresh with the last untouched bastions of the Labour movement; the trade unions who funded Labour and local government where the left still had power.

The National Union of Mineworkers (NUM) occupied a special place in the heart of the Labour movement. The conditions in the mines, the union and the communities they fostered are all celebrated in the Labour movement. Even today, the annual Durham Miners Gala celebrates the pits and branches of the union. The NUM was created in 1947 and operated as a federation of regional coal fields with their own local power structures. It had taken part in two national strikes that were instrumental both in bringing down Edward Heath's government and in propelling the Yorkshire Miners' leader, Arthur Scargill, to national prominence. Scargill had developed the tactic of flying pickets – bussing hundreds of strikers to critical points in a dispute to close down a target. This won a pitched battle with police outside the Saltley

Gate fuel depot in 1972 and led to his election as South Yorkshire President in 1973 and President of the NUM in 1981.

It is difficult to know who hated Scargill more, Margaret Thatcher or Neil Kinnock. Kinnock was a lifelong member of the Labour party, Scargill had been in the party since 1962 but had previously been in the Young Communist League and, even in the early 1980s, was a supporter of the Soviet Union against organisations such as Solidarity in Poland. Kinnock was the face and voice of the centre-left whilst Scargill was a supporter of the New Left. Kinnock was of South Wales and Scargill, Yorkshire. Scargill also loved playing to the gallery. He was planning to oppose a second conservative term and called for extra parliamentary action against it. In 1981, the miners faced down Thatcher's first government over pit closures but between 1981 and 1984, 41,000 jobs were lost. Despite this, Scargill's repeated calls for strikes in 1982 and 1983 could not gain the necessary majority in a ballot of his members.

Margaret Thatcher knew that the trade union she had to defeat was the NUM. Her predecessor had lost twice, but she had a huge parliamentary majority and a battle plan written in 1977 by Nicholas Ridley after the 1974 strike. This document suggested contingency planning, stockpiling coal at power stations, recruiting non-union lorry drivers and using non-union ports, cutting off financial support to strikers and for the training and equipping a large, mobile squad of police, ready to employ riot tactics in order to uphold the law against violent picketing. In March 1984, the National Coal Board (NCB) announced that twenty collieries would be closed at the cost of 20,000 jobs.

The government had followed the Ridley plan by stockpiling coal and preparing the police for serious levels of conflict. An unofficial strike began in Yorkshire and Scargill took the bait to push for national support. Critically, he also took the decision that a strike would be ordered without a national ballot, with delegates at the NUM conference in April 1984 voting by sixty-nine to fifty-four not to hold a ballot and leave it to the different regions to decide. This decision had a huge impact on the strike and the union. For the miners, it split their ranks. Some areas aggressively pursued the action, especially Yorkshire, Scotland, South Wales, North East England and Kent. The Midlands and North Wales were less involved. The real trouble was in Nottinghamshire where miners who did want to go on working were faced by picket lines sent from other parts of the country. Conflict broke out – miner against miner, police against miner – and violence filled television screens night after night. This came to a head in the Battle of Orgreave in South Yorkshire in June 1984. The coking plant was supplied by lorries bringing in supplies. The striking miners, flying pickets and police were prepared for war – 5,000 miners and at least 6,000 police, some of whom were on horseback. The battle was ferocious with repeated mounted charges by the police against the pickets. It was repeated throughout the rest of the year as confrontations between flying pickets and flying police squads became more localised. There were numerous arrests and injuries.

Eventually, a combination of factors led to the defeat of the NUM: the government's tactics, the decision to call the strike in the summer, the fragmentation of the NUM with the Nottinghamshire miners creating a new union allowing them to work, the failure of the pit safety union NACODS to strike that allowed some pits to remain open, and finally Scargill's refusal to compromise over any pit closures. To add insult to injury, the courts ordered the sequestration of NUM funds. The aristocracy of the trade union movement had been beaten. It was the most important industrial confrontation of the last fifty years and changed trade unionism as we know it. It was fought under the auspices of a Conservative government that had planned its tactics and timing for maximum damage. It destroyed communities and smashed the unity of the union movement. It also destroyed the coal industry in the UK. Scargill's more fantastic speeches were discounted when he predicted the end of the coal industry but, in truth, he was right. In 1983 there were 171 collieries. By 2015 there were none and Britain now imports its coal.

For Neil Kinnock, the strike was cataclysmic. It started within six months of his leadership. It was at the heart of his emotional and personal commitment to the Labour movement and his own family, who were South Wales miners. He faced a horrible dilemma. Thatcher made the strike an issue of legitimacy for both her government and for the NUM. Its decision not to hold a national ballot played into the narrative that Scargill and the NUM executive were politically motivated, and the flying pickets were their shock troops. The Battle of Orgreave, the picketing in Nottinghamshire and the death of one non-striking miner, when a concrete block was dropped on his taxi on his way to work in the Merthyr Vale Colliery, contributed to that narrative. Kinnock, as Labour leader, was acutely aware of the impact on strikers' families who had been denied welfare benefits, as well as the effect on the NUM and the Labour party. He was caught between his heart and his head. He could not support Scargill, who had initiated the strike without a national ballot, yet he saw the end of the way of life from which his family had come. Thirty years later, in 2009, the two men were still fighting about the causes and impact of the strike with Kinnock admitting that in 1984 he had felt helpless. Speaking in 2018, Peter Mandelson said of Kinnock at that time:

> Can you imagine what it was like, a man from the South Wales valleys coming from that – mining and the left-wing tradition. Neil had to spend the first years of his leadership distancing himself from his own side, the left. His own people. Which reassured the public that he was not of the Scargillite left, but it crippled him emotionally, it vexed him. He was dancing on the head of a pin for a year.

Meanwhile, Tony Benn was back. In 1983, despite having lost his parliamentary seat of Bristol East, he had retained his seat on the NEC with the highest vote from the constituency section. Now he was elected to the parliamentary seat of Chesterfield in a by-election on 1 March 1984 and fully supported Scargill against Kinnock. At the same time, the left was having to evaluate its position as other challenges were made to its strongholds.

Although Margaret Thatcher had seen the miners as her main target, another more recent centre of the Labour party also came to her attention. The Greater London Council (GLC) had, since 1981, been under the control of a group of the New Left who had been active in Labour politics in London through the 1970s. Organisations such as Labour Against the Cuts, formed in 1975, and London Labour Briefing, launched in 1980, had brought together Ken Livingstone, Tony Banks and Jeremy Corbyn. In 1980, a centrist, Andrew McIntosh, beat Livingstone by one vote to the leadership of the Labour group on the GLC and in 1981 won the election on a manifesto that was markedly to the left of his own views. On the first meeting of the Labour group, McIntosh and his supporters were ejected from the leadership positions and replaced by the left. Livingstone became leader and a 29-year-old called John McDonnell became chair of the GLC finance committee and deputy leader.

In the following two years, as the left came under increasing pressure at national level, the group at the GLC rose in prominence. Livingstone, McDonnell and Tony Banks were targeted by the national press for their support of a wide range of organisations championing women's, gay and ethnic minority rights, that in the early 1980s were seen as totally eccentric. When they invited Gerry Adams of Sinn Féin to London, they were also seen as dangerous. This was accompanied by an open denial of the Conservative government in parliament across the river. London's unemployment figures were prominently displayed on the upper terrace of County Hall directly across from the House of Commons. John McDonnell, speaking as shadow chancellor in 2018, reflected on the strategy of the GLC and its youthful leadership. He used the GLC's revenues from rates to create a new economic model:

> We had the resources that I could shift to redistribute income and wealth across London. This gave us the opportunity to discover how we could put money in people's pockets, reduce their costs, particularly on transport, and start investing in

the economy. Our emphasis was on the delivery of cost-effective public services. We wanted to demonstrate that the left could run an administration effectively and that was my job.

The best example of this was the 'Fares Fare' policy, promised in the manifesto and then quickly implemented. It dramatically reduced fares on London's buses, underground and British Rail services and created the concept of a railcard that could be used on all services. This was subsidised by a 5 per cent increase on the rate of the GLC precept that was added to borough rates. There was a 10 per cent increase in usage of public transport and a decrease in road traffic by 11 per cent. It was a much more assertive use of traditional local government funds taken from central government grants and local rates. Speaking in 2018, McDonnell recalls the GLC having a wider agenda:

> We had the theory of 'in and against the state'. The state is a set of institutions. It's also a relationship with dominance by the state of the individual. So, the theory of in and against the state was basically that you get elected into the state and you transform the relationship. So when we got elected, the whole purpose was to throw open the doors of County Hall and invite people in. Every night, every room would be packed because people were talking; talking about policing, about lesbian and gay rights, about housing and transport. We had people turn up saying what a housing programme would look like, what industry and employment should be developed in London.

The GLC was a prime target for Conservatives. Eventually the London Borough of Bromley took the GLC to court on the basis that it was failing to meet its fiduciary duty of balancing the advantages of decreasing fares with the need to avoid higher burdens on ratepayers. The case ended up in the House of Lords and the GLC lost on the basis it had not acted in the interests of the ratepayers of Bromley.

The GLC leadership tried and failed to get the law changed and a group of ten GLC councillors launched the 'Can't pay, Won't Pay' campaign that encouraged civil disobedience around the newly increased fares. This did not work but it led to a fundamental breach between the group and Livingstone. By 1982 the campaign had failed and Livingstone had consolidated control against the GLC councillors. This split became relevant when a series of Acts were passed to allow central government funding to be cut from local government. By 1983, the GLC had lost all of its central funding and was reliant only on its own power to raise money by increasing its domestic and business rates. The Rates Act of 1984 then introduced rate capping which prevented councils from raising funds above a set level. This put it on collision course with thirty-one councils that simply refused to set a rate until the cap was lifted. They had all been elected on manifestos that advocated greater taxation and spending. Within the GLC, John McDonnell advocated refusing to set a rate despite the GLC's legal obligation to do so. It was a choice between honouring the manifesto or setting a rate and making cuts. Livingstone chose to sack McDonnell from the deputy leadership and make the cuts. Of the thirty-one councils, only Lambeth and Liverpool did not back down and under the power of the Act. The leader of Lambeth Council was prosecuted, fined and banned from office for ten years. The final act in the drama was in 1985 when, having forced the end of Fares Fare and reduced the GLC's ability to raise and spend money, the government decided to abolish it all together. The Local Government Act 1985 was narrowly passed in parliament, setting the end of the council for 31 March 1986.

Neil Kinnock had watched the resurgent Thatcher defeat the miners and act decisively against the Labour party in local government. Tony Benn was back in parliament from 1984 and the Campaign Group was challenging him over the lack of support for Scargill and the future direction of the party. Leading figures from the GLC were also entering parliament. Tony Banks in 1983 was followed by Livingstone in 1987 who was part of the inner circle around Benn. Livingstone was also elected a member of the NEC in 1987. If Labour stood any chance of winning, Kinnock believed he had to act to clean up and control the party, clear out Militant and any other groups that would undermine Labour's position and prepare to take on Thatcher for the real battle for power. Between 1984 and 1987 he consolidated authority around the leader's office. In 2018 he explained the fight as follows:

> The important thing to recognise is that the contest in the Labour party was between people who put a priority on getting power *in* the Labour party, and those who put a priority on getting power *for* the Labour party.

The first step was to win votes over the left in the NEC through his union allies:

> There were occasions in those first four years up until 1987 where the only way I won votes in the Home Policy Committee and the Organisation Committee was if Alec Kitson deliberately went to the toilet and Sam McCluskie popped out for a smoke. And because they were really solid comrades of mine, they did that often against the mandate of their own unions. So, they were absolutely crucial.

It was necessary to create new alliances between those on the right of the NEC, and detach erstwhile allies of Benn to a more centrist position.

> What I had to do was to get an alignment of all those who actually wanted to win an election for the Labour party to realise that that wasn't a vague ambition. This had everything to do with the survival and prospering of the Labour party. And that's how I managed to pull in right-wingers like John Golding and people on the left like Tom Sawyer.

In the years between 1983 and 1987, the centre of gravity of the party shifted. In his first conference as leader in 1984, Kinnock tried to get one member one vote for the purpose of mandatory reselection in the constituency parties, replacing the general committees with votes by all members of the constituency party. This was a clear move against the activist left and it achieved a small majority on the NEC, but was then beaten in conference as the unions voted against it. This setback merely activated him and his allies even more. In December 1983, organisation reforms were introduced to replace the NEC's subcommittees with new policy committees consisting of both shadow cabinet and NEC members giving the leader far more control. In 1985, Larry Whitty was appointed by Kinnock as general secretary of the party.

A campaign strategy committee was also formed to plan broadcast, polling and campaigns independent of the NEC and party headquarters. Tony Benn's diaries in this period show the gradual migration of key allies to Kinnock. For months, the NEC had been battling it out over the aftermath of the miners' strike, which had left a residue of personal hardship and bitterness for striking and non-striking miners and devastation of the union's own funds. It also had to contend with the attack on Labour local councils and with it the activities of Militant in Liverpool. The consolidation of power was seen in the appointment of three new directors of the Labour party at central office. They included a man who Tony Benn came to distrust immensely, the 32-year-old Peter Mandelson, as director for campaign and communications.

That year was the last year of the left fighting effective battles on the NEC. All the issues of the previous two years – the miners' strike, the banning of the Liverpool and Lambeth councillors and the activities of Militant in Liverpool – came up and were defeated. Neil Kinnock argued against committing a future Labour government supporting the sacked miners and returning the NUM's sequestered funds. The vote was fifteen to fourteen in favour of his position. As Tony Benn reported in his diary, 'with Michael Meacher voting against, any residual links I had with him are finished and done with.'

Kinnock followed these narrow victories with a famous speech at conference in which he condemned Militant in Liverpool. His position in public was set; he was dragging Labour into electability as the holder of the centre ground and would reform the party to focus on this. Speaking about this in 2018, Kinnock said:

> The Militant battle helped because it drew another thick dividing line between those who called it a witch hunt and those who understood that unless and until the ultra-lefts and sectarians were eradicated, there was no hope of them ever being part of a winning team.

For the left, Militant was proving to be a fight too far. Its sectarianism made it impossible to support for most of the left. Jon Lansman had seen the fragmentation caused by the issue as he reflected in 2018:

> There were Trotskyists who you could work with sometimes on some things. We never agreed. Vladimir's attitude was they're people who work incredibly well. You need someone to mend the fucking duplicator, you find an old Trot. You can't expect to agree with them, but they do a lot of your work. There was a lot of division over Militant, understandably it was a dividing factor because they were unpleasant people who never had any time for Benn anyway.

For Kinnock, from 1985 to 1987, the focus was on redefining the Labour party to take on Margaret Thatcher as she sought a third election victory. In the twentieth century, no one had won three consecutive terms and it was seen as an opportunity to beat her if Labour could be repositioned as a centrist party that had driven out its extremes. Up stepped Peter Mandelson. In the New Labour years, Peter Mandelson famously defined himself as the third man. In the years under Neil Kinnock and in the run-up to the 1987 general election, he could justifiably claim to have been the essential guru of the Kinnock project. He masterminded the Fulham by-election win over the Conservatives and SDP in 1986. He brought in a new style of campaigning with the creation of the Shadow Communications Agency (SCA) run by Philip Gould and Deborah Mattinson who were, for the next twenty years, New Labour's pollsters and guides to the public mood. He formulated the process of dealing with the media that came be to known as 'spinning' – or blatant manipulation and bullying. All of this was new and, when launched, his first big policy document, 'Freedom and Fairness' was both slick and totally different from anything Labour had done before. This makeover led to the introduction of the SCA in all aspects of Labour's campaigning and image. Tony Benn records, in March 1986, his encounter with the strange new world of Peter Mandelson:

> I went to the party's Campaign Strategy Committee where four men and a woman from something called The Shadow Agency [sic] made a presentation entitled 'Society and Self'.

A survey had been done with 240 non-committed Labour voters:

> They flashed up screen quotes which were supposed to be typical of Labour votes for example:
> 'IT'S NICE TO HAVE A SOCIAL CONSCIENCE BUT IT'S YOUR FAMILY THAT COUNTS'.
> What we were we being told was what you could read every day in the Sun, Daily Mail, Daily Express, Telegraph and so on. What was required in the party leadership was decisiveness, toughness and directness; people wanted a tough person at the helm. Who was the leader and what did he look like. It was a Thatcherite argument presented to us as 'You had better be more like Thatcher if you want to win.' I came out feeling physically sick; I'm not kidding . . . because if that is what the Labour party is about, I've got nothing whatever in common with it.

Appointing Mandelson was a brave decision by Kinnock. He pushed all the old Labour boundaries, and this had the effect of trying to make the leader a cult for Labour as much as Thatcher was for the Conservatives. This was not totally successful given Neil

Kinnock's personality – he was far more a man of the movement than a cult. The makeover was based on deep research by the SCA, Mandelson's handling of the media and a new presentational style.

At the 1986 conference, the NEC elections moved further away from the Bennite left. Eric Heffer and Margaret Beckett (then seen as a left candidate) were ejected and Benn himself was knocked off the top spot. However, the sheer nerve of Mandelson and his advisors was displayed in dropping the red flag as Labour's symbol and replacing it with a red rose, culminating in Neil and Glenys Kinnock throwing red roses off the stage. It was politics as high camp and produced a furious entry into Benn's diary that night:

> At the end Neil and Glenys threw a whole mass of red roses at the delegates from the platform. It was a disgusting spectacle and I couldn't stand it, so I rushed out.

The second spectacle was to come at the general election the following year in *Kinnock: the movie*, a brilliant piece of American style political advertising focused on him, completely unlike anything seen before. It featured his speech in the 1985 conference attacking Militant and ended on one word, 'KINNOCK', rather than 'LABOUR'. Mandelson had taken Labour from the 1983 campaign that was essentially set in the 1960s and produced a forerunner to twenty-first century campaigns.

The 1987 general election saw the return of Labour as an electoral force, but not nearly strong enough to win. Its share of the vote increased to 31 per cent with a drop of the SDP-Liberal Alliance to 23 per cent, but the Conservatives still had a huge share of 42 per cent, almost exactly the same as in 1983. Labour's vote had increased from the dismal 8.4 million in 1983 to 10 million, but the Conservatives had also increased their vote to nearly 14 million. For all its makeover, Labour had increased its number of seats by only twenty to 229, compared to 376 for the Conservatives. It was a big defeat, but as Kinnock's first attempt and only two years into the makeover, he didn't hesitate to stay on as leader and to plan to fight the next election. His control of the party was now complete.

The new shadow cabinet was the real forerunner of the New Labour era. In 1987 the last big beast of the 1970s cabinet, Denis Healey, retired, leaving only two ministers from 1979: Roy Hattersley as deputy leader and John Smith as shadow chancellor. A new raft of faces began to emerge: Bryan Gould, Jack Straw, John Prescott and Frank Dobson; and the fast-rising members of the 1983 intake, Gordon Brown and Robin Cook. Two years later, a reshuffle saw the introduction of Tony Blair into the shadow cabinet. Within this new group, the title of 'moderniser' began to be used. Peter Mandelson and Philip Gould, Tony Blair and Gordon Brown, Charles Clarke and Patricia Hewitt as Kinnock's policy co-ordinator, began to plan a new beginning.

From 1987 to Kinnock's resignation in 1992, three trends were evident. First, the rapid alienation and collapse of the left into a small pocket of resistance; this was the start of the wilderness years. Second, the increasing power of the leadership at all levels of the party balanced with a countervailing pessimism over Neil Kinnock's chances of winning. Finally, the rise of the modernisers who believed that a much more radical view had to be taken about Labour's future. These three trends, so different from only five years earlier, were to lay the course of Labour for the next twenty years.

6

The Wilderness Years Begin

After their successes of the late 1970s, the rise of Kinnock was the worst thing that could have happened to the left. CLPD receded into the background, leaving only pockets of activism. Jon Lansman was by now working as a freewheeling consultant within the left, whilst watching all the victories of the previous five years being reversed:

> We fought [Kinnock] all the way. We fought him to retain what we had won, to defend what we had won all the way through his period of leadership. I think we still were fighting all the way through. The left was still strong in local government throughout the eighties but it was in retreat all the time at national level.

This had a big impact on individuals and organisations that had supported the New Left in the constitutional battles.

> People began to drift away towards the end of the eighties. They were fed up with Kinnock. After we lost in 1987 and there was continuing retrenchment by Kinnock and further moves to the right, I think people began to get fed up with it. And so we became less strong. Also, the left became increasingly divided. With hindsight, we made the massive error of not giving the soft-left a road back. We marginalised ourselves.

Tom Sawyer and Michael Meacher were detached (Meacher left the Campaign Group when he joined the frontbench in 1983), and in parliament new MPs who might have been allies such as Robin Cook and Claire Short were forced to choose. The Bennite wing had become a rump. Lansman describes Benn himself having:

> . . . the actions of someone who accepted defeat and saw his role as keeping the standard flying for the left and encouraging people and giving them hope rather than trying to win again. I think he saw it as an encouraging strategy, as one that would keep the fires burning in the Dark Ages.

In 1988 the Campaign Group decided, at a meeting chaired by Jeremy Corbyn, that it had to run candidates against Kinnock and Hattersley. Benn didn't really want to run again, but he and Eric Heffer had both been nominated. This led to the resignations of Margaret Beckett, Clare Short, Joan Ruddock and Jo Richardson from the Campaign Group. As usual, Lansman ran the campaign ('Not one of my best') and it was a disaster. Benn received only 11 per cent of the vote and Heffer a mere 9 per cent, coming third behind John Prescott and Roy Hattersley. Lansman was losing faith. Reflecting back on this time in 2018, he said:

> I felt very alienated because I was someone who was trying to keep the left together, for various purposes, and it gave me an almost diplomatic role in trying to oil the wheels that prevented sectarianism from just blowing everything apart. That was hard to do.

The attack was not on people like him who were long-standing, non-Trotskyist members of the party. They were never under threat of expulsion, just irrelevance.

> They attacked us, but they didn't try to exclude us. At no point did they try to exclude anyone but Militant at that point. It's hard when you're marginalised, which we increasingly were,

particularly from Kinnock's election onwards. We were eventually hounded out of local government in the early nineties. Shortly after Blair's election, we were completely marginalised.

Despite this, at no point did he consider leaving the party:

> The Labour party was an instrument for political change. It wasn't a great instrument when it was run by Kinnock, and it was an even worse one than when it was run by Blair, but it was less bad than the alternatives, which were leaving the Labour party and starting something else, and that never made any sense. As Eric Heffer used to put it, it seems like a good idea until you think about what the founding conference would be like. When you know that you would have the most absurd arguments with the fucking sectarian bastards who would fill the hall. It was never going to be a good idea. The Labour party was always the least bad option, so you had to hang on in there for the long haul.

For John McDonnell, the end of the GLC meant he needed a job and, in 1987, he became chief executive of the Association of London Authorities, then merged with the Conservative Association, so it became the Association of London Government. Speaking in 2018, he described how the pillars of the left were eroded by Neil Kinnock's control, but there was always a glimmer of support.

> I never thought the left was over, never had done. We were certainly relatively isolated in terms of the parliamentary Labour party, and elected office in local government as well. There was still the rank and file left that was active on the ground, as best it could. In the PLP there was still an active Campaign Group, and we worked and campaigned around that. It was undoubtedly a cold climate, both in terms of what was happening in the PLP, and in terms of what was happening in some unions as well, because we lost left control of those unions. But there was still a base of

rank and file support for the left, within the constituencies, that was what we had to fall back upon for a long period.

McDonnell himself was trying to find a seat to fight in 1992. Kinnock's control of the party had extended to candidate selection where several members of the left had been excluded and in 1991 the final expulsions of Militant, including sitting MPs, took place.

> All selections were tightly controlled in terms of parliament, which was the most difficult element of it. But what we had to fall back on was maintaining an element of mobilisation for the left, constituency by constituency, and bringing them together on different campaigns, and in different left organisations.

Ironically, as Lansman and McDonnell were isolated and reduced in influence, so the other side of the Labour party was starting to move away from Neil Kinnock. He had assembled a coalition of soft-right and soft-left to defeat the Bennite left. He had routed Militant, been the face of Labour's mild resurgence and brought in a fresh wave of talent, but somehow it wasn't enough for his modernising protégés. In his autobiography Mandelson said:

> In the eighteen months or so after the election I gradually lost heart. Intellectually, Neil understood the need for change. The trouble was his heart and more so his soul weren't in the scale of change needed.

Kinnock proceeded to roll back the policy of the 1970s and early 1980s (especially in 1989) over unilateral disarmament and continued the process of expelling members of Militant. In 1990 he amended the rule on mandatory reselection that had been the New Left's victory in 1979 and had never been used. Now a 'trigger' ballot had to take place which made it easier for a sitting MP to keep their seat. If they lost this ballot of local branches they would have go to mandatory reselection, but if two thirds of local branches voted in the ballot to retain the sitting MP then there would be no mandatory reselection process. Under Tony Blair this bar later got reduced to 50 per cent. In reality, mandatory reselection was dead. The control also began to spill into candidate selection. Martha Osamor was removed as candidate for the Vauxhall by-election and was replaced by Kate Hoey. Thirty years later, Osamor was made a Labour member of the House of Lords by Jeremy Corbyn, her daughter, Kate Osamor, was a Labour MP and Kate Hoey was a leading Labour rebel in favour of Brexit. All the changes Kinnock had made were not enough for the party to be the natural party of government and he began to attract internal criticism from the right as well as the left. Mandelson reported a row with Roy Hattersley, John Smith and Donald Dewar over dumping Kinnock. He didn't support it, but the seeds were sown.

Mandelson commissioned *Labour and Britain in the 1990s* which analysed a desolate future for the party. More than a quarter of those polled voted for Labour out of historic loyalty. The reasons people had left the party included extremism, trade unions, defence policy and weak leadership. The Thatcherite revolution in fighting the miners, the GLC, and being strong on defence had combined with aspirational politics over home ownership to make Labour look irrelevant in the modern world where things were changing incredibly quickly. Ronald Reagan had been replaced as US president by George H. W. Bush, but this was of secondary importance to the rise of Mikhail Gorbachev in the Soviet Union who, from 1985, launched *glasnost* (openness) and *perestroika* (restructuring) within the USSR that slowly but surely spread to the East European states under Soviet influence.

In 1989, the last Russian troops left Afghanistan and Poland was ready to allow elections. By April 1989, this fever of liberalism had spread to China and Gorbachev became the first Soviet leader to visit China since the 1960s. Students occupied Tiananmen Square for a month only to be crushed by Chinese Army tanks on 4 June 1989. In August that year, F. W. de Klerk became the State President of South Africa, leading to the release of Nelson Mandela in February 1990. The Berlin wall opened in November 1989.

It was incredible; the world had transformed. These were the most dramatic changes since the second world war.

In Britain, 1989 saw the start of Margaret Thatcher's hubris. She introduced the poll tax in Scotland, which was ultimately to be the main instrument of her downfall. Throughout this period, Kinnock was preparing his party for the election that would define his time as leader. If 1987 had been the election that had partially eradicated the memory of 1983, the next election would be decisive. However, he was also hampered by doubts. Peter Mandelson reflecting on this in 2018:

> I took him to our agency of advertising volunteers to meet the creative teams who had developed three different creative campaigns for the general election campaign, and he said 'They're all marvellous. I couldn't tell you which one is best because I think they're all absolutely brilliant but they're all going to fail because of me.' Nobody agreed with him but they didn't know what to say. And, you know, you could've heard a pin drop.

As Kinnock stayed his course, so Mandelson followed his. With Tony Blair's help, he secured the parliamentary nomination for Hartlepool and was promptly asked by an irate leader's office to leave his job.

In 1990, popular fury over the poll tax resulted in demonstrations and battles on the streets. The power of the demonstrations led Margaret Thatcher to face a leadership challenge, after which she was deposed and replaced by the comparatively unknown John Major. Suddenly, it looked like Labour had a chance, and opinion polls through 1990 gave it big poll leads. By September 1991, these had softened and by January 1992, the two parties were neck and neck. John Smith, then shadow chancellor of the exchequer, took the blame for a shadow budget in 1992 that appeared to be promising substantial increases in taxes. This raised memories of Labour in the 1970s at just the wrong time for the 1992 election, especially as he failed to defend it properly. The election was fought on the basis of traditional party positions. The Conservatives attacked Labour for tax, spend and extremism. Labour attacked the Tories on poverty, unfairness and the poll tax. Already the signs were not looking as good for Labour as had been expected, and by the middle of the night it was obvious that the Conservatives had won a fourth term. It was a devastating night for Kinnock. When asked about it in 2018, Kinnock replied, 'It was awful, but I knew it was going to happen. That's the awful bloody thing.' Labour had increased its share of the vote from 31 to 34 per cent and to 11.5 million voters, but John Major had still managed to get 42 per cent and 14 million. Labour increased its seats to 271, a gain of forty-two, and the Tories had lost forty – but Major still had 336 seats and was able to form a government.

It was clear that all the reforms under Kinnock had taken the party halfway towards electability. It was not enough to just reverse the power of the left; Labour needed to do more to show it was a modern and relevant political force. It had nowhere to go but up. It was a great opportunity, but it needed radical thinking beyond anything that had gone before. Peter Mandelson, Gordon Brown and Tony Blair were desperate to act.

PART THREE

Power:
The New Labour Revolution

'We are not going to win despite our beliefs.
I want to win because of our beliefs'
Tony Blair 1994

7

The New Generation

Neil Kinnock's defeat had been expected but was still devastating. Spencer Livermore, who was later a senior figure under Tony Blair, Gordon Brown and Ed Miliband, remembers the depressing impact of this defeat.

> I was too young to vote, but I supported Labour in the 1992 election, and was absolutely devastated. I lived in Basildon which was the deep iconic seat for 1992. I used to go on the bus to school through the council estates and there were Labour pictures everywhere. I was absolutely convinced that Labour was going to win. I was sixteen, I didn't know much about it – and I was absolutely devastated. Just devastated, because I really thought it was going to happen. And so, my fear then was: could Labour even survive after four defeats?

Clearly Kinnock would step down, and John Smith was his probable successor. The new intake of MPs included the new member for Hartlepool, Peter Mandelson, working closely with his political consorts Gordon Brown and Tony Blair. Now, the first strains between Brown and Blair began to show. Brown was the dominant figure of the younger generation and had been winning elections to both the NEC and the shadow cabinet. Could he stand for leader against Smith? He couldn't bring himself to do it and the idea of standing for deputy leader was a non-starter as you could not have two Scots, following a Welshman, at the top of the party. You could, however, have a new, young, middle-class Englishman. Tony Blair for a brief moment wanted it. He was stopped by party support switching to Margaret Beckett. By Mandelson's account, Brown had not been supportive. It showed that Blair was a possible alternative leader to him in the future. Smith ran against Bryan Gould and won 91 per cent of the electoral college.

For the first time, the left did not run a candidate. The Campaign Group in 1992 was depleted. It had seen its ranks thinned out by death (Eric Heffer and Pat Wall), loss of seats and expulsions (Ron Brown for criminal damage, Terry Fields and Dave Nellist for membership of Militant) or deselection. John McDonnell had failed by fifty-three votes to get into parliament in Hayes and Harlington. The bar had also been raised. In 1981 when the electoral college had been introduced, any candidate needed to have 5 per cent of MPs to be nominated; by 1988, following Tony Benn's challenge to Kinnock, this bar had been raised to 12.5 per cent. The left had both no candidate and no ability to get one on the ballot. It was marginalised. The main action was now between the traditionalists and modernisers.

Over the next two years of John Smith's leadership, the context for every decision was how Labour could win the next election. John Major's government was torn apart by economic chaos and Europe. On 16 September 1992, Black Wednesday, the government pulled out of the European exchange rate mechanism (ERM) after spending billions to stop the pound depreciating. The impact on interest rates was immediate. In the course of a few hours they were increased from 10 per cent to 12 per cent and then to 15 per cent. Only by leaving the ERM that night did the government take pressure off the pound and rates were reduced to 10 per cent again. The Conservatives' claim to be the party of economic competence was fundamentally damaged. Its collapse in the opinion polls was immediate and lasted until the next election. Suddenly Labour was electable, but unfortunately there was no election in sight.

Gordon Brown had been promoted to shadow chancellor and Tony Blair to shadow home secretary. They, with Mandelson, saw up to four years in opposition under Smith's leadership. However, the patterns of behaviour they had started to exhibit under Kinnock remained. They were frustrated with Smith for being too slow to modernise, saw the trade unions as an impediment to change and the sense of competition between them began to grow.

John Smith was an exceptionally able politician and lawyer who came from the moderate wing of the party and held middle-of-the-road views within it. He was an older generation to the modernisers and made this apparent by the dropping of the Shadow Communications Agency. Smith relied far more on appeals to the traditional wings of the party and a projection of competence against the apparently incompetent government. He allowed Blair his head at the Home Office and 'Tough on crime and tough on the causes of crime' was a classic rallying cry against the home secretary Michael Howard. Brown had a more difficult time against Kenneth Clarke, who became chancellor in May 1993 and was successful in the role.

It was in the internal battles that John Smith incurred his colleagues' displeasure and showed his greatest leadership. The link with the unions had been seen by Philip Gould as a clear problem in the public's opinion of Labour. Blair, as employment spokesman, had irritated the union chiefs with his lack of desire to unwind the Thatcherite legal changes concerning secondary picketing. Since 1982, the unions had been seen as the bulwark against the left. In 1993, he viewed them as a bulwark against modernisation of the party.

Kinnock had failed in his ambition to get one member one vote (OMOV). Smith became convinced that it was needed for both candidate selection and the leadership elections. He wanted to work with the unions to get it through. The modernisers wanted far more radical moves away from the unions. They leaked Philip Gould's research that purported to show that separation was the main goal of the party, to the media. As usual, a review was ordered by the NEC and the argument came down to OMOV in candidate selection. For Smith it became a critical issue of leadership. He won over some key unions at that year's TUC by committing a future Labour government to a charter of union rights and full employment. These promises were seen by Blair and Brown as inherently dangerous, but they paved the way for Smith to go to the Labour conference looking for the vital last pieces of support. He attached all-women shortlists to the package to gain some CLP support. Then John Prescott delivered a barnstorming speech to conference that argued they had to back Smith and reaffirm the link with the unions. This did the trick. It went through 47 per cent to 44 per cent. OMOV was finally included within Labour's constitution. As important was the agreement to change the electoral college proportions from forty/thirty/thirty to parity between the Unions, PLP and CLPs with a third each. This changed the balance of voting in the electoral college until 2014 when it was abolished. The left's great victory at Wembley in 1981 was dead and buried.

Smiths' victory reaffirmed his position of primacy within the party. The respective positions of Brown and Blair began to shift. Brown was tougher in his dealings with colleagues and with the media and had the policy detail and the need to win. Blair had a lighter touch but also a desire to win. None of which mattered when Smith was senior to both and looked a likely prime minister at the age of fifty-five. Neil Kinnock reflecting on this period in 2018:

> They had been unnerved by what for them was an unexpected defeat in 1992. They divided into the 'one more heave' school to which John belonged, which generated criticism amongst the other group who thought it was much more than one more heave. There was a period in which John was the subject of murmured, rumoured, leaked criticism. John and I talked about that and actually the last meeting I had with him was a long discussion in which we sketched out a plan for him rebutting this stuff to show that there was a lot of life and energy in the leader and what he stood for. He died a week later.

John Smith died of a heart attack on 12 May 1994. It shocked the country and the Labour party. His presence had been one of balance – between the party and the unions, between left and right, between the modernisers and the traditionalists, and especially between the ambitions of the younger members of the shadow cabinet. Once he was gone, so too were the restraints and Labour politics of the next twenty years were reset. Paul Kenny from the union movement, later to be general secretary of the GMB:

> John Smith's death was a big tragedy because I think a lot of the unions had a lot more faith in terms of what John would deliver for them. He was your friendly bank manager.

For the left, already demoralised within parliament, it was a blow. Jon Lansman:

> John Smith was a decent, principled bloke. He was of the right, but he was also more in tune with the Labour movement than Kinnock was. He was more in tune with the unions. He was a Labour person. That's why he got rid of Mandelson, because he hated the politics of spin. It was tragic when he died, and we were all mortified. It was tragic because it was such an untimely death, but it was also tragic politically.

The shift in leadership was not just of a generation, it was of a whole political style and ideology. The modernisers had to unify around a candidate who could win. Possible opponents were Robin Cook, John Prescott – who eventually stood for both leader and deputy leader – and Margaret Beckett who, as deputy leader at the time of Smith's death, became the temporary leader of the party. The modernisers had one candidate who was the obvious heir to John Smith, the leading policy thinker of his generation and a man clearly of the Labour movement: Gordon Brown. Except he had also big negatives. He was a dominant figure who liked to dominate. He had legendary feuds stretching back years, Robin Cook being the main example. He was not an emollient figure with his colleagues.

From 1992, Tony Blair and Gordon Brown had a pact not to stand against one another in the event of a leadership battle.

Blair's appeal to both middle England and the PLP was stronger. He slowly but surely overtook Brown within the Labour party. From the day of John Smith's death on 12 May to his funeral on 20 May, the two men and their acolytes were building support. Peter Mandelson was applying media pressure for Blair behind the scenes. He had made his choice. On 31 May, at dinner at Granita, an Islington restaurant, Gordon Brown accepted the reality that Tony Blair would be the candidate for leader.

The Blair-Brown relationship sat at the heart of New Labour and ultimately led to its destruction. Brown's never-ending belief was that he should be leader and his price for stepping back in 1994 was absolute control over domestic economic and social policy. Blair agreed to this on basis that it would mean peace between them. This created a partnership in government that, when it worked, had a hugely positive impact over the next ten years. The more corrosive assumption was that Brown would succeed Blair at some point in the future. This was not written down and it was not a specific agreement. It had no timetable and later became explosive. A generation of politicians coming in their wake became defined by their loyalty to one leader or the other. The timing of Blair's departure became an article of faith for Brownites and something to be ignored by Blairites.

In July 1994, Blair won the leadership race easily with 57 per cent of the electoral college in a three-way race with Prescott and Beckett. Prescott became his deputy. The young lawyer, who had advised Michael Foot on the expulsion of Militant and stayed in the Labour party when he could have joined the SDP, was now leader of the party at the age of forty-one. He was to lead the Labour party into a completely different, modernising agenda and had three years to prepare for power. For the left it was going to be a turbulent period of being further marginalised and demoralised.

8

New Labour Takes Control

At the 1994 Blackpool Labour party conference, the scene of the great drama of 1980 when the left had won its constitutional changes, Tony Blair set out his leadership vision.

> Politics is moving to our ground. Across the nation, across class, across political boundaries, the Labour party is once again able to represent all the British people. We are the mainstream voice in politics today. This is my socialism and we should stop apologising for using the word. Above all we must conquer the weakness of our economy that holds our country back. It can only be done by a dynamic market economy based on partnership between government and industry, between employers and employee and between public and private sector.

But the sting in the tail of the speech was his vision to his own leadership.

> Some of you will think we are too modest in our aims, too cautious. Some of you I hear, support me because you think I can win (laughter). Actually, that's not a bad reason for supporting me, but it is not enough. I want more. We are not going to win despite our beliefs. I want to win because of our beliefs (applause). There is no choice between being principled and unelectable and

electable and unprincipled. We have tortured ourselves with this
foolishness for too long. We were right to introduce one member
one vote last year and that change is now done. It is time that we
had an up-to-date statement of the objects and objectives of our
party. If that statement is accepted then let it become the object
of our party for the next election and let it take its place in our
constitution for the next century.

This speech was the template for the next seven years, through
opposition and his first term in government. He set out a clear
break from the New Left of the 1970s, the Kinnock years of
internal strife and pessimism, and even the John Smith era of slow
and cautious preparation for government. In October 1994, when
he made this speech, Labour was consistently 25 to 30 per cent
ahead in the opinion polls over the Conservatives. This lead never
really dropped for the following eighteen months. Blair could own
the agenda, and he did.

The team of Blair, Brown and Mandelson that had worked so
closely together was now fragmented by Brown's fury at Mandelson
for supporting Blair as party leader, but this was still secondary to
the goal of winning the next general election. They created strategies
for reforming and managing the party. Even if Tony Blair didn't
command total support, he would be given the benefit of the doubt
on almost anything. The first test was replacing Clause IV of Labour's
constitution. No one had realised he wanted to drop the commitment
to 'common ownership of the means of production, distribution and
exchange', that had been part of Labour's soul since 1918, and replace
it with a wider definition. He saw it as a logical extension to dropping
the red flag for a red rose as Kinnock had done. It was modernising
the image of the party. The days of the NEC promising to nationalise
Britain's top twenty companies that had led to the creation of CLPD
were well and truly over. In an interview with the *Guardian* the day
after Blair got the amendment to Clause IV, he said:

I know my Labour party very well now. It may be a strange thing
to say but before I became leader I did not. The Labour party is

much nicer than it looks. Labour often looks as if it is about to engage in class warfare in fact it is full of basically rather decent and honest people.

The two biggest unions, the Transport and General Workers Union and Unison, had voted in favour of keeping Clause IV and Blair predicted that the block vote would be reduced from 90 to 50 per cent at the party conference and that the NEC could not be allowed to become an opponent to a Labour government as it had in the 1970s.

The importance of changing Clause IV is seminal because it liberates the Labour party from dogma and sets us free to think and I want us to be free to think the unthinkable.

This declaration on May Day 1995 set off the constitutional changes that would make the party more governable in Blair's image. New Labour was obsessed with driving individual membership, open ballots on policy, low membership fees and open primaries. Membership increased from 300,000 in 1994 to 400,000 in 1996 to 405,000 in 1997. In his three years of opposition, Blair appointed a new generation of advisors and managers. Tom Sawyer, once of the left and NUPE, was now general secretary and the later appointment of Margaret McDonagh as his deputy and successor confirmed a new level of active control of the machine. He had the formidable presence of Alastair Campbell, who acted as campaign director and spokesman and after 1997 acted as Downing Street press secretary, and then director of communications. The three years before the next general election were spent asserting the modernisers' control of the party. Tony Blair and his team had seen how the New Left had used the annual conference, the NEC and the use of constitutional amendments to push against the Labour leadership in the 1970s. This was not going to be repeated under his leadership.

Blair had inherited three internal party institutions: the NEC which had been a continual thorn in the side of the Labour leadership in the 1970s but tamed under Neil Kinnock, and two new bodies created by John Smith, the Joint Policy Committee and the National Policy Forum. They were designed to move policy debate away from the annual conference and allow more control by the leadership over the policy development of the party. In 1996 the leader's office and shadow cabinet created the 'Road to the Manifesto' that agreed Labour's policy positions for the next election with the NEC and National Policy Forum. Party members were balloted on the proposals. When the result was announced on 5 November 1996, there was a 95 per cent vote in favour. It was seen as an exercise in party management and spin, and the use of open primaries and policy votes was established. The means by which motions could be submitted to conference were also now far more restricted. Vladimir Derer's tactics in the 1970s were not going to be used against the new leadership in the 1990s.

On the NEC itself, the constituency section had always been a stronghold of the left. Tony Benn regularly topped the poll as an MP elected from it. In 1997, Peter Mandelson stood for the CLP section of the NEC against Ken Livingstone. Livingstone won. The immediate response was to abolish the right of MPs to stand in this section which henceforth be only for 'rank and file candidates'. Over the next two decades, the constituency section generated slates of relatively unknown left activists who stood under the banner Grassroots Alliance (GRA). The GRA always managed to get a small number of candidates, such as Pete Willsman and Christine Shawcroft, elected.

The New Labour machine originally put up an alternative slate every year and over the years, various celebrities were brought in including Michael Cashman, Tony Robinson and more recently, Eddie Izzard. All of them were serious candidates and Cashman as an MEP played a big role. As a former actor in *EastEnders,* he was an example of people with different professional backgrounds and aims coming into the big tent of New Labour. In 1988 the Conservatives introduced the Local Government Act that included section 28, which banned local councils from promoting, teaching or publishing any material 'with the intention of promoting homosexuality'. It was only repealed in Scotland in 2000 and the rest of the UK in 2003. Michael Cashman:

> Section 28 came along famously repressing lesbians, gays and bisexuals. It was the first anti-LGBT law in 100 years. I became involved in that campaign. That brought me into contact with Neil [Kinnock] and members of the shadow cabinet, particularly because around at that time there was confusion in Labour as to whether they should support section 28. I intervened very quickly to say, 'Absolutely not.' . . . I became really deeply politicised through the miner's strike and through section 28, particularly playing a gay man on television and breaking the mould in that respect.

The use of these slates in NEC and conference arrangement committee elections by the party machine became proxy wars for power of the machine against the grassroots left. The overreach in control also inevitably backfired. As Blair continued as leader and then prime minister, more and more of the left removed themselves from the party and the balance towards the centre became stronger. Participation in the voting for the NEC had declined between 1997 and 2001 by a staggering 71 per cent.

New Labour also became obsessed with candidate selection. Over the New Labour years, candidates were chosen on a general basis of who would be supportive of either Blair or Brown. Many candidates were on a standardised journey from Oxbridge to policy unit or special assistant to MP to ministerial office. The princes and princesses of New Labour were generally from a background of media, law or working within government for the previous generation. Those elected to parliament in the three elections won by Blair and who went onto cabinet or shadow cabinet posts included Yvette Cooper, Ruth Kelly and Ben Bradshaw, all of whom came from a media background. By 2001, Labour was creating its own succession with policy advisors David Miliband and Andy Burnham, along with Shaun Woodward who combined a media background with being a Conservative MP before being placed into a safe Labour seat. James Purnell had come from the policy unit of the BBC and Tom Watson, just to mix it up, from a Labour party and trade union background. In 2005, Ed Balls and Ed Miliband were both selected after working for Gordon Brown at the Treasury. Paul Kenny of the GMB:

> It was corrupt in a way that I'm not sure anyone's ever really analysed. They had no intention of allowing any more working class sons or sisters of toil. They knew about and controlled vacancies in constituencies.

Notable cases of candidates being forced out by the party machine for parliamentary seats included Liz Davies, a member of the NEC, who won an open selection in Leeds North East only to be dumped by command of the leadership. She left the party. By 2018 she had returned and became a prominent lawyer in the enquiry over the Grenfell Tower disaster. The control of selections and favouritism of candidates would be a long-running sore, both during and after New Labour's rule. The unions and the left always remembered it and were prepared to do it themselves when they got the chance.

New Labour also took a more radical view of its relationships at the centre of British politics. In 1988 the Liberals and SDP had merged to initially become the Social and Liberal Democrats and then in 1989, the Liberal Democrats or 'Lib Dems'. Paddy Ashdown was elected leader. Some former Labour members who had joined the SDP after 1981 came back to the Labour party under Blair, some stayed in the new party. The political atmosphere it produced took two forms that would have been inconceivable under any of Blair's predecessors: a rapprochement with the Lib Dems, and a genuine consideration of proportional representation. Part of the coterie around Mandelson was his old friend Roger Liddle, who had been an SDP candidate, and later the SDP adherents Derek Scott and Andrew Adonis. They all returned to the Labour party as advisors. Blair had a close relationship with Roy Jenkins, which led to detailed conversations on proportional representation and some form of power sharing. When the 1997 election was over, the Lib Dems joined a cabinet consultative committee and on 1 December the Jenkins commission was created to look at proportional representation.

The radical alliance in the centre ground of British politics was designed to ensure the left never came back. Pro-European, socially liberal, radical about modern Britain; all of these applied to Blair and Ashdown. It was in the Roy Jenkins tradition going back to his rebellion over the EEC in 1971. Peter Mandelson:

> We wanted the centre, and the left, to come together in a progressive alliance. We did see a liberal tradition in New Labour ... Attlee, post-war, Keynes, Beveridge; these were people who were important reformers from the centre, and we needed to draw those strands into what we were doing.

The other sign of the big tent was to bring people from other parts of modern life into the plans for government. David Triesman, general secretary under Tony Blair:

> Well it certainly was about competence ... Tony Blair so often talked about having a big tent, he wanted people who'd been in business. He wanted people who'd been in unions. It was the creation of a new broad church, but it was created not just out of believers but out of doers and I always thought it was a do-tank even more than a think-tank.

People like David Sainsbury were brought into government for their expertise and competence. As New Labour continued in office this led to more controversial appointments.

As control was being ramped up so the style of the party was changing. The introduction of corporate style became a feature of the New Labour years. Out went t-shirts, beards and dungarees and in came smart-suited, corporate style for both employees of the party and the companies they attracted. Clean-cut had replaced half-cut, although there were exceptions. Jeremy Corbyn regularly won beard of the year and, as events were to show, alcohol was not entirely absent from the House of Commons. Barbara Follett, who became a Labour MP in 1997, became the face of the New Labour makeover. Michael Cashman:

> Members of the shadow cabinet and others were 'Folletted' . . . People were sent off to have their colours chosen for them, the styles that were right. We all used to traipse off, very willingly, to their beautiful house in Cheyne Walk, where we would plot strategy on benefits, but you were always clear that Barbara was looking at the colours you were wearing, the shapes of what you were wearing, as to whether you should be Folletted.

Byron Taylor, who would later play a major part in the trade union relationship with Labour, had a different experience at the lower end of the party before the 1997 general election:

> I went to a Young Labour event in 1994 and the 1995 Conferences, and was surrounded by young men in suits, which was completely alien to me. This was the first time I'd been surrounded by people my own age dressed in suits.

The image fit into the wider strategy of the message put out by new Labour. Michael Cashman again:

> Blair often used the term 'script'. 'We have to write you into the script. We have to write this into the script.' And there was a real sense that there was a script, there was a story and there was a production and they were production values. There was huge distrust within the party. It's interesting for me that when I stood in 1993, I was portrayed by the right as this crazy left-winger interested in lesbian and gay rights. We then get to 1998 and I'm portrayed by the left as this crazy right-winger who believes in Tony Blair.

The evolution of economic policy that would underpin the first term was dominated by Gordon Brown and his advisor, Ed Balls.

They were driven by the memory of John Smith's shadow budget before the 1992 election that had allowed the Conservative attack on tax and spend. Brown was determined to avoid this trap, and could rely on the fact that Kenneth Clarke, as chancellor, had done an effective job in cleaning up the economy since 1993. The break with the past and with traditional Labour norms were all central to Brown's thinking. Everything would be controlled through the prism of first winning, then of prudence in public spending. This led to his announcement on 20 January 1997, four months before the general election, that Labour would keep the Conservatives' top rate of income tax through the lifetime of the parliament. This commitment would obviously constrain the first Labour government's spending plans and here Brown also promised that he would stick to the Conservatives' spending plans for the first two years in power. This new realism was confirmed in the 1997 manifesto, with a foreword from Tony Blair that laid out his mission, accompanied by a description of a new politics with a new and different Labour party that would own the centre ground of politics and business.

> That is one way in which politics in Britain will gain a new lease of life. But there is another. We aim to put behind us the bitter political struggles of left and right that have torn our country apart for too many decades.

He equated the growth of New Labour with growth for Britain:

> I want a country in which people get on, do well, make a success of their lives. I have no time for the politics of envy. We need more successful entrepreneurs, not fewer of them. But these life chances should be for all the people. And I want a society in which ambition and compassion are seen as partners not opposites – where we value public service as well as material wealth. The old left would have sought state control of industry. The Conservative right is content to leave all to the market. We reject both approaches. Government and industry must

work together to achieve key objectives aimed at enhancing the dynamism of the market, not undermining it.

There was also a pledge card to do five specific things:

- Cut class sizes to thirty or under for five, six and seven-year-olds by using money from the assisted places scheme.
- Fast-track punishment for persistent young offenders by halving the time from arrest to sentencing.
- Cut NHS waiting lists by treating an extra 100,000 patients as a first step by releasing £100,000,000 saved from NHS red tape.
- Get 250,000 under-twenty-fives off benefits and into work by using money from a windfall levy on the privatised utilities.
- No rise in income tax rates, cut VAT on heating to 5 per cent and inflation and interest rates as low as possible.

The 1997 election saw Labour increase its share of the vote from 34 per cent to 43 per cent and the number of votes increase to 13.5 million. It won 418 seats. It was the last general election to achieve a national turnout above 70 per cent (71.3 per cent). Even the fact that election day was on May Day played into New Labour's hands. Tony Blair became the youngest prime minister since Lord Liverpool in 1812. The face of politics was changed forever by all-female candidate shortlists that had been introduced by John Smith in 1993. This selection process was introduced in half the seats where sitting male MPs were retiring and half the seats that appeared to be winnable. It produced a record number of 101 women Labour MPs.

There have been three great cyclical moments of political shift since 1979: the election of 1979 that brought in Margaret Thatcher and Conservative dominance of a generation; eighteen years later, in 1997, the election of Tony Blair and New Labour which ended that dominance; nineteen years after that, in 2016, the vote for Brexit, the consequences of which are still uncertain.

New Labour is a matter of huge debate between its adherents and critics. It's full of contradictions and disputes but when it won the general election that electric night in 1997, it was full of hope and promise. It's worth reflecting what it meant to some of those who later became important figures in Labour's drama. As Conservatives lost their seats, particularly cabinet minister Michael Portillo, to a young Labour unknown, Stephen Twigg, it was a special moment – even for the members of the left who had been frozen out. Jon Lansman:

I was delighted when Labour was elected. It was a euphoric night. Who wouldn't be euphoric at the end of Tory rule, after that number of years? It was of course a fantastic victory.

For the unions, any doubts about New Labour could be set aside against the win. Paul Kenny:

People in (the union) leadership were desperate for a Labour government and if that meant Blair was going to win the election, then that's what they wanted. In 1997, people, the electorate, everywhere you went were sick and tired of the Tories (who) were absolutely bankrupt. People just couldn't wait to get to the polls. I've never seen anything like it since . . . There wasn't a soul in the country who was a Labour supporter, or a trade union activist, who didn't revel in the prospect of people like Portillo getting kicked out. Let's be honest about it. I still think it's a great moment in politics.

One 16-year-old, Emilie Oldknow, wasn't that bothered:

I went to bed. Sixteen-year-olds don't care. My dad came and got me up out of bed, we went downstairs and he said, you have to watch this, this is like, you know . . . And I'd never seen, I don't think, anybody be so overwhelmed and joyous . . . shouting at the telly.

PART FOUR

New Labour:
The Good, the Bad and the Ugly

'It was a title for victory, not for rule . . . they made an
ideology of the absence of ideology'
Neil Kinnock 2018

'It's wrong for Neil to say we didn't have an ideology,
that's completely wrong. It was rooted in strong social
democratic beliefs and values'
Peter Mandelson 2018

'Immediately you saw that actually it wasn't just a
marketing ploy to get into government. It wasn't just
"We'll tone down our ideas and when we get into
government, we'll implement real Labour policies."
They believed in it'
John McDonnell 2018

9

What was New Labour?

New Labour's achievements were huge, its impact great, and it was victorious in 1997, 2001 and 2005. Its parliamentary majorities were always large enough to ensure its agenda would be met; its opposition came not from the other political parties as much as from its own side. The title 'New Labour' emerged in 1994, but it became the principal ideological and branding exercise in 1996 when the party manifesto *New Labour, New Life for Britain* was published, and it became the mantra of the new government in 1997. This was the reformation that Mandelson, Gould and the Shadow Communications Agency had been pushing since 1987.

It is impossible to escape the shadow New Labour still throws. Within the Conservative party, Margaret Thatcher created a neo-liberal consensus around rolling back the state, ignoring 'society' and putting private wealth and profit at the heart of taxation and spending policies. Even forty years after she was first elected, it means something to be a Thatcherite in the modern Conservative party. In today's Labour party, no one would use New Labour as a means of gaining support. It has become such a damning term of abuse that even its natural heirs try to avoid it. Yet Blair and Thatcher both won three elections for their parties and were heads of radical and reforming governments. It took only sixteen years from 1994 for New Labour to be repudiated by Ed Miliband in

2010, but it remains a hugely significant part of Labour's past and influence on its politics now.

One prominent New Labour figure recently said of a leading Corbynista shadow cabinet member, 'They really hate us.' The levels of opposition within the Labour party have always run deep but New Labour induces levels of hatred from the left that is truly exceptional. Tony Blair, Gordon Brown and the people around them had a clear vision of what they wanted to be and how to achieve it. Tony Blair:

> What we did with New Labour was create a modern, progressive, social democratic party and that's what the 21st century requires on the progressive side of politics.

This would mean working as a reforming and modernising part of the current economic system. It would mean utilising both the market and the state. Alastair Campbell:

> New Labour was the understanding that a modernised Labour party was the key to modernising Britain because it was the means by which we took progressive values but allied them to an acceptance of and appreciation of market economy.

Stewart Wood, an advisor to Gordon Brown and later Ed Miliband, viewed it as a skilful trade-off:

> It was a political project to make Labour safe again for England and it was done primarily through a kind of Faustian pact with the City or with business in general. Lightly regulate, you pay the tax, we do the redistribution. Everyone's happy.

For Spencer Livermore, it was a necessary correction to the past:

> It was about reconnecting the Labour party both to its traditional values and to the people it was founded to represent. Prior to Neil Kinnock, the Labour party had gone on a sort of ideological

holiday, where it indulged itself in all of that sort of dogma. This amused the middle-class intellectual socialists but had absolutely nothing whatsoever to do with real people.

Except some traditionalists like Neil Kinnock himself saw it as a rebrand without a real soul:

> It was a title for victory, not for rule . . . They made an ideology of the absence of ideology.

Peter Mandelson, unsurprisingly, had an opposite view:

> It was a modernising, radical, social democratic project, based upon a progressive alliance of people on the centre and the left of British politics. Therefore it's wrong for Neil to say we didn't have an ideology; that's completely wrong. It was rooted in strong social democratic belief and values. We needed New Labour rapidly to become a governing project. Neil's project – a successful one – was more about saving the Labour party and beating the hard left.

Andy Burnham, who served as a cabinet minister under Blair and Brown and then mayor of Manchester, saw it change over time:

> It was Labour in touch with the real world, at the beginning, because later it became something different . . . There's a difference between early New Labour, middle New Labour, and late New Labour. Certainly, early New Labour was about Labour values, but completely connecting them to the mainstream current of society.

Anna Yearley, later political secretary to Ed Miliband, saw it as a new means of hope:

> The way the Labour party wins elections is from the centre of British politics, and in order to do the radical things you want

to do to help natural Labour voters, you need to appeal to the people. What Tony Blair represented was the personification of New Labour, an alternative and hope, and I know that sounds incredibly clichéd, but I think when you're fifteen, you do feel like that.

For Paul Kenny, general secretary of the GMB and union baron; it was about winning:

> It was a new style. The smart, young, clean-cut style. It was designed to appeal, it was an architectural design of some sort of new centrist party. They had this idea of balance that if you get the centre, never mind about the underclass and the poor at this end, and don't worry about the super-rich, but everything in between, we are effectively on the same level. It was an election machine.

And for the left then and now, it was a betrayal of Labour values and nearer to those of Margaret Thatcher. John McDonnell:

> It was a neo-liberal party within a party. When Tony Blair announced 'New Labour' we knew that was a new party being formed from within. We knew then, as his ideas were developed, especially the economic ideas, that they were largely dominated by neo-liberalism. So, elements of trickledown economics, public sector bad, private sector good, privatisation, PFI's, were all on the agenda. Others like Gordon Brown who did have a left background, almost had a Faustian pact with Blair and others, that this was a way of getting into government. I think Blair believed it.

Jon Lansman:

> It was completely devoted to market economics, almost uncritically. And it had no commitment to change anything, no commitment to any kind of fundamental change in society. It had no mission.

And from the man who eventually inherited it, Ed Miliband, leader of the Labour party from 2010 to 2015:

> New Labour was an economic acceptance of much but not all of what had gone before, combined with a determined commitment to invest in public services and redistribute, as well as a sort of sentiment of modernisation.

New Labour was powerful enough in 1997 to convince almost everyone that it could change the Labour party and Britain for ever. That lasted thirteen years.

10

The Good

In 1997, the new government had all the advantages: a growing economy, a new and youthful leadership, control over its future, electoral success and a genuine desire in the country for change. New Labour started by representing the hope and desire to make Britain a fairer, more equal and open society. For the early part of the thirteen years in power, this was a genuine aspiration that succeeded. Blair and Brown were a duopoly who shared a mutual vision of change, reform and economic competence. It is worth remembering that after eighteen years of opposition, there was very little experience in New Labour. They were unfettered with governing experience and given this, or perhaps because of this, it is remarkable how self-confident government policy was and how many risks were run.

As chancellor, Gordon Brown practised immense activism. Three days after entering government, he made the Bank of England independent in setting interest rates through a monetary policy committee. His first budget created a windfall tax on private utilities and pensions that was balanced by an announcement of an extra £3 billion on education and health. The following year he introduced the working families tax credit and a national minimum wage of £3.60 an hour. In his second term, he put extra charges on National Insurance to fund substantial increases in spending on public services. His three-year comprehensive spending review in 1998 controlled spending in all government departments and by the end of the first term this prudence, combined with a fast growing economy, meant he had a war chest that allowed a pre-election budget in 2001 of £40 billion extra in health spending alone.

He also took a strong position against Britain joining the Euro as this would have meant losing the pound, agreeing European budget targets and having borrowing limits of no more than 3 per cent of GDP. Brown first ruled out joining for the lifetime of the first parliament, and then set five tests that would theoretically lead to a referendum on joining. As intended, this never happened.

By 2001, the years of prudence had allowed all of Labour's 1997 manifesto pledges to be met. No increases in income tax, the introduction of a new, low rate of ten pence in the pound, VAT reduced on fuel to 5 per cent, inflation held to 2.5 per cent throughout the first term and economic growth continued throughout the first term and into the second.

New Labour had a substantial role in reducing poverty and increasing public expenditure on key social services. The first term and the first few years of the second term saw a huge number of new schemes and rising levels of expenditure fuelled by a growing economy and Gordon Brown's use of stealth taxes. In one area alone, children and young adults, New Labour used tax credits and benefits to target poverty. A report for the Child Action Poverty Group in 2010 stated that without the tax credits conferred by Brown, poverty would have affected 4.3 million children. Instead it fell from 3.4 million to 2.5 million – 900,000 children taken out of the poverty trap was a huge achievement. Measures such as the introduction of Sure Start in 1998 poured money and resources into early age services though healthcare, education and home-based support for families suffering high levels of deprivation. Two hundred and fifty Sure Start local programmes reached up to 150,000 children. This scheme was repeatedly extended and by 2003 was put under the control of local government.

Similar targeted schemes were created for other age groups, with free nursery care for 615,000 preschoolers and class sizes reduced for five to seven-year-olds. The Fresh Start policy for failing schools combined with a building programme that rose from £683 million in 1996 to more than £3.5 billion by 2004. National literacy targets for English and maths were introduced. The New Deal workfare programme created training schemes for 345,000 under-25-year-olds. All of this pointed to the fundamental purpose of New Labour at its height. It allied economic competence with ambition for change in key areas of social policy. This could fairly be said to be Brown's achievement. His dominance over economic and social policy was immeasurable. His claim to be a full partner with Blair in government was understandable. His repeated claims in this period were that New Labour had ended the cycle of boom and bust. This became a boast that would come back to haunt him.

The 2001 manifesto was the high point. It made commitments about public services that combined economic stability with substantial investment. Annual spending on education was to rise 5 per cent in real terms, on health by an annual average of 6 per cent, on transport systems by 20 per cent for the following three years. The police were given an extra £1.6 billion by 2003-2004 and up to £400 million was set aside for local government in return for targets to improve local services. Increases in staff in front line services included 20,000 more nurses, 10,000 more doctors, 10,000 more teachers and 6,000 extra police recruits. The minimum wage was to be increased to £4.20 an hour, along with a child trust fund for every child at birth. The ten pence band of income tax was widened and training schemes were established to help 750,000 adults achieve basic skills. These were levels of investment and renewal that are unique in modern British political history.

Alongside the economic management were New Labour's other ambitions. It is often forgotten that Tony Blair had a remarkable ability to seize the public mood in his early years as prime minister. This was shown as early as August 1997 when Diana was killed and he named her 'the People's Princess'. It could be said he helped save the dysfunctional royal family at that time by guiding them through the public mood of hostility.

New Labour introduced wide-ranging constitutional and social changes and the tone was set for a far more inclusive and liberal society. Lesbian, gay, bisexual and transgender rights were opened up. The government tackled homelessness. Everything from pensioners to ramblers' rights were extended. The attempts to create the big tent with the Lib Dems had led to the creation of the Jenkins Commission on Proportional Representation, but ultimately Blair pulled back from implementing it. There were other major constitutional changes: the creation of the Scottish Parliament and Welsh Assembly was followed by partial reform of the House of Lords with most hereditary peers removed; elected mayors in major cities and a partial Freedom of Information Act were introduced.

On the international stage Britain acceded to the presidency of the European Union in New Labour's first year, and Blair spoke French well enough to address the French National Assembly. He projected youthful vigour and ambition on the world stage and created an alliance with Bill Clinton – the third way – that led to what some may regard as his greatest achievement, the Good Friday agreement in 1998. The impact of this, ending thirty years of troubles in Northern Ireland and creating a completely new dynamic within the island of Ireland, should never be underestimated and lives with us today.

By 2001, the electoral team of Blair, Brown and Mandelson could fight the Conservative's William Hague with total confidence that the five pledges of 1997 had been met and that they would win. Labour won 413 seats, down only 5 from 1997, and 40.7 per cent of the vote from 43.2 per cent in 1997. The Conservatives under William Hague only won one more seat (166) than in 1997 and went to 31.7 per cent, a mere one per cent increase. The worrying trend, however, was that overall turnout had dropped by 12 per cent from 1997 to only 59 per cent. The impact on the Labour vote was a huge drop from 13.5 million votes to 10.7 million. This was lower than in both 1992 and 1979 when Labour had lost elections. After only four years of government, something was going wrong. Somehow the electorate was sensing there were problems lurking beneath the glossy surface.

11

The Bad and the Ugly

From the earliest days of 1997, the government's lack of experience had produced self-inflicted wounds that bubbled into the public consciousness. Finance and money, spin and obsessive control all came to haunt New Labour. The lure of money was to become an early issue, and from 1994 to 1997, attracting business support was a prime objective. This was partially to offset trade union funding and partially because New Labour loved business and business people quite indiscriminately.

The modernisers had abiding memories of the 1970s, with trade unions influencing government policy and then turning on the Labour government during the winter of discontent. They were determined to bring in the world of business through the employers' organisation, the CBI, as a balanced partner in government policymaking. The anti-union legislation of the 1980s was not repealed and the emphasis on keeping to the Conservative's spending plans, not increasing the higher rate of income tax, and getting filthy rich was all fine – so long as taxes were paid. This was not in the Labour tradition. However, it was a policy that could be defended at a time when the economy was booming and government spending was benefitting everyone. Why worry about it if taxes were being paid?

Where it became far more problematic, as was often the case for New Labour, was in the atmospherics. Both Brown and Blair had their favourite businessmen and women who clustered around them both socially and politically. Throughout their time in office, the honours system was used to reward business people and trade unionists who had shown support. Some of these were bound to be less salubrious than others. Tony Blair and Gordon Brown, who themselves were entitled to honours when they left office but didn't take them, used the system in a way that was open to accusations of cronyism. There were plenty of people given honours by New Labour: Fred Goodwin, Philip Green and Alan Sugar to name a few, who would not have been thought of as natural recipients of honours from a Labour government. This hero worship for 'wealth creators' and 'people who get things done' took on a much more insidious form when it came to party finance.

The desire to raise money led to the first problem, when it was revealed in January 1997 that Bernie Ecclestone, then chief executive of the Formula One Group, had made a £1 million donation to Labour before the election. In October Ecclestone lobbied Tony Blair to exempt Formula 1 from a ban on tobacco advertising – the ban was a key plank in the Labour manifesto. F1 was granted the exemption in early November but when the donation became public it was an embarrassment. Blair couldn't explain this away and finally confessed it was a mistake, insisting he was still 'a pretty straight sort of guy'.

Labour was always running out of money unless the big unions stepped up, but they were often slow to pay. David Triesman was party general secretary in 2002 and explained the dilemma.

> The next problem was that the party was very, very heavily in debt. And the moment for me when that became particularly telling, was when the bank told me that we would not pay the salaries next month. At the height of New Labour, Labour couldn't afford to pay its salaries because the unions would pay very, very late and usually with some conditionality around it. . . . I would have to go back to the very big donors and then people would say, 'This is in the hands of the very big donors'. If you can imagine really trying to run this quite big machine which was visibly very successful, but with more or less no

money and technically probably beyond the point which you would see we're insolvent. That was very difficult.

By the early 2000s, the Labour party gave itself over to corporate money. Everyone wanted a piece of New Labour. Kevin Maguire wrote this article in 2001 for the *Guardian*:

Tony Blair last night triggered a potentially damaging row over Labour's increasingly close links with big corporations after it emerged that he is to attend a £15,000 reception at the party's annual conference paid for by the burger chain McDonald's. It agreed to sponsor the food and drink for 450 guests at a high-profile event in Brighton to celebrate Labour's 100th conference only after receiving assurances that the prime minister would attend. The Labour MP John McDonnell, a critic of transnational corporations such as McDonald's, said: 'It turns my stomach, I don't know how low we can sink. It just shows how out of touch the Labour leadership is with the rank and file of the movement'.

For sale: access to captive audience
Examples of New Labour sponsorship 'opportunities' at the party's annual conference:

Chair's reception NEW! 8 p.m. to late. A major reception celebrating the 100th Labour conference. The event will be hosted by the party chair and general secretary and will be attended by up to 450 guests in the Hilton Metropole's Balmoral Suite **£15,000**

Policy fringe – education A question and answer-style event with the education team **£10,000**

Ambulance service NEW! Enjoy a positive profile through an association with the vital emergency service provided by the local ambulance service **£5,000**

Conference dinner – flowers Branding opportunity on every flower arrangement provided for the 700 guests **£3,500**

Relaxation zone NEW! This increasingly popular relaxation therapy facility is free for all visitors and delegates. A unique branding opportunity to a captive audience **£7,500**

Leader's speech video screen A unique promotional opportunity for the special video screen provided for hundreds of delegates to watch leader's speech **£4,000**

Branding opportunities on relaxation and flower arrangements! It was enough to burst a blood vessel of any self-respecting critic of New Labour.

By 2001, New Labour's image was becoming tarnished. This had been compounded by the peculiar political fate of Peter Mandelson, who had to resign twice in the course of the first term through accusations of unethical decisions in office. He was brought down by the very spin he had created and journalists were dying to get him as the face and voice of New Labour. He also had been the given the poisoned chalice of making the Millennium Dome work.

In *Talking to a Brick Wall*, Deborah Mattinson of the Shadow Communications Agency described a focus group discussing the Dome and its reported £700 million cost. The sheer fury and incredulity people felt about it caused her, in 2000, to write a briefing to the Labour party:

> The Dome continues to be a weeping sore. Its potential to damage the government is immense. The recent injection of £29 million has generated voter fury about profligacy. It tells them the government is out of touch with ordinary people.

The harder the criticism, the harder New Labour fought to control the message. The spinning operations conducted by Mandelson, Alastair Campbell and the people around Gordon Brown such as Charlie Whelan and, later, Damian McBride, were of a different nature to anything that had been seen in British politics before, or since. Hugely aggressive central control of messaging throughout government was brilliantly effective, until it got out of hand.

Off-the-record briefings worked well until they took place against members of the same government. Bullying and insertion of threats against television producers, newspaper journalists and editors only worked when the power to bully was reinforced by truth.

By the second term, when the government got into trouble, its friends were few and far between. No wonder the media wanted to get Mandelson and any other victim of the various feuds, New Labour made it so easy to do. At the same time, Blair and his inner circle made every attempt to work with Rupert Murdoch and his empire in an attempt to nullify the press attacks from his stable of newspapers. The underlying stresses these actions created were only manageable when the central project held together. After 2001, the cracks began to appear.

12

Conflict

After winning its second victory in 2001, New Labour entered into a series of spasms that ultimately brought the project to an end. The all-powerful combination of Blair and Brown, the most effective political pairing of their time, indeed of almost any time, would slowly but surely strangle New Labour. Of course, they were not alone and the fights between their two camps of loyalists were legendary. However, although the division was driven by personality and the desire to win, it was also based on policy. The areas that gradually split New Labour and alienated the wider constituent elements of the party were foreign policy, especially Blair's conviction to be an interventionist on the world stage, the role of reform, and the role of private capital in public services.

All prime ministers want to play on the world stage. It appeals as a way to create history, rub shoulders with the global elite and take selfies at conferences. For Tony Blair it started well. With Foreign Secretary Robin Cook he established what he called an 'ethical foreign policy'. He and Brown created the Department for International Development. By 2007 the overseas aid budget had more than doubled and, in 2005, when Blair hosted the G8 conference, 100 per cent debt cancellation for African countries was agreed, along with huge increases in aid from the other G8 countries.

In Europe, Blair was immediately involved in tearing up the UK's opt-out of the EU social chapter and vowed to put the UK 'back into the heart of Europe' after the tension of the Conservative years. He became a significant figure in European politics and was in favour of enlarging the EU and reinforcing its institutions. At the same time, he failed to get Gordon Brown to approve the Euro and to make the British people understand why membership was to the UK's benefit. The longer-term consequences of this – the rise of UKIP, the difficulties of immigration policy and Cameron's referendum in 2016 – can all, in part, be explained by a certain complacency about the EU under New Labour.

His biggest impact, however, was alongside two US Presidents as a global interventionist. By 1999, the bloody civil war in the former Yugoslavia had claimed tens of thousands of lives and two million refugees a mere three hundred miles from the EU's own borders. The nationalist Serbian leader, Slobodan Milošević, had pursued the most violent and brutal war on European soil since world war two. The ultimate target of the Serb aggression was Kosovo. The US tried to get a negotiated settlement but, by June 1998, President Bill Clinton believed the threat from Serbia was too great. Blair lost no time in agreeing that NATO could execute limited air strikes. By March 1999, peace talks had failed and a bombing campaign under NATO (but not UN) authority was begun. This included attacks on Yugoslav units on the ground but also in Belgrade, resulting in hundreds of civilian casualties and the bombing of the Chinese Embassy. Blair was prepared to put NATO ground forces into Kosovo and 50,000 British troops were put on alert, but lack of Russian support forced Milošević to accept the terms of an international peacekeeping plan.

Blair had taken a hugely active part in this conflict and when he visited a Kosovan refugee camp, was treated like a hero and mobbed. He had, within two years of becoming prime minister, become a sponsor of military action. A small group on the left of the party, led by Tony Benn and Jeremy Corbyn, condemned it as imperialist aggression, but overall the action was supported by the political mainstream.

In April 1999 Blair made a speech in Chicago that sought to further establish his global credentials. He highlighted the danger of Milošević and another potential threat, Saddam Hussein. He argued for the need for intervention on both moral and pragmatic grounds and also made it clear that he would do it again. He stated, however, that action would only be taken based on five tests to guide British involvement in intervening in conflict. First, the certainty of the case. Second, had all the diplomatic options be exhausted? Third, were there military operations that could be undertaken sensibly and prudently? Fourth, was there a long-term strategy rather than just an exit strategy? Finally, were national interests involved? These tests were applied to interventions after Kosovo. By the end of the first term British armed forces had also been used in Sierra Leone.

He fought his second general election in June 2001, clear about his role as a global interventionist. His commitment to this role was emphasised on 11 September 2001. He was about to give a speech at the Trades Union Congress when Alastair Campbell told him to turn on the television, and they watched the planes hit the twin towers. The US had a new president, George W. Bush. That night, Blair broadcast that 'we here in Britain stand shoulder to shoulder with our American friends.'

It was quickly established that the attack had been made by Al Qaeda, an organisation based in Afghanistan. The decision to go to war was made and the US and its allies started to bomb Afghanistan on 7 October. It ignored the five tests as well as the lessons of history. No one since Alexander the Great has fully invaded and subdued Afghanistan. The British involvement has continued there to 2018 in one form or another. The decision to attack Afghanistan could be defended on the basis that Al Qaeda was an international threat and support for the US was of paramount national interest. There was little mainstream disagreement in 2001 that the UK should take part, except from the left who created a new organisation to protest against it, The Stop the War Coalition.

The events leading up to the next war were far murkier and their consequences much more pervasive. Four months after the bombing began in Afghanistan, George W. Bush made the State of the Union address in which he attacked countries he deigned the axis of evil: Iran, North Korea and Iraq. The pressure exerted from the vice president, Dick Cheney, secretary of defence, Donald Rumsfeld, and their neo-conservative allies, was to attack Iraq. Blair met Bush in Crawford, Texas in April and the discussion began in earnest. Blair urged Bush to get a UN resolution that would give legitimacy to any attack on Iraq. This did not happen.

The Chilcot report, published in July 2016, could not be more damning about the ensuing events. In the run-up to war, peaceful methods of diplomacy were not used, intelligence reports pointing to the stockpiling of weapons of mass destruction (WMD) were inaccurate and the nuances and uncertainties within the intelligence were ignored. The dossier justifying the war based on this intelligence came to be known as the 'dodgy dossier': the claim that Iraq could launch a WMD within forty-five minutes was wrong, Saddam Hussein did not pose an immediate threat, and the UN security council supported continuing weapons inspection and monitoring. The legal process to go to war without a security council resolution was 'far from satisfactory'. For Tony Blair, the overriding desire to be the key ally of the US, dating back to Kosovo, meant that he overestimated his influence and did not agree a post-conflict plan that would be a condition of UK involvement. In retrospect, his private memo to Bush which read 'I will be with you whatever' could not be more damning. The impact on domestic politics was to be seismic.

If Iraq was affecting New Labour, domestic strategy was also beginning to cause friction. The 2001 manifesto had not only promised huge increases in public expenditure, it also focused on the role of choice and of external, private funding in public services. In education, there was to be increased support for city academies and church schools, with more testing for eleven to fourteen-year-olds. In health, more power was to be given to NHS health trusts and waiting times were to be cut. New hospitals were to be created either by the NHS or the private sector, and successful NHS hospitals would be allowed to take over unsuccessful ones.

This was the next stage of the modernisers' agenda. The emphasis from now on was *choice* and it could be supplied from numerous sources. The 2001 manifesto stated:

> Services need to be highly responsive to the demands of users. Where the quality is not improving quickly enough, alternative providers should be brought in. Where private sector providers can support public endeavour, we should use them. A 'spirit of enterprise' should apply as much to public service as to business.

Pat McFadden MP, a Blair advisor and then minister:

> A lot of the public service reforms were about empowering the consumers of these services. We were conscious that those with power and money could buy their way out of any dissatisfaction that they would have from public services provision. So that might mean sending your child to private school, or having your operation done privately, but if you didn't have money you couldn't do those things because they're expensive. And so were trying to empower people without money with the same kinds of . . . 'choice' and 'voice' and 'exit' and terms like this, that people who had money exercised.

In 2003 Blair spoke to the Fabian Society and framed the reform of public services as his big task.

> Our supposedly uniform public services were deeply unequal as league and performance tables in the NHS and schools have graphically exposed. The affluent and well-educated meanwhile had the choice to buy their way out of failing or inadequate provision . . . It was choice for the few, not the many.

His response was:

> . . . to open up the system, to end the one-size-fits-all model of public service, which too often meant one supplier fits all,

with little diversity, irrespective of how good new suppliers – from elsewhere in the public sector, and from the voluntary and private sectors – might be.

This meant bringing in new elements to provision: city academies, new suppliers into the NHS and new, flexible employment. He was unleashing the forces of change on public services whose unions were key supporters of the Labour government. He was backing the use of private money and firms in the provision of services as competitors and he was encouraging the use of private-public partnerships. Over the next four years of his premiership it also became a structural problem within New Labour, as specific proposals came from different ministries at a bewildering speed and intensity.

In education, there was a flood of consultations, white papers and secretaries of state. In 2004, tuition fees in Higher Education created a rebellion of Labour MPs that saw the measure passed by only five votes. As money poured into the NHS it was accompanied by a series of reforms and edicts that made its management ever more complex. Reorganisation followed reorganisation. Polly Toynbee, in the *British Medical Journal* in 2007, summed up the conflict between the desire for reform and the need for efficiency:

This has been a decade of turmoil, with zigzag reforms dictated from the top, only to be countermanded again from the top. The history of his (Blair's) 'reforms' hardly bears repeating. First he dismantled general practice fundholding and some aspects of the Tory internal market. He set up primary care groups, remade them into primary care trusts, and then merged them again into half the number. Demolished regional health authorities were resurrected as twenty-eight strategic health authorities and then merged again back into the original ten regions. The public health director for the south west region provides one graphic example of what has happened on the ground in this breathless deckchair shuffling. He has held the same job since 1994 but has had to reapply for it seven times since then because of reorganisations.

Once the money dried up, the NHS was deeply vulnerable and all of the reforms that were supposed to make it more efficient and consumer-focused made it exactly the opposite.

In 2006 Tony Blair told a conference in London, 'There is a basic deal here. Investment for results.' He wanted private companies such as Sainsbury's, Lloyds, TSB and GlaxoSmithKline to give their time and expertise to the trusts. For the private sector it was money to be earned. This was the most radical departure from the traditional Labour model. Its justification was that more testing, more private financing and more third-party involvement in education, transport and health would benefit those services and the people using them. If the services did not work properly or the contracts with private suppliers were not effective, the system would be open to failure and very high costs.

Nowhere was this seen more clearly than in the areas of public-private partnerships and how they were financed through private finance initiatives (PFIs). It was an agreed policy within New Labour that private money could be brought into major construction projects. For the Treasury it appeared to be win-win. The building of new schools and hospitals paid by partnership with private money. For the chancellor, it kept huge amounts of public spending off the government's books. It allowed large amounts of infrastructural build at what appeared to be much lower risk and it met both fiscal targets and the desire for reform. The National Audit Office (NAO) published a report in February 2018 that showed quite staggering figures. There were 700 operational deals with a capital value of £60 billion and *annual* charges paid by the government of £10.3 billion in 2016-2017. The Department of Health was responsible for debts of £13 billion, Ministry of Defence £9.5 billion and Department of Education £8.6 billion. The NAO reported that interest payments were huge. Even if no new deals were made, future payments would continue to 2040 and amount to £199 billion.

Private companies built up high numbers of contracts with the government to the benefit of their shareholders and executives. Hospitals, schools, roads and back office functions all came under this net. If costs ran over, the private company had to bear the risk and was vulnerable to huge losses, but the government would still act as the backstop and would be left with a failed project that was intended for public use. The use of private finance enhanced the risk profile for the state. In the case of one company, Carillion, this heady mix led it to grow to 43,000 employees and list on the stock market before it went bankrupt in 2018.

Throughout the second term, Tony Blair, Gordon Brown and their ministers grappled with the dilemma of keeping the New Labour project radical and relevant. Huge investments in public services and attacking poverty still united them, but Iraq and a differing view on the range and role of the market in public services began to crack this unity. Nevertheless, the power of New Labour as an electoral force was still overwhelming. Whilst the opposition within parliament was nullified, inside the Labour movement, it began to stir.

13

Opposition: The Left, the Unions and the Media

By 2003, the hopes of 1997 had evaporated and the memories of eighteen years of opposition turned into disquiet about the actions of the Labour government. The left had been in retreat since 1983. By 1997, it had been forced almost entirely back into a tiny rump in parliament, some representation in local government and some trade union support. It was a hard time to be in the party and many activists had left. New Labour's mantra was to avoid the mistakes of the 1970s, including challenges to the leadership from the NEC, the unruly conferences, the pockets of the left's activity in the constituency parties, the unions and the dress code. This control was accepted almost entirely before 1997 because everyone wanted Labour to win after four failures. Peter Mandelson:

> We had to reassure that we were different, that we were not 1970s old Labour, that we were not the fratricidal Labour of the 1980s, that we really were modern, sensible, centrist and united. That was the task. What happened in the 2000s is that Iraq disrupted our progressive alliance. This alliance was working class/middle class, educated/less educated, centrist/left, Trade Union – on a good day, not every day – socially liberal, northern/ southern; I mean it was an amazing alliance. Iraq disrupted that, particularly from the point of view of the more educated middle class, urban, inner-city people.

And the left?

> By the 1990s, that battle had been done and dusted, it wasn't
> relevant any more. Tony was not sectarian in the way that
> Kinnock was, he didn't need to be, nor was it in his culture
> or soul. He didn't need to worry about it. These had become
> yesterday's people, and he felt that the Labour party now was
> so decidedly settled New Labour it didn't really matter, that this
> fight was not his priority.

Yet even in the early days of New Labour, there were signs of
dissent within parliament and the wider labour movement. John
McDonnell, an MP after 1997, was relentlessly pushing the left's
agenda. McDonnell speaking about this in 2018:

> I was chair of Socialist Campaign Group which gave the base
> of the organisation within parliament. We operated as trying
> to ensure there were effective alternative voices heard both in
> parliament and in the party. So, from 1997 onwards, there was
> always a left campaigning voice in the party, issue by issue. After
> the elation of winning the election in 1997, incrementally you
> find that disillusionment setting in. We were recognising that
> there could be significant improvement with the right policies.
> The policies were being introduced but within each policy there
> was a setback and there was an undermining of confidence
> that this was the right direction. People were increasingly
> disillusioned, policy area by policy area.

On first being elected, Gordon Brown's commitment to the
Conservative's spending plans for the first two years of the new
parliament had caused him to cut benefits to single parents. In
December 1997, this caused the first rebellion. Forty-seven Labour
MPs voted against the government, some 100 abstained, one
minister and two Private Parliamentary Secretaries (PPS) resigned
their posts and a ministerial aide was sacked ahead of the crucial
vote. John McDonnell:

The first serious vote when we got elected in 1997 was cutting child benefit. That was the first vote and that was a test, and as soon as they knew they could break us on that, as soon as they knew that they could get the PLP and a majority voting for that, they knew they had a relatively free hand.

He saw New Labour as a serious threat to traditional Labour principles:

Immediately you saw that actually it wasn't just a marketing ploy to get into government. It wasn't just 'We'll tone down our ideas and when we get into government, we'll implement real Labour policies.' They believed in it.

Over the next three years of the first term, there were a series of clashes within the PLP. The imposition of tuition fees, changes on incapacity benefit, increasing the state pension, the Freedom of Information bill and nationalisation of the air traffic control system each had sizable rebellions but were always containable, as the government had a majority of 179. However, the biggest challenge came from outside of parliament when New Labour's control went too far.

Constitutional changes had taken place in Scotland and Wales to create the new devolved governments, and it was proposed to extend this to directly elected mayors starting with London. In Scotland, Donald Dewar moved seamlessly from secretary of state for Scotland to being elected the Labour leader in Scotland and then the first minister of the devolved parliament. Dewar died after only eighteen months in office. Labour had lost a major figure and its future in Scotland was to become much less secure without him. In Wales, Alun Michael was imposed first as secretary of state and then as first minister. The favourite had been Rhodri Morgan, who was a well-liked MP. The uproar this caused only lasted a few months because Morgan replaced Michael, who had to resign amid threats of a motion of no confidence in his leadership of the Welsh Assembly. The blatant nature of the meddling by London was inexplicable, as Morgan was completely in the mainstream of Labour politics.

The saga of the first London mayoral election in 1999 and 2000 was even more damaging. In 1998, a referendum created the first elected London-wide institutions since the removal of the GLC by Margaret Thatcher in 1986. The GLC's radical policies had become mainstream over the previous fifteen years. Women's and LGBT rights were now embraced by the Labour government. Fares Fare was fondly remembered, with rail cards serving as a reminder. Ken Livingstone was regarded as a much more acceptable figure to Londoners.

Livingstone was discovering that being a backbench MP in a New Labour government was ill-suited to his desire for power and authority. Anyone who had known him as leader of the GLC would not have been surprised by this, but New Labour definitely didn't want him as the candidate. In May 1999, it was confirmed that the selection would be on a basis of one member one vote. By this point, Glenda Jackson MP was a candidate and Frank Dobson, the secretary of state for health, was pushed into running by Tony Blair. Why did they care so much? Simon Fletcher, who worked with Livingstone, and later Ed Miliband and Jeremy Corbyn:

> They thought Ken wanted to be mayor to do to Blair what he had done to Thatcher, which would be a point of opposition. Whereas Ken wanted to be mayor to be mayor, because he wanted to do things, and he was bored of being a backbench MP. There was a massive debate in the leadership about whether to block Ken or whether to allow him onto the thing and then stop him . . .

The mechanism for stopping him was an electoral college. In November 1999, after forty-eight hours of meetings and two interviews, Ken Livingstone was allowed to be on the shortlist for the Labour candidacy. By this point, he was repeatedly denying he would stand as an independent if he lost. Despite the earlier announcement of OMOV, the Labour leadership created an electoral college to help their preferred candidate. This had two sections for individual members and unions as well as a third block of MPs, MEPs and GLA candidates. Dobson very honourably declared that he wanted OMOV. He was furious with being the apparent patsy of the leadership and he accused it of messing up his campaign. He went on to win the nomination in an extraordinarily divided electoral college. On both rounds of the voting, Livingstone dominated the party members' and trade union sections. On the second ballot, he won 60 per cent to Dobson's 40 per cent among members and 72 per cent to 28 per cent in the unions section. Among the elected officials, however, Dobson won 86.5 per cent of the votes which was enough to get him through overall by 51.5 per cent to 48.5 per cent.

Livingstone immediately cried foul and two weeks later announced he would stand as an independent. He was expelled from the party. With Fletcher acting as his campaign manager, his campaign had substantial support from Labour activists, media celebrities and a small group of advisors from Socialist Action, an unusually effective Trotskyist organisation with close connections to Fletcher. Livingstone won with 58 per cent of the vote. Dobson, the official Labour candidate in London, came third. This mess was a prime example of the weakness of New labour's desire for control. It tried everything to stop a Labour candidate who it knew would win. The ministerial career of Frank Dobson ended after he was made the sacrificial lamb. Even more recklessly, they created a focus for the left outside the party. In 2004 when Livingstone was up for re-election, they finally admitted the true depth of their stupidity when Tony Blair sued for peace and readmitted him into the party in order to have a Labour mayor in London. This decision was not universally liked. Michael Cashman was on the NEC:

> The party leadership and the general secretary decided that Ken should be brought back into the fold because they wanted him as the candidate. I thought they were wrong. And that's why me and Dennis Skinner were the only two who voted against Livingstone returning, because you have to be consistent in the

application of the principle . . . So Livingstone was a reminder that actually, for us in the party, he was a convenience.

Livingstone was to reappear frequently in the next fifteen years both a winner and loser in London, as a maverick presence within the Labour left and then as a problem who finally resigned from the party.

Through the second term pressure from the left grew. The pattern of rebellions can be seen over the three terms of New Labour in the voting records of Jeremy Corbyn and John McDonnell. Corbyn's record was:

1997-2001 – 77 rebellions out of 889 votes or 8.7 per cent
2001-2005 – 172 rebellions out of 720 votes or 23.6 per cent
2007-2010 – 238 rebellions out of 949 votes or 25.1 per cent

McDonnell had a similar pattern:

1997-2001 – 72 rebellions out of 1028 votes or 7.0 per cent
2001-2005 – 161 rebellions out of 873 votes or 18.4 per cent
2007-2010 – 205 rebellions out of 824 votes or 24.9 per cent

Any government with a large majority would expect rebellions in its second term, but the decision to go to war in Iraq blew the small embers of resistance within the Labour movement to a full fire, both within parliament and among the public. Months of negotiation and the pressure to act were counterbalanced by demonstrations organised by the Stop the War Coalition. Originally formed after 9/11 to oppose the war in Afghanistan, it included most of the usual names from the left when it came to opposing what it saw as American imperialism and aggression: Tony Benn, Tariq Ali, Harold Pinter, George Galloway, and two figures who would work together from 2015 in the Labour leaders' office: Andrew Murray and Jeremy Corbyn. The war with Iraq had galvanised a mass response. Marches held worldwide were estimated to have included as many as 30 million people. In London, the estimated scale of those marching against the war was anything from 750,000 to over 2 million. For the first time since being elected an MP in 1983, Jeremy Corbyn found himself on the side of a majority opinion. For Blair, the key vote was held in the House of Commons on 18 March. Two hundred and seventeen MPs, 139 of whom were Labour, voted for a motion against the war. The opposition included many from the left of the party, but also former ministers and those who would normally be regarded as loyalists.

Robin Cook led a number of resignations from the government. This signalled the deepening split between Tony Blair and his parliamentary party, and the beginning of the end for his command of the internal machine. Although he won parliamentary approval for the invasion of Iraq, claiming that his information was good and his moral duty was clear, it soon became obvious that Iraq did not have weapons of mass destruction. The war and its aftermath tarnished Blair's reputation and moral authority. It also gave Jeremy Corbyn a greater profile and a sense of authenticity, which was to prove invaluable twelve years later. Iraq became a defining issue. Ed Miliband, who was not even an MP when the vote took place, used it in 2010 against the other leadership candidates who had voted for it, including his brother. Jon Lansman on its wider impact:

I can understand the pressure for trying to keep people on-message, but I think in the prevention of any dissent, the Blair regime was more Stalinist than anything outside Albania for several decades in Europe. It wasn't just aimed at us, we were a marginalised fringe. It was aimed at a very broad range of people, some of whom you wouldn't even identify with the left. In the Iraq war, more than half the parliamentary party were against it in the key vote. Then, with Tory support, they defeated the majority of the parliamentary party, never mind the Labour party outside, who of course were more against it.

Different groups were created to address different factions. In 2003, John Cruddas, who had become an MP in 2001, set up Compass. Its manifesto *A Vision for the Democratic Left* argued that New Labour had gone too far in allowing unaccountable and unacceptable concentrations of wealth and power. It was a traditional soft-left grouping. In 2004, John McDonnell chaired a new group using a very old name; the Labour Representation Committee was set up by CLP activists and a group of left unions to advocate its agenda. Meanwhile, the left was still without a clear leader. Tony Benn was president of the Stop the War Coalition but had retired from parliament in 2001. Corbyn and McDonnell were active on a wide range of causes, but neither was the stand-out leader of the left in the way that Benn had been. From his position in London, Ken Livingstone was a national figure but not a leader of the wider left, due to his association with Socialist Action and the degree of animosity he was capable of generating.

By 2007, membership had dropped from its peak of 405,000 in 1997 to 176,891. The campaign against the Iraq war showed that there was resistance to New Labour and a much wider constituency outside the Labour party that one day could be mobilised to rejoin it. This was the constituency that would be mobilised in 2015 in support of Jeremy Corbyn.

The great anchor of the Labour movement throughout its history had been the unions: as funders, as political organisations and as natural supporters of the status quo. Throughout the period of New Labour, they were supportive yet wary. There was a game to be played by Tony Blair appearing to be independent of them whilst working with them. Paul Kenny was a senior union official who not only became the general secretary of the GMB but also chairman of TULO (Trades Unions and Labour Party Liaison Organisation):

> I remember saying to Blair once that I understood that there were times when it was quite healthy for him if we disagreed in public. I wouldn't take it personally if he gave me a slap in public, just as long as, in private, we got legislation that improves the lots of workers. They needed unions around at that time, but only in a particular box.

Over the years, the unions' frustration was eating away at the relationship.

> I got to see Gordon during the years he was chancellor. They were responsible for effectively allowing PFI, they were promoting it in a way the Tories had never done. Gordon was a good guy in many senses, but how did he ever allow that process to arise? I mean I argued unbelievably with Gordon, I mean to the point of fisticuffs almost, and I realised that was deliberate policy. They hadn't made a mistake. It was about appeasing business and making money.

And when it came to formulating policy it was a constant standoff:

> Everything was eked out of them. When you got the national policy forms, you would sit there for two days, and all the unions would put forward particular areas of policy. You'd get nothing.

Byron Taylor, worked as the Labour party organiser before becoming the communications director of TULO from 2002, and its managing director from 2008-2016.

> If you look at the unwritten rules of the movement, the trade union leaders had to play this strange game of talking to their members on the one hand, and dealing with the Labour party on the other, and that's a very fine balancing act. As they became more isolated from the Labour party leadership, they realised that they were not getting what they needed out of the relationship, and it was becoming much more difficult for them to justify the Labour party to their grassroots. As you move from the 2001 election, you start to get a wave of leadership elections inside the trade unions that create the awkward squad, and the awkward squad would start to say, 'Okay, how can we seek change in the Labour party?'

The unions were to start playing a more important and difficult role in the politics of the movement as the decade went on.

The media's response to New Labour had also changed since 1994. The early New Labour sheen had attracted many supporters from the media industry, but this did not stop Alastair Campbell and his media operation, who worked to control both messaging from government and its representation in newspapers and the broadcast media. After getting into government, this rose to a new level of control and aggression. His operation quickly gained a reputation for exaggeration and spin. This came to a head in 2001 when Jo Moore, a New Labour spin doctor who worked for the Trade and Industry Secretary of State Stephen Byers, was revealed by a colleague to have described 9/11 as 'a very good day to get anything out we want to bury'.

It was a small example of the ways in which New Labour had become a victim of its own spin and excesses. An understandable distrust of the Tory press had led them to trying to neutralise it, but it had got to the point where public perception was open to believing any accusation and trust dropped like a stone. In 2002, the accusations just kept coming. Blair was accused of helping an Indian billionaire buy a steel company just months after a donation to the Labour party of £125,000. In May, the party accepted a contribution of £100,000 from Richard Desmond, a press baron who owned the Labour-hating *Daily Express* and a bunch of pornographic television channels and magazines. John Reid, as chairman, stated:

> If you are asking if we are going to sit in moral judgement, in political judgment, on those who wish to contribute to the Labour party, then the answer to that is no.

The cult of control and antagonism reached its apex when the New Labour government fought the BBC in the aftermath of the Iraq war. The BBC had two Labour supporters in its chairman of the governors and director general. Gavyn Davies was not only a major donor to the Labour party, he was also married to Gordon Brown's private secretary, Sue Nye. Greg Dyke had been an early supporter of Tony Blair and contributor to his private office.

In the aftermath of the war, the BBC reported that the dossier used to persuade the public and MPs that the war was justified had been embellished or 'sexed up' over the key intelligence assertion that Iraq had weapons of mass destruction capable of launch within 45 minutes. *The Today Programme* was the first to make the allegation through its reporter, Andrew Gilligan, who was interviewed in the early morning on 29 May 2003 by John Humphrys. It was repeated on the *Ten O'Clock News* and *Newsnight*. Alastair Campbell went into attack mode as the BBC stuck to its story, citing a source. The row became more and more ugly, driven by the personalities of the combatants; neither of whom would back down. On 1 June, Gilligan repeated the main thrust of the story in the *Mail on Sunday* accusing Campbell as the driving force behind the alteration of the dossier. This was a serious charge. It was compounded on 17 July by the suicide of Dr David Kelly, who had been named in the press as Gilligan's source, from leaks within the Ministry of Defence.

An enquiry was appointed under Lord Hutton on 1 August and it exposed the innermost workings of both the BBC's editorial process and Downing Street. It was deeply wounding to both sides. Campbell had become the story and resigned in August 2003 as director of communications, although he claimed this was a coincidence of timing and had nothing to do with the enquiry and public row. Throughout the next four months, various attempts were made to bridge the gap between Downing Street and the BBC, but Greg Dyke was intractable on the issue.

In January 2004, Hutton's report exonerated the government and refuted the accusation of the dossier being 'sexed up'. It confirmed that Tony Blair had chaired a meeting at which it was decided to release Kelly's name if asked by journalists. The report slammed the BBC. Both Davies and Dyke resigned. The BBC was supported by many newspapers who called the Hutton report a whitewash. The damage done to the government was in further evidence of the overweening power of Campbell's communications department and a deterioration of trust in Blair. In the evidence he gave to the Hutton enquiry, Blair said he would have resigned if the enquiry had upheld the BBC claims.

The honeymoon with the media was over, the unions were disgruntled and internal opposition was beginning to come alive, but New Labour still had the power to continue its agenda. The only thing that could really bring it down would be losing an election, (and that was unlikely given the weakened state of the Conservatives who had also supported the Iraq war) or a self-inflicted injury. The next surprise would come from Tony Blair himself.

14

The Beginning of the End

By the time of the Labour party conference in September 2004, Tony Blair was prepared to take on his critics and lay out his short-term agenda. In his conference speech he addressed some of the obvious issues. He defended the core of his second term domestic agenda and admitted he was partially wrong on Iraq.

> I want to deal with it head-on. The evidence about Saddam having actual biological and chemical weapons, as opposed to the capability to develop them, has turned out to be wrong. I acknowledge that and accept it. And the problem is I can apologise for the information that turned out to be wrong, but I can't, sincerely at least, apologise for removing Saddam. The world is a better place with Saddam in prison not in power. So, it's not that I care more about foreign affairs than the state of our economy, NHS, schools or crime. It's simply that I believe democracy there means security here; and that if I don't care and act on this terrorist threat, then the day will come when all our good work on the issues that decide people's lives will be undone because the stability on which our economy, in an era of globalisation, depends, will vanish.

This speech, ten years after his accession to the leadership, marked the beginning of the end for New Labour. The following day he added the next stage, as reported by Michael White in the *Guardian* on the day, that Peter Mandelson's Hartlepool seat was up in a by-election:

> Tony Blair last night reshaped the landscape of British politics by announcing that he will fight the coming general election and, if re-elected, serve a full third term as prime minister, but stand down before the likely election of 2009. Asked whether his announcement helped the chances of Mr Brown, the chancellor, succeeding him, said: 'I have a huge respect for Gordon . . . I'm sure there are lots of people who want to do the job and I think he is very very capable of doing it, don't misunderstand me at all. But the reason I want to stay is to see the job through, I've begun it; I want to see it through.' Mr Brown had not been given any prior warning and was informed of Mr Blair's dramatic decision as he stepped off the plane in Washington last night for a meeting of the International Monetary Fund. Other cabinet members were informed by phone by Mr Blair's staff an hour before the news was broadcast. Mr Blair, his staff revealed, had been thinking about the decision for more than a month but the timing was only clarified this week.

It was a unique moment in British politics. A prime minister announces that he will fight the next election that could be eighteen months away, and then stand down at some point in the future that was not defined, but would be before a fourth general election. Michael White further pointed to Gordon Brown not being informed in advance and that there may be other, Blairite, contenders. Unsurprisingly, this brought the full problem of the Granita dinner ten years earlier back onto the political agenda. The battle was well and truly on: from one side to prepare possible Blairite contenders for the throne; from the other to crush any contenders other than Gordon Brown and to get Blair to stand down as soon as possible. The nature of these differences, with armies lining up for the post-Blair era, became personal. Every decision was politically charged. The 2005 general election became a focus for full-scale sulking. Patrick Loughran:

> It became very difficult in the party at that time. Tony made his announcement of a third term and appointed Alan Milburn to run the election, which caused great ructions and basically the Treasury withdrew cooperation in terms of the party campaign.

Despite this, Tony Blair won the 2005 general election. New Labour had a majority of sixty-six with 355 MPs. This was won with only a 35.2 per cent share of the poll, the lowest of any majority government in UK history. Labour's popular vote dropped to 9.5 million. The Conservatives were on 32.4 per cent or 8.7 million votes. It was very close. In Scotland the redistribution of boundaries had reduced the number of seats from seventy-two to fifty-nine. Labour won forty-one on nearly 40 per cent of the vote. Without those seats it would have been in trouble. The Conservatives won 198 MPs, up by thirty-two, but also won the popular vote in England and were narrowly beaten by the Lib Dems in a number of marginals. The Lib Dems, the only party that voted against the Iraq war, won sixty-two seats. Blair had won three elections; an unprecedented achievement. He was only fifty-two. It should have been a triumph but the only question was when he would leave.

There was incredible pressure from the Brownites for Blair to go, together with a series of events which kept going wrong for Blair. In late 2005, he suffered his only defeat in the House of Commons when, after the 7 July London bombings, forty-nine labour MPs voted against terrorist suspects being held for up to ninety days without charge. In March 2006, the Labour party revealed the names of twelve businessmen who had given it £14 million in secret loans before the 2005 election, some of whom had subsequently been recommended for peerages. A series of unconnected ministerial resignations then took place that included potential Blairite leadership candidates David Blunkett and Charles Clarke. Brown's position as heir apparent was strengthening. By August 2006, the knives were out for Tony Blair and to deflect the pressure, on 1

September in an interview with *The Times*, he claimed he had 'no intention of leaving Downing Street' and said dismissively that he was not going to go 'on and on' about it. This appeared to indicate that he intended to serve out most or all of his third term.

A coup was mounted by an acolyte of Gordon Brown, who would become a notable figure in the Labour party in the following decade. Tom Watson featured in the Miliband and Corbyn eras as a serial fixer, plotter and eventual deputy leader. He activated the campaign, known as 'the Curry House Coup' to push Blair into announcing his departure by a series of pre-planned resignations from the government. Watson resigned as a defence minister and seventeen MPs, in a round-robin letter, called for Blair's resignation. David Miliband and Hilary Armstrong declared, on Blair's behalf, that that he would resign before the 2007 conference a year later. On 6 September, the *Sun* broke the story that he would go even earlier, in May 2007.

This was not enough for Brown, who demanded a departure schedule and, remarkably, that Blair endorse him as his successor. The sheer brutality of it still resonates. John McDonnell described it at the time as an episode of *The Sopranos* and, on behalf of the left, he pledged to stand in any leadership contest. Tony Blair, in 2018, explained why he succumbed to the pressure:

> I did it for these reasons, genuinely. I felt I was going to break the Labour party unless I went, I'd been leader for ten years and I thought that was a long time . . . I think one of the reasons that we governed for so long – we governed for twice as long as the previous Labour government – is because the opposition was inside, and he [Brown] was a pretty reasonable face of it. So to me, the round-robin letter, that's just politics. It happens in all political parties all the time where people feel 'It's time the guy moved on'. I've never had a problem with that.

Being under constant attack had finally got to him. He left the political arena to his partner-and-rival, Gordon Brown, and for the legacy of New Labour either to be continued or replaced by something else. Brown had finally got within inches of his prize. His success in removing any pretenders to the throne became clear after Blair's resignation. As one advisor commented:

> Every time someone dipped into double figures in a poll as a good future Labour Prime Minister, the guns came out for them, and the operation kicked in to do the assassinations.

Labour held a special conference on 24 June 2007 to elect its new leader, but it was more of a coronation as not a single minister stood against him. John McDonnell, as chair of the Socialist Campaign Group, had signalled his desire to stand against Brown from the moment Blair announced he would depart in September 2006. The bar for getting nominations was forty-five MPs, or 12.5 per cent of the parliamentary party. Michael Meacher also decided to have a run as the left candidate. This produced a typically divided house from the left, who had not put up a candidate for the leadership since Tony Benn ran in 1988.

Jon Lansman had been out of front-line activity for a long period. He had never left the party but was raising his three children and doing a master's degree at Birkbeck. He re-emerged by going to see Gordon Brown at a party meeting:

> Quite a lot of people on the left had the expectation that Brown would be significantly better than Blair . . . Before it was clear that Brown was going to have a coronation, I thought I'd like to hear what he had to say and get the vibe of the people there. It was a little meeting. There may have been a hundred people there. I was really turned off by it because he was surrounded by fawning, careerist acolytes, it really was nauseating. And I thought, 'This isn't going to be any different from what's come before.' I threw my lot in with McDonnell as a result.

McDonnell and Meacher were both failing to get enough nominations as different parts of the left disliked them for different reasons. Lansman continued:

John and Michael were getting slightly different combinations. They were each on about twenty-one, twenty-two. I think when you put them together you didn't get the sum of the two because they each had people who weren't supporters. So neither of them were going on the ballot paper. They agreed to show the nominations that they had to each other. It turned out that John appeared to have more than Michael.

John McDonnell saw a concerted campaign to keep him off the ballot:

But the reality was, Brown moved heaven and earth to keep me off. I thought if we got on the ballot paper we could demonstrate about 30 per cent support and on that basis send a message out to the Left that we're still here and we've got a base that we can build upon. That's why Brown was adamant, absolutely adamant, to the point of the day of closing nominations, phoning people up at half past five in the morning and stuff like that.

The end result was that Brown received 313 nominations for the leadership and McDonnell twenty-nine – sixteen short of the bar. Gordon Brown was crowned King without a fight. The memory of this latest failure of the left to clear the bar would have a direct impact on the 2010 and 2015 leadership elections.

Where there were signs of resistance, as in 1981 with Tony Benn, was in the race for the deputy leadership. There were six candidates for this position following the resignation of John Prescott. They were across the political divide with one possible left candidate. Jeremy Corbyn had announced that he might stand but ended up nominating Hilary Benn. The other candidates were Hazel Blears, Peter Hain and Alan Johnson, each with strong union and ministerial ties, and Harriet Harman as a strong advocate for women (following Margaret Beckett as deputy leader under Blair). The most interesting candidate was one put up by Byron Taylor as a voice for change: Jon Cruddas. Having set up Compass, Taylor saw him as an independent candidate who could beat the machine.

In the balloting, Cruddas was the overall leader of first preferences on 19.4 per cent and retained the lead among the union section in the second and third rounds. On round four he reached 40.9 per cent of the union section, but was last in both others and was knocked out. Harman became the surprise winner over Johnson in the last round by the tight majority of 50.4 per cent to 49.6 per cent. This is despite only winning the members section, but with sufficient second preferences among MPs that she was able to squeeze through.

Two lessons were learned from this election. The unions and the left could see that a candidate with their support could make inroads with an anti-New Labour agenda (as John McDonnell had assumed in the leadership race if he could only get over the bar). It also showed the importance of second and third preference votes to achieve final victory. This was a lesson for 2010.

15

Gordon Brown: The End of New Labour

On 24 June 2007, Gordon Brown made his first speech as Labour party leader, three days before he became prime minister. It deliberately tried to re-engineer New Labour.

> It is only by engaging people in the decisions that matter to their lives, only by a new government building trust by involving the British people that we as a country will meet the new challenges of 2007 and beyond. So as people's aspirations and priorities change, we the Labour party must renew ourselves as the party of change.

He focused on the key issues: housing, college and university entrance, affordable child care, the NHS and greater democracy.

> For people wanting a stronger democracy, we will meet the challenge of change. And we will govern for all the people of our country. This week marks a new start. A chance to renew.

Brown saw this as his chance to renew New Labour without the deviations by Tony Blair. Spencer Livermore explained why this, and the subsequent speech at Downing Street, marked the start of a new era by going back to an old era.

> My view is that New Labour 1994 to 2000 is original New Labour. Gordon was a return to that early phase. [It] was about

returning the conversation to everyday needs of ordinary people. We had lost our way. So, if you look at Gordon's speech, it's all about returning to the things that matter: housing, education, the health service, the economy, stability, all of that. That's very much what Gordon was all about.

Gordon Brown's premiership, after the longest term as chancellor in two hundred years, could be seen from entirely different angles depending on the perspective of the onlooker. For the Blairites, still smarting from the brutality of 2006, he had an opportunity to take New Labour to a new level, but he did not do so. Peter Mandelson:

> The problem is that Brown, in many ways, although he was instrumental in the creation of New Labour, did not really share the same conviction or mindset as Blair. He wasn't as passionate as Tony about New Labour. They were quite different people and when Blair went, Gordon was, at best, indifferent to New Labour and certainly did nothing to rekindle, or nurture, the New Labour project or brand. He didn't think in those terms for three reasons. One, he wasn't a complete believer, he was more 'old school Labour'. Secondly, in his head, New Labour was Blair. It was identified with him and he wanted to replace anything that was to do with Blair. And thirdly, he had throughout very busily set about stoking up the forces in the party, either on the left, or on the right and in the unions who were not New Labour, and he did so because he felt he needed a constituency that was separate from Blair.

This, however, caused Gordon Brown a conflict about his own positioning. Peter Mandelson:

> His problem was that while he wanted to distance himself from Blair and New Labour, he hated being seen as a throwback, as an anti-moderniser. There was an ambivalence in Gordon that made people uncertain what he really stood for.

Alastair Campbell thought this ambivalence meant he focused on the wrong target. David Cameron had been elected in 2005 as the fourth Conservative leader to face New Labour, but for Gordon Brown he was not the real threat; it was the lingering ghost of Tony Blair, and that preoccupation worried New Labour veterans.

> We had doubts, but we thought once he was free of Tony's shadow, he'd emerge in a different sort of way. When he came in, I felt he defined himself against Tony, maybe far too much, rather than against David Cameron.

For Brown's supporters who had worked so hard to get him into power, the desire was to move on from the Blairite vision to something new, to get back to a refocused vision of reform and investment in the future. In 2007, ten years of growth made this look possible and the key question was whether the mandate of being elected by coronation was enough. Soon after his accession, key advisors to Brown were raising the idea of calling a snap general election. Spencer Livermore again led the charge. Brown himself had a very strong run dealing with terrorist attacks, floods and other crises with assurance. The idea of the election 'not flash just Gordon' captured his appeal well. Tony Blair had won three and left him with a majority of sixty-six seats. Spencer Livermore:

> I was the first person to suggest it, and I wouldn't let it go. My view was that it would be a crime not to consider it. I said, 'We should go early' and he said, 'What do you mean?' and I'm like, 'This year' and he's like, 'Crazy.' So then it was dropped. I went away and I thought, that was dismissed too easily, we've got to come back to it. I wrote a note and set up a case for and against. At the time, there was absolutely a strong case. And I think that the most important thing to remember is that Gordon had wanted to be prime minister his whole life.

But he did not want to gamble the future.

> Gordon wanted that ability to say he'd won an election, every politician would. But don't forget, if we held the election with the majority of sixty-six, we thought we would come out with a majority of thirty-five. If he'd done it, everyone would have said he was the man who squandered the majority of sixty and had gone for thirty. So, it was sort of a lose-lose situation.

The case was made for an autumn election in 2007. This would have been nine months before the crash of 2008 that changed everything for the government. Gordon Brown was around in 1978 when James Callaghan, also elected Labour leader and prime minister by his party and not the country, teased the Labour movement only to lose his nerve at the TUC in September 1978 and see his government subsequently fall apart. The parallels are startling. Throughout the summer of 2007, the party and trade unions got geared up for an election after the conference season. Paul Kenny:

> Not only were we geared up, the cheques had been written, the leaflets had been printed. We'd had the council of war and basically the gun had been fired. And then for some inexplicable reason, because the Tories had a bump over inheritance tax and stuff like that – I mean the bulb went. It just did. I honestly do believe he would have been re-elected. He wouldn't have a huge majority, but he would have been re-elected.

Brown didn't think he would lose. He feared he wouldn't win as decisively as Blair had. In the end, his indecision was final. The stories of his time in government are constantly about his brilliance as a thinker and politician offset by his indecision and his desire to throw off the Blair shadow. The inherent problem was a matter of personality and of chronology. Like the later years of the Attlee government, Brown had been in power for over ten years. He was exhausted and so was his government. No new mandate, no new policy initiatives and a sense of impending political failure dogged him in the early months of 2008. Spencer Livermore, who left Downing Street after the general election that didn't happen:

> I think that part of the decline of New Labour in power was simply a case of running out of steam, running out of ideas. We'd been in power for thirteen years. When Gordon became prime minister he had pretty much had achieved everything he wanted to achieve while he was chancellor, because he was chancellor for much longer than he had planned. And when he became prime minister, he didn't have very much left. He would have been far more successful as prime minister had he become prime minister earlier, because he would have had big stuff left to do.

The disillusionment was compounded by internal changes such as making Harriet Harman, the deputy leader, party chairman and appointing six new deputy chairmen. To the fury of the left, the party was even more tightly controlled. There were low-level scandals involving donors to the Labour party under Tony Blair, not Brown, but the public perception affected Brown's government. Trust was eroded in politicians in general, and gradually Brown faced more and more challenges within the PLP and the unions. In May 2008, the Crewe and Nantwich by-election was lost and Labour slipped to third place in the local elections behind the Conservatives on 44 per cent, the Lib Dems at 25 per cent with Labour only polling 24 per cent. Then, in July, the Glasgow East by-election saw Labour lose a 13,000 majority to the SNP. This led to the first of three attempted coups. Byron Taylor from TULO:

> Tony Blair used to attend the AGM on the eve of the Labour party conference every year. Gordon Brown came to his first TULO AGM and opened his speech by saying Tony Blair used to tell me that he got a better reception on the West Bank than at TULO AGM. There was lots of laughter and that started the relationship off on a good footing. But it descended quite

quickly when it became apparent that Gordon was seeking further reforms to the Labour party structure and constitution and the election that never was. And then we had the [Glasgow] by-election in the summer of 2008. We thought he was fatally damaged and probably wouldn't survive the summer, so we planned for a [leadership] election that September.

Jon Cruddas was their preferred candidate:

Because he'd won first preferences in the 2007 deputy leadership. The agenda he was espousing was there. It was popular and that popularity was growing. We could see that. The question was how we could get the Blairites out and get David Miliband to knife Gordon first so that he took the flak, and we could put Cruddas in.

David Miliband wrote a barely coded article in July 2008 which pitched for a change of leader and style, and by September, twelve Labour MPs were pushing for a change of leader. Miliband backed off after his detailed planning was leaked to the *Daily Telegraph* and Brown's allies then moved against TULO. Charlie Whelan, Brown's long-time ally, was placed as political director in the newly named Unite, a merger of Amicus and the Transport and General Workers. There would be no further trouble from that source for Brown. However, events started to run away from him. In April 2009, Whelan, Derek Draper and Damian McBride, who worked for Brown, were involved in an email exchange discussing how to smear Conservative frontbenchers. 'Smeargate' meant McBride had to resign. By June 2009, after a set of disastrous Euro elections when Labour came third with only 15.9 per cent of the vote, behind both the Conservatives and UKIP, another coup was attempted. James Purnell resigned as a cabinet minister in a direct challenge to Brown's authority but turned around to find no support. At the PLP meeting, twenty-one speakers spoke in favour of Brown and five spoke against him. The man who reportedly rallied the troops in favour of Brown and stopped any wider Blairite attack was Peter Mandelson, who

Brown had brought back from the EU, where he had been trade commissioner, as a member of the cabinet. He became first minister.

Finally, in 2010, the great goose dinner coup took place, or didn't. Geoff Hoon and Patricia Hewitt wrote to every Labour MP arguing for a change. This was apparently dreamt up at a New Year's Eve dinner at the Suffolk home of Harriet Harman while they ate goose. Yet again, the Brownites were too strong and both Harman and Miliband failed to back the coup itself. Gordon Brown's years of plotting against Blair had given him and his supporters the experience to fight off every challenge. The Blairites couldn't find a way to beat him when their natural leader, David Miliband, failed to grasp the opportunity on every occasion.

Throughout 2008 the government was faltering, but Brown's moment came in an international crisis that he was uniquely qualified to handle. The seeds of economic chaos were being sown in September 2007 when Northern Rock ran into trouble and was finally bailed out by the government in February 2008. The US investment bank, Bear Stearns, was also rescued by JP Morgan. In March 2008, the US Treasury secretary, Hank Paulson, stated, 'I do believe that the worst is likely to be behind us.' The unseen and unexpected contagion of subprime had only just begun.

Brown, as chancellor and then prime minster, had presided over a decade of growth and sound fiscal management. The statistics from 1997 to 2007 on the economy were extremely favourable. Northern Rock was the forerunner to a crisis within the global banking system that was unlike anything seen for seventy years. Since Bill Clinton's period as US President, banks had been increasingly deregulated and encouraged to engage in greater and greater risk. This had taken the form of higher levels of mortgage loans driving up household and commercial debt. This was then packaged up as collateral, in a variety of abstruse financial instruments, and sold throughout the international banking system at higher and higher levels of risk. In the UK, deregulation had also taken place under Brown, but at a lower level of risk.

Banks infected banks with what were essentially false assets. Sooner or later the house of cards was bound to collapse, and this occurred with resounding force in September 2008 when the US government had to take over the two huge mortgage lenders, Freddie Mac and Fannie Mae, that had issued thousands of subprime mortgages. A week later, Lehman Brothers filed for bankruptcy. More banks came close to collapse on both sides of the Atlantic and in every major western economy.

In Britain, HBOS was taken over by Lloyds in a rescue mission. By October, the crash was in full swing worldwide. The US started a $700 billion bailout operation, Ireland's banks had to be underwritten. Iceland's three commercial banks collapsed and, in a move that made him hated in Iceland to this day, Gordon Brown used anti-terror legislation to freeze their assets in the UK. The Dow Jones collapsed; eight banks cut their interest rates. Amid the worst ever week for the Dow Jones, eight central banks – including the Bank of England, the European Central Bank and the Federal Reserve – cut their interest rates by 0.5 per cent in a coordinated attempt to ease the pressure on borrowers and banks. The British government bailed out the Royal Bank of Scotland, Lloyds TSB, and HBOS. The crisis management was thrashed out over the weekend and well into the small hours of Monday morning.

Throughout that week, Brown and his chancellor, Alistair Darling, became central to the global efforts to save the banking system. They worked through the G7 with European and US leaders to get a global agreement to reinforce collapsing banks. The G20 met in November for the first time since Lehman Brothers had gone under. This meeting was compared in significance to the Bretton Woods summit in 1944. Paul Krugman writing in the *New York Times* in October 12, 2008:

Has Gordon Brown, the British prime minister, saved the world financial system? OK, the question is premature — we still don't know the exact shape of the planned financial rescues in Europe or for that matter the United States, let alone whether they'll really work. What we do know, however, is that Mr Brown and Alistair Darling, the chancellor of the exchequer have defined the character of the worldwide rescue effort, with other wealthy nations playing catch-up. This is an unexpected turn of events. The British government is, after all, very much a junior partner when it comes to world economic affairs . . . But the Brown government has shown itself willing to think clearly about the financial crisis and act quickly on its conclusions and the combination of clarity and decisiveness hasn't been matched by any other western government.

Gordon Brown could claim huge credit and, unfortunately, he did just that in December in the House of Commons. 'We not only saved the world . . .' In a slip of the tongue at Prime Minister's Questions, he revealed how highly he rated his role during the financial crisis. He had some justification, but the impact of the crash was felt for the rest of his time in office. Every plan had to be rewritten and the impact on public debt and borrowing was massive. This could be seen in two key statistics of the British economy.

Public debt as a percentage of GDP:

1997-1998: 40.4 per cent of GDP or £352 billion
2007-2008: reduced to 36.4 per cent or £527 billion
2010-2011: increased to 60 per cent or £902 billion

The budget deficit which became the subject of attacks by Conservative spokesmen against Labour in 2010:

1997-1998: £7.8 billion
2007-2008: £40.3 billion
2010-2011: £145.1 billion; an increase of £100 billion in only three years

Peter Mandelson on its political impact:

It was a problem for us because it was used by those in the party who wanted to characterise New Labour as a sort of pro-business, neo-liberal, market infatuated, aberrant political phase of the party's history.

For the rest of his time in office, Brown won global plaudits and UK opprobrium in equal measure. His government, like Callaghan's in 1979, saw the end of an era of social democratic government. It was rocked by a parliamentary scandal over expenses that affected MPs of all parties, enraging the public and party members alike. The Blairites were unable to act without a leader, the Brownites were determined to hold onto power. The left was still in its bunker but slowly gaining support and traction.

There began to be pressure from the unions and TULO for a change in the relationship with the government and within the party. Membership was dropping off. CLP representation at party conference declined every year in this period. Five hundred and one in 2007, 465 in 2008, 444 in 2009 and 412 in 2010. The unions' new crop of leaders and TULO pushed for constitutional change within the National Policy Forum. The left had swung behind the idea of one member one vote as a means of beating the New Labour machine. This was one indicator for the future but there were also indications of the politically estranged beginning to revive. Jon Lansman was by now working from Michael Meacher's office in the House of Commons editing *Left Futures*, which was beginning to be influential as a house blog of the left. John McDonnell's Labour Representation Committee and Socialist Campaign Group were active. As Lansman said:

> We were surviving. We were fighting the elections. We were pushing for OMOV elections. Because it was democratic, and it was to our advantage because the grassroots were more pro-us. Blairites never had strength on the ground.

The unions were beginning to move away from New Labour with:

> . . . a leadership that was more open to challenge, challenging the party leadership, because they were so sick of having got so little out of New Labour. By the end of it, from thirteen years of New Labour government, what did they have to show for it?

In May 2010, Gordon Brown called the last general election of New Labour. It was expected to be a Conservative walkover after thirteen years of Labour rule and the financial crash only two years before, but it was much more unpredictable than that. The Conservatives won 306 seats, an increase of 96 over 2005 and 36.1 per cent of the poll. Labour dropped to a miserable 29 per cent of the vote but retained 258 seats, a loss of ninety-one, and the Lib Dems on 23 per cent won fifty-seven. Within a week, the Conservatives and Lib Dems had created a big tent of their own and created the first coalition government since the second world war. New Labour was out of time and out of office.

The 2010 general election held a number of indicators for the following period of British politics. The Conservatives' attacks on Brown were on the increases in government debt and his use of indirect taxation over the thirteen years of Labour rule. This was compounded by attacks on the union funding of the Labour party. The economic section of the manifesto made it clear that they were going to hang the impact of the crash round Brown's neck. They continued to do this throughout the next five years as George Osborne brought in austerity as the main plank of government policy. He advocated a one-year public sector pay freeze, changes to pension rights, stopping tax credits to families with income over £50,000, cutting spending on Child Trust Funds for all but the poorest third of families and ending dependency on welfare. It was the clearest possible repudiation of New Labour' s policies.

During the campaign, Cameron and Osborne were never quite convincing enough against the heavyweight figure of Brown and the slick presentation of Nick Clegg as leader of the Lib Dems. However, Brown had his worst moment of the campaign over immigration. Gillian Duffy, a Labour voter from Rochdale, asked him about people not receiving benefits that were otherwise going to East European immigrants. He batted her away but kept a *Sky News* microphone on and was recorded as calling her a 'bigoted woman who says she used to be Labour'. This plunged him into a frenzy of apologies to her and to the public. Immigration as an issue was now here to stay along with New Labour's economic record, Europe and the relationship with the major unions as the main funders of the Labour party.

The years since 1994 had seen Labour rebrand, refresh and win three general elections. Tony Blair and Gordon Brown had created a political machine that was unique in Labour party history and yet its legacy was to be attacked almost from the day it ended. Predictably, the Conservatives would do so. Unsurprisingly, the left would also do so. What was not expected was that the greatest repudiation would come from one of its own protégés. Its legacy was now up for grabs.

16

Judging New Labour

From the moment in 1983 that Tony Blair moved from his office with Militant's Dave Nellist to share with Gordon Brown, the two men represented the future of the Labour party. They were unchallenged masters of their political era, with a combination of skill and intellect rarely seen in British politics. This was to be their opportunity and their undoing. Winning power was not enough. Each had to claim that their version of New Labour was dominant.

The unravelling of New Labour after 2010 showed that there was a fundamental flaw in its heart. It succeeded at times of economic boom that ended in the crash of 2008, but the repudiation of New Labour was not just over its economic policies. Iraq had eroded trust. Exhaustion played its part, as it always does when political parties have been in power for a long period, but the fundamental problem was New Labour itself. The internal policy differences were slight compared to those who hated New Labour – the Conservatives and the left – but the need for Gordon Brown to be prime minister, his desire not to be history's second fiddle even though he had a substantive record as chancellor, was just too much. Blairites and Brownites alike concede that Gordon Brown did not want to carry on as Tony Blair's heir. He wanted to be different. The questions remain, what were their differences and why were they enough to kill the New Labour project?

For those who were not natural Blairites it was a mixed picture. Neil Kinnock, who had spotted their talent and promoted both from the backbenches in the 1980s, saw them failing to apply the values of the traditional movement:

> Tony is real Labour, there's no doubt about that. If you cut Tony Blair open, you'd see Labour running right through him. It's just that this was never really asserted in his thirteen years in government.

Andy Burnham, who had been in both Blair and Brown cabinets:

> I think it was very personality driven, and the personalities of the camps, a kind of strange fundamentalism that grew up around both of them . . . Labour was my first loyalty always, and therefore I was a Blairite when Blairite was the mainstream agenda and then I was a Brownite. What always used to surprise me was how much I was the exception, rather than the norm. . . . The arrogance of both sides was shocking. Really shocking. I thought I was working in the Labour party. I had no sense I was working for a working-class movement, which is what I thought I was doing. The arrogance, the elitism – and that goes for both Tony's camp and Gordon's.

Spencer Livermore, advisor to Brown and Miliband:

> Tony Blair saw much more of a role for markets and public services, Gordon Brown saw a limit to that. But at the time, of course, those things were magnified by their personalities. It felt profoundly different. You look back and you think, what the hell were we doing.

About Brown:

> I think we should just pause and say what a phenomenal achievement it is to be the heir apparent for seven or ten years. I mean it is one of the unrecognised, most significant political achievements – who else has done that? Who else has remained as chancellor, the heir apparent, for ten years and then come

in and won the leadership without even a contest. That is a phenomenal piece of political survival.

Stewart Wood, advisor to Brown and then Ed Miliband:

> The biggest argument they ever had was actually over tuition fees. Iraq a little bit, but mostly tuition fees and then the Euro. Of those three, tuition fees were the only philosophical difference between them. Iraq was a tactical, handling issue with Gordon feeling upset that he wasn't involved as part of the core inner kitchen cabinet. The Euro was a profound difference but that's because Gordon saw the world essentially through an economic lens and Tony saw the world through a great game of geo-politics lens. That's not an ideological difference, and temperamentally they were poles apart, but essentially, they were cast from the same mould.

Why did it end?

> There were three deaths of New Labour. The Iraq war was the most profound moment probably in post-war politics because it destroyed the faith of a class more generally. The second death was Tony leaving because New Labour without Tony Blair always was a very, very poor political project. Blairism without Blair was never a substantive political force in the Labour party. The third death – the Gordon part of New Labour – was essentially the political economy deal and that was destroyed in the crash. And that was the real death of New Labour.

Ed Miliband:

> Blair was very much a sort of unifier. He wanted to be for everybody. He wanted as big a tent as he could possibly have. That was both his success and his vice. Part of him was happy that Gordon was doing what he was doing and part of him was frustrated by it. He was definitely more open to the role of the private sector in public services. That said, Gordon made the

Faustian pact with business and with the economic settlement. So, I don't think there was a fundamental difference on economic policy. I think there was a difference on the redistribution . . . the role of the private sector in public services.

Yet for many the impact of New Labour was far more positive and inclusive. Ayesha Hazarika, senior advisor to Harriet Harman and Ed Miliband:

For me, what New Labour represented was the fact that they managed to convince people like my mum and dad to vote for the Labour party. My mum and dad, classic, small 'c' conservative, Indian-Asian, socially conservative, who had very much believed in a strong economy, aspiration and working hard, had always probably distrusted Labour because they thought it was lots of union shouting men, and not really for them. They had stuck with the Conservatives for a long time. . . . Then Tony Blair comes along and he brings all of this stuff together. He provides them a home to go to which they feel is economically confident and savvy, and they can trust him on the economy, yet he is kind, he is warm, and he has invited in these new groups of people. You can come and be part of our club now. We're not an exclusive white, posh, dismissive, privileged group of people. At that point, that's sort of what I felt New Labour was. It was this very, very broad church. . . . It became like a lifestyle choice, like a sort of a brand. If you were a New Labour person, a New Labour adviser, you were quite corporate in your attitude, and you wanted to be corporate. That really professionalised New Labour, but I think it was its downfall in the end as well. I think we became too corporate. We became like a series of sort of lobbyists who were stuck in government.

Peter Mandelson:

New Labour, I would say, captured the minds of the party. I'm not sure that we were as successful in capturing the heart and the soul of the Labour party. We were good at constructing a very successful governing project with many radical policies, we achieved a huge amount, no question about that. But then, did we equally succeed in putting down roots, as deeply laid as they needed to be in the party? No. Did we promote and develop and nurture a successor generation? No.

Tony Blair:

There was a policy difference between myself and Gordon in the end.

About public service reform?

Well, that was just a symbol of a deeper disagreement which is that I could see society moving in what I thought was a much more individualistic direction, which is not to say people didn't want the social bonds strong, but you had to do it in a different way. It was a different governing philosophy.

From the left there is a radically different view that went to the narrative of judging and damning New Labour after 2010 and in 2015. Jon Lansman:

Labour in power is always better than Tories in power. But Labour in power when it doesn't try to fundamentally change anything is not doing its job well, and it's building up problems for the future, which is precisely what it did. It alienated its core voters to the long term detriment of the left in this country. We're still paying the price for the alienation that Blair's government caused in the left-behind areas which voted Brexit which are disinclined to vote Labour. It actually moved public opinion in the wrong direction in certain key areas. On the welfare state, by being relatively generous in terms of child benefits, anti-poverty measures and benefits in general, whilst at the same time pursuing the narrative of 'strivers not scroungers', it turned public opinion against the welfare state. On immigration, they had an open-door policy and, at the same time, they talked tough on migrants and refugees. Their spin was running deliberately contrary to their policy, and they used that to try and soften the blow of their policy for the *Daily Mail* readers in the Home Counties. What that did was push public opinion in the wrong direction.

New Labour was still subject to violent disagreement about its motives and achievements after sixteen years leading the party and thirteen in power. The desire within Labour to move on was about to be demonstrated in a leadership election and subsequent repudiation of New Labour that would, in only five years, lead to its traditional enemies taking control of the party and totally reject its memory and achievements. Yet this only happened after the closest leadership election in Labour's history when the heirs of Blair and Brown were to stand up and fight for the future.

PART FIVE

The Miliband Interregnum:
Between Power and Protest

'This will require strong leadership. It won't always be easy.
You might not always like what I have to say.
But you've elected me leader and lead I will.'
Ed Miliband, 2010

17

The Last Electoral College

The 2010 general election was the first since 1979 when all three main party leaders were new to the role. Gordon Brown was fifty-nine, had been on the national stage for twenty years, was Labour's main electoral strategist for most of that period, but only the leader of his party for three years. David Cameron and Nick Clegg were both a decade younger. Cameron was forty-four, had been an MP for nine years and leader of his party for five. Clegg was forty-three, an MP for only five years and leader of his party for three.

In the five days after the election, the Conservatives and Lib Dems moved to a coalition – the first since the second world war. Brown and Mandelson tried and failed to resurrect the big tent. On 10 May, Brown announced his resignation as leader of the Labour party and on 11 May, as prime minister. Labour was in opposition for the first time in thirteen years and Harriet Harman was made acting leader. The last time Labour had lost office was in 1979. It had not had a competitive leadership election since the PLP had its last vote in 1980. The leadership elections in 1983, 1988, 1992, 1994 and 2007 had all been won by huge majorities and by the front runners Kinnock (twice), Smith, Blair and Brown. Now the game was wide open.

The qualification to stand was still 12.5 per cent of the PLP, or thirty-three MPs needing to nominate. Clearly David Miliband was going to stand as the inheritor of the Blairites. Having failed to challenge Brown, his moment had come. He announced his candidacy on 12 May. A week later, Ed Balls as the main supporter, ally and inheritor of Gordon Brown's legacy also announced he was standing. He received thirty-three nominations. The surprise announcement was on 14 May. Health secretary Andy Burnham had decided he was going to stand. His strategy was to be the candidate who was neither a committed Blairite nor Brownite. He would stand as a 'Labourite'. At the only cabinet meeting held by Brown in the five days between the general election and leaving office, Burnham saw his opportunity.

> I had worked out that David was definitely going to stand, and Ed Balls was definitely going to stand, and I felt that neither of them were right as leader of the Labour party. I used to stand up at those hustings and say, 'I'm the only one who supported Tony and I supported Gordon wholeheartedly.' No one else on this thing can say that. For that reason, I saw David [as a] Blair continuity candidate, Ed Balls [as a] Gordon continuity candidate; and here's the problem, here's my mistake: I had, perhaps from a northern, working-class sensibility, assumed that Ed wouldn't stand against his brother, because I would never. I can't get my head around that. . . . But that's where I made a mistake: it was the day we were going out for the one cabinet meeting we had after the 2010 General Election. And the bizarre thing was Ed rang me that day and said, 'I'm going to stand', and I was taken aback, I was like, 'What? You're what? You're standing?' And at that point my ground had gone; any ground that my campaign would have had had gone, because I knew he was probably more liked and more well-known than I was.

Ed Miliband announced two days after his brother. The decision to stand against the front runner, the assumed potential prime minister, was a bold one. The fact that the front runner was his older brother was astounding. Various theories have abounded about this, including the obvious one, that the party could only elect one Miliband as leader. If Ed was going to run, this was the moment. He and David had grown up in different political camps within New Labour. Could Ed be tough enough and use the campaign to strengthen alliances to master the complexities of the electoral college? The psychology behind the decision is probably only known to the two brothers. Even in the annals of Labour party history it resonates as a unique act.

Harman had decided that the nominations would open on 24 May, the ballot would take place between 1 and 22 September and the results would be announced on the first day of conference, 25 September. The process was nearly five months long. There were never-ending hustings (fifty-seven) and four television debates. The real work, of course, was in positioning, personality and deals. In this, Ed Miliband's small team of advisors were critical. Anna Yearley had worked for Gordon Brown and the PLP before becoming director of political relations for Ed Miliband. She was one of a small group around him when he started to plan his strategy and the first step was to show he had support from a large enough group of MPs in the nomination process.

> David was going to get more MPs nominating him as first preference. He was more well-known. We had to show that we were a contender in this. And so we had a really clear strategy to get as many people as possible.

The left had two potential candidates. John McDonnell who again saw the opportunity to establish the left as a real force in the electoral college if he could get on the ballot. He was nominated by sixteen MPs but could not get across the line of thirty-three. He was just too much of a threat. Diane Abbott, who had a completely different profile on the left, announced she would stand and had two advantages. Ayesha Hazarika, who was working for Harriet Harman as deputy chief of staff at the time looked back on this in 2018:

> We were very neutral on it. Jonathan Ashworth and I, on Harriet's instruction, got Diane Abbott onto the ballot paper

because we wanted a woman but we also thought that the members should have a broad choice with someone from the left of the party. I bumped into somebody who was helping Diane Abbott in the cafe downstairs, and she was saying, 'Look, Diane's really struggling to get the nominations, and what does it say about our kind of party when a black woman can't get on the ballot.' I remember thinking this really didn't seem right, and I spoke to Harriet about it, and she felt exactly the same way, and we thought actually there was nothing ignoble in trying to help Diane, to give the members as broad a choice as possible.

David Miliband also threw his own nomination and those of some of his supporters to get Abbott on the ballot. She was never going to be a threat to him and might draw some votes from other, more dangerous candidates in the first round. Abbott got thirty-three MP nominations and eventually, in the electoral college, only seven MP's votes. Ed Miliband received sixty-three nominations, only eighteen behind his brother. This allowed him to start repositioning himself as the alternative candidate to both David and Ed Balls. Burnham had been correct; he was squeezed out as the change candidate. Ed Miliband had been shoulder to shoulder with Ed Balls at the Treasury from 1994 to 2005 (with a break to go to Harvard), and then as an MP was quickly promoted to ministerial jobs and the cabinet. He had not been an MP when the Iraq vote took place in 2003, but neither had Ed Balls. He had been a fully signed up member of the Brown faction, as had Balls.

The differences lay in personality. Ed Miliband had more evident charm that allowed him to make fewer enemies than either of his rivals. Personality counts in politics, as Gordon Brown discovered in 1994 against Blair, and Jeremy Corbyn was to find in 2015. You don't have to be more liked than your rivals, you have to be less disliked. A good example of Ed Miliband's less tribal and more consensual approach was described by Paul Kenny of the GMB, who had both significant votes and influence with other union leaders. This took place earlier, before a National Policy Forum where the unions would meet ministers before the full sessions to agree positions. Gordon Brown had sent his team. Paul Kenny:

Ed Miliband and Tom Watson were given the job of meeting the unions. It was a policy forum, but the unions always met the party leadership and negotiated. Within minutes, Ed, who was not skilled at this at all and didn't really understand what we did, basically said, 'Well you know, you're privileged to be here.' Apart from trying to stop someone from belting him, we just said 'Okay, if that's how you want it fine no problem' and we walked out. I was making an argument about trade union rights and stuff in the work place. Ed wrote a note saying, this seems very reasonable, we should agree this and Tom went back and said tell them they can't have it. Gordon had said (give them) nothing. That was I think Ed's first experience at being thrown into a negotiation with the unions.

What happened next? Kenny continued:

Ed rang me up and said perhaps we could have a meeting. I said to him, well what's the point of that. You don't get us, you don't understand, you don't get it. And he said, no I don't but I'd like to. So we met. He arranged for them to open up the cafe in St James's Park early, and we sat there and he just asked me about my background and where I came from and what we did and the things that the union did. And I thought to myself, well at least you've had the courage to ring, which very few of them ever did. We met for about an hour and then he went off to the cabinet. I met him a few times after that and we went in for discussions and I found that he was listening.

Kenny found Ed Miliband's approach in distinct contrast to that of his brother, David, who tended to channel Sir Edward Grey in 1914.

David would say you must come up and see me at the Foreign Office. You'd go up to there, and you'd have a chat and then you know, the door would open after twenty minutes. You knew the routine, you were out. He always used to take us to this little window, and he used to say, this is the window from which the foreign secretary at the time said the lights are going out all over Europe. He gave me the same story at the end of the interview. And I remember saying to this guy who was going to see him, as soon as he starts telling you about the lights going all over Europe and takes you to the window, you'll know you're out the door. It's about fifteen seconds to the door. Sure enough this guy said, yeah he did exactly the same to me.

Kenny favoured Ed:

The choice between David and Ed was really simple for people like us. Because David was just more of the same. All the speeches he'd made in the hustings were all, basically, don't ask me for anything. I'll let you know. It was just so repetitive of what we'd been through and frankly we were sick to the back teeth of it. We were having regular meetings at the time and we spelled out that if it was to be more of the same, whoever the new leader was, we were off. What's the point of us doing anything when we were getting nowhere, we weren't getting any of the stuff through.

Lucy Powell, a key Ed Miliband advisor and, from 2012, MP:

What I observed was the diffidence and impatience of David. He was a busy man with a lot of pressure on him. In contrast was the apparently relaxed and empathetic attitude taken by Ed Miliband.

David Miliband was aware of the need to throw off the Blairite tag but he couldn't just repudiate the previous thirteen years of government. Ed could at least present himself as the change candidate which was a strategy that required a lot of finesse. Stewart Wood:

Ed Miliband was trying to do this extraordinarily ambitious thing which was to be a change candidate, having been in the bunker for fifteen years. And at the beginning, he was a change candidate because we picked things to show differences on, in particular on Iraq, but other things as well.

As Ed Miliband said himself in 2018, 'I was the "moving on from being the New Labour" candidate.' This positioning allowed him to appeal to the left. Although Diane Abbott had got on the ballot, she was not a unifying candidate. Some small unions, such as Manuel Cortes's TSSA, were prepared to vote for her on the first ballot.

> The reason for that was that she was the only person who was in that ballot paper that came out unequivocally and said that if she became leader of the Labour party, our policy would be to nationalise the railways. The importance of that to our members is obvious. I thought what was even more defining than that was that she was prepared to say that an incoming Labour government would undo vital elements of the Thatcherite economy settlement. Something that New Labour had failed to challenge in any significant way. New Labour had run its course. Why did the average member of the Labour party go along with New Labour? Because it could win general elections. The moment it couldn't, it was dead in the water.

Ed Balls had his best moment in the campaign in a speech at Bloomberg responding to George Osborne's policy of austerity and the need to sharply reduce the deficit. Balls defended the record of the Labour government, accepted the need to cut the deficit over a much longer period, and attacked Osborne's growth forecasts. It was a forerunner of the arguments between the parties for the next five years but it was too late for Ed Balls in this election. One group led by Ken Livingstone with Seumas Milne of the *Guardian*, Billy Hayes of the Fire Brigade Union and Jon Trickett MP, discussed voting for Balls but he didn't get much traction with the left, unlike

Ed Miliband whose team had meetings with different groups and individuals such as Michael Meacher and Jon Lansman. Anna Yearley was focusing on the possible second preference voting:

> I remember the person we sent to go and talk to John McDonnell about second preference was Hilary Benn because John liked Hilary.

And it worked. John McDonnell:

> Those of us who dealt with him on a number of issues, we could see that Ed Miliband was different. He was different from what went on in New Labour. He had a spark about him that made you realise things would change. You knew that. He understood the traditions of the Labour party even though he was young and not part of those traditions. He understood them and he actually understood that he had to have radical policy change. Because he had been around for the Blair years, I think he was waking up to the fact that it hadn't worked. That's why, when it came down to it, he was most probably the optimal candidate for the left.

The trade unions were heavily in support of Ed. The rules said promotional material for any one candidate could not be placed *inside* the envelope with the ballot paper. You could put it in a bigger, second envelope with a picture on it. Ed's breakfast with Paul Kenny had paid off. Anna Yearley:

> It was Lucy Powell who is the person to take credit for that. She's the one who said, 'Well, put him on the envelope then.' Which is what they did to get around the rules. And they were allowed to do that. And so, we knew that he would hopefully win the union section.

The public clashes and polling began to break the candidates into groups. The two brothers and the rest of the field. Tensions grew. At the last televised debate on *Question Time*, Roger Mosey, a senior BBC executive, witnessed this:

> I was the BBC meet-and-greet person for the 2010 Labour leadership debates which took place in London. Before the debate, David and Ed Miliband were in the room and were at exact opposite ends of it and didn't exchange a single word through the whole of the pre-programme of drinks and discussion. Then when they went onto stage, they took part in the debate. At the end of the debate, in front of the audience, Ed moved over to David and embraced him, took him by the arm and they chatted as they were in front of the audience. Then we all went back up the green room upstairs where, again, they were at total opposite ends of the room and never spoke to each other at all. Didn't even say goodbye to each other.

Who could blame them? By the time the interminable process (the last leadership or deputy election featuring an electoral college) came to an end, it was as difficult to predict, as Healey-Benn had been in the first electoral college vote in 1981. David had led in the polls all the way, but Ed had the momentum. In the last poll before the vote taken by YouGov on 7 to 10 September, Ed was narrowly ahead by 51 to 49 per cent having won both the members and affiliates (union) sections. In the real election two weeks later, the results were announced over four rounds. Abbott and Burnham were eliminated in the first two rounds. In the affiliated section, where Ed had a commanding lead from round one, he ended up with 59.8 per cent of the vote, a huge margin in a two horse race. In the members' section where David had led on every round (unlike in the YouGov poll), David won by 54.4 per cent to 45.6 per cent. The real battle ground came down to the section featuring the MPs and MEPs. By the third round David led 47.3 per cent to Ed's 36.4 per cent, a wide lead that meant he was 42.7 per cent to 41.3 per cent in the college overall. After Ed Balls was eliminated in the third and penultimate round, the key question was where his forty-three voters would go in the last round. David gained fifteen votes to take him to 140 and 53.4 per cent of the section. Ed gained twenty-six to take him to 46.6 per cent. Although he had lost two of the three parts of the college, as with Harman in 2007, he had one huge win in one section – the unions and affiliates – which was enough to carry him home to victory by a margin of only 1.4 per cent: 50.7 per cent to 49.3 per cent. It was sensational. His small team gathered around him as David's team were in shock. Ed's ruthlessness and ability to make alliances worked in the particular circumstances of an electoral college. David's perceived arrogance, his Blairite credentials and his failure to seize the day over the previous three years all counted against him. To win was one objective, to lead was another. This was not going to be easy. Ayesha Hazarika:

> He had no honeymoon period at all. Literally no honeymoon period. On the night that he was declared leader, in the lobby of the Midland Hotel in Manchester there were people striding around, women in tears, men threatening to punch each other. And you have the David Miliband people, who are finger-pointing at the Ed Miliband people, saying, 'You've ruined this party. You mark my words, this is the beginning of the end.' So he gets no honeymoon period. You know, he doesn't get the chance to bask in the thing where you become leader, and you sort of wander round, and everyone's wanting to shake you by the hand. Right from the off, the tabloid newspapers had their name for him, 'Red Ed', so that's like day zero. I mean, you've not even started, and it's Red Ed, and so he wore that very heavily. He tried to sort of brush it off, but he was very conscious of it.

Anna Yearley:

> We'd done really well in the PLP. We hadn't won it, he did very well in the MPs' second preferences, and then in the trade union section. He won that as we knew he probably would, given the turnout was always going to be low in that section and given

that the unions had been pushing. But it was very disappointing that he hadn't won the membership section. So, he became leader without the majority of the PLP supporting him. Not by a huge margin, but people were quite disappointed. I remember at conference they organised a meeting of the PLP and it was a stand-up reception. We went in with Ed and lots of people there were polite, nice people . . . but, you know it was not particularly lovely. It wasn't like this homecoming of any leader. You had this leader who didn't have the vast support of the membership, didn't have the support of his colleagues in parliament. Not overwhelming support. And the unions were like, 'Yeah, that's fine he's won.' But there was no particular love for him from the trade unions either.

Ed Miliband had to define himself early and stake out a clear position both against his internal critics and the coalition government. His first step was his conference speech in 2010. He opened by referring to a new generation taking control. He then told the story of his family; his father, Ralph, was a noted academic and leftist who had arrived in Britain as a penniless, Jewish refugee in 1940, had learned English and served in the British army. His mother was from a Polish-Jewish refugee family who had seen the Nazis invade Poland. He talked about the defeat of 2010 and how lessons had to be learned:

We have to understand why people felt they couldn't support us. We have to show we understand the problems people face today.

On the need for leadership:

This will require strong leadership. It won't always be easy. You might not always like what I have to say. But you've elected me leader and lead I will.

He then spent a good section of the speech praising Blair and Brown and the achievements of New Labour, but then came the pitch to be the change candidate, moving on from the errors of New Labour:

> But we have to ask, how did a party with such a record lose 5 million votes between 1997 and 2010? It didn't happen by accident. New Labour, a political force founded on its ability to adapt and change, lost its ability to do so.
>
> Let me say to the country: You saw the worst financial crisis in a generation, and I understand your anger that Labour hadn't changed the old ways in the city of deregulation. You wanted your concerns about the impact of immigration on communities to be heard, and I understand your frustration that we didn't seem to be on your side. And when you wanted to make it possible for your kids to get on in life, I understand why you felt that we were stuck in old thinking about higher and higher levels of personal debt, including tuition fees. You saw jobs disappear and economic security undermined, I understand your anger at a Labour government that claimed it could end boom and bust. And I understand also that the promise of new politics of 1997 came to look incredibly hollow after the scandal of MPs' expenses. And we came to look like a new establishment in the company we kept, the style of our politics and our remoteness from people. I stand before you, clear in my task: to once again make Labour a force that takes on established thinking, doesn't succumb to it, speaks for the majority and shapes the centre ground of politics.

He moved onto foreign policy and Iraq:

> I've got to be honest with you about the lessons of Iraq. Iraq was an issue that divided our party and our country. Many sincerely believed that the world faced a real threat. I criticise nobody faced with making the toughest of decisions and I honour our troops who fought and died there. But I do believe that we were wrong. Wrong to take Britain to war and we need to be honest about that. Wrong because that war was not a last resort, because

we did not build sufficient alliances and because we undermined the United Nations.

As conference roared its approval, David Miliband was captured on television rebuking Harriet Harman for applauding since she had voted for the war. His frustration was visible. In this speech were all the themes that ended up defining Ed Miliband's time as leader. His powers of leadership and control within the party, immigration and social policy, economic policy in the face of constant Conservative attacks on New Labour's record as a justification for austerity, his own public persona and his position on New Labour and its repudiation. For the princes and princesses of New Labour, those from the generation who rose to ministerial office and power under Blair and Brown, the defeat in 2010 forced them to choose whether to defend or disavow their political heritage and find something to replace it. For Ed Miliband, his conference speech and subsequent attempts to move on was a logical political position because his election was based on being the change candidate and because he believed that seeking to defend the record was less important than finding a new political position against the coalition. In 2018 he said:

> No government is perfect. The financial crisis revealed that New Labour's bargain, which was, 'Okay we'll have a minimum wage and New Deal. It's not Thatcherite economics.' It's too simple to say Thatcherite economics or neo-liberal economics, but the compromise of low corporation tax, low capital gains tax, business is good, all of that. It was very problematic, and the financial crisis is one of the things that revealed that. . . . And I also feel this about being leader of the opposition, you have such little air space until the general election and the party conference, just such a little window to be heard, I didn't want to be heard on, 'New Labour was actually really quite good.' Although I didn't accept that it was New Labour overspending, I did accept that we didn't regulate the banks properly. The financial crisis happened on our watch, and I don't think anyone was then going to say, 'Well it wasn't really their fault.'

This refusal to defend the economic record and try to find other weapons to attack the Coalition causes bemusement and fury among New Labour adherents to this day. Tony Blair:

> I wasn't sufficiently aware of the degree of repudiation, funnily enough, until much later. But actually, what was as bad as the repudiation was the tacit acceptance that we had caused the financial crisis. In my time, the borrowing was lower than it was in the previous ten years of the Conservative government, so that was actually the thing because that was a repudiation of Gordon as well. I just never understood that one, I have to say, because it seemed to me a) obviously not correct and b) politically damaging.

Peter Mandelson is much more direct about the Blairite view of Ed Miliband:

> Ed Miliband, even though he was absolutely part of the Gordon Brown Treasury and its financial reforms, laid the deregulation of the financial markets at our door and by implication that we had precipitated the financial crisis. That took some nerve. . . . Ed punted this and other claims that New Labour hadn't fought inequality and that we just sucked up to business throughout his leadership. His own complicity in New Labour policies whilst working with Gordon at the Treasury went unacknowledged. His abiding aim was to delegitimise and kill off New Labour, without replacing it with any alternative, coherent, cogent thinking of his own.

In Peter Mandelson's view, the new generation were there to repurpose New Labour and failed:

> Their job was to assemble a new modernising agenda, to take all the fresh policy challenges that we were facing, post-2010 onwards, and say, 'Right. Let's take the New Labour rubric and apply it to these new challenges having learned lessons from what

we've done in government so as to create a new programme, a new agenda and platform.'

For the people around Ed Miliband, who had supported him in the leadership race and were of a younger generation, there was a need to find a new purpose and quickly. Lucy Powell:

> I thought at the time that Ed understood that we needed to move on from New Labour. And I'm not a critic of New Labour, I think it was a thing of its time, but if New Labour was anything, it was about keeping ahead of yourself and reinventing yourself. I felt we needed a kind of reinvention, and I thought that Ed understood that better than David.

The problem with denying New Labour was that there had to be a strategy to replace it, and a united opposition to deliver the messaging. Ed Miliband now had to rebuild the party, his shadow cabinet, and create a set of policies to replace what had dominated his party for the previous sixteen years.

18

Where are the Milibandites?

One of the vagaries of the Labour party was that, until Ed Miliband changed the rules, the shadow cabinet was elected by the PLP. Leaders had to find jobs for people who may well not have elected them. There was also a quota for at least six of nineteen appointments to be women. In the 2010 elections, not a single shadow cabinet member in the top ten had voted for Ed as a first preference. Of these, Yvette Cooper naturally voted for her husband Ed Balls, followed by John Healey, who also voted for Balls, then Ed Balls himself and Andy Burnham. Of the eighty-four who had voted for Ed Miliband in the first round, only six other than Miliband himself made it into the first shadow cabinet and, arguably, none of these were in the top jobs except Rosie Winterton as chief whip and Sadiq Khan as shadow justice spokesman. Lucy Powell:

You think that Jeremy Corbyn had some hostility from the PLP, it was almost the same as Ed Miliband had within the party staffing structure and the PLP and the shadow cabinet. Ed's approach, his personality, his demeanour is someone who tries to resolve. He's a peacemaker, he's someone who wants to kind of create consensus. He found himself the leader of a very ego-filled cohort in which perhaps none of them really accepted that he was the senior player. There was the dynamic of his brother. There was the dynamic of trying to be a one term opposition against this whole new thing. The first two years after Ed's leadership election, no one was even vaguely interested in the Labour party because it was all about coalition. It was all about Lib Dem-Tory relations.

He took the decision to appoint Ed Balls not as shadow chancellor, but shadow home secretary. David Miliband was out of contention as he had declared his intention to leave politics. Three months later, Alan Johnson resigned as shadow chancellor and Balls was brought into the job. The two Eds declared they would share a suite of offices to show they were not repeating the Blair-Brown splits of yesteryear. Cooper was made shadow home secretary and Douglas Alexander shadow foreign secretary, but the split in the shadow cabinet between the Brownites and Blairites was evident. Miliband and Balls were constantly referred to as the two Eds but there were also two Ed Milibands. Stewart Wood:

> There's Ed Miliband, the son of Ralph Miliband, and there's Ed Miliband the special advisor in the Treasury for ten years. The first Ed Miliband is radical, sees what Labour does as in a sort of strong tradition of social justice and combating inequality. Inequality is what gets him out of bed in the morning. The second Ed Miliband is tactically incredibly cautious. Essentially, that tactical Ed Miliband made a lot of decisions for very good reasons, which were massively risk-averse.

Ed Miliband agreed in 2018 that it was a problem:

> I was trying to hold in both hands the need to do what was right, according to my principles, but also, I probably fell between two stools. I should have been more radical. I used to say, we're trying to steer between the rocks that say, 'There's no difference', and the rocks that say, 'You're not responsible and you can't be trusted.' In a way it turned out to be a very narrow, white-water rafting expedition.

When Blair, Brown and Mandelson took power in the Labour party in 1994, they had a clear agenda. They were battle-hardened after the upheavals of the 1970s and were running a party that had lost four general elections and was going to agree to almost anything to get into power. Ed Miliband came from exactly the opposite position. He had won by explaining what he was not: New Labour and his brother. However, he came without a clear programme. He had almost no support among his rivals and inherited factions – he never had a group of Milibandites. This meant managing a party that was never properly owned by him. The real party management was placed with Tom Watson and his Brownite coterie and staffers until 2013 when the Falkirk crisis occurred. Miliband's office was also lacking in clear direction. It was divided between different strands of policy wonks (including Ed himself). There were no adults in the room to create clear messaging or clear strategy or to enforce that strategy. This meant he was swayed by differing advice, prey to short-term strategic decisions and vulnerable to attack.

Paul Kenny:

> The Blairites were quite open that he would have a fall of some sort and that David could be ushered back. He did have an insecurity to a certain degree about his legitimacy, I'd say that, Ed got it. He grew much, much more into understanding. He got the issues for the first time maybe since he'd entered the Commons. He actually got a whole range of social issues, that it wasn't just, 'Oh isn't this terrible', these poor people in bad housing. He got beyond it, how do we change that?

Andy Burnham:

> I think people shouldn't underestimate how tough it is to come out of government. It's a bit like a bereavement. It was galling to see Cameron and Osborne and we were struggling with all of that, and so I think actually, Ed did a respectable job of getting

us back as a fighting force pretty quickly without us all falling to bits, so I wouldn't necessarily run straight to a narrative of, it was awful. It wasn't, actually, I mean, for a first-term opposition, we didn't fall to bits, we kept in the game and the different wings of the party stayed broadly united.

That was never enough. Miliband's indecision impacted different aspects of policy but it was most clear in the ways in which Labour dealt with two major policy areas. The government's austerity plan and immigration and social policy. The fundamental conundrum was where to pitch the attacks on the coalition's economic policies that were, in turn, based on ferociously blaming everyone else. They would both hate this description, but George Osborne in many ways resembled a younger version of Gordon Brown. Both had been shadow chancellor (Osborne from the age of thirty-four for five years). Both were chancellor for lengthy periods (Osborne for six years) and both held sway over all government domestic policy, appointments and political strategy. They were the spines of their respective governments. Both had prime ministers who were more superficially attractive to the electorate, but both ran the machine and were the key political strategists. In later years, John McDonnell was to play a similar role as shadow chancellor to Jeremy Corbyn. Osborne's economic mantra of severe cuts to address the deficit had the political upside that he could blame Labour. In his 2011 speech to the Conservative party conference, he promised to ride out the storm of the deficit on which he blamed others' mistakes:

> There were three above all – and they are all connected with each other. First, the last government borrowed too much money. They saddled the country with the worst debt crisis in our history. What a catastrophic mistake. The second mistake was made by banks who ran up staggering debts of their own, buying financial instruments even they couldn't understand. . . . And there was a third mistake. Our European neighbours plunged headlong into the Euro without thinking through the consequences . . . For

generations to come, people will say: thank God Britain didn't join the Euro.

It's noticeable that Osborne didn't give Balls (or Gordon Brown) the credit for keeping Britain out of the Euro with the five tests created in the Treasury in Labour's first term. The main point of attack kept coming and both Eds failed to come up with a coherent response. Ayesha Hazarika:

> I think they were so conscious of the mantra that the Tories used against them which was, 'These guys crashed the car. Why would you give the keys back to the guys that crashed the car?' I think they both felt, Ed Balls probably more than Ed Miliband, that they couldn't give the Conservatives openings to attack them in that way. Remember, on top of all of that, Ed Miliband had won with a message which basically said, 'What went before me was bad'. That allowed the Conservatives, particularly Osborne, who has a ruthless strategic brain, to work out very, very quickly that was the way to completely box us in.

In the face of this onslaught, Miliband and Balls tried to come up with a coherent set of policies that would attract voters while attacking the deep cuts made in government spending. It is worth remembering that Osborne had his own misfortunes, such as the omnishambles budget in 2012 in which he cut the top rate of income tax and launched a series of failed initiatives for other tax changes. The Conservatives had launched cuts and alterations in the welfare state that outdid anything attempted by Margaret Thatcher. One example that lives with us today is the extraordinary incompetence and impact of Ian Duncan Smith's Department of Work and Pensions that attempted to combine benefits into one payment: universal credit. This not only failed as an administrative process, it failed in its core attempt to redefine welfare and caused, over a number of years, untold damage and social deprivation. Osborne's cuts were deep and affected all aspects of government: the NHS, education, the police and even areas of traditional Conservative interest such as defence. But they had one political advantage; they took time to work through the system. Lucy Powell:

> The full effects of austerity were nowhere near being felt through any of Ed's era of leadership. Although as politicians, as economists, as thinkers, as policy makers we understood that would come, we were sort of trapped between a rock and a hard place of making an argument for a time in the future when we were also trying to win an election in the present. That was actually the fundamental challenge.

What Miliband was trying to do was explain a new sort of economic theory for the post-crash world. He had to balance the need to attack austerity, which was demanded by his party, and the perceived view of the voters who blamed Labour.

> I think it was very tricky for us, because austerity was very problematic for the country. The cuts the Conservatives were making were pretty sharp and intense. We were trying to offer some reassurance, but it wasn't enough for the voters who wanted mega-reassurance and self-flagellation. It was too much reassurance for the people who wanted radicalism and not enough for those who said 'We're going to fight austerity with every sinew of our being and we want no cuts at all.' We were caught between our instincts, which were pretty anti-austerity, but the electoral necessity was that we perceived to offer some reassurance and say, we are going to cut the deficit.

In 2011, the first full year of his leadership, Ed Miliband showed his best and his worst instincts. In July, it was revealed that Rupert Murdoch's newspaper empire, run in the UK by his son James and Rebekah Brooks, had engaged in extensive phone tapping of public figures and victims in the news. The *News of the World* had been a particularly keen exponent of this practice as well as being accused of bribing police officers and targeting the families of murdered schoolgirl, Millie Dowler, and the victims of the July

2005 bombings in London. Miliband attacked both Murdoch and David Cameron, whose chief communications officer was Andy Coulson, a former editor of the *News of the World*, who was eventually imprisoned. On 6 July 2011, Cameron announced the establishment of an enquiry under Lord Leveson which spent nearly a year cross-examining leading members of the press and then publishing its report. Ed Miliband can claim responsibility for pursuing and challenging the government all the way.

The other side of this was his habit of making mistakes that just shouldn't have been made. Even when he had a clear message, it got lost in its presentation. In his 2011 conference speech that was plagued by delivery issues, Miliband tried to redefine himself as willing to 'break the consensus rather than succumb to it'. He promised a 'tough fight to recast a new capitalism built around British values that reward the hard-working grafters and producers in business, and not the asset-stripping "predators."' This immediately led to him having to define British companies as 'good' and 'bad'. However, the attacks on the government could work when specific, and targeted on unfairness and consumer unease. Stewart Wood:

> I think there was a turning point in 2013 which is the conference when we did the energy price freeze and that was, in a way, our best moment in terms of an announcement, because I was telling the journalists beforehand and they were astonished that we were doing this. We baited Osborne to give the exact reaction, who accused us of being Marxist. We were like, okay here's the poll we've just done showing 80 per cent of the public agrees with us, where are you going to go now? As a political moment, it was fantastic for us.

The choice was to come up with radical ways of managing a shrinking economy that appealed to consumers and emphasised economic fairness. Over the five years of his leadership, Labour floated redistributive ideas about low pay, a mansion tax, boosting the national minimum wage to more than £8 an hour, a ban on zero-hours contracts, price regulation in the energy sector and reforming public services. It proposed bringing back the 50p tax rate for the income tax band over £150,000 and also proposed a new British investment bank. The essential trade-off was to accept the need for short-term cuts but promise longer-term investment and rebuilding of the infrastructure. After launching twenty-two policy reviews in 2010, they had settled on 'the squeezed middle' as a target group. It was all too secondary against the clarity of the Conservatives cuts. Labour's position was to agree the need for cuts, but phased over a longer term. This stance also meant that a public sector wage freeze of 1 per cent and other cuts that looked like austerity would have to be accepted to appear to be responsible in government, just as Gordon Brown had done in 1997 in accepting the Conservative's spending plans. Jonathan Ashworth, elected as MP in 2011, said in 2018:

> I think the problem was that we ran a campaign for five years focused on stagnating wages and on the lack of economic growth and then when it came to the general election, our economic policy was not radically different enough from Conservative policy. In 2015, the position of our party was to keep the public pay freeze in place as an example of how we too were going to be tough on the economy. Yet the previous four or five years, we'd been attacking it and saying that people's wages across the public sector and the private sector were stagnating.

If Labour was torn between a new radicalism and innate conservatism, the actual Conservatives throughout these five years managed to blame either their partners in coalition, or the Labour opposition for its past. The Lib Dems had finally got into power, but were blamed by their younger voters in university seats for the rises in tuition fees which they had pledged to oppose. In government, twenty-seven Lib Dems voted for the increase, twenty-one against and eight abstained. Their role in blocking other extreme Conservative measures was not really seen or counted by the electorate. Increasingly, Lib Dem voters moved to Labour and neutrals blamed them for keeping the Conservatives in power.

The coalition agreed the Parliament Act that set five-year fixed-term parliaments. This established the date of the following election as the first week of May 2015. It now needed 66 per cent of the House of Commons to vote for an election before the term was up; a piece of legislation that would have long-term ramifications for both Labour and Conservative parties from 2017 onwards.

The Lib Dems had demanded a vote on proportional representation and secured the promise from David Cameron that the coalition would vote for a bill allowing a referendum. It failed to secure a guarantee that the Conservatives would support it in the actual referendum. In the event, 67.9 per cent voted against, 32.1 per cent in favour. Neither major party officially supported it and David Cameron actively campaigned against it. The same night in 2011, the local elections showed the way the wind was blowing. The Lib Dems were decimated, dropping 11 per cent in the polls to Labour's gain, but the Conservatives also gained seats at their expense. Labour was 2 per cent above the Conservatives in the poll.

On the same night in Scotland, the news was far more dramatic and would have a far greater impact on Labour. The Holyrood electoral system, which was itself based on PR, had been designed for a permanent coalition government when set up in 1997. The Scottish National Party, led by Alex Salmon, smashed this assumption by winning sixty-nine seats over Labour's thirty-seven, the Conservatives fifteen and Lib Dems five. The combination of constituency votes and regional lists slightly disguised the true nature of the victory. The swing to the SNP was over 12 per cent. The potential impact of Labour's chances in a UK general election was too damaging to think about in 2011.

The other electoral challenger was UKIP and, in a series of elections in 2013 and 2014, it became a frightening challenger to each of the main parties. In the local elections of 2013 it won 17 per cent against Labour's 31 per cent and the Conservatives' 29 per cent. In 2014, it increased its vote in local elections to 20 per cent, just behind Labour's 21.1 per cent and ahead of the Lib Dems' 13.8 per cent. The more shocking result was in the Euro elections on the same day.

UKIP won the most seats: twenty-four. It also got the most votes: 27 per cent of the poll. It was the first time a political party other than Labour or the Conservatives had won a national election since 1906. The Conservatives had dropped to 23.1 per cent, its lowest ever share in a national poll. Labour edged into second with 24.4 per cent. The shock was to drive both major parties into problematic positions. The Eurosceptics in the Conservative party started to push for an electoral alliance with UKIP. In January 2013, David Cameron had promised an in-out referendum by the end of 2017. Now the pressure was put on him to hold it earlier, in 2016. In 2014 he rejected this idea. Miliband had already refused the idea of a referendum if Labour got to power. For Labour, UKIP's challenge reinforced the dilemma within the party both on its immigration policy as well as membership of the EU. Labour northern heartland seats were regarded as being under threat. Frontbench spokesmen, including Balls and Miliband, were under constant pressure from their constituents. This was a problem for all sorts of emotional and political reasons dating back to the 1960s, but also a more recent memory of 2010 and Mrs Duffy with Gordon Brown. Ayesha Hazarika:

> We really lost our way on what our narrative should have been on immigration. We were very, very aware of how difficult an issue it was for us, particularly with very high populations of the ethnic vote, but we also got very spooked by UKIP. At that point, UKIP was at the height of its powers, and we even set up a little UKIP working group, a meeting of key shadow cabinet people and there was a big division over how we should handle the UKIP thing. There were some people saying we should never even mention their name, let's not give them the oxygen of publicity, let's just ignore it and it will all go away, and we mustn't talk about immigration because it's all racist. There were other people, saying, 'Look, this problem is really not going away. This immigration stuff, it's coming up on the doorstep.'

Miliband could see in constituency meetings that he was facing a challenge from the white working-class Labour voters who had always been Labour's core support. This was a hugely emotive issue so he tried to recast it as a mainly economic issue. Miliband reflected on all this in 2018:

> When I launched my leadership campaign, I said, 'Immigration is an issue'. Why does Britain, among all other European countries, have so much more of a problem with intra-European migration? It's because of the collision of a highly deregulated labour market and immigration. . . . I was defending free movement, but that was why my focus tended to be on, what do we do in the labour market? What do we do about agencies? What do we do about jobs being advertised first abroad? What do we do about people not paying the minimum wage? That doesn't mean you don't think immigration is good. I was trying to talk about the issue, and I used to spend a long time really thinking, 'I don't want this to be a dog whistle, I've got to be true to what I believe, and true to my background.' You celebrate the positive things of immigration, we can't not talk about it. But it clearly wasn't successful.

Stewart Wood acutely felt the problem:

> Some of the most unpleasant meetings we had as a team were when our strategy and focus group people would come in saying 'Ed you really need to make a speech about this because people think you have nothing to say on it and that you're running away from it.' He would say, 'I don't want to talk about it, I've done my speech, I did a speech last year on this.' It became a very sensitive topic because he didn't want to go to this other place. In a way he was being true to himself, but the party needed someone to say something bigger. We should be much more liberal. He could have done it in different ways, he may have got credit for being himself about it much more vociferously, but he couldn't.

By 2013, the need to get a clear focus and a full policy slate also meant new people were joining the team. Simon Fletcher, having run two successful campaigns for Ken Livingstone in London and then two losing mayoral elections against Boris Johnson in 2008 and 2012, was brought into the Miliband office by Anna Yearley. It was a joke in the office that Ed Miliband was the most left-wing person in it until Simon Fletcher joined, but Fletcher was to play an important role with the unions over the next two years. Patrick Loughran and Spencer Livermore of the Blair and Brown leadership teams were also approached. Loughran said no, it wasn't his project. Livermore finally said yes to role of the election organiser and to 'make the trains run on time'. In a strange way, appointing the left-wing Fletcher and the centrist Livermore sums up the approach of Miliband. Both were highly capable but neither were natural Milibandites. The internal policy debates and formulations continued but in late 2012, something else was to come up that would deflect the leadership for over a year and have a huge impact on the future of the party, and it all began with a drunken brawl.

19

Falkirk and Collins

The Miliband era may well be remembered only for the fundamental reform that led to a transformation of the party from 2015. The events leading up to the Collins report are somehow uniquely Labour. The essential division between being a party of protest and of power can be seen in the events of 2013 and 2014, and in the introduction of one member one vote. The unexpected consequences were a mass movement, and the return and election of the left after so many years in the wilderness.

The internal changes started in 2010. Ed Miliband always saw himself as a reformer and, on becoming leader, he appointed Peter Hain, the shadow Welsh secretary and party elder, to investigate how to turn Labour into a mass party. Hain produced a paper, 'Refounding Labour', which he presented at the 2011 conference. It pointed out that despite gaining some new members since 2010, the party had suffered a huge drop in the New Labour years. Constituencies were in danger of getting moribund and were sending fewer and fewer delegates to conference. He touched on the role and use of social media, but the focus was to drive new people into some degree of association with the Labour party. This became the registered supporters' scheme. Supporters could be signed up but not have any rights to vote until they became members or their numbers would be so significant that they could have a section of the electoral college.

This set of proposals passed but never really took hold except to establish the idea of registered supporters being a viable way to get more involvement in the party. It was to become much more relevant after 2014. A new general secretary, Iain McNicol, replaced the outgoing Ray Collins. In 2012, he introduced sweeping reforms that reduced staffing at Labour HQ but also introduced an executive board designed to link the HQ at Southside more closely to the leader's office. The left had high expectations of change. Jon Lansman:

> We had hopes that there might be a bit of democratisation, but there wasn't. Actually, what Miliband did was even more centralisation and the obvious bit of that was creating these new executive directors of the party, who sat in the leader's office. It further centralised control.

The left continued to watch and wait, but then Falkirk happened. Anyone who worked around the Palace of Westminster in the 1970s or 1980s was used to heroic amounts of drinking in the various bars. Twenty years later, there were always a few hardy souls lowering standards. On 22 February 2012, Eric Joyce, the Labour MP for Falkirk, was arrested for attacking six Conservatives in the Strangers' Bar, in the course of which he smashed a door while resisting arrest. He was suspended from the Labour party the following day and, on 12 March, announced he would not stand for re-election in 2015. This triggered the Falkirk episode, a quintessentially Labour crisis. It was entirely self-inflicted, involved huge egos, big hatreds and unexpected consequences.

Simply put, after 2010, Tom Watson had become Labour election coordinator and Miliband's chief fixer in the party. His private office was run by Karie Murphy, a former chair of the Scottish Labour party. Watson also shared a flat with the new general secretary of Unite, Len McCluskey, who was a good friend of Karie Murphy. Jim Murphy, (no relation) a leading Scottish MP, shadow cabinet member and Blairite, had a long-standing rivalry with Tom Watson and a mutual hatred of Len McCluskey. After

Joyce had declared his departure, Karie Murphy announced she would stand for the nomination for Falkirk. Stevie Deans, Unite's chair at the local Grangemouth refinery, also became chair of the Falkirk constituency party. The two of them campaigned actively for her to become the candidate. This included signing up new members for the constituency in a local pub. Unite then posted large batches of new Falkirk membership applications to Labour's head office for approval and paid the fees. The CLP membership doubled in size as Unite members at the refinery signed up. None of this was outside the rules of either Unite or the Labour party. As a Unite report proudly and openly stated in December 2012:

> We have recruited well over 100 Unite members to the party in a constituency with less than 200 members. A collective effort locally, but led and inspired by the potential candidate.

It was an established principle that unions could sign up new members and pay their fees in advance. The critical accusation made was that some new members did not know they had been signed up and their applications were false. Labour HQ staff raised the issue but were told that this had been approved and to allow new signatories the right to vote. This instruction apparently came from a 'senior figure'. Accusations started to fly within the Scottish Labour party and from supporters of other potential candidates, one of whom, Gregor Poynton, later admitted that he paid a cheque for eleven new members to join the party. Poynton himself was married to a Labour MP in Jim Murphy's team and was a member of the Blairite wing of the party. This quickly become a proxy war between the supporters of the Blairite Jim Murphy and Len McCluskey for power in both Falkirk and the Scottish Labour party. The announcement that the nomination would be an all-woman shortlist seemed to seal it for Karie Murphy and the membership forms had been accepted at Labour HQ, no matter how dubious they were alleged to be.

At the same time, a bigger political issue was brewing over candidate selection in marginal constituencies. Following years of resentment of New Labour's control of candidate selection, the unions were now flexing their muscles. Unions such as Unite and the GMB were becoming far more successful in getting candidates selected who were sponsored by them.

In February and March 2013, the Falkirk nomination was scrutinised by the NEC and an internal report commissioned. The process in Falkirk was suspended. On 25 June, after receiving the report, the CLP was put into 'special measures' to 'uphold the integrity of the Labour party'. This included freezing the membership of anyone who had joined it since March 2012 and suspending Murphy and Deans. By this point, the whole mess had been made public. Peter Mandelson had used a progress conference in which questions were raised over union influence in parliamentary selections, to attack Unite and its activities in Falkirk.

On 27 June, Len McCluskey attacked the NEC and accused Labour of undertaking a smear campaign against the union. He threatened legal action if necessary. At Prime Minister's Questions (PMQs) on 3 July, David Cameron lost no time in taunting Miliband of being the creature of Unite:

> We have a situation in this country where we have got one of our political parties where it has become apparent votes are being bought, people are being signed up without consent. All done by the man – Len McCluskey – who gave him [Miliband] his job.

Rumours abounded that a backbench Conservative MP was to refer Unite's campaign in Falkirk to Police Scotland. Even by Labour's standards this was unusual. There were considerable efforts within Labour HQ to reach an accommodation with Unite, not to refer anything to the police and to lift the suspension of Karie Murphy, but part of the summary of the NEC's report was leaked to Channel 4's Michael Crick. This created panic in the leader's office and Tom Watson resigned as Labour election coordinator, having felt compelled to support Unite. On 5 July, Ed Miliband announced the party was to refer its own internal report to Police

Scotland. Three weeks later, Police Scotland reported that it would not pursue any action concluding there were insufficient grounds.

Events now took two parallel courses. The resolution of the Falkirk issue was arranged by Anna Yearley and Simon Fletcher. At this point it was being suggested that Unite might have to disaffiliate from the Labour party. Simon Fletcher:

> I came into that job with high ambitions to change the dynamic of the relationship between the unions and the party leadership, to create a more collegiate approach so that we could bury the arguments of the last couple of years and get together to win a general election. That was my high ideal, and then six months later comes this situation. It clearly needed some sort of intervention given the strength of personalities of those involved, especially Len McCluskey.

On sending the report to the police: 'It shouldn't have happened.'

The pragmatists in Labour's HQ and the leader's office wanted Falkirk to be resolved and swept away. Whatever the personal reasons were for the row, they had resulted in Cameron's attack at PMQs, a huge amount of bad publicity, internal faction fighting and the resignation of Tom Watson as election coordinator. Miliband's attempts to hold the centre of the party and his own authority were being undermined. Yet the row was also an opportunity for him to seize greater control of the party. It was well known that in the 2010 leadership election, numerous voters had voted multiple times (including for him). Party financing had been discussed with the other parties for two years, but it hadn't gone anywhere. He was still sensitive to the accusation that he was the creature of the unions due to his failure in 2010 to win either the constituency or parliamentary sections of the electoral college. The time had come to act, to show independence and possibly to create new primaries and to make Labour a more attractive party to potential supporters. It was a New Labour view going back to the early 1990s.

A few days after Cameron's attack and the referral to Police Scotland, Miliband and his close advisors decided to act. It was all done in a huge rush. At a barbecue at Miliband's house, plans were made to change the relationship between the party and the unions. Instead of the union paying fees on the assumption of their members supporting Labour, those members would now have to 'opt in'. They also decided that the next candidate for the London mayoral election would be selected by a primary. Phone calls were made between Miliband's private office and Labour party officials, during which the impact of these decisions were pointed out. If the unions stopped paying the current level of fees, Labour would lose substantial funding.

Miliband's speech, given to the St Bride's Foundation on Tuesday 9 July, was designed to address the issues of funding and allowing new supporters or members into the party. According to the electoral commission report in 2014, Labour's membership was just under 190,000 in 2013 and its income £33.3 million, of which the unions had supplied about a third. Using Falkirk as the lever, Miliband proposed the opt-in for trade union members who wished to be individual members of the Labour party.

> Trade unions should have political funds for all kinds of campaigns and activities as they choose. But I do not want any individual to be paying money to the Labour party in affiliation fees unless they have deliberately chosen to do so. I believe we need people to be able to make a more active, individual, choice on whether they affiliate to the Labour party. So we need to set a new direction in our relationship with trade union members in which they choose to join Labour through the affiliation fee: they would actively choose to be individually affiliated members of the Labour party and they would no longer be automatically affiliated. . . . I believe this idea has huge potential for our party and our politics. It could grow our membership from 200,000 to a far higher number, genuinely rooting us in the life of more people of our country.

He made the move to a primary in the London mayoral election in 2016. This would be the earliest date to bring in new supporters.

If we are to restore faith in our politics, we must go further in involving members of the public in our decision making. We must do more to open up our politics. So I propose for the next London mayoral election, Labour will have a primary for our candidate selection. All Londoners of voting age should be eligible to take part. All they will need to do is either be a party member or register as a supporter at any time up to the day of the ballot.

A raft of other ideas included a new code of conduct for parliamentary candidates, spending limits in candidate election contests and agreements with unions in constituencies so that they are not under 'undue pressure'. This would create a party:

> . . . where everyone plays their part and a politics in which they can, a politics that is open, transparent and trusted – exactly the opposite of the politics we saw in Falkirk. That was a politics closed, a politics of the machine, a politics hated – and rightly so. What we saw in Falkirk is part of the death throes of the old politics. It is a symbol of what is wrong with politics. I want to build a better Labour party – and build a better politics for Britain.

He announced that Ray Collins would lead the follow-up work and report back to a special conference in 2014.

This speech got a mixed reception. At party HQ, the reaction was one of outright concern. On the other hand, some people liked it. Tony Blair issued a statement that afternoon:

> I think this is a defining moment. It's bold and it's strong. It's real leadership, this. I think it's important not only in its own terms, because he's carrying through a process of reform in the Labour party that is long overdue and, frankly, probably I should have done it when I was leader. But at the same time what he's doing, and I think this is also very important for the country, is that he's sending a very strong message to the country that in the end

he will do what's right, he'll govern for all the country and not simply for one section of it. This is big stuff and it takes a real act of leadership to do it.

Paul Kenny, as Chair of TULO, convened the main trades unions. He stood between Miliband and McCluskey, but when it came down to it couldn't see what Unite had done.

Falkirk's really simple. The hostility between Len and Jim Murphy was legendary. I was talking to Len, I was obviously talking to Ed. Honestly, I could not see what it was exactly that Unite had done. I have never seen anything that stands up in daylight about it. At the time I was thinking, we know what's going on, you're talking about people making allegations about Unite making inappropriate behaviour.

In his view this had always happened under New Labour. The favoured could always find a way to get a parliamentary seat. How was this different if a union was doing it? He tried to calm the row down but then came the St Bride's speech which he saw as a direct threat to the unions in the Labour party:

There were long conversations between me and Ed. And I'll be honest with you, I really needed him not to make that speech. I think if you look at it, his advisors will have said to him, 'Well of course if you go for one member one vote you're free. The unions elected you and controlled you, well now you're free.' But by the time it took place, we'd already worked out what the end game was. I told him not to do it. I pleaded with him not to do it and I explained to him that once he did this, this really was the box. If he opened this box it was not closable.

Ray Collins was the person asked to make these proposals a reality. Miliband's speech and his brief to Collins was originally about finance and how to bring in new supporters without the unions controlling access. The process of electing the leader was not on the original agenda at all. Yet in the following six months the Collins review was the final nail in the coffin for the parliamentary party's ability to determine the election of its leader. Ray Collins met with a wide range of party members and officials, but the biggest stumbling block was always going to be the unions. The leader had made his position clear, but how the opt-in and new supporters' scheme was to be implemented without damaging the link with the unions as the largest funding entities of the party had to be resolved somehow. Ray Collins saw the origins of all of this, as a former trade unionist and Labour party general secretary, as just bad leadership and communication. In politics everything is personal:

> Before the Falkirk issue, what was the relationship between Ed Miliband and Len McCluskey? I suspect if you ask Ed Miliband, he would say, 'It was fine. I got on well with him. Liked him'. If you asked Len McCluskey, if he was honest, he would say, 'Well, the guy doesn't have time for me'. Did they ever spend any time together? Did Ed Miliband ever take Len McCluskey out for dinner?

Ray Collins thought it was badly handled from the start:

> They planned a speech and they planned a review, and the speech was going to sound radical but was the review going to be particularly radical? They had lined up trade union leaders, apparently, and they'd lined up somebody to do the report. It was all looking hunky dory. And then, when the press release of the speech went out, all these trade union leaders that had been approached in advance, who were comfortable, went absolutely ape shit. Because the speech was reaching conclusions. The worst thing about the speech, which I found incomprehensible, is that he didn't attack trade union participation in the party. He didn't attack the fact that trade unions controlled 50 per cent of the vote of conference. Didn't even mention that. He attacked the money. This is after two years of talking to the Tories about trying to take big money out of politics.

Collins was caught in the middle:

> I tried to square a circle. What I tried to do – maybe clumsily, but most people thought I managed to pull it off – was to protect the money. I thought the electoral college had reached the end of its day because it made no sense. When you have an electoral college where actually the same people are a member of each part of it, and you have individuals with six or seven votes, each with a different value, my starting point was, you can't defend the current system. It doesn't work.

The union leaders were reaching a similar conclusion. Allow lots of people to join, but make sure the problems with the electoral college could be dealt with, and it could mean a move to something that would actually benefit the unions. Paul Kenny wanted to protect the unions' control over 50 per cent of conference votes. It didn't matter which union was the biggest or the strongest at any moment, it was their collective position, and the link with the Labour party that mattered. If they had to accept thousands of new individuals joining the party, they would get a trade-off that would significantly reduce the power of MPs influence over electing the leader.

> Collins came to see me and he said we have to deliver this for Ed. I said we're not going to deliver it. He'd made a decision, he may well get turned over at the party conference, because it's not a good decision. This dance went on for about three weeks, with Collins under pressure to get things going but knowing effectively the unions had to be lined up. Eventually, the deal was struck in my office between me and Collins. It was a very simple one which was that if they were proceeding, the golden vote goes, absolutely goes.

What was the golden vote?

> The golden vote meant one MP's vote is worth 30,000 trade union votes. And so, if it was going to be OMOV, it would

be OMOV and that meant an MP had no more clout than an ordinary member or a trade union member, they all would be exactly the same.

The idea of the new registered supporters' scheme didn't worry him:

> Oh absolutely, it was crystal clear. If they're worried about a few Unite members in a constituency, there are now going to be hundreds if not thousands flocking into the party and particular constituencies. You knew exactly what was going to happen.

The impact of that could be managed. The unions were prepared to accept the removal of the electoral college to take away the final vestige of MPs' power to influence the election of the leader. The creation of electoral college in 1981 was seen as the left's greatest victory. For the first time, MPs had lost the unilateral right to elect the leader of the party, but by 2010 they still held a third of the college, which meant an individual vote by an MP had more weight than anyone else. In the first two decades of the college when leaders won with huge majorities, this didn't matter, but in 2010, the individual MPs' votes in the final rounds counted enormously.

The introduction of OMOV to elect the party leader would have a far greater impact than anyone could predict but even in this early stage, Ray Collins saw that there might have to be some control mechanisms to manage the process. Firstly, controlling who could join the party by setting the fee: the lower the fee the more potential supporters you could attract, but the less control you may have. You could also delay giving any new supporter the right to vote until they had been in the party for six months; a freeze period. Secondly you could control who was eligible to stand for the post of the leader by the setting a high parliamentary bar for nominations. The introduction of the 12.5 per cent bar on nominations to the leadership in 1988 had prevented any left candidate getting on the ballot in 1992, 1994 and 2007. In 2010, Diane Abbott had only succeeded with support from David Miliband and Harriet Harman. Twice John McDonnell had been stopped. This bar still would give some protection to the PLP depending on how high it was set. Collins went back to the leader's office with a new set of proposals. Anna Yearley:

> Ray's going around negotiating with the general secretaries, meeting all the different stakeholders. The thing that then started coming up was scrapping the electoral college. I was concerned about that, because the safeguard of the electoral college is the weighting of the PLP section and the lock mechanism on that was the nomination threshold. The nomination threshold that we had first proposed as 25 per cent of the PLP, which didn't seem unreasonable, that was the number that Ray was talking to people about.

As the initial proposals were circulated, Ed Miliband came under pressure from two opposite ends of the political spectrum in the form of the unions on the left and the Blairites. Both wanted the bar to be much lower than 25 per cent. Miliband's team opted for 20 per cent but then came the pressure. Manuel Cortes of the TSSA, a left-leaning general secretary:

> We were at the TUC congress. And there was a very heated exchange between union general secretaries, and Ed Miliband. Clearly, he was in a room full of negotiators, and he wasn't a particularly brilliant one. What started off as being an attempt to disenfranchise unions ended up in what I thought was a very good deal for unions. Because we got rid of the electoral college.

In a party with a mass membership, the unions can have a big impact on new supporters;

> Unions can mobilise in those elections. They can mobilise over a quarter of a million, 300,000 people. We just looked at a different way to influence. Out of those 600,000 Labour party members, a significant number of them are union members and they will be influenced by us.

A parliamentary bar can always be further lowered in the future:

> Because once you set a bar, all you can do is you can reduce the
> bar. We knew that if you put the bar at 15 per cent, a Labour
> party conference some day is going to get that down.

If the left could see having a low bar would work to its advantage so
could the Blairites who were worried about undue union influence,
and a possible problem with getting a leadership nomination for
their future candidates. Ed Miliband also came under pressure
from them as he explained in 2018

> Falkirk became a big problem. I think it was inevitable that I got
> dragged into it. It didn't make sense to me that we still had this
> single thing called the electoral college system. Nobody really
> liked the electoral college system. We had to find a new way of
> funding things. Falkirk had raised a number of problems about
> our funding model. As Ray was doing this review, the idea of
> electing a leader getting rid of the electoral college arose. . . . The
> left liked it, because they thought it would radicalise the choice
> of leader, and maybe diminish the MPs. The right liked it, and
> then hated it afterwards.

As for the parliamentary bar dropping from the Collins proposal
of 25 per cent to Miliband's office wanting 20 per cent and then
pressure to reduce this even further:

> It went from 20 per cent to 15 per cent because the right of
> the Labour party, in particular a couple of shadow cabinet
> members said to me, 'This 20 per cent's terrible, it means that
> if there's a Progress candidate, they won't get on the ballot.'
> And I ended up agreeing to 15 per cent. I remember going to
> a PLP meeting, where everybody thought I was going to be
> saying it was twenty, and saying it was fifteen. And they were
> all really relieved.

The decision to drop the bar to 15 per cent may look like an obscure point but it was to prove a game changer in the history of the Labour party only a year later. If the original Collins recommendation of 25 per cent had been undertaken it is certain Jeremy Corbyn would not have been nominated in 2015; he even would have had problems at 20 per cent. Ironically he would have a lot to thank the Blairites for in 2015.

Collins had assumed that all of this could take five years to bed in. Moving away from affiliated fees to new supporters should be phased in on a sensible basis. The first big call would be the London mayoral elections in 2016 with an open primary. This would give the party time to organise it and the NEC could take its time to decide the fee levels and the freeze period. His final report was taken to a special conference in February 2014. It included all the changes that no one had foreseen six months earlier. Ray Collins:

> Len McCluskey was incredibly supportive of Ed Miliband's position. He supported the review, supported when Ed was talking about greater engagement and membership involvement. He supported that. I had the difficulty explaining to Ed Miliband why Len McCluskey supported him, and I don't think people around Ed Miliband fully understood why Len McCluskey supported him.

Len McCluskey, like the other union leaders, saw an opportunity of removing the power of MPs and building a mass party that the unions would be best organised to manage and to attract a New Left supporter network. Other figures on the left did not like the Collins report as much. The special conference to approve the measures was called for 1 March 2014. Jon Lansman, writing in *Left Futures* the previous month, slammed it. He wrote 'Eight reasons to vote against the Collins report'. There were objections about the administrative process, the ways to vote on rule changes, but the key objections were the attack, as he saw it, on the unions' power within the party, which is where the left had most influence.

The one-day conference overwhelmingly supported the changes by 86 per cent to 14 per cent. The big three union leaders warned that they would not agree to any more reforms of this type. Paul Kenny had already put his money down in September 2013 by cutting the GMB's affiliation fees to Labour from £1.2 million to £150,000 on the assumption that only 50,000 out of 650,000 of its members would opt in. Miliband was taking a huge gamble. Within the PLP there was a muted reaction apart from a few who realised they were losing any influence as a parliamentary party. Very few MPs raised objections to opening up the party to a flood of new supporters who could easily impact the structures of the party. Pat McFadden:

> I got a call quite late in the day from someone who was involved in it. I said 'I understand why there's an impetus to get rid of the [electoral] college [but] all they're doing here is getting rid of the MPs' power. I see no logic to what you're doing, unless you're going to move from the college to a one member one vote system where all our votes – MPs, party members, union members – are exercisable only by being a member of the Labour party. That's a one member one vote system. There's a logic to go into that system, but there isn't a logic to doing what you're doing.'

McFadden spotted that it would give the trade unions too much influence:

> The system that you're giving them is going to empower them significantly and more than they're empowered in the current system. And the trade unions have wanted to do that for a long time. I think I was one of the few MPs not to go to the special conference to cheer this on.

Ray Collins, in 2018, reflected on the fact that his plan had been overtaken by events. The control mechanisms that were to set the joining rate for new supporters and the decision as to whether there would be a freeze period, had not been set or agreed. Collins assumed that there would not be a leadership election for years, that the process of affiliations would take at least five years and that the London mayoral primary would be the first test:

> What we ended up with was immediately going to a leadership contest. I actually regretted very much that they used the leadership contest to recruit. The supporters' network wasn't about electing the leader. Its purpose was not to elect a leader of the Labour party. Its purpose was for the party to engage with the most important relationship it has, i.e. the voter.

Lucy Powell MP:

> In hindsight, party reform should have been done over a longer term and should not have been done in haste as a response to a perceived media storm at the time. It wasn't properly calibrated and thought through. The one thing I advised Ed at the time, when he told me what he was proposing, was that I thought the MP threshold needed to be much higher if you were going to go down that road. I know there are certain people on the right who want to say this was all Ed Miliband's fault. They are wrong and it's unfair and it's unkind and it was the push from the right at the time who wanted this sort of opening up.

The reforms were the most radical since the creation of the electoral college in 1981, and were to have huge unexpected consequences in 2015. Between the St Bride's speech in July 2013 and the special conference on 1 March 2014, the very definition of reforms had changed from union funding to the role of the PLP. Paul Kenny had managed to reduce the amount his union paid to Labour while enhancing the power of the big unions within Labour. A remarkable achievement, but with an outcome he couldn't predict. The control mechanisms originally wanted by Ray Collins were unpicked. The NEC and Harriet Harman as acting leader in 2015 were to have the last word on the control mechanisms after the general election and Miliband's departure. Falkirk, the resulting rush to reconcile funding, and mass mobilisation, meant that the PLP's final level of control over the leadership was eroded. The irony was that it was both the unions and the Blairite wing of the party, traditionally opponents, who had between them reduced the bar from 25 per cent to 15 per cent. The unexpected impact of this was to become apparent within eighteen months of the special conference, after Ed Miliband ceased to be leader. In the meantime, from March 2014, he had an election to plan and policies to set.

20

The Road to 2015

Once the Collins report was approved the next target in 2014 was to prepare for the general election, set for 7 May 2015. Policy had to be finalised and set out in a manifesto. This was debated through discussions with the trade unions in the National Policy Forum (NPF) in Milton Keynes. Anna Yearley and Simon Fletcher represented the leader's office. Simon Fletcher:

> In the run-up to that NPF, we were determined never to go back to the previous NPF experiences, which were 3 a.m. high noon-type standoffs with guns put to their heads. So we developed a different approach at the general secretary level to take them through a collective process of what were their priorities, and had a series of meetings with them so that we went into the NPF with the unions essentially signed up.

Rail nationalisation was a major goal for the unions and policies on housing and Trident were agreed. Among the visitors was Jon Lansman who, although not a delegate, decided to turn up with a friend to lobby for a debate on austerity. Anna Yearley:

> He wasn't actually a member of the NPF, so he couldn't access the conference hall. They were in a camper van in the car park sleeping in there, trying to hand out leaflets, and then he'd

managed to get himself into the NPF dinner and Angela Eagle as the chair of the NPF let him, but made him pay twenty-five quid. This was how on the outside they were.

He did enough to get an amendment on the agenda for the following day. A delegate was given one minute to move a motion calling on a Labour government to reject Conservative plans on austerity and pursue a policy of investment and jobs after 2015. Ed Balls, the shadow chancellor, also had one minute to respond and it was defeated by fourteen votes to 145. The unions were not going to support any policy that was not pre-agreed with the leadership.

The party was, however, becoming more open to the left along with greater union support for left candidates selected in winnable constituencies. Ed Miliband had met with Michael Meacher, for whom Jon Lansman was still working and the door was slightly more open. Jon Lansman:

Michael had a good relationship with Ed from the beginning. It became more difficult for him to get a meeting with Ed as the gatekeepers started locking down. The only left-wing ones were Simon Fletcher and Jon Ashworth, but because we were always trying to influence him, we never directly confronted Miliband. . . . We became increasingly alienated but it was always a judgement because was it redeemable? The unions had worked very hard on selections, and with some success. We didn't have the resources. We didn't have the people on the ground. . . . We were going into an election which we thought we'd win, where we had a leader who was publicly committed to breaking with New Labour. And although he hadn't departed that far from it, he had departed from austerity and he had made more concessions to the unions on certain things. There was an opening up of debate on policy issues, and we knew we'd have more strength in the PLP. The Blairites were on the retreat. It was the brightest position we'd been in for years.

John McDonnell agreed. Labour under Miliband was not perfect, but it was moving:

> The atmosphere within the party changed with Ed Miliband, there was a lot more freedom, discussion, debate. In addition to that, we weren't having a scale of parachuting in that we had in the past. So, things eased up. It was a lightening up. He opened the door up more to the left and had a discussion with the left on individual policy areas. So that was a breath of fresh air, in comparison with the way we had been treated, certainly under Brown and certainly under Blair.

The NPF meeting was closely followed by the local elections in 2014 where Labour narrowly beat the Conservatives by 31 per cent to 29 per cent, and UKIP still beat the Lib Dems. Neither major party could get traction against the other. By now, Spencer Livermore was involved in general election planning, but was getting frustrated with Ed Miliband:

> We tried to get him to be more electable but he wasn't interested. After the 2014 local elections, it was very clear that we were not on course to win. The prevailing view within the Miliband office was, you can't lose, because the Lib Dem voters are going to come to you, and everything will be okay. There was an extraordinary complacency, really, in that respect. And 2014 was the first big wake-up call. We used the local election as a sort of test run for various systems, and what we should do and how we should run the campaign, or what worked and what didn't. And the performance was poor. It wasn't what it needed to be to win.
>
> After that we had a big meeting with Ed at his house, and Ed thought that it was some sort of coup. All his advisers were of the view that we needed to up our game. We all arrived there and the atmosphere was like death. It was a sunny, Sunday afternoon, we're all cooped up in this living room in

north London, and it was just the most ghastly meeting. He was incredibly defensive and somehow thought that we were coming to tell him to stand down.

This only got worse in the party conference that coincided in 2014 with the Scottish referendum on independence from the United Kingdom. David Cameron had agreed to hold a referendum and right up to the last minute, the polls indicated that the Yes vote for independence would win. The initial success on the No campaign had been eroded by the Scottish National Party (SNP) which had become increasingly dominant. Only a late intervention for the Union campaign from Gordon Brown who still had the political weight and skill to carry voters in Scotland, seemed to halt the tide. Hours before the votes came in, it was thought the Yes campaign had won. Not for the last time, the polls were badly wrong. 55.3 per cent voted No and 44.7 per cent Yes. Brown had saved the union. The campaign was marked by two pointers for the future: the aggressive tactics of the SNP's Yes campaign, particularly against Labour in Scotland; and the negative tactics of the No campaign which stressed the downsides of leaving the UK. The use of very strong negative arguments became known as 'Project Fear' and was a tactic increasingly used in the next elections in the UK by David Cameron and his advisors.

In Manchester, Ed Miliband had to digest this news whilst launching Labour's five pledges for the general election in a deliberate attempt to emulate Tony Blair in 1997. They were:

1. A strong economic foundation
2. Higher living standards for working families
3. An NHS with the time to care
4. Controls on immigration
5. A country where the next generation can do better than the last

These pledges were about as vague as it was possible to be. Unfortunately, they were overshadowed by the disaster of the conference speech when Miliband, as was his habit, memorised his speech rather than use an autocue and this time forgot key parts on both the deficit and immigration. It was a public humiliation and meat and drink to the Conservatives and his critics inside the party.

In the months following the conference, there was greater focus on foreign policy. Over the previous five years, a series of upheavals in the Middle East under the banner of the Arab Spring had seen regime after regime come under pressure from their populations. In 2011, this had caused David Cameron to leap on the bandwagon of regime change in Libya within an international coalition. Labour had supported this intervention but the subsequent failure to support Libyan rebuilding and infrastructure had caused a significant rise in refugees crossing, and drowning, in the waters off the coast of Greece and Italy.

In August 2013, when evidence came to light that that chemical weapons had been used by President Assad's Syrian regime against the Syrian rebel groups, David Cameron agreed to support the US in a bombing campaign against the regime. This was taken to a vote on the House of Commons in which both coalition government parties were split: thirty Conservative and nine Lib Dem MPs joined Ed Miliband and 220 Labour MPs in voting against air strikes. It was defeated by thirteen votes. This was the first test of Ed Miliband's post-Iraq strategy. He was not going to follow in Tony Blair's footsteps as an interventionist. The UK failure to support the US meant that the threat of bombing was withdrawn. The carnage in Syria continued and refugees flowed in increasing numbers towards Europe.

At a speech at Chatham House in April 2015 during the general election, Ed Miliband tried to make his foreign policy distinct from both New Labour and the Conservatives. He declared his support for remaining in the EU. He saw a distinction between Libya and Syria. He was for multilateral action, if any action had to be taken, but was clearly for a non-interventionist foreign policy. At this stage of the general election campaign Miliband and his team had a sense of hope, which was surprising given the odds against a party reclaiming power one election after being in office for thirteen years.

The attempts to distinguish Miliband's Labour from New Labour had some success. The Conservative's policy of austerity was beginning to bite. There might be a way to become the biggest party. The variables, though, were greater than in almost any election. Although Labour and the Conservatives were close in the polls and the Lib Dems were dropping votes, UKIP was still capable of taking votes from all the established parties and the SNP was a huge potential threat to Labour in Scotland. It looked like Labour stood a chance to at least be the largest party in parliament with Ed Miliband leading a minority government. He, David Cameron and Nick Clegg were all leaders of the same generation and would be competing for years to come. There was all to play for in this election campaign.

The first referendum in 1975,
Tony Benn against Roy Jenkins.

Vladimir and Vera Derer
at home in Park Drive.

Best of enemies: Michael Foot
and Tony Benn.

Best of friends: Chris Mullin,
Caroline Benn, Claer Lloyd-Jones,
Tony Benn and Jon Lansman
enjoy lunch in Brighton in the
midst of the deputy leadership
election in 1981. Jon Lansman
went back to the same fish bar
during Jeremy Corbyn's first
conference as leader in 2015.

The good old days, Labour party conference 1981, the unfashionable years.

The GLC leadership in 1982 with a stylish John McDonnell.

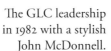

The counter-revolution, Glenys and Neil Kinnock with Peter Mandelson.

A very fringe meeting, Jeremy Corbyn and Tony Benn.

© Tom Stoddart, Getty Images

© Steve Eason, Getty Images

New Labour heading for victory with, from left to right, Ed Balls, Peter Mandelson, Alastair Campbell, Tony Blair and Gordon Brown.

The dynamic duo, Tony Blair and Gordon Brown in 1999.

Dominance, Tony Blair at the Labour party conference 2002 (clean-cut replaces half-cut).

© Scott Barbour, Getty Images

His last day, Tony Blair announces in Sedgfield that he is stepping down, 10 May 2007.

His first day, Gordon Brown commutes to work, 10 May 2007.

Brotherly love, the 2010 leadership election.

The pain and the pleasure, Ed Miliband delivering a conference speech.

Camper man, Jon Lansman at the National Policy Forum 2014.

Where are the meerkats? Harriet Harman with Ayesha Hazarika during the 2015 leadership election.

A kinder form of politics? Jeremy Corbyn singing 'The Red Flag' at 2015 Labour party conference; Iain McNicol on his far right.

Glastonbury 2017.

The rise of the movement; Momentum.

The rise of the movement; The World Transformed.

The rise of the movement; Love Corbyn Hate Brexit.

Always watching, Seumas
Milne from LOTO.

Enough is enough,
Luciana Berger leading the
antisemitism rally.

Out of the wilderness,
Jon Lansman 2018.

The class of 1983.

21

The 2015 General Election

Ed Miliband had spent five years trying to establish his persona with the electorate. David Cameron and George Osborne may have presided over austerity and a fragmented Conservative party, but they looked the part in government, which had helped them through the previous five years. Miliband had been dogged by a series of missteps. The memory lapses of the 2014 conference speech, the unfortunate photo opportunity with a bacon sandwich and, during the campaign, the faintly ludicrous 8ft 6in slab of limestone with Labour's campaign promises 'carved in stone' that was not only mocked as his 'Moses' moment but cost a reported £30,000 and was reported to the electoral commission. He was the successor of the slickest, most effective election machine in Labour's history that had won three elections in a row, and yet was still struggling to get a fair hearing, having become a media target.

During the election campaign he was interviewed by Jeremy Paxman who quoted 'a bloke on the tube' who cited Vladimir Putin putting Miliband 'on the floor in pieces' because he wasn't 'tough enough'. Miliband started off handling it well by stating how he had stood up to Cameron and Barack Obama over the bombing of Syria, but he noticeably reverted to the intonation of his youth in a London school playground by adding 'right' at the end of each sentence, ending with 'Hell yes, I'm tough enough'. Responding to Paxman without Olympian calm is never a good idea. Jeremy Corbyn demonstrated this two years later when, in the 2017 general election, he was asked whether he wanted to abolish the royal family. Corbyn swatted the question away. Miliband fell into the trap. In events in front of an audience he was generally a better performer, but in a BBC *Question Time* debate, he lost all his preparation when asked about New Labour's management of the economy. The audience were on the offensive as much as Paxman had been.

The Conservatives had rolled out their latest version of Project Fear by alleging that Labour would go into a coalition with the SNP if it was the largest party and that Labour would be the Trojan horse for the SNP breaking up the UK. To the UK electorate, this was presented as a more dangerous position than a UKIP-influenced Conservative party opting for a referendum that might break up the EU. Despite Miliband's protestations, the SNP charge would not go away.

On 6 May, the day before the election, the polls were still showing the two major parties running at around 34 to 35 per cent each. The three traditional combatants – the Lib Dems still had fifty-seven seats – were joined by UKIP, the SNP, the Greens, Plaid Cymru and the Northern Irish parties in a mosaic of competing interests in different parts of the country. It was a confused picture that the polling failed to capture accurately on a national basis. Even on election night it looked to Labour insiders that they might make it. The Labour teams assembled in London and Doncaster. Preparations had been made for a variety of outcomes. Anna Yearley:

> We believed we were going to win because Ed had been consistently told that there was mathematically no way that Cameron would be prime minister. We'd gone up to Doncaster the night before. Ed had voted in the morning. We were knackered because we'd been working for weeks. We did a bit of door knocking and then slept quite a bit. That night, we went to Ed's house and had chilli con carne. We were discussing the exit poll, saying if it's bad what we would all go and do. I remember saying, 'I might go and set up a florist'. I got an NVQ in floristry when I was sixteen.

(She didn't. Anna Yearley now runs Reprieve – a global charity campaigning against use of the death penalty.) The election was a perfect political storm. The Lib Dems were crushed, losing forty-nine seats going from fifty-seven to just eight. The Conservatives gained twenty-four seats to reach 330. Labour dropped to 232, twenty-six seats fewer than the 2010 general election.

David Cameron had won 36.8 per cent of the poll, the highest Conservative percentage since 1992, Labour had 30.4 per cent, a marginal improvement over the 29 per cent of 2010. The Lib Dems had dropped from 23 per cent to 7.9 per cent in only five years. UKIP had 12.6 per cent of the vote but only one seat. Its impact was in taking votes from the main parties. The biggest shock came from Scotland. Labour had depended on Scotland for decades to supply its MPs, its leaders and its political and industrial strength. Even in 2010, it got 42 per cent of the vote and forty-one of the country's fifty-nine MPs. The SNP had built on its previous successes over the previous four years. It had become the governing party in 2011, fought a powerful albeit losing campaign in the referendum in 2014 and now had a visibly competent new leader in Nicola Sturgeon. Labour's Jim Murphy had overcome the fierce opposition of Len McCluskey to become Scottish Labour leader in 2014 and, although he knew he was in a fight, no one expected this. The SNP gained fifty-six of Scotland's fifty-nine seats. Labour collapsed to one seat, the same as the Conservatives and the Lib Dems. The SNP won 4.7 per cent of the UK vote and gained fifty-six seats making it the third biggest party in the UK. Cameron had an overall majority of twelve seats over all other parties.

It is difficult not to feel sorry for Ed Miliband. He could not have predicted the variety of elements that would lead to this result. He and the people around him were in shock. Anna Yearley:

We stayed at Ed's for a bit. Sky News and the BBC were all outside Ed's house in Doncaster, in this little cul-de-sac, doing live pieces to camera. There were blaring lights outside, and we were all making sure the curtains were shut so they couldn't see us. There were all sorts of uncomfortable silences, Jeremy Vine (of the BBC) doing that thing where he would show you the seats that Labour was going to lose.

Trying to make decisions in that environment was not easy. Miliband took soundings from Neil Kinnock, who had lived through this in 1992. There were arguments for staying on as a caretaker leader but it would be horrible, as Miliband described in 2018.

> The truth is that most of the people who wanted me to stay on, wanted me to stay on for just a few months. I felt I'd given everything I had to give, and I'd lost. I think we weren't expecting to lose in the way that we lost. I think I talked a bit to Neil about him staying on . . . and how purgatory was. I thought people are going to need to debate not just the direction of the party but my performance as leader and I thought that it would be better and easier if they did that without me sitting around the shadow cabinet table trying to tell them what to do. It was just going to be incredibly awkward for everyone concerned. So I don't think I could've stayed on as leader, I don't think it would have been fair to my family to stay on as leader.

He resigned the morning of 8 May 2015.

> Whatever the qualities of my leadership, I thought some of my ideas were quite good and it turns out, maybe I was right, in the sense that lots of people are adopting them. I thought the analysis I had of society and what the problems were with society . . . the extent to which things which were controversial, predatory capitalism, inequality being a problem, 'left behind' and everything like that. All of that stuff is now commonly accepted. It's quite paradoxical.

The immediate fallout from the election was a huge transformation of the PLP. Overnight, a political generation that had grown up under New Labour had been smashed. Thirty-nine Labour MPs lost their seats including Ed Balls, Jim Murphy and Douglas Alexander. The real shift happened with new Labour MPs coming in from seats in which the unions had been much more active in selections. As in 1983, with this shattering loss came a new generation that was to have a big impact. Fifty-three new Labour MPs won their seats. They included a group who would become the basis for the shadow cabinet in only eighteen months. Figures like Richard Burgon, Dawn Butler, Peter Dowd, Clive Lewis, Rebecca Long-Bailey, Angela Rayner, Keir Starmer and Kate Osamor would all rise to prominence. Others, such as Stephen Kinnock, Jess Philips and Wes Streeting, would stand out from the backbenches and one, Jo Cox, for the shocking way in which her life and career were ended. On 8 May, the party was reeling in shock as Miliband resigned and the new rules of the game were being considered.

An interview in *Vice* magazine two weeks before the general election demonstrated that nobody had a clue what was about to happen. It interviewed two backbenchers on how they could, under a Labour minority government, have a much bigger sway over policy. Jeremy Corbyn and John McDonnell were quite open about using their Socialist Campaign Group of MPs (maybe thirty members after the new intake) to stop a minority Labour government continuing with austerity. It was the same tactic used by the Brexiteer Conservatives two years later under Theresa May's minority government. The *Vice* interview included some great insights. Would the two MPs join Labour now if they were young? John McDonnell said no, adding 'I think you can see why not. People are pissed off at the Labour party, especially young people.' Corbyn saw the problem as the PLP, and felt that Labour should be a broader movement. The Greens had a manifesto that was far more socialist than the Labour manifesto. When asked if Ed Miliband would remain as leader, Corbyn replied, 'He's the leader, it's not going to change.' McDonnell added:

> Let's be clear, we don't believe in leaders . . . we believe that leaders should be following the masses. We only ran leadership campaigns to get our ideas across, to use it as a platform. One of

PART SIX

The Four Summers of Jeremy Corbyn: The Summer of Love

'Be not afraid of greatness. Some are born great, some achieve greatness, and others have greatness thrust upon them.'
Twelfth Night, William Shakespeare

22

The Establishment

In the aftermath of the election defeat, with a Conservative party now resurgent, Labour was thrown back into its internal processes. Harriet Harman was acting leader again and her decisions would have a considerable impact on how Labour was going to adjust to this new reality. The positions of leader, deputy leader, London mayoral candidate and Scottish Labour leader were all up for election. There was a parliamentary party of 232 of whom fifty-three were new MPs. David Cameron's government was now a purely Conservative one; he had used and abused the Lib Dems to their virtual parliamentary extinction. The Queen's speech three weeks after the election promised an EU referendum bill that would give British voters a choice of remaining in or leaving the EU. It also proposed a Welfare Reform and Work bill that would include a reduction to the welfare cap from £26,000 to £23,000 and the scrapping of automatic housing benefit for eighteen to twenty-one-year-olds.

The immediate question facing Harman and the NEC was how to handle the internal selections. Ray Collins had always envisaged the London mayoral process as the first step. It would have an open primary with three groups of voters, all of whom had to 'support Labour values'. The three groups would be:

- Fully paid members of the party; *who could take part in any activity in the local CLP*

- Members of affiliated organisations who were not already party members but who could take part in the ballot if they registered with the party as affiliated supporters; *by opting into the Labour party as trade unionists through their local branches*
- Individuals who were not already party members or members of an affiliated organisation now could take part in leadership elections by registering with the party as a supporter. *Who by paying only £3 could vote for the highest posts in the party but no other activities unless they were full members.*

The Collins Report had assumed that there would be a year to figure out the London selection process and that this would influence any national selection, which would be at least five years later. Miliband's resignation had not been factored into any of this thinking and the logistics were not in place. The NEC would have to step up. It had already agreed that the new supporters in London would pay a £3 fee. In the week between the general election and a special meeting on 13 May, Harman was taking advice on how to manage the national elections. The critical decisions would be the fee for individuals to join to vote, whether these new entrants would be subject to a vetting process and whether there would be any freeze period in which they would have to wait before becoming eligible to vote. The final and most critical decision, which was hotly debated, would be the length of the campaign. Would the campaigns in London, Scotland and the national posts be short campaigns of a couple of months or lengthy ones as in 2010, culminating in a special conference in September?

Harman wanted as long a process as possible. The objection to this was that, as in 2010, it would allow the Conservatives free reign over the politics of the next five months. The arguments in favour were that a period of reflection would allow enough time to consider the candidates and new people who needed time to build up campaigns to come forward as candidates in each campaign. For the leadership these might include Chuka Umunna, Tristram Hunt and Dan Jarvis against the probable front runners Andy Burnham and Yvette Cooper; for the deputy leadership, Stella Creasy against Tom Watson; and for the London mayoral race, Tessa Jowell against Sadiq Khan. Of course, this is exactly what happened. There was a new entrant who would also use the long campaign to his advantage. Except in early May 2015, no one in the leadership saw that coming from the left.

The NEC was called to meet for a special gathering on 13 May. The London mayoral candidate contest was confirmed with results to be announced on 11 September. The electorate for the primary in London would include full members, affiliated members and the new supporters who would be charged £3. This was now extended to all new supporters for every election. The Scottish posts would be declared on 15 August, London on 11 September and the national leader and deputy leader posts on 12 September at a special conference in London. There would be no freeze period for new supporters, but they would need to be vetted to stop members of other parties, such as the Conservatives, flooding in. They had to join by 12 August to be eligible to vote, which would allow some time to verifying them. There was no sense that these new supporters would add up to much – it was anticipated to be a few thousand and all felt that the party machine could handle that. Ayesha Hazarika, then Harriet Harman's chief of staff:

> It was horrendous because it was completely unchartered territory, and we thought this £3 thing was such a weird gimmick. At the beginning, we were trying to encourage people to join up as £3 members because we thought there was no interest in it. We did an interview with the *Sun* saying we want *Sun* readers, who may want a Labour government at some point, tell us who you would like as your leader. We did a big speech saying, 'We've got to reach out as a party, and actually these £3 members give us a unique way of communicating with a broader group of people from just within' but then suddenly everything started changing. . . . These £3 members just started going through the roof, and it got to the stage where we were starting to have crisis

meetings with our team up in Newcastle. There was not enough staff to even physically process all these new members, and of course, because of the Collins review, we had new rules about how you verify these new affiliate supporters to make sure that they actually had been signed up. . . . The whole thing morphed from a normal leadership contest, with all the heat and the fury and the passion, to a nightmare logistical exercise as well. We had people signing up pretending to be llamas, cats, meerkats, other animals, all kinds of things. It was absolutely extraordinary, and then of course in all of this, right at the beginning of the story, *Newsnight* rang me up and said, 'Right, Ayesha, you're acting chief of staff of the Labour party. You've just done this interview about you wanting to bring the public in. Let's really bring them in. Let's televise these hustings,' and of course we say, 'That's quite a good idea. It will democratise the whole process. It will encourage more people to get involved.'

The publicity was certainly going to change the course of the leadership election, but in the meantime, potential candidates were trying to figure out what all this meant and who should stand. The 15 per cent parliamentary bar for nominations now meant that a candidate for leader and deputy leader had to have thirty-five nominating MPs. The week after the general election Andy Burnham was at Goodison Park watching Everton with his kids:

A lot of people were speculating, would I stand? Middle of the game, the phone goes, Harriet Harman. And I said 'Sorry, can I ring you back? You know, middle of the game.' Harman said: 'I'm taking some early decisions about the leadership election, and obviously there are rumours that you're going to stand, so I need to know.' I said 'Oh, thank you, Harriet, that's nice of you.' She continued: 'We're thinking of running it into conference, and doing the—' and I said 'Oh, whoa, hang on a second, the one thing everybody said after 2010 leadership election was "Way too long!"' It went on and on.

Liz Kendall, the Blairite candidate, announced on 10 May. Andy Burnham and Yvette Cooper on 13 May. None of them had an inkling as to who else might apply. It was suspected that the longer the campaign, the more vulnerable the front runner might become as other candidates would be encouraged to stand. Burnham, at this early stage, was the front runner and did not want a long campaign.

However, various possibilities for leader were counting themselves out. The deputy leadership had more candidates (eventually five) of whom Tom Watson was the early front runner. The race for leader was so limited that two new backbench MPs, Stephen Kinnock and Jo Cox, argued that the party would be damaged by a two-horse race and wanted others to enter. What was needed was an insurgent campaign that would shake things up to galvanise the membership and these new supporters.

23

The Insurgents

At 10 a.m. on the morning after the 2015 general election, Jon Lansman had called Pete Willsman of CLPD who, not owning any modern conveniences, had not heard the results. They discussed the need to find a candidate if Ed Miliband resigned. The three names thrown around were John McDonnell, Diane Abbott and Jon Trickett, a veteran Labour frontbencher on the left who also had worked closely with the New Labour leadership and Ed Miliband.

This conversation followed a long tradition. From 1981, Tony Benn's deputy leadership campaign had been run less in the expectation of winning than in the need to protect the electoral college and show the left's muscle. In subsequent leadership and deputy leadership races, the left had always sought to put up a candidate to show that it was still alive and kicking. In 1983, 1988, 1992, 1997 and 2007, candidates had either lost heavily (1983 and 1988) or more recently had been blocked by the parliamentary bar. In 2007 and 2010, John McDonnell had failed to cross the threshold, and in 2010 Diane Abbott had only got on with a combination of nominations from David Miliband and Harriet Harman, neither of whom supported her in the actual election.

This disguised the gradual movement to the left under Ed Miliband's leadership. The PLP was changing, the union leadership was more supportive and the new voting system might encourage people to rejoin Labour and vote for a left candidate. There was a movement outside of dissatisfied former members who might be incentivised to come back with the right campaign. Jon Lansman:

> There were going to be these registered supporters we immediately thought we could recruit. Was this a way that we could track people back? Not so much because we thought we could win but because we could build the left and encourage people back. We really wanted our own candidate but we knew we might settle for a candidate that was, if we couldn't get ours, second best.

The preferred candidates were counted out. John McDonnell had suffered a heart attack and had failed twice before, Diane Abbott was standing for the London mayoral selection, Michael Meacher was suffering from cancer and although no one knew this at the time, he was noticeably absent from the discussions. New MPs, such as Clive Lewis and Keir Starmer, were too unknown. This led to a group of leftish MPs who could be supported. Jon Trickett and Ian Lavery wouldn't stand, Angela Eagle had some support but decided for the deputy leadership, Owen Smith was considered as he had some leftist credentials in Wales. However, with two weeks gone it was a sign of the weakness of the Campaign Group that there was really no candidate even as attractive as Ed Miliband had been in 2010 who was open to influence from the left and had a chance of winning. Jeremy Corbyn was not considered, according to Jon Lansman:

> Jeremy . . . although he'd been an MP for a very long time, was seen almost like an activist. Jeremy is a nice guy. He turns up. He talks to people like he's the same level as them. He doesn't have airs and graces. He does ordinary things.

There were three Socialist Campaign Group meetings with very little time to go before nominations had to go in. The longer they waited, the more people would be committed to the three existing candidates. Lansman missed the first meeting and assumed that no candidate would be found who was even marginally viable to get support. Before the second meeting, however, he attended a TULO reception hosted by Byron Taylor on 26 May. Taylor had known Corbyn and the Socialist Campaign Group for years.

> Jeremy was a friend of mine. In 2015, my constituency, South Basildon, was not a marginal. We knew we weren't going to win it, so no one was going to come and visit, but the parliamentary candidate wanted a bit of external support so I asked Jeremy to come and visit Basildon. And he did. . . . On the way back from that event I had a conversation with Jeremy about what would happen if we lost the 2015 general election. Ever since Collins in 2014, that had been the topic of debate in TULO. What would happen if we lost the general election? There would be civil war and we would have to fight an election. . . . And I said to him 'You should run. Think about it, Jeremy'. And he was like 'Oh well, I'll see'. And it was all very comradely.

Three weeks later, Taylor hosted a TULO reception:

> I met Jeremy in one of the meeting rooms in Portcullis House and told him why he had to run. The conversation took place at the TULO reception when Jon Lansman turned up and came over to me to say, 'What are we going to do?' I thought, it's got to be Jeremy. Jeremy's got to win. He's the man. We can get nominations for him, I can probably pull some union support. I mean it was desperate stuff, but Burnham was in the city talking to business and making clear that he was going down exactly the same route as New Labour and Ed Miliband had done.

Jon Lansman:

> Byron said Jeremy Corbyn . . . Jeremy's got no enemies . . . he will get on the ballot paper . . . and I thought, I've never taken Jeremy even remotely seriously. Byron was not a rabid left-winger. He was a trade union bureaucrat who had been a party bureaucrat under New Labour, and he was saying Jeremy Corbyn would get on the ballot paper, and it just made me think, actually. I mean he

hasn't got enemies. Everyone likes him, even people who thought he was a left-wing loony. He was a nice bloke, you know . . . he was never nasty to people. He didn't fall out with people.

Lansman went to the next meeting of the Socialist Campaign Group, the following day:

I argued for it. No one argued against it. This sort of light bulb moment happened. It happened for me . . . I don't know if it was a light bulb for everyone else, but I think it was, OK, Jeremy's turn. We were already ten days into the nomination period. Lots of left-wingers, Michael Meacher included, had already committed to Andy Burnham. (MPs) Ian Lavery and Cat Smith had signed up to Burnham and so, when Jeremy said he would stand, of course, some people were reluctant because they'd already committed. It's an indication that people didn't expect him to cross the threshold.

Outside parliament, Len McCluskey of Unite had also already committed to Burnham. By the third meeting on 3 June with only twelve days to get thirty-five nominations, Jeremy Corbyn formally announced his campaign for the leadership of the Labour party. Very early on he showed that he was not just a puppet. His thirty-two years as an MP addressing hundreds if not thousands of meetings had prepared him for hustings in the way that none of his rivals could emulate. If anyone could command a room with a clear exposition of his views it was Jeremy Corbyn. Ayesha Hazarika was still trying to run the mechanics of the various selections and the flood of new applications of supporters, while *Newsnight* wanted to hold a live husting:

We had lots of meetings internally about organising these hustings, which I then went off and organised with the broadcasters, but at one of our very early internal meetings, somebody said, 'Well, hang on a minute. How soon do we want to do these hustings?' And I said 'Well, look, there's a huge appetite from the media. From a press point of view, as an opposition party that's just been smashed, I think we should take the opportunity.' Somebody quite rightly pointed out, 'Well, the only thing is, if we go too early, and we do a televised hustings, let's say, for example, some joker like Jeremy Corbyn is thinking about running, right? Just imagine we have a public husting with someone like Jeremy Corbyn. I mean, come on.'

Then we have a hustings for the PLP, the peers and the MEPs. This was not televised, and this was when Corbyn still didn't have enough to get onto the ballot paper. He walked in, and everybody was like *Mean Girls*, sniggering at him, laughing and pointing, and I have to say, he stood up and wiped the floor with everybody at that first internal hustings. Everyone gave the same version of a mangled, triangulated 'on the one hand, on the other hand', nobody gave a straight answer on anything. He stood up, was clear, passionate, fluent, coherent, had an argument which you knew he was invested in, you know, you could feel the authenticity just singing through every word, and I remember at the end of that meeting, a couple of advisers and myself gathered, and there was this kind of nervous laughter, and everyone was like, 'Well, I'll tell you something, if he can get on the ballot paper, he might just win the damn thing.'

This was followed by another hustings in Dublin at the GMB's annual conference. Jon Lansman:

> Jeremy was there with all those candidates. It was important that it was before the closed nominations because he did fantastically well at it because he was relaxed. He answered questions from union reps who are people he had more in common with than the others on the panel . . . and he answered the questions honestly. He told them what he thought whereas they just gave safe politicians' answers. So, he got a rapturous reception from the GMB, which is a right-wing union.

Other appearances started to show that he was exactly the opposite of what people expected. He was more coherent and less apologetic than other candidates. He had clarity of position and was so far removed by political generation and so strikingly unlike any of the other candidates that he stood out. The struggle was to get thirty-four fellow MPs to nominate him. Although he was so late to the game, his advantage was that he had neither enemies nor expectations. No one thought he could win, he was much more neutral a figure than McDonnell or Abbott, and there were deals to be done with candidates running for other offices. Jon Lansman:

> We only had about ten days. There were some that were easy, there were some that should've been easy but we didn't get because they were already committed and there were some that we lost because Jeremy was utterly incapable of making phone calls. I think Jeremy had agreed to stand without any thought that he would actually get on the ballot. He thought it was just another repeat of John McDonnell's failure. We were determined to get him on the ballot.

The candidate's reluctance to chase votes was a problem. In the case of one MP who eventually didn't nominate him, Lansman continued:

> Jeremy was supposed to ring her, and he promised on the Thursday before nomination. He didn't ring her by Thursday. Then, she said alright, I'll give you until Friday lunchtime, and then I'm going to nominate someone else. And by Friday lunchtime, he still hadn't rung her.

If you review the list of thirty-six who finally did nominate, no more than fifteen were Socialist Campaign Group or loyal supporters of the left. Some votes were trade-offs. Four candidates for Mayor of London all nominated him (Tessa Jowell was no longer an MP and therefore could not nominate) and when Mary Creagh pulled out of the leadership, three of her supporters moved to him.

> So there was a bit of negotiation, which John McDonnell and I did. For example, a deal we did with Rushanara Ali whereby

Jeremy and John both nominated her for the deputy leadership, and she gave us one nomination for our cause. We tried to do another deal with Angela Eagle, but she wasn't into doing deals.

There were the obvious unlikely nominators who knew Corbyn, had nothing to lose and believed in the democratic principle, for example Frank Field, Margaret Beckett and Jon Cruddas. There was also the overwhelming view from the other candidates that allowing Corbyn on the ballot would do no harm. He wouldn't win. They would allow their natural supporters to nominate him. It would be a gesture to the left. The nominations were due to close on Monday at noon. On the Saturday the sheer pressure of the campaign was beginning to tell on Lansman, McDonnell and the few support staff around them including Alex Halligan, a Unite organiser from the North West and Jack Bond from Corbyn's constituency office. They were exhausted and frustrated. Jon Lansman:

> John, by 7 p.m., decided that it wasn't fair to Jeremy to carry on. We should stop and call it all off. Alex [Halligan] was the one who persuaded me that I couldn't give up. Alex talked me into it, but I went to bed still thinking, fuck it. I woke up in the morning thinking, get everybody into a room and that'll do it, and we'll maintain morale and regroup. I rang John, and it worked.

Thirty-five years of being in the wilderness, of failing to be noticed and still ploughing on gave a level of resilience. Lansman and McDonnell were prepared to keep going and so was Jeremy Corbyn. On Sunday they regained morale and had the last big push into Monday. The missing piece was the front runner for deputy leader, Tom Watson. The Falkirk actors were still on the stage: Len McCluskey as General Secretary of Unite and Karie Murphy in Watson's office. Jon Lansman:

> I rang Karie on the Sunday. I didn't have that close a relationship with Tom at that point, but I suggested it to John. He said, 'Yeah, phone him.' So, I spoke to Tom the following morning,

and he gave me the bum's rush. So, I rang Karie and she rang Len, and Len rang Tom, and then Tom rang me back and said 'I want to know every name you've got, and if you're lying, I'll take away two for every one I've given you . . . and you've got to tell Alicia the name of everyone.'

Alicia Kennedy worked as Watson's chief of staff. Lansman was about to be a kidney donor and on Monday morning was giving blood.

And then, I took off to my appointment. I went in, and they're taking blood out of me and stuff, so I've got a tube coming out of me and I'm texting with my left hand, which I can't do, and I'm texting the names to Alicia, and when I come out, having done that, I tell Tom 'You fucking bastard!'. I explained the situation, and he laughed. And, to be fair, he has a sense of humour.

Throughout the morning, more and more MPs turned up to nominate Corbyn. By 11 a.m. there were twenty-six names, by 11.40 a.m. thirty names. With a few minutes to go he was up to thirty-three names but a few MPs were waiting to decide to be the final voter if he only needed one more. Watson was texting people (but did not nominate himself). According to Alex Nunns in *The Candidate,* McDonnell went on his knees to beg four of his fellow Labour MPs to vote. In fact, he hadn't checked the names of those who had already done so; he already had thirty-four and needed only to get the final nominator. With ten seconds to go, Gordon Marsden and Andrew Smith voted, making them the thirty-fifth and thirty-sixth votes because, absurdly, no one had kept an accurate number. An incredible result that was seconds away from not happening.

Now the left had a campaign to run. The other components had to come together: union support, organisational support and, most important of all, reaching the electorate that was growing and changing every day. The next three months were to be explosive.

24

Throwing it Away

After the frenetic search for parliamentary nominations, the role of the unions in the left's fledgling campaign was beginning to be much more important. They had felt betrayed by New Labour but still wanted an electoral winner to support. Andy Burnham looked the obvious candidate for unions on the centre-left, with Yvette Cooper potentially commanding support from the centre-right. The Collins report had created a situation where individual voting replaced the electoral college, but the unions still had money, resources and influence over their members.

At the start of the campaign, Andy Burnham had received verbal support from Unite's Len McCluskey. Then, on 21 May, Burnham issued a declaration turning down any union financing for his campaign.

> I am not going to take any money from the trade unions in this leadership campaign. No money has been offered, but if it was, I would encourage it to be given to the Labour party to assist the rebuilding after the election. But I am actively seeking the support of individual trade union members and am pleased they have a bigger say in this contest.

He wanted to stress his independence and assumed that as there was no candidate to his left, the unions would either have to support him or remain neutral.

the young who had never been in the Labour party. His clarity of message against New Labour, against Tony Blair and the invasion of Iraq gave him a kind of historical validity. This was also the generation that, since 2010, had suffered from hikes in tuition fees, cuts in benefits and the overall impact of austerity. It was a prime target market if it could be reached.

A strange reversal had taken place. The generation of New Labour ministers: Yvette Cooper elected in 1997, Andy Burnham in 2001 and even Liz Kendall who had been elected in 2010, appeared to be the old guard. They were too invested in the politics of the previous fifteen years. Corbyn, first elected in 1983 but who was comparatively unknown to the non-political world and had never been in office, looked fresh, new and authentic. There was a generational movement taking place in politics but in the opposite direction to normal. Between 2015 and late 2017, a group of fortysomethings – Miliband, Clegg and Cameron, were to be replaced by two leaders aged over sixty – Jeremy Corbyn and Theresa May, and one over seventy – Vince Cable.

The campaign around Corbyn was run by people who had nothing to lose and who had not expected to win. It was in stark contrast to the three other campaigns run by candidates and supporters who had always worked at the top of the party. If you're in a fight, get battle-hardened veterans who've tasted defeat for thirty years. Once the nominations were closed, their sheer desire and drive to win was of a completely different order to the other campaigns. The mechanisms to achieve this were run by a tight knit-group at the centre of the Corbyn organisation, using a new means of reaching a new audience: social media. The traditional tools within an electoral college of leafleting, lobbying, touring conferences and influencing trade union barons were swept away by a phenomenon that allowed outreach on a constant and targeted basis. Where once you could reach dozens or hundreds of potential voters, now you could reach millions. The new rules meant a targeted campaign would bring in over 100,000 new supporters in three months; social media gave the opportunity to talk to them. In 2015, there was only one campaign that did this effectively.

Lansman and McDonnell had only a small team through the two weeks of the nominations process: Alex Halligan, Jack Bond from Corbyn's constituency office and Ben Soffa from the TSSA. It was felt that more experience was needed. Simon Fletcher and Anneliese Midgley had run four London mayoral campaigns for Ken Livingstone and, in 2012, Fletcher had joined Ed Miliband's team. After the 2015 general election they were both open to offers. One possibility would be to work on a fifth London mayoral campaign but John McDonnell called and offered Fletcher the role of campaign manager. Anneliese Midgley:

I said 'You've got to work on Jeremy's campaign. Obviously, we're not going to win, but this is a really important opportunity for the stuff that the left has been espousing through Ken to come through.' And the campaign had started, Jeremy got onto the ballot paper, there was that *Newsnight* debate where it panned across the politicians and there was Andy Burnham looking like a politician, Yvette Cooper looking like a politician, Liz Kendall looking like a politician and Jeremy Corbyn, like an ageing beatnik. . . . There was a question about austerity, is it more important to pay down the deficit than to put roofs over people's heads? The other three dodged the question but basically said it's really important to pay down the deficit, and Jeremy said 'No of course it isn't, it's more important that people have food to eat, a roof over their head, clothes to wear.' The audience erupted, and my mum texted me, she's a working-class woman in Liverpool. 'I know you said this Jeremy Corbyn's got no chance, but he's just been really good on the *Newsnight* thing. Are you sure?' And I said, 'Mum, he's definitely not going to win but we've got to try.'

Anna Yearley was no supporter of Jeremy Corbyn, but she knew Simon Fletcher and for her that was a sign that it was a serious challenge. The *Newsnight* hustings had also made a big impression on her:

I absolutely knew the second that Simon said he was going to join Jeremy's campaign, because he's brilliant and a campaigner and a tactician, so I knew he'd know how to work out how to get maximum support for Jeremy. Then I remember watching the first hustings. Jeremy was authentic. It might have been bullshit what he said, and it might not have been said very well, and he might have his hands in his pockets and had one of those yellow shirts on and all of that, but he sounded totally authentic, and the party members loved it. I was watching this on telly, because it was a live hustings, and he got a standing ovation, constant weeping and cheering, and it was like, 'Shit'.

Jon Lansman, for the first time since the RFMC in 1981, had a real operation to run.

Well, we had a serious campaign. I was building an organisation. I was director of operations. John and I recruited Simon Fletcher. I wanted to get the data right, and I worked with Ben Soffa who worked for the TSSA and was later recruited by the Labour party. Alex [Halligan] did the field work so he was running the organisers. I got Gordon Nardell, who was our QC who helped us navigate the data protection legislation, and we had Jack Bond who got into social media.

The compliance work on the data management turned out to be the most important part of the operation.

Right from the beginning, the strategy that we adopted for maximum data retention was to set up a data company which was the publisher of the website and which was the owner, you could say, of any data that we collected. When you wrote to someone on the Labour party database and they interacted with your website, you pressed a button. It took you to a microsite, part of our website, and we harvested data based on the privacy policy of that website, which they could access if they clicked the right link. It was all the right information, and so, we were entitled to keep that data there. That was my idea. That was my intention.

Simon Fletcher was getting stuck in:

We started to phone bank, and so we piloted our phone banking script with some student volunteers the day before we ran proper phone banks. We deliberately chose a constituency where they would be as far removed from Jeremy Corbyn supporters as you can imagine. We ran the pilot and the students came back to me halfway through the evening and said, 'It's going really well' and I said, 'Sorry?' and they said, 'No, no. It's getting a really warm reaction.' So I looked at the data. This was before the mass recruitment. These were existing party members, so this was not even the party members who were recruited, it was the existing party members.

The campaign also was extended to left-leaning unions that could at least be persuaded to vote for Corbyn as their first preference and then Burnham second. The big prize was Unite. On 5 July, despite Len McCluskey's previous support for Andy Burnham, the executive voted to support Corbyn. Suddenly Corbyn's campaign had offices and resources that dwarfed the other campaigns. Anneliese Midgley:

That was serious and people didn't think that was going to happen. Andy still thought that he could get Unite's nomination. Len knew Simon and Jon Lansman. It was clear that the left was coalescing around Jeremy and momentum was building up around him. Within the union, the left were very strongly supporting Jeremy Corbyn and with the team that Jeremy had built around him, although we still didn't think at that point that Jeremy was going to win, his had become a serious candidature. Simon said to Jennie Formby (who was political director at the time), Andrew Murray and Len 'Unite giving Jeremy their support will make a huge difference.' So you had on the one hand Jeremy's team saying Unite was very important, it was key to the left and building on this, and you had Andy Burnham on the other hand saying the unions can go fuck themselves but I still want your support.

The problems for Burnham were about to get worse. The Conservative's welfare bill had been announced in the Queen's speech. Its first reading was on 9 July and second reading 21 July. It contained a slew of proposals cutting or abolishing £12 billion of benefits mitigated by some language on apprenticeships and full employment. Harriet Harman decided that Labour had to demonstrate it understood the electorate's apparent concern about high welfare costs. Andy Burnham knew that this would be a political problem for him and insisted on a discussion within the shadow cabinet. Harman agreed but positioned Yvette Cooper next to her as the first speaker. By the time it got to Burnham he had lost the tactical argument. Ayesha Hazarika:

> I think what Harriet was trying to do was just to show that Labour wasn't a party that just opposed everything. There were some things in that bill that we did agree with as well. There was stuff on apprenticeship targets, there was stuff on full employment. These bills are never single issue, but it was just an impossible situation.

The official position would be to abstain rather than vote against the government's proposals. There was an overly complex voting tactic about voting for an amendment to stop the second reading but then abstaining on the main bill, but no one outside the PLP understood this. Burnham, Cooper and Kendall all abstained on the second reading. Forty-seven Labour MPs voted against it and one acted as teller for the noes along with the SNP and Lib Dems and minor parties. Andy Burnham was stuck in a position that he knew was untenable. He could resign, he could tough it out, or he could try to explain to the wider parliamentary group. This is what he sent to them on the day of the vote:

Dear Colleague,

I wanted to update you on my position ahead of today's vote on the Welfare Reform and Work bill. The party has come to a position over the last week and we now have a reasoned amendment which sets out our opposition to the bill. As you know, I was very clear last weekend that we could not simply abstain on this bill and that we needed to set out where we have agreement with reforms, but more importantly, where we strongly disagree. For example, I have said that, as leader, I will oppose the two-child policy.

I also strongly oppose the changes in this bill that will increase child poverty whilst at the same time abolishing the child poverty reduction target. I will always defend our record as a Labour government of supporting low-paid people in work, and into work, through our tax credits. For these reasons, I have led calls for the party to change its position.

Our reasoned amendment sets out clearly our opposition to many aspects of the bill. In truth, it could be stronger, but it declines to give the bill a second reading and, therefore, voting for it tonight is the right thing to do. The Tories want to use this period to brand us in the way they did in 2010. We must not allow that to happen.

Collective responsibility is important, and it is what I would expect as leader of our party. It is why I will be voting for our reasoned amendment and, if it is defeated, abstaining on the bill.

But I can reassure you that this is only the beginning of a major fight with the Tories. I am determined that we will fight this regressive bill line by line, word by word in committee. If the government do not make the major changes during committee stage, then, as leader, I will oppose this bill at third reading.

Yours sincerely,
Andy Burnham

John McDonnell was pretty clear what he thought as he said in the debate:

> I would swim through vomit to vote against this bill. And listening to some of the nauseating speeches in support of it, I might have to.

Burnham, Cooper and Kendall were operating under the assumption that they were appealing to a Labour electorate that would still want to see leadership after the New Labour model, a government in waiting that would appeal to the centre ground. It was a delusion that assumed the politics of 2015 were unchanged from the New Labour years. Why didn't he resign?

> I've agonised about that ever since and I was advised to do that but the difficult thing for me would've been changing who I was and how I operated to win and that felt antithetical to me. You could argue it out on shadow cabinet, as we did, and come to a compromise which I thought was enough for me because it was opposition, which was a reasoned amendment; but in the black and white in the world that we were in it wasn't. But I'd have had to take all my supporters in the shadow cabinet through a different lobby to Harriet, to resign en masse, and I wasn't prepared to do that to the party.

Over the following two weeks, union support moved away from Burnham. Unison, the most centrist of the big unions, had a large membership of low-paid workers from the public sector many of whom were women depending on additional benefits to survive. There was an active left organisation in the union and when Dave Prentis, its general secretary, allowed a consultation of its eleven regions, nine of eleven came out for Corbyn over Cooper. Burnham was nowhere. The GMB was still run by Paul Kenny, who was just knighted for services to trade unionism. He had invited Corbyn to his annual conference in Dublin, despite thinking Burnham would win. He moved to a position of neutrality:

I wasn't going to rip our union apart arguing about it, so I just said, well, we'll open all the books, have the hustings and people will vote. I've known Jeremy thirty years and he's always been a decent bloke. But there's a hell of a difference between that and leading this outfit. . . . As it started steamrolling, I was convinced Burnham would win it. I thought [Corbyn] might come third. It was clear that he was going really around the place. He was saying things from a Labour platform that hadn't been said by a senior Labour politician standing for high office since Tony Benn.

The GMB, which was so instrumental in backing Ed Miliband and pushing through Collins, now took a position of neutrality. This was tantamount to a victory for the left. By the end of July, six unions affiliated to Labour had nominated Corbyn as well as three other unaffiliated unions. This was an overwhelming majority through which affiliated supporters would come. Manuel Cortes of the TSSA:

In the original round, I think other unions were thinking of supporting him. When all this started, and I called for him to be on the ballot paper, I thought it was going to be maybe one, or maybe two or three unions that would support Jeremy. In the end, I think every union with the exception of three came behind him.

The upsurge of support came from the social media campaigns that sprang up organically outside the official campaign and within it. Different individuals and groups have claimed they were the true creators of this phenomenon. The outriders came from different, left-orientated groups who created their own campaigns. They started a fledgling online campaign on Facebook and Twitter. One contributor came up with #JezWeCan. This was a campaign to get Labour MPs to nominate Corbyn. Pat McFadden was always going to vote for Liz Kendall but found himself experiencing the new forms of campaigning:

I was getting all these direct Twitter messages from people who obviously hadn't met me, saying 'Please nominate Jeremy Corbyn so we can broaden the debate'. And that was my first experience of that, where you can sort of bombard somebody. Now I was impervious to these appeals . . . but not everybody was.

The central office had Jack Bond liaising with different groups. By the end of the three-month campaign, one Facebook page had 70,000 likes, the top post reached 750,000 people and on a weekly basis, the Facebook posts reached 1.5–2 million people. It was highly engaged – around 200,000 a week and up to 600,000 in late July. They were posting ten posts a day along with videos. At the same time, Ben Soffa was creating a new canvassing app as reported in the *New Statesman*:

Ben Soffa developed the Canvassing App, a website that allowed volunteers to set up a phone bank anywhere with an internet connection, so long as they were signed up to the Corbyn campaign. It contained the details of every Labour party member in the country, with one person at a time's name, constituency and phone number appearing on the screen, along with simple instructions for volunteers: what to ask and how to record the person's views. Once the data was input and fed back to the central system, the volunteer's screen would refresh with a new person's details, and the canvasser would be unable to go back and contact the last person again, protecting their privacy.

For Jon Lansman, the power of social media combined with volunteers signing up for phone banks and the mass interest in joining the Labour party was everything he had set the campaign up to do, apart from winning. That was never a serious consideration until early July when the social media campaigns were generating unexpectedly high numbers of volunteers and levels of support. The campaign HQ initially operated from the TSSA offices in Euston until Unite switched to Corbyn, when it moved there with its hundreds of volunteers and phone banks.

The machine was being built and the data was beginning to come in. As the Labour party was getting new supporters signing up, the campaigns had access to the data and they could, if they chose, follow it up. Amazingly, it appears only Corbyn's campaign had the resources and skill to do this on any substantial basis. Nowhere was this seen more than in the sheer number of volunteers. Kat Fletcher had been a friend of Corbyn's in his constituency party for twenty years, his election agent in 2015 and the organiser of volunteers for Ed Miliband in 2010. At the start, she thought she would be doing a couple of days a week volunteering, building a left network in the party. Within a week, Simon Fletcher asked her to manage the volunteers and data collection. She set up a test to see how many would come on short notice.

> The first time I realised it was going to be extraordinary was when loads of people were pushing to get involved. The thing you do to test the water is set up a little phone bank. We were still at the TSSA with central London volunteers only; a small pool of 500 people. There was a tube strike and I gave them less than twenty-four hours' notice. That first night, sixty-two people turned up. I'd never seen that before. The last day of the Ed Miliband (campaign) when it was on a knife edge we might have got that number but not on a first day. It spiralled, and we were getting hundreds of people in the evenings on the phones. It evolved. At the start we were just collecting data and then we pushed it out to more activities – running the shop, the main telephone line, the core team of super volunteers.

One volunteer who became a super volunteer was journalist, James Schneider:

> I joined the Labour party three days after the 2015 general election and before the candidates were selected. When I joined, the party was moving right not left. I didn't think it was going to go well.

He messaged the Jeremy for Leader Twitter account but there was no advice on how to become a volunteer. He attended a solidarity rally for Greece against the EU, where Corbyn was a speaker, and handed out leaflets and finally:

> The Unite office opened at the end of June and wanted volunteers. I tried to go on Saturday but it was shut. I tried to go to TSSA, but it was shut.

On the Monday he got into Unite:

> I thought I would be there for two weeks. The first phone bank was in purposely selected CLP seats that were adjacent to the three other candidates. (I was) expecting hatred and derision but instead 20 to 25 per cent said we quite like him, 25 per cent just laughed, 25 per cent said no, fuck off and 25 per cent said I have no idea who he is and who are the other ones? I thought that was really good. The aim at the beginning was if you can come third that's amazing.

Kat Fletcher's phone bank regime was using data bought from the Labour party in an increasingly sophisticated way. It started by telling volunteers:

> Here are ten numbers, find out how they're voting. The campaign bought the sheets from the Labour party initially getting people to go to CLPs to endorse Jeremy and then we moved onto general voter identification, first and second preference voting and then nuancing the data.

And if people couldn't do this?

> A dozen older members couldn't phone bank. Everyone who had contributed at least £10 to the campaign got a letter of thanks from me headed and signed by an older volunteer in a hand addressed envelope. Hundreds of letters every day.

Schneider was soon a super volunteer:

> Every night, I would select where we were phone banking in the
> Unite office and we would input all of the data and I would see
> it come in day after day after day with fewer people laughing at
> you. There was something very odd and very special going on
> and more and more volunteers coming in. We ran phone banks
> at 5 and 8 p.m. Monday to Friday all day in one or two or three
> rooms every day. By the end, five or six hundred people were in
> the Unite building, on burner phones, every single bit of space
> with calls sheets and things. It felt like magic.

There was no sense of exhaustion; an 8 p.m. finish and then
everyone went to the pub, fostering a sense of comradeship. At the
TSSA building they were getting more and more data. This was
kept to a very small group of senior individuals. Jon Lansman:

> In mid-July, we did an analysis of our candidate's returns, and
> we did it in a way that we compensated for all the biases in
> the data because we could look at the Labour party database.
> We were given new data in waves, all the time giving us data
> on new joiners. I always wanted to collect it for our purposes
> in a way that both satisfied the public regulation of data and
> which satisfied the Labour party's restrictions. So that we were
> legitimately gathering data on Corbyn supporters to build an
> organisation after the election, including people who were not
> fully members but who might be persuaded, later, to join.

The other campaigns?

> God knows what little they did with it. They did pretty much
> nothing. We were organising the phone banking. We were
> collecting data. We were analysing data. And we produced our
> first figures, which only Alex and I looked at, and we didn't
> reveal these to anybody else. We didn't tell Simon. We didn't
> want people to know how well we were doing. It did scare us

because we couldn't believe the figures, you wanted to pinch yourself and say, 'Can it really be this good?'

They did not initially tell either Jeremy Corbyn or John McDonnell because they were terrified that the data have been giving false readings. Apparently it was not: *The Times* published the first poll on 22 July taken by YouGov over the previous week. It showed that even in the first round, Corbyn had a lead over all the other candidates with 43 per cent against 26 per cent to Andy Burnham, 20 per cent to Yvette Cooper and only 11 per cent to Liz Kendall. His lead among affiliated and newly signed supporters was 57 per cent to Burnham's 21 per cent, Cooper's 14 per cent and Kendall's 8 per cent. The more people joined the party, the greater his lead. By the final round in this poll he was 53 per cent to Burnham's 47 per cent and, among new signers, 69 per cent to Burnham's 31 per cent. On every measure he was ahead and the internal data was validated. The external shock was huge. Now the world knew what only a very few people in the campaign had spotted.

At the same time the leadership based at the TSSA building were not letting anything be taken for granted. Jon Lansman:

> Don't exaggerate the certainty that we were going to win the leadership. We knew it was possible. We always knew, however, that things could change and one of the really important factors was that if we ended up with a single opponent, then the tables could, perhaps, be turned. Which, is why we strived so much to . . . keep both Yvette Cooper and Andy Burnham as close to each other as possible.

Up to this moment there had been unofficial discussions between the campaigns about second preferences. When trying to get the nominations together, Lansman had reached out to the other candidates and deputy leadership candidates. Now there was bartering for second preference votes. They did not want candidates to drop out and unify the anti-Corbyn vote. Up to the end of June, chats were happening with the two other campaigns; but then the data was published. Jon Lansman:

> They were interested in our second preferences and we promised that we would make a decision by the end of June. We kept stalling and at the end of June, we postponed it further. But, of course, by the time we got to July, they knew that they were both behind. People were switching from Andy to Jeremy and so Andy – who, of course, started in the lead – was slipping back, whilst Yvette was holding her ground a bit better. We did win some transfers from Yvette. But it was much more from Andy and essentially keeping her in the race and keeping up with the possibility that we would favour her did help to sustain the two of them.

If the left could figure this out, why didn't their opponents? The three other campaigns were in turmoil and, at the end of July, Burnham and Cooper took holidays. Both had been in the forefront of the 2015 general election campaign and both had young families. Cooper's husband, Ed Balls, had lost his parliamentary seat, and this campaign was already months old; none of which applied to Jeremy Corbyn, who did not go on holiday. However, this did not prevent tactical discussions between them.

Andy Burnham had gone to a waterpark in Mallorca with his kids. He was contacted by Chuka Umunna who was supporting Liz Kendall for the leadership. Kendall was prepared to pull out if Yvette Cooper did as well, so there would be one anti-Corbyn candidate. Burnham spent most of the day on the phone, but when it came down to it they could not agree. There was also an approach from one intermediary in Corbyn's camp, suggesting that if Burnham stood down, he would get support two years later for another run. How official this was is unclear, but it shows the uncertainty around the process, even in the Corbyn camp.

Instead of unifying to stop the insurgent campaign, the establishment candidates fought one another on top of the party machine, which was trying to handle the flood of applications before the 12 August deadline. Ayesha Hazarika was watching the Corbyn campaign whilst getting flak from all sides:

> We were so out of touch with where the party was at that time. They did a brilliant job of tapping into the emotions that people were feeling in our party, and we were tone deaf to them. I was just trying to oversee the process. We were trying to make sure that we were interpreting the new Collins rules in the right way. There were so many logistical issues, and there was also what Andy's team and Yvette's team did. Instead of actually rolling up their shirt sleeves thinking, 'We've got the fight of our lives on my hands, we've got to get ourselves around every single thing, get out there' they started to just challenge the rules the whole time. I spent a vast amount of the time having people shouting at me from Andy and Yvette's team. I thought it was so telling that instead of just thinking, 'Right, how can we literally get in, and campaign the shit out of this?' We had angry MPs the whole time going, 'You've got to stop this process. This is out of control. He's getting so much traction. There's something wrong with the rules,' and it was like, guys, this is what it is now, and you would be better off out campaigning. I mean, I remember there was one time at the beginning of the campaign when the refugee stuff in Calais was just beginning to kick off, and actually that would have been an amazing point for Yvette.
>
> Even Corbyn hadn't quite plugged into this, and Yvette was shadow home secretary, so it would have been perfect for her to go out, and it would have been great lefty credentials. We're here with these terrible displaced people. A classic Labour message, our kind of message that we would believe in and agree with and which our members would have loved, but her team was like, 'No, no, she's not focusing on that. She's doing something completely different.' Sadly, both Andy and Yvette's teams had the arrogance and the complacency of the incumbent.

The *Guardian* reported on 17 August, with one month to go:

> Andy Burnham's campaign chief has accused Labour leadership rival Yvette Cooper of clinging on in the contest 'out of pride' as the two candidates fought publicly over who was best placed to defeat frontrunner Jeremy Corbyn.
>
> Michael Dugher, who is also the shadow transport secretary, added that Cooper's team should stop talking up the possibility of her becoming leader, arguing that 'the Yvette campaign remains in complete denial as to the fact that they cannot possibly win'.
>
> Dugher's aggressive intervention prompted an immediate counter-attack from Cooper's team, with a spokesman for the shadow home secretary accusing Burnham's campaign of 'old-style bullying from the boys' and saying it was he who 'needs to step back and leave it to Yvette' if he is not prepared to offer an alternative to Corbyn.

The events of 2015 are deeply reminiscent of 1980 and 1981, when the establishment opponents of the left saw the threat too late and were too divided to take effective action. In 1981, this led to one group walking out and setting up the SDP. The group of centre-left and centre-right led by Neil Kinnock and Roy Hattersley had learned their lesson and unified, stayed and fought, which led to New Labour ten years later. The generation that had grown up as ministers under New Labour hadn't learned any of these lessons. The left had learned in its political wilderness that the historic divisions and sectarianism could be set aside if there was a clear goal. It was uniting around an incredible campaign. Its opponents were drowning under levels of ego and denial.

The Corbyn bandwagon was moving on and faced its biggest potential threat: how many new joiners would be disbarred. In August, the flood of applications had been processed enough for the party to tell the four campaigns that 1,200 members and supporters of other parties had been excluded and a further 800 were under investigation, but this was the tip of the iceberg. Eventually, 56,000 were rejected, but of that number, 45,000 were not on the electoral roll (presumably including llamas, cats, meerkats and other animals). In this first one member one vote election, the tidal wave of new supporters and members was enough to overcome the doubts of the process of disbarment. A year later, for the second election, this would be a much hotter issue.

The power of Corbyn's message was getting through. Anti-austerity, anti-Trident; a new kind of politics away from New Labour and triangulation. The nature of his delivery, the sense that a tangible figure was about to replace the prince and princesses of New Labour was driving him to victory. His refusal to engage in personality politics added to his authenticity. It was a return to pre-Blairite politics supercharged through the prism of social media. Jon Lansman:

> Jeremy loved the campaigning, and, of course, as you had bigger and bigger audiences, you know – it's exhilarating. And so his confidence rose, and he grew into it. It was the message. It was anti-austerity, it was hope. It was not triangulation. It was politics that inspired, not politics that was designed to triangulate *Daily Mail* readers in the Home Counties, and it was left politics. You know, the people could feel enthusiastic, refreshed by things they'd never heard before; it was from twenty years before they were born. So, even if they were old ideas, the alternative economic strategy hadn't had a hearing for decades.

By the end of the campaign the estimated contacts to potential supporters, as captured on the database by data harvesting from connections made by mobile phones, emails and texting was, according to Jon Lansman:

> Something like 130,000, most of whom were new. We were communicating in that election. We had their mobile phone numbers, their email addresses, and so we interacted with them electronically by email and text and we got responses from them and so, most of the data harvesting was electronic.

The moment of truth was on 12 September 2015 at the Labour party special conference in the QEII conference centre in London. The results showed the scale of Jeremy Corbyn's victory. On the first and only round, he won over 50 per cent of the vote in a four-horse race; 59.5 per cent or 251,417 votes. Burnham won 19 per cent, Cooper 17 per cent and Kendall 4.5 per cent, the three losing candidates only won 16,000 votes between them.

Among the individual types of supporters he had huge leads:

- Party members, he won 49.6 per cent or 121,751 votes
- Registered supporters, he won 83.8 per cent or 88,449 votes
- Affiliated supporters, he won 57.6 per cent or 41,217 votes.

Kat Fletcher:

On the day, forty or forty-five super volunteers assembled around the corner and I put him in the middle of them and we marched into the conference hall, straight into the world's press. I was screaming '*Keep moving*' as we got into the venue. And then the announcement. That hall was not a friendly Jeremy place. We all went to the pub. Pete Bond [Jack Bond's dad] was a cabbie, he took Jeremy to a demonstration.

She went on to stay with him as he became leader: 'It was a mad journey but there no way you could turn it down.'

In 2014, two lions of the Labour left had died. In March, Tony Benn at the age of eighty-eight, and in June, Vladimir Derer, aged ninety-five. Neither of them lived to see the victory achieved by their political heirs, Jeremy Corbyn and Jon Lansman. The parliamentary and non-parliamentary parts of the left had never worked together so effectively to pull off a victory that no one could have predicted. Falkirk had led to Ed Miliband's speech, which led to the Collins report, which led to the nomination bar of 15 per cent and to thirty-six MPs putting Corbyn on the ballot believing he would not win.

Even with this confluence of events, the campaign had to be fought and won with new weapons that would change the Labour party overnight. Jeremy Corbyn had been a politician for thirty years but had never been regarded as a leader – he was an activist from the backbenches whose moment had come. What no one had expected was how he had seized it. By July they knew they were going to win but that moment in September was extraordinary. For the veterans of the left who had been in the Benn campaign, CLPD, the GLC and all the other groups in the 1970s and 1980s, it was an incredible summer. Jon Lansman:

> It did become increasingly exhilarating. Of course, we were winning it but not with the people who had been around for all of those years. The few of us who had been running it were old. Now it was mostly young people. Frankly, it makes me want to cry about all the years that had been wasted. (He did.)

John McDonnell had tasted victory before in the GLC in 1981. He more than any of them knew that you had to seize the moment and move on. The next nine months were going to test that resolve within parliament and in the wider movement, but for the time being, it was just an extraordinary moment:

> Get ready, start preparing now because what happens then is you realise after all those years in opposition on the left, all those years of defeat and failure, the responsibility is on your shoulders, absolutely on your shoulders. And if you don't get this right, the left will be out for another generation. For God's sake, we've got to get ready.

PART SEVEN

The Four Summers of Jeremy Corbyn: The Summer of Redemption

'Momentum was very, very rocky. It could have collapsed at many moments.'
James Schneider, 2018

25

From Swarm to Momentum

The victory was so unexpected that its authors were unsure about what to do next. The leadership of the campaign was almost entirely devoid of any experience in running large organisations. John McDonnell had been the finance chair of the GLC at the age of twenty-nine, but that was between 1981 and 1985. Simon Fletcher had run the mayor's office in London from 2000 to 2008. The unions were large organisations who could flow in support but there was a skeletal structure for the new leadership. The first nine months of Jeremy Corbyn's leadership demonstrated how fragile the left's victory had been. The movement outside parliament created a new organisation that could have collapsed at any time. The position within the PLP was fragile since Corbyn was completely unused to power, the tools of leadership or the parliamentary process. He struggled in the face of Conservative contempt and internal opposition.

Against these internal pressures there were several major events: Syria, terrorism, the continuation of austerity under a newly emboldened Conservative party, local elections, the referendum on Europe and the murder of Jo Cox. All of this from September 2015 to June 2016. The culmination of all these events was the second extraordinary summer for the left and for Jeremy Corbyn. He was to be saved by the weakness and lack of understanding from his opponents. By September 2016 the left would survive these tests and emerge far stronger.

It was clear that a new army that had been signed up. The leadership campaign had generated 17,000 volunteers, up to 130,000 supporters and over 250,000 voters. For the old left, the campaign had started as an exercise in galvanising support for future battles. Now it had to consider what to do with the unexpected success of this strategy. Jon Lansman looked back to the glory days of 1979 and CLPD:

> I think, in my head, before Momentum was established, I saw it as a kind of hundred times bigger, modern version of CLPD. That was probably my conception. There were lessons I'd learned about getting the left to work together, but that was what was in my head. That wasn't the way it turned out.

In August, they hired some consultants to think of a name for a new organisation. Various names were thrown around: Straight Talking, Catalyst and Swarm. It is difficult to think why anyone would have wanted 'Swarm'. Eventually Momentum was chosen; brilliant in its brand in that it describes forward movement without specifying the aims of the organisation. It could mean many things to many different people. The name was, as it turned out, the easiest part of the process. The extraordinary success of the campaign between May and September had been in uniting the fractious left with one common goal. After thirty-five years of failure, it now had a vast number of new entrants, some of whom were returnees – old ultra-leftists, but many of them were young, new and unused to any sort of Labour party organisation. The strains were to become very apparent very quickly. James Schneider came from the body of 17,0000 volunteers who had joined the Labour party in May 2015:

> Momentum was very, very rocky. It could have collapsed at many moments. It was a lot about personalities. Jon had a long-standing plan we first heard about in early August to funnel everybody into CLPD and revitalise CLPD; at the same time, in the volunteers' office, two or three of us tried to write an alternative proposal for 17,000 volunteers – don't demobilise, you

need some vehicle for continuous mobilisation and continuous political activity.

Whereas Lansman saw it as a traditional left organisation within the Labour party, fighting for constitutional change and supporting an anti-austerity programme, the new generation saw it as something quite different; the way to harness energy among much more disparate political groupings. James Schneider:

> The idea was to create a new series of social unions allied to the party, tenants' unions, carers unions, citizen assembly type things. There was an opportunity to strengthen progressive forces. The other aspect [was that] we had all these new people in the party who needed a political activity to keep them involved, yet constituency meetings were hostile, new people were not welcomed.

There was a need to get some form of central management in this. The new leader's office was going to need staffing. The volunteers and all the data on the supporters could be used and there were dozens of local groups that had been formed around the leadership campaign, but no formal structure existed to bind them together. The corporate structure had been organised around two companies and the campaign had been very careful to collect data legally to keep for further use. One company was set up to handle staffing and administration matters and had Lansman and Simon Fletcher as directors. The other company which held the data on Corbyn supporters went through several name changes over the next two years but had remained with Lansman as sole director. It was a multi-purpose vehicle allowing Momentum to build website activity but, as Momentum grew, so did the number of individuals signing up with its data service. In September 2015, two key individuals joined the process: Adam Klug and Emma Rees, 28-year-old teachers who were on the long summer break. Adam Klug:

> We both joined the campaign when it was in full force because we were teaching in schools in Birmingham, and the school year

doesn't finish until the end of July. The campaign existed, but it was growing rapidly all the time. We both started off as phone bank volunteers in the Unite offices.

Many people of their generation were joining, not because of Iraq, but because of the financial crash of 2008. Emma Rees:

> Obviously, I knew about the Iraq war and I was a bit upset about it, but it wasn't something that really mobilised me or got me engaged. For me it was the 2008 financial collapse. I think that was a really politicising experience.

They were introduced to Jon Lansman. Adam Klug:

> We organised Jeremy's arts policy launch on 1 September, before the end of the campaign, that was trying to get popular culture, music, poetry and art all coming together. Jeremy asked 'Will you work with Jon Lansman to build this new organisation?' Jeremy and John [McDonnell] kept talking about a social movement. Jon envisaged a faction within Labour. In those early days we were thinking more about the fact that we brought all these people into Labour, we got more people politicised and we won elections for Jeremy Corbyn's Labour, but we didn't have a coherent enough strategy or, indeed, a deep enough understanding of the party itself. We were representatives of this huge swathe of people coming in. There wasn't an organization. There was no purpose or set of goals and there was no strategy document that we were working to. It was kind of a free for all. I mean, that was just a reflection of the fact that you had a 200/1 odds on us to win, everyone was focusing on the election.

Although they had no experience, it was an inspired move to bring them in. Adam Klug: 'I think the classroom was a great preparation'.

Emma Rees on being linked with Lansman, 'It was like an arranged marriage or something. You know, put them together, give them no money, just see what happens.' However, James Schneider,

Adam Klug and Emma Rees could not have been more different to Jon Lansman. He had been in the Labour party since 1974, they from 2015. Two different generations with a very different view of the nature of political organisation and the movement. Two groups were represented – the movementists and the institutionalists. James Schneider:

> The first time I met Adam and Emma was the day before Jeremy won. The first proper meeting was going through Jon's paper and we thought it was terrible. Jon was carrying on with souped up CLPD plus souped up Left Futures. By the end of the meeting he added on a third element. food banks – not very good. We kept volunteers, the fifty to sixty core people every day. We kept that going for three weeks. Not being paid. Trying to work out what do we do with 17,000 people and the other 83,000 people on the database.

From this tiny group a new organisation began to evolve, bringing in very talented, very inexperienced, very young activists who were learning as they went along but had an extraordinary level of commitment. Over the next six months, they were to became the core of Momentum. There are three other examples of those who came, never left and were to become formidable political activists and none of them were from the traditional ranks of Labour activists of yesteryear.

Beth Foster-Ogg was sixteen when she joined the Labour party in 2014, making her a party veteran compared to all the others. She bought a ticket to the Labour party conference and started an internship at Citizens UK in Whitechapel, where the fledgling Momentum was camped out:

> We're in this tiny attic room in this massive venue in Whitechapel. It had no heating, no internet, no tables, three chairs. Adam Klug walked in. I had been following Momentum online. I was really enthusiastic. I'll come volunteer for you if you want. I went to the Euston office the next week, and I was instantly in love with

the whole thing . . . For the first six months everyone pitched in for everything. There was pretty much complete transparency about everything. Which was, I think, why so many volunteers came in and then stayed, because you could be anyone from any kind of walk of life and experience and they would treat you completely equally. We all had a very shared experience and responsibility for the whole thing. You instantly had massive buy-in.

Rachel Godfrey Wood, a more experienced activist with a background in the environmental movement, had a similar story:

I joined the Labour party a few days before Momentum was formed. One of the first things I went to was a meeting of London Labour left. I sat next to someone there who said, 'At tomorrow midday we're going to be launching something.' That was Jon. At first there was a sense of being isolated from the other key people or actors in the movement. And of not being that aware of their relative strengths. Second, a feeling of being under attack and under siege and being aware that Jeremy was under attack and not quite understanding what our role was.

Harry Hayball, another complete newcomer who had completed his PhD in history at London University, was more motivated by Iraq:

I was going on a post-PhD trip for about a month, and I saw Corbyn and I just thought, the leader of Stop the War is now a leader of the Labour party, which was the party that led us to Iraq. So, if you can achieve meaningful political change on these issues, and with a more left-wing agenda and anti-interventionist, then that's obviously the chance, once Corbyn's been elected.

The Labour party's decline in membership from 400,000 in 1997 to 200,000 in 2013 had created an organisation dominated by local rules and veterans who disliked newcomers. Three hundred and fifty thousand new people had joined. This was bound to cause friction and indeed it did, as Harry Hayball quickly discovered:

> I went along to my first constituency Labour party meeting which was the local Annual General Meeting and there were huge numbers of people there. But it was a super boring meeting and they didn't do anything to engage anyone. I became secretary of my local branch of the Labour party because they didn't have a secretary and I offered to do it. They kept trying to shut us up. They changed the rules so you couldn't speak if you weren't a delegate. All that kind of stuff.

Momentum became a home for individuals who were to have a major impact on the development of the Labour party and the left. When working for Tony Benn in 1981, 24-year-old Jon Lansman stood out because he was younger, more articulate and more motivated than many of his peer group. Forty years later, when he was the same age as Vladimir Derer had been in setting up CLPD, he was now the veteran institutionalist having to deal with a group of people from the movement who were all a reincarnation of his younger self. There was an inevitable clash of styles and understanding of the new world dominated by social media. Just like CLPD in 1979, the more successful Momentum became, the more the accusations against it grew: of being ultra-leftists, Trots, commies (to quote several Labour MPs and supporters of New Labour), but the truth was that this inner group did not conform to these labels. Emma Rees:

> The Labour right had played this whole situation so badly in my view. I think if they'd just been really nice to all those new members – mostly people who just joined the party because they didn't like homelessness and thought the local libraries should stay open – if they'd been welcomed in, invited to tea and coffee mornings and so on, they wouldn't have necessarily been in the mindset of some kind of factional war in the Labour party.

But the systematic shutting out of new members over those two years hugely expanded the number of people that thought 'No, we have to organise, and we have to take control of this local party. We need to vote in internal elections, and make sure that Jeremy's legacy will actually be about people who share our political platform.' I think that increasingly happened.

Momentum was launched on 8 October 2015, four weeks after Corbyn's election, with no formal structure and a divided house between Lansman and the trio of Rees, Klug and Schneider. As Lansman explained in 2018:

> We didn't have any kind of governance structure, we didn't have any kind of regulation of local groups, we didn't have any kind of membership. So how did we make decisions? Adam, Emma and James Schneider were the three core ones who effectively, became full-time.

They thought he was obsessed with structure, he thought they were lacking in any sort of organisational ideas. Lansman was the product of the left's history, its hierarchies, of CLPD, of running slates and party organisation. He had kept the left alive over thirty-five years. They were born of the new movement from outside the structures of the party. These two strands became one within Momentum and Emma Rees became its first national coordinator, but in those early months everyone was fighting for their vision, as Lansman admitted:

> They wanted a complete open-door policy. They wanted it to be a totally horizontal organisation, totally anarchic. They had no experience of left-wing sectarianism and to be fair, my attitude was also completely wrong. Because my conception had been of an organisation that was kind of a mass CLPD and one that would preserve Jeremy's leadership, that would do the democratisation that CLPD would do, that would run slates, that would attempt to win at constituency level. It was a kind

of continuous battle over a period of many months, developed with increasingly shared understanding. But it was hard, in the early stages.

There had been no formal process to set up a staff or even a chair of an organisation that itself had not been properly established. Although there was a steering group of new MPs, it had a very loose structure. No one was getting paid and for an old activist like Lansman, this was also part of his past and his attitude toward the volunteers who were now full-time:

> When I left university, I went and worked for CLPD for ages and never got paid anything. My approach was, 'Well, you know, we haven't appointed you. We haven't had a process. We can't just pay you. We'll give you some expenses and pay you in lunch money and stuff like that.'

Even in his own case it was unclear:

> Who'd appointed me? The answer is John McDonnell that appointed me. I was the person who'd been asked to set it up by John McDonnell who had been the campaign chair.

Momentum needed to live up to its name despite these teething troubles. There was a danger that it would fall apart without any sort of clear focus, exactly as the Rank and File Mobilising Committee had done in 1982. It needed another challenge to pull it together, and in late 2015 one presented itself.

26

Learning on the Job

September 2015 was a remarkable series of firsts for Jeremy Corbyn. He was elected leader of the official opposition, his appointment to the Privy Council was announced (although not enacted until November), he had his first PMQs and he appointed his first shadow cabinet.

The role of any political leader is to appoint the shadow cabinet and the private office. Jeremy Corbyn had no personal experience of this. He had come from thirty-five years on the backbenches in which he had very little immersion in the parliamentary party, the structures or organisation of the party. He did exactly what Ed Miliband did in 2010; appointed his friends to his office and his enemies to the shadow cabinet. In the fevered parliamentary party, this is not always a successful strategy, but he had very little choice and very little control. Some refused to serve: Yvette Cooper, Liz Kendall, Tristram Hunt, Rachel Reeves and Ed Miliband. The horse trading was undertaken by Rosie Winterton (the reappointed chief whip), Corbyn and his newly appointed chief of staff, Simon Fletcher. John McDonnell was appointed shadow chancellor over the wishes of unions such as Unite. This was a sign of Corbyn's loyalty to his oldest political ally but it also, by common consent, turned out to be the best appointment of any. John McDonnell became the rock of the new leadership. The rest of the initial shadow cabinet consisted almost entirely of people who had not voted for it. In the three senior jobs McDonnell was joined by Andy Burnham as shadow home secretary and Hilary Benn as shadow foreign secretary. Angela Eagle was hastily given the title first secretary, despite the fact she was shadow business, innovation and skills. This was to offset the lack of women in the nominal top jobs.

In his first Labour party conference speech as leader, Jeremy Corbyn thanked everyone including his three rivals plus Ed Miliband, Harriet Harman and Iain McNicol, and announced a new style of politics:

> First and foremost, it's a vote for change in the way we do politics. In the Labour party and in the country. Politics that's kinder, more inclusive. Bottom up, not top down. In every community and workplace, not just in Westminster. Real debate, not necessarily message discipline all the time. But above all, straight talking. Honest.

He attacked the Conservatives over austerity and backed his new shadow cabinet even when they were not his supporters: Lucy Powell at education, Maria Eagle at defence, and John Healey at housing. It appeared that a truce between wings of the party was possible. For three months this shadow cabinet held together, but the problems were there from the start and were soon exacerbated by the one area where Corbyn could bring in his allies, LOTO – the leader of the opposition's office.

Every leader chooses a staff reflective of the personality and ideology of that leader. Kinnock, Smith, Blair, Brown and Miliband all surrounded themselves with a praetorian guard that they trusted and could work with. The office is an extension of the leader. In Corbyn's case, as he had come from the far reaches of the Labour movement, it is not surprising that he sought out people who were as close to his views and tastes as possible. Simon Fletcher and Anneliese Midgley joined from the campaign and Jack Bond and Kat Fletcher moved from Islington North. These were unsurprising appointments. They were of the left but essentially pragmatic individuals with a history of making things work. The bigger surprise was Seumas Milne brought in as the executive director of communications.

Seumas Milne of Winchester, Balliol and the *Guardian*, the son of a former director general of the BBC, was at first sight an unlikely ally, yet he perfectly demonstrated the concerns of Corbyn's enemies. He had once been the business manager of *Straight Left*, the house magazine of the Communist Party of Great Britain – a pro-soviet magazine. He had not been a member of the Communist party but over thirty-five years his columns in the *Guardian* perfectly echoed Corbyn's world view: anti-imperialist, anti-American, anti-capitalist and anti-Israeli. Anyone reading his collected columns in *The Revenge of History* could be left in no doubt about his politics. They were clearly to have an impact on Corbyn and Labour in a range of policy areas, including the upcoming EU referendum in 2016. Milne and Corbyn brought in Andrew Fisher, who was suspended almost immediately after it was revealed that he had put out several tweets attacking Labour MPs and had backed a rival party, Class War, against Emily Benn, Tony Benn's granddaughter in Croydon South. He continued working for Corbyn as head of policy even while the suspension took place and, after a year, it was repealed.

These appointments were publicly attacked by MPs and the press alike. One headline in the *Independent* read, 'So Jeremy Corbyn, what made you appoint Seumas Milne, an apologist for murderous dictators?' However, as much of the problem was the impact they had on Corbyn himself. Milne and Fisher reinforced his bunker mentality, including his habit of reading off a screen in meetings in the shadow cabinet, rather than engaging with colleagues. The alienation was considerable, and it was compounded by his performances week after week in the House of Commons, which were patchy and weak against a resurgent and cocky David Cameron.

The first big test came in November when a series of terrorist attacks rocked the world. The so-called Islamic State (ISIS) in Paris on 13 November 2015 killed 130 people, as well as seven terrorists, and injured a further 413. This followed previous incidents in

France in January. An international coalition led by the French and Americans declared air strikes on ISIS in Syria. The UK had already been involved in bombing ISIS in Iraq. Corbyn, true to his non-interventionist past, argued strongly against further military attacks and suggested that negotiations should take place to stop the carnage of the Syrian war. This was entirely consistent with his world view. It also had no possibility of either being carried out by either the US or UK governments. Two years after his failure to join the US in bombing Syria which had been defeated in the House of Commons in August 2013 David Cameron wanted again to join the bombing campaign against ISIS and again went to the House of Commons on 26 November. The shadow cabinet was completely divided with Hilary Benn, the shadow foreign secretary, arguing in favour of the government's policy. Corbyn agreed to give Labour MPs a free vote on the issue as the only way to paper over the gulf between the two wings of the party. The fledgling Momentum organisation re-emerged to put pressure on Labour MPs to vote with Corbyn against military action. James Schneider:

> That was a significant public campaign where we organised lobbies. We got thousands of people to turn up in Parliament Square at a very short notice.

The Stop the War Coalition, led by Andrew Murray, marched on Westminster on 1 December with various supporters such as Richard Burgon and the old anti-war horse George Galloway. On the night of the vote, sixty-six Labour MPs defied Corbyn's leadership and voted with the Conservatives to authorise bombing on ISIS targets in Syria. They included Tom Watson and Hilary Benn, who made a final conclusive speech in favour of standing up to fascists. This was a substantial indication of the true split within the parliamentary party early in Corbyn's leadership. Eleven members of the shadow cabinet voted with the Conservatives.

During the previous week, Momentum had come under substantial criticism for allowing different local groups to protest against their MPs. Accusations of bullying and intimidation were voiced. Tom Watson appeared on Radio 4's *Today* programme to discuss Labour's by-election victory in Oldham (caused by the death of Michael Meacher) and attacked Momentum saying it 'looks like a bit of a rabble to me'. Momentum issued a statement the following day stating 'We are pleased that the majority of Labour MPs and the shadow cabinet did oppose David Cameron's proposal'. It claimed it had initiated 30,000 people to email their MPs to vote against. Momentum's statement went on to say:

> Momentum strongly disapproves of anyone who engages in abusive behaviour against MPs or anyone else. Momentum is not a threat to MPs who voted for bombing. We have made it clear we will not campaign for the deselection of any MP and will not permit local Momentum groups to do so. The selection of candidates is entirely a matter for local party members and rightly so.

Within Momentum, the pressure was building. In February, it announced a code of conduct that excluded members of other parties from voting in internal elections but still allowed them in the organisation. It now had a paid membership structure in which supporters had to agree the aims and values of the Labour party, but it was not a formal constitution. It created a fifty-two-person national committee and a steering committee of fourteen that included Christine Shawcroft from Labour's NEC and the Grassroots Alliance, and Jill Mountford of the Trotskyist Alliance for Workers' Liberty, with Jon Lansman as chair. A budget of £243,000 would be set aside for eight full-time members of staff, including a national coordinator. Emma Rees would become the first holder of the post. She, Adam Klug and James Schneider were still there challenging Lansman, but the mood was getting worse. During this period, the three wrote a letter to John McDonnell asking for Lansman to be removed. McDonnell didn't get involved and this forced the four of them to work it out. Without the events of that summer, it probably would not have been resolved, and

Momentum would have gone the way of many left groups in the previous thirty years.

Both Momentum and Corbyn's office made important changes as the battle lines were being drawn. Two of Corbyn's opponents, Michael Dugher and Pat McFadden, were ejected from the frontbench and three junior spokesmen resigned in support of McFadden. That month, Karie Murphy was appointed to Corbyn's private office, which was a significant moment. Corbyn had his intellectual support with Milne and Fisher. Murphy was a link with Len McCluskey and Unite, which was to become ever more important in the internal faction-fighting over the next three years. Murphy was an aggressive fighter whose management style was highly unlikely to blend with the more measured and cerebral Simon Fletcher. She may have started with the title of office manager, but she was to become chief of staff whilst Fletcher was moved to a different role. Murphy and Milne insulated and protected Jeremy Corbyn, but they also isolated him.

In March, a list of Labour MPs was leaked from someone in the leader's office that designated Labour MPs by their loyalty. The five groups went from 'The Core Group' right over to 'The Hostile Group' and included a number of shadow cabinet members as either 'Negative' or 'Hostile' including Chief Whip Rosie Winterton and Shadow Foreign Affairs Spokesman Hilary Benn, or merely 'Neutral' such as Andy Burnham. Only nineteen were listed as Core Group, one of whom was Jeremy Corbyn and another Michael Meacher, who was listed as 'RIP'. It did not point to a solid group of supporters.

It was during these few months that LOTO decided to allow a film crew from *Vice* to record the first few months of Corbyn's leadership. Milne had overruled Fletcher to allow this. The programme displayed the inexperience of the new leader in PMQs and in challenging David Cameron and George Osborne. The campaign in the local elections in May 2016 did show Corbyn's enthusiastic support from the army of new members and their belief in his powers of victory, but Labour won a mere 31 per cent of the vote against 30 per cent for the Conservatives, 15 per cent for the Lib Dems and 12 per cent for UKIP. More relevantly, Labour did win mayoral elections in Bristol, Liverpool, Salford and London. Sadiq Khan won in London after a Project Fear campaign fought by the Conservative, Zac Goldsmith, who destroyed his own liberal reputation with a campaign condemned as Islamophobic, even by Muslim members of his own party. Khan crushed him. The Conservative's negative tactics in elections were beginning to lose their potency. Labour came third behind the SNP and Conservatives in Scotland. This was not a triumphant victory for the new leadership.

One month later, the UK returned to the ballot box to vote on the referendum on staying in or getting out of the European Union. Forty-one years earlier, in the 1975 referendum, Labour had been split between the pro-Europeans in the centre and right of the party who became the forerunners of New Labour and the anti-EEC left whose political heirs now led the party. Those historic divisions were to resurface all over again.

27

The Referendum

The 2016 referendum campaign and its aftermath was one of those unexpected generational moments in British politics. Two years earlier, UKIP had scored a stunning victory in the European elections and both major parties learned to fear its impact. Within the Conservative party, the anti-European faction had become more vocal and more threatening to David Cameron. Following his run of victories in the referenda on proportional representation in 2011 and Scottish independence in 2014, Cameron saw no reason why he couldn't use the device to quell the internal debate in his own party. Ed Miliband had rejected the idea but, under Harriet Harman's temporary leadership, Labour supported the 2015 European Union Referendum Act. Only the SNP had voted against it. Cameron marched off to Brussels with a shopping list of proposals designed to show he was listening to his party. They included limiting benefits to European migrants in the UK, reducing the impact of further European consolidation and helping competitiveness within the UK. There was no fundamental change in the relationship between the EU and the UK but it did allow him to come back and claim he was negotiating for Britain and the UK should stay in. The referendum date was set for 23 June 2016.

The referendum was described as advisory and not constitutionally binding, and the interpretation of what Brexit could be was entirely up to any future government's ability of negotiate the exit. By using the referendum as a party management device, Cameron balanced the government's official position behind the Remain campaign while allowing his cabinet ministers the right to campaign in any way they chose. If he won the referendum, he could move on with his second term against a weak Labour leader and with a renewed agenda.

Cabinet unity and collective responsibility went out of the window. The known leavers, Iain Duncan Smith (who resigned from the cabinet before the referendum), Chris Grayling, Theresa Villiers and John Whittingdale were not particularly prominent among the public. Michael Gove joined them in February, despite his close relationship with David Cameron. Three weeks later, Boris Johnson announced his last-minute conversion to the cause. Having taken the decision, Gove and Johnson had no choice but to lead the Leave campaign with vigour.

Cameron and Osborne countered this with Project Fear, which depended on a combination of economic arguments and the fear of the unknown. Pushing the economic consequences of leaving the UK in Scotland in 2014 had helped achieve a 'No' result in the Scottish Independence referendum. It also helped in the 2015 general election, when using allegations of the SNP running Ed Miliband's agenda had led to a Conservative victory.

The official Remain organisation was the latest example of the big tent envisaged by Peter Mandelson and Tony Blair in 1994. It was staffed, funded and driven by veterans such as David Sainsbury and Mandelson, run by Will Straw (the son of Jack Straw) and, as the campaign developed, Craig Oliver from Downing Street. It embodied the political class of the previous twenty years: New Labour, Lib Dems and centrist Conservatives divided by policy but united by political outlook; liberal, European, pro-business.

Johnson and Gove were not going to be temperate. They had made their choice and now had to fight for it. On their flank they had Nigel Farage of UKIP who could now be as unrestrained as he liked. During the campaign, the claims of the benefits of leaving became more exaggerated from the Conservative renegades and enhanced the more extreme fearmongering from UKIP.

On the Labour side, there was a new leadership quite different from Blair, Brown or Miliband, both in its view of Europe and of unifying with other members of the Remain big tent. For Jeremy Corbyn, Seumas Milne or Andrew Fisher to work with Conservatives or Lib Dems on a campaign would be bad, to work with New Labour would be beyond their political comprehension. This was not just a political issue, it was ideological. Corbyn came from the wing of the left that had always regarded Europe as a capitalist project designed to unify the forces of capital and business in a much larger market. Protection of workers' rights and other benefits were useful, but the Bennite view of the 1970s from which he sprang was fundamentally against the institutions of the EU. For Seumas Milne, the collapse of Greece and the refugee crisis was the latest example of the EU failure. Over the previous four years he had repeatedly written about it in the *Guardian*:

'The Elite still can't face up to it; Europe's model has Failed'; A Tory-led exit for Europe would unleash a carnival of reaction.

The nationalist right has long set the agenda. Labour should back a referendum and make the progressive case for change.

What has been almost entirely missing from the mainstream British public debate has been the progressive case from fundamental change . . . in the 1975 referendum. The left case against the then common market was that it was a cold war customs union against the developing world that would block socialist reforms, but the modern EU has gone much further, giving a failed neoliberal model of capitalism the force of treaty, entrenching deregulation and privatisation and enforcing corporate power over employment rights.

No one, including Milne, knew that he would be the intellectual driving force of the leader of the opposition less than a year later.

It's not surprising that he and Jeremy Corbyn would be at best lukewarm when it came to supporting a Conservative- or New Labour-led campaign to stay in the EU. The various left and right fringe parties, including the Socialist party (previously Militant) and the Communist party all campaigned to leave.

When he was running for leader, Corbyn had advocated a policy of 'wait and see' toward Cameron's negotiations with the EU. As the Conservative splits over Europe grew in early 2016, he could afford to remain on the sidelines. However, he faced the problem that Miliband had struggled to resolve; large numbers of Labour voters were showing signs of agreeing with Leave. The Remain campaign was fixed on the Conservatives' economic arguments and Project Fear pushed the Treasury argument of economic disaster. For traditional Labour voters in the North and the Midlands, immigration was a red button issue and UKIP was pushing those buttons.

As the campaigns continued, the Leave camp drove the rhetoric. It claimed EU membership cost the UK £350 million a week that could be saved to spend on the NHS. Turkey was close to membership of the EU which would bring increased immigration. In the last stages of the campaign, Farage put up a poster with pictures of a long line of refugees from the Syrian war and the slogan 'Breaking Point', pushing the idea that floods of immigrants would be entering the UK.

In the face of this onslaught, the government fought back with a volley of establishment appeals. A pro-EU information document was sent to every home, the Treasury warned that every house would be £4,300 a year worse off on leaving the EU and Barack Obama was persuaded to back Remain in his last visit as US President. The problem was that the sheer emotion of the Leave campaign overwhelmed these appeals from the establishment. David Cameron had lost his sense of the electorate – as the London mayoral election had demonstrated, Project Fear had been overused. Johnson, Gove and the other Conservatives all attacked their own party leadership without restraint.

Labour's involvement in the campaign was fronted by Alan Johnson and Hilary Benn, neither of whom were compelling or authoritative enough. Jeremy Corbyn was persuaded to take part on 14 April. His speech focused on workers' rights and reform of the EU, he was not particularly concerned about immigration. He argued that on balance, it was better to stay in:

> Just imagine what the Tories would do to workers' rights here in Britain if we voted to leave the EU in June. They'd dump rights on equal pay, working time, annual leave for agency workers, and on maternity pay as fast as they could get away with it. It would be a bonfire of rights that Labour governments secured within the EU.

Kate Hoey, the Labour MP in favour of Leave, immediately responded with, 'We know first that he doesn't really mean it, no matter how much he tries to pretend he does, and secondly, that it is not in the interest of the Labour movement.' For the next four weeks the Remain campaign had Labour involvement but no thrusting attack, compounded by Corbyn's refusal to share a platform with Tony Blair. By the time it got to the last week before the referendum, the polls were neck and neck.

As the *Guardian* reported:

> The 'Labour fightback' had a promising start, then went awry after a couple of days. An event with Corbyn, his shadow cabinet and trade union leaders on 14 June was overshadowed by an internal Labour row about whether free movement of workers – an axiom of EU membership – should be up for renegotiation. . . . Corbyn, meanwhile, was retreating into non-cooperation. Gordon Brown had devised an initiative to bring Labour leaders past and present together for an event – but Corbyn refused to share a platform with Tony Blair. Even when Blair's involvement was downgraded to a statement read by someone else, Corbyn would not budge.

Two days later, only hours after Farage's 'Breaking Point' poster was put up, the emotion of the campaign was heightened by the murder of Jo Cox MP. She had worked in Brussels for Glenys Kinnock and then for Oxfam. She had been elected to Batley and Spen in 2015, nominated Jeremy Corbyn for the leadership and voted for Liz Kendall. If anyone exemplified the reasoned centre of the Labour party, it was Jo Cox. Her maiden speech was on the diversity within her constituency. Her attacker shouted 'Britain First' as he shot and stabbed her. The sheer ugliness and brutality of the murder demonstrated the divisions in the country and the campaign was suspended for three days. Politics of the centre were being swept away.

In the last few days of campaigning, the polls were close but the overall assumption from the media, pollsters and commentators was that Remain would just about pull it off, that the risks of leaving the EU would be enough for most voters to ignore the paucity of the Remain campaign. The challenges to political orthodoxy as represented by Corbyn's election, the rise of social media that created alternatives to established media to reach the electorate, the sheer zest of the Leave campaign given a patina of respectability by some Conservative politicians despite its blatant exaggerations and untruths – all these factors were not seen as quite enough. A poll by YouGov on the eve of the referendum gave Remain a four-point lead.

By 4 a.m. on the morning of 23 June 2016, a revolution had occurred. Leave had won by 52 to 48 per cent. Only in the regions of London, Scotland and Northern Ireland did Remain win. Even in areas that had been the recipients of EU funding or inward investment, the electorate voted to leave. The highest voting area for Leave was Boston in Lincolnshire, with 76 per cent, the highest to Remain was Gibraltar with 96 per cent. Over 70 per cent of those aged under twenty-four voted to Remain.

At 8 a.m., David Cameron walked out of 10 Downing Street and resigned. He had used the device of a referendum and the tactic of Project Fear one time too many. The campaign had been misjudged and undermined by members of his own party, but his decision to push for a referendum had been rooted in his over-confidence and desire to resolve the internal fights over Europe that had lasted fifty years in the Conservative party. He will be remembered not for liberalising the Conservative party, as he attempted to do with social reforms such as legalising gay marriage, but for presiding over a period of austerity and creating the circumstances for leaving the EU. He will also be remembered for walking away with a typical old Etonian insouciance: now it was someone else's mess to clear up.

Cameron's statement at 8.00 a.m. was preceded by an interview by Jeremy Corbyn at 7.30 a.m., in which he made two statements that would come back to haunt him.

> The British people have made their decision. We must respect that result and Article 50 has to be invoked now so that we negotiate an exit from the European Union. Obviously there has to be strategy but the whole point of the referendum was that the public would be asked their opinion. They've given their opinion. It is up to parliament to now act on that opinion.

The Labour leader also defended his performance during the referendum campaign, saying his 'seven and a half' level of support reflected the views of the electorate.

Invoking Article 50 so quickly and admitting his campaign was at a level of seven and a half was the last straw for many in the PLP. The accusation of being half-hearted over the referendum and the indecent haste to move ahead with the two-year withdrawal seemed to confirm the lack of grip he had shown in the nine months of his leadership. He was detached from most of his MPs, and his office was even more detached. The time had come to re-establish the primacy of the PLP and reverse the mistake of 2015.

At 8.15 a.m. on Friday 24 June, the Conservative leadership was in disarray. Cameron had fled the battlefield. His natural successor was George Osborne, but if anyone shared this defeat it was

28

The Chicken Coup

The history of the Labour party is littered with examples of an utter lack of understanding by different groups of each other. No one outside the left understood the potency of the 2015 campaign until it was too late. In 2016, a total lack of comprehension of Corbyn's motivation led to the most incompetent attempt to remove a party leader in political memory. In the words of John McDonnell, 'as plotters they were fucking useless'. It truly can be said that Jeremy Corbyn, his 2018 shadow cabinet and Momentum all owe their prominence and power to the events of June and July of 2016, through the opportunity created by their internal party opposition.

After the events of 24 June 2016, Margaret Hodge decided someone had to act. She was in a unique position as a former leader of Islington council where Corbyn had been an MP since 1983, and as the former chair of the Association of London Councils, had hired John McDonnell as its CEO in 1987. Like many others in 2015, she did not quite realise what was going on with Jeremy Corbyn until it was too late:

I was incredulous when he got on the shortlist but I thought great; a debate! I've known Jeremy since the 1980s. I had a perfectly nice relationship with him as leader of the council. The decent side of Jeremy was that he never attacked the council. He wasn't that interested, much more in Nicaragua; he was foreign policy focused. John is the brains, very, very able which

Jeremy isn't. When he got elected in 2015, I knew it would be a nightmare. But how cleverly they used social media!

She and a fellow MP Ann Coffey decided on Friday 24 June to move a motion of no confidence in Jeremy Corbyn as leader. Hodge explained why they did it so quickly:

> He had no confidence within the PLP, there were a lot of groups meeting before the referendum as he wasn't promoting a Remain agenda. We were meeting for support and plotting, a bit of both. The general view was the time to move was 2017, but I was rung up by a key mover and shaker, I had nothing to lose, I had guts, would I move the motion of no confidence? I slightly panicked but if you think back on that day, Corbyn was blamed for the referendum going wrong. It felt like an opportune moment in which to move against him. The decision was literally taken that morning, we had to put it in that day.

Over the previous seven days, the PLP had seen one of its MPs murdered, the referendum gone horribly wrong and its leader unable take advantage of the government collapsing into its own leadership chaos. It is no wonder that all political judgement went out of the window.

> It was a judgement. We probably had people against Corbyn anyway and [we thought] young people in Momentum would be cross about the referendum and wouldn't support him. We miscalculated. It was a moment. It wasn't pre-thought through. Would 2017 have been more successful? I wasn't a leader of this. I was a follower. The next generation should lead it but I was happy to play a role. If it had it gone right it would have been brilliant, when we got it wrong, it was condemned.

The next generation, however, didn't know what was going on. Some of them had other things on their mind. A curious feature of that weekend was that the middle-aged of the PLP were partying in Glastonbury whilst the young leaders of Momentum had gone abroad on holiday. In both cases they had believed that the referendum was a foregone conclusion. Lucy Powell was Labour's education shadow secretary of state. She went off to see Adele:

> I was out in Glastonbury thinking it was going to be fine. It was Thursday and we were having cocktails, I was having a nice time with my friends, then stuff started coming through from Sunderland at midnight. I woke up at four or five in the morning with my phone going. Margaret Hodge and Ann Coffey tabled the no confidence motion on Friday. I was still travelling from Glastonbury at that point as a member of the shadow cabinet and I thought God, this is a stupid thing to do. Why are they doing that? It's the last thing that we need. I think at that point most people just thought we don't need this, this is a mad thing to do. I decided to come back from Glastonbury on Friday. I had a few phone calls with a few members of the shadow cabinet on the way back about this motion of no confidence and the referendum generally. There was no way we're all going to resign on Sunday, no not at all. But we knew this is quite a big moment.

As Lucy Powell made her way back from Glastonbury, which was also attended by Tom Watson, Ed Miliband and various new MPs such as Clive Lewis, there was no organised coup. Hodge and Coffey had put in their motion that would be enacted the following week, but no one was planning to resign. On Saturday night the *Observer* reported that Hilary Benn was calling his colleagues to rally support for a change of leader and that he would threaten to resign, with other shadow cabinet members, if Jeremy Corbyn refused to go. They believed that the failures of Corbyn's leadership would somehow persuade him to stand aside at a regular PLP meeting on Monday before the no confidence motion set for Tuesday. Lucy Powell:

> With hindsight it was a series of small triggers that mushroomed in a very febrile environment.

What you've got to remember is, in the build-up, there was a lot of disappointment about Jeremy's role in that referendum campaign, particularly for those of us that were working closely with him. We should have all been a bit more generous to him because it happens to any leader, but in terms of chairing the shadow cabinet, in terms of leading a discussion, leading anything, we had seen first-hand that he would come along to shadow cabinet meetings, especially when it was a difficult meeting, with a pre-written out script that he would read and then sit back and that would be that. That happened quite a few times and we'd had this Syria vote, there'd been quite a lot of difficult things. Jeremy was at that point totally out of his depth. That was the context. Then the front page of the *Observer* came out about ten o'clock on a Saturday saying that Hilary Benn was organising to get rid of Jeremy. Over that night, everyone was ringing everybody else.

Heidi Alexander resigned on Sunday morning as Labour's shadow health secretary. Hilary Benn was gone later that afternoon. In a completely disorganised fashion, the ball started rolling and a competition started for who could resign first but with no plan for how to actually remove the leader. Lucy Powell:

We obviously knew we were going to be creating a kind of crisis. By mid-morning on Sunday several people resigned and you're racking your brains, thinking what are you to do? Len McCluskey rang me. People were ringing me from both sides to persuade me. I don't think I saw it as a permanent state. I always saw it more as a protest that would shake things up, and the shaking back down again it would all fall back into place.

Lucy Powell and a group of able, ambitious, frontbench Labour politicians who should have been the next generation of leadership, all fell into a race to resign as a protest with no plan, no leader and no understanding of the forces against them. Corbyn argued at a shadow cabinet on Friday and throughout the weekend that the Conservative leadership election could spring a surprise general election, but the pressure was building as resignations started to flow.

At eight thirty on Monday morning, Emily Thornberry went from shadow defence to shadow foreign affairs. Young and completely unknown MPs from the 2015 intake were shovelled into jobs as quickly as they became vacant: Kate Osamor into international development and Clive Lewis into defence (unlike Lucy Powell he had stayed at Glastonbury). At 9.00 a.m. Tom Watson (now back from Glastonbury) met Jeremy Corbyn and told him he had to go.

Later that morning, five soft-left MPs went to meet Corbyn in his office at the House of Commons. Lisa Nandy, Nia Griffiths, Owen Smith, Kate Green and John Healey were reported as not wishing him to stand down. They wanted assurances on how he was going to work with the soft-left and the PLP in the future. Corbyn's private secretary outside the door was Laura Parker, who was to become a key figure in Momentum later, but at the time was letting in the five plus John McDonnell. If there was one person who was not going to give in without a fight, it was John McDonnell, who knew his role as a defender of the leader. As he said:

> My job was to look after the shop. I joke about it and I get accused of being a bureaucrat, but that's what I am. It's to live through the politics, through bureaucracy.

McDonnell was also conscious of the tactics used by Tom Watson in an earlier coup.

> There was no way that it was going to get traction within the rank and file of the party. There was no way whatsoever. In terms of the parliamentary Labour party, even then the bulk of people actually just wanted to get on with the job. But when the coup occurred, the best way to describe it was that it was like *Lord of the Flies*. People were influenced in a way, there was almost a herd mentality. There was like a stampede – they were worried

about their seats, some of them were exploited and therefore the coup and the coup organisers manipulated the situation.

That Saturday I got a call from the media saying Hilary Benn's resigning and so are others, and we were trying to chase him all day. Jeremy eventually got hold of him near midnight, said what's happening? Remain in place, no consequences brought and he said no. And then after that, we then had them resigning in batches every four hours. And that was the strategy that Tom Watson used against Blair in 2006. So all we had to do was keep on filling shadow cabinet places, and the big issue for us was could we fill in the frontbench? Could we form an administration?

When the soft-left delegation went to meet Corbyn, McDonnell was ready:

They asked him to stand down. I came in and said no way. It's not going to happen. And a couple of them burst into tears and all that sort of thing. I wasn't in any way nasty, I just said this is not happening we're not doing any of that. Get used to it.

All five resigned, and by lunchtime fifteen other resignations had come in. One newspaper report said that a reshuffle list had been leaked at 1.05 p.m. showing forty-one names to be removed, and only twenty minutes later it was out of date. Even David Cameron, who was having his first day as a lame duck prime minister, made the joke 'and I thought I was having a bad day'. By 6 p.m. the PLP meeting took place with repeated denunciations of Corbyn from veterans such as Alan Johnson. By the end of Monday, forty-seven frontbenchers had resigned. The following day, the motion of no confidence in his leadership was passed by 172 votes to 40. Lucy Powell:

There wasn't a strategy around it. If there had been a strategy, we wouldn't have done it. It was a kind of domino effect that was a massive strategic error. Because we didn't have a strategy, it was quickly possible to label it a coup. We were the absolute opposite of careerists, but there was no one leading that process. For those few days, we tried to coordinate media management by adding pressure in terms of what was going to come next, but that was hard to do because what came very quickly were potential leaders emerging. There was no collective endeavour, then it became this sort of individualist pursuit which all went horribly wrong.

It all depended on Jeremy Corbyn resigning.

It really did get to him. Jeremy didn't enjoy the day-to-day parliamentary rigour of the role. What he really enjoyed and what he was actually very good at was the out and about there, the rallies, the selfies, the meeting people. Plus, he'd just done nine months of horrible hard slog with PMQs every week. Chairing meetings, having people coming in lobbying him. That's not Jeremy, that's just not him at all. I don't think he really enjoyed the job really at all at that point either. The referendum had been difficult for him because of what he felt and what was happening. I think it got to a point where he felt just let the next person do it. He was persuaded against that at the last minute by John McDonnell.

The shock to the system would be enough to shake any leader and Corbyn was no exception. However, the chicken coup was to have unexpected beneficial consequences for him, his supporters in the House of Commons and the wider left. Those who resigned, as Lucy Powell explained, did not think it was forever. They had left the frontbench denuded of talent and people. They also did it in a particularly brutal way. The memory of June 2016 influenced a substantial number of people who were suddenly thrust into the responsibility of leading the Labour party. One of them was Rebecca Long-Bailey. She and Angela Rayner had been elected in 2015, shared a flat and were of different wings of the party. Within hours of being elected they were plunged into a leadership contest. Rayner supported Andy Burnham and got a job as shadow member for pensions. Long-Bailey decided to follow her political instincts from day one as the leadership contest happened and nominated Jeremy Corbyn.

She was quickly spotted by John McDonnell and appointed to a junior job in the shadow treasury team and had a researcher called Olivia. The coup took place just as the finance bill was going through parliament, needing a line by line debate about its hundreds of clauses. The Treasury team had divided the bill into clauses that each of them would handle in committee, and the research and answers were saved on a shared hard drive. Long-Bailey was working with another, more experienced Labour MP, Rob Marris.

> We were in the finance bill committee, going through each clause line by line. He was going to do the first half of the session, I was going to do the second half. He got to Clause 20, stood up and publicly announced to the chair and to all the Tories and Labour MPs who were there that, 'He didn't have any faith in Jeremy Corbyn and he resigned forthwith' and walked off.
>
> So I'm in this finance bill committee thinking 'Oh my God!' You know, keeping a poker face, because I don't want the Tories to see that I'm perturbed by it. I started to get a bit worried and was thinking, 'We've got 180 clauses yet to go on the finance bill, and he's had responsibility for some of them'. We were concentrating on each section ourselves. Something in my gut told me something wasn't right. So, I ran back to my office and said to Olivia, I said 'Check the shared drive' which she did and all the clauses and the all the notes were gone. . . . I said to Olivia, 'If they think that they're going to get rid of us like this, they've got another thing coming, we'll stay up all night going through these clauses and re-writing the notes if we have to.' And that's what we did.

The level of anger was building.

> I could see that they were trying to do, they were trying to make us completely ineffective as an opposition. They didn't reckon

on us working twenty-hours a day so that the next day we could walk in and actually do the finance bill and do a good job of it. I remember poor Angela Rayner in my office at 3 o'clock in the morning eating a Domino's pizza, saying 'When can we go home?' to which I replied, 'We're not going home!'

Not only did the resignations have an immediate impact on legislation, they also meant that the whole frontbench had to be covered by inexperienced MPs covering multiple roles.

We didn't have enough people on the frontbench to cover everything, so we were working every single day, on every single piece of legislation. I'd be running from a committee to make sure we were sat on the frontbench because if you don't have a frontbench spokesperson sat there when a debate starts you're in serious trouble, because then the PLP, or whoever wants to declare themselves the opposition, can say 'We're the real opposition, not them. Look, they haven't even got a spokesperson there.' So, it was a constant battle of having rotas and making sure that everything was planned militarily to within an inch of its life, so that we had people in places twenty-four hours a day, so that we were covering things. It was quite an exhausting time.

The consequences of these actions were to be long-lasting. The plotters had failed to get rid of Jeremy Corbyn. If he could hang onto the new shadow cabinet made up of a large number of the new generation, it would have to step up and, having gone through the fire, would be stronger over the long term. The impact in parliament was a state of constant civil war. As Rebecca Long-Bailey said:

We'll never forget the position that many of us were put in. On some of the debates that I was speaking in on the Treasury team, I know that there was a whipping operation to make sure that nobody came. Debates that I would speak on the frontbench, and there wouldn't be one soul sat behind me on the Labour benches. So, I'd be facing a baying mob of Tories with no support at all. It was immediately hostile.

If events in parliament were getting exciting, the people who had been responsible for supporting the campaign in 2015 were also getting mobilised. It had gone into a quiet phase with just over four thousand members, who had been activated for the rather disappointing local elections. Adam Klug and Emma Rees were in Spain.

> We hadn't been on holiday or had a day off really, since Momentum started, and we very foolishly thought, 'Oh, I know, we'll wait until the EU referendum results are in, and surely everything will just go back, it will be very politically calm after that, so we got on a flight that evening of the EU referendum results. We found out the result as we landed.' And then we just saw our holiday disintegrate in front of us. We didn't bring a computer. We had our phones, and we instantly had to organise the rally.

They set up a WhatsApp group, organised volunteers to contact every Momentum group, organised coaches and key contacts. All from Spain on mobile phones.

> Within forty-eight hours of initially setting up this WhatsApp group, suddenly we watched on the news ten thousand people out demonstrating in Parliament Square. It was unbelievable. We came back after five days to 'Keep Corbyn: Build Our Movement'. The whole thing was we needed to build this, and we needed to grow.

Beth Foster-Ogg was supposed to be on her gap year.

> I left two days before the Brexit referendum. I was going to have five weeks in Cuba, come back, do a couple more weeks with Momentum, and then go to Uni. That was the plan. We got a

text to say that Brexit had happened and my phone exploded. It was actually vibrating, because I'd been put in all these group chats about the coup. I rang Adam. 'What the hell is going on?' He was on a beach in Spain. 'There's a coup, we're probably going to have a leadership election. I don't know but I will keep you in the loop.' He rang back two days later. 'There's a leadership election, we need everyone here. You've got to come home.' I had a forty-eight-hour journey and eventually got back to London. During that process, Adam had rung me and said we've got you a job on the campaign. You're going to be Jon Lansman's PA and he's going to be the director of the campaign.

Momentum burst into life. The demonstration in Parliament Square initiated a new burst of activism that probably saved the organisation. 1,700 Corbyn supporters joined it within twenty-four hours, a 27 per cent increase. It had doubled in size from 4,000 to 8,000 members between April and the end of June. It launched a petition over the weekend that gained 56,000 signatures over three days.

Events started to move at a fast pace. After the motion of no confidence was passed by the PLP, the plotters assumed that Jeremy Corbyn would simply resign. His frontbench was barely full, with a few veterans and many new entrants. He was shaken by the level of personal animosity. He did not particularly like the job and could possibly have gone if an approved successor could be found, but such a figure did not exist. John McDonnell did not want to do it and there was no one else from the left. Tom Watson was a master of plots but unacceptable to the left. Everyone else had resigned. The plotters had failed to appreciate that without having a clear path for resignation, Corbyn's allies in the unions and among the constituencies saw their actions as the betrayal, not as Corbyn's failure to fight Brexit. Margaret Hodge, who had started this chain of events a week earlier:

We had never been in a situation where after such an overwhelming motion of no confidence, the leader didn't resign. There were two issues: firstly, we just assumed he'd resign. Secondly, in the anti-Corbyn group there was a conflict. When he refused to resign what we should have done was to create our own PLP and select our leader. The person who prevented us from doing that was Tom Watson. I was used. I was a tool of it. I thought they were more organised.

Amidst all this turmoil, the political world continued to revolve. On 30 June 2016, two days after Labour's vote of no confidence, the Conservative party nominations for leader closed and Michael Gove completed his cycle of turning on his friends by announcing he would stand against Boris Johnson who immediately pulled out. Gove had been his campaign manager up to that point. The Conservative soap opera continued into the following week with two ballots culminating in Theresa May beating Andrea Leadsom on 7 July. Four days later, May was leader of the Conservative party and on 13 July, the new prime minister.

Meanwhile, two reports were published that had a big impact on Labour and Jeremy Corbyn. On 30 June it published Shami Chakrabarti's report on antisemitism. The following week the government published the long-awaited Chilcot enquiry report on Iraq in which Jeremy Corbyn both condemned Tony Blair and apologised for his party's role in the war. It was a reminder of one of the main reasons he had become leader.

The real battle was whether he would face a challenger and how the process would work. There was only one real way to stop him. The NEC had to decide whether he would automatically be on the ballot as the sitting leader or whether he needed to be renominated, which would require MPs and MEP's standing by him. Although he had overwhelming support outside parliament, this would be the big test. The coup had failed in its first attempt to persuade him to go. In the words of one Corbyn supporter, Manuel Cortes, who had been the first trade union leader to support him in 2015:

A coup needs two things: it needs to be fast and it needs to decapitate. Neither of these things happened. This turned into a slow, lingering death. And that always favours the leader.

The first thing to do was find an alternative candidate. Between 30 June and 11 July various names were bandied about but the front runner looked to be Angela Eagle, who had resigned from the shadow cabinet and was seen as a reasonable candidate from the soft-left of the party, not a New Labourite, and who could be acceptable under other circumstances to the wider party. She had some national profile after standing in for Corbyn against Cameron at PMQs. After she declared, and it was rumoured that Owen Smith would also declare, the general secretary Iain McNicol called an emergency NEC meeting for 12 July. There were accusations that it was too short notice and not all the delegates would be able to get back from their holidays. At the PLP meeting on Monday night, Tom Watson accepted that he had failed to get Corbyn to stand down. He was quoted in the *Guardian* as saying, 'For years I've been known as a fixer. I have tried to fix this, and I have failed.'

On 12 July, the day before Theresa May became prime minister, Labour's NEC met to resolve critical questions about the leadership. Would Jeremy Corbyn be allowed to automatically be on the ballot in a new leadership election? Or would he need to get new nominations from Labour MPs and MEPs to get on the ballot? It's an anomaly of the rules that any *challenger* needed 20 per cent (fifty-one nominations) of MPs and MEPs to get on the ballot against an existing leader, whereas if a vacancy appeared (as with Ed Miliband in 2015) only 15 per cent (or thirty-five nominations) were needed. There was a debate about which Corbyn would need if he was not on the ballot automatically. Although even if he needed only thirty-five MPs, would he get them? It was entirely unclear given that 172 had signed a motion of no confidence.

The second question was whether those members who had joined the party in 2015 and 2016 would be allowed to vote in this new election. Or, unlike in 2015, would there be a freeze? Would there be a repeat of the £3 supporters' entry fee to broaden the electorate again? This was the most important moment for the NEC to decide the future of Corbyn's leadership and every part of the movement was getting stuck into managing the outcome.

spokesmanship. At the same time, every union delegate on the NEC was being approached. Manuel Cortes had one delegate from the TSSA who was on holiday. He arranged a cab to bring her into London for the vote. Before the NEC even met, two members of the shadow cabinet tried to stop the proceedings. Andy Burnham and Debbie Abrahams proposed a forty-eight-hour delay and an independent mediator to avoid the leadership contest but, as NEC member Anne Black said, 'Thirty-two of the thirty-three NEC members were present on crutches, back from holidays, taking time off work and could simply not come back on Thursday.' The NEC voted seventeen to fifteen to hold a secret ballot after some expressed fears of intimidation and online bullying.

Jeremy Corbyn addressed the meeting but then agreed to withdraw. Now the real mess began and contradictory legal advice was taken. One barrister that said Corbyn had to get 20 per cent of MPs and MEPs as with any other challenger, another said only challengers needed to have new nominations. After hours of debate, the secret ballot was held and the vote was eighteen to fourteen to allow Jeremy Corbyn automatically on the ballot as leader. This was a huge win for him from an NEC that did not have a built-in majority of his supporters. Jonathan Ashworth:

> People assumed that when the NEC voted for a secret ballot that meant that Corbyn would be automatically off [the leadership ballot]. I think a lot of people thought it was reasonable and fair enough that a leader who had been elected by OMOV, less than twelve months earlier, should have the right to put himself forward again.

The NEC then voted on whether to continue to allow supporters to join for £3. There was 'near unanimous opposition' to this. A one-off fee was finally set at £25. Then the vote to create a freeze period on new members voting began. This was a critical issue given how many new members had voted for Corbyn in 2015. The first vote was on whether to allow anyone who joined before 24 June

2016 to vote, the day after the referendum. This was tied fourteen to fourteen and failed. The NEC then agreed a much earlier cut-off date of 12 January 2016. This disbarred anyone joining after that date from taking part in the new leadership election. It was a messy way to decide the issue. Although Corbyn and his supporter Jon Trickett had been at the NEC when it voted to keep him on the ballot, they then left to address his supporters gathered outside and missed the votes on the fee and the freeze. Reactions to these decisions were mixed. John McDonnell was prepared for the fight.

If Jeremy was not automatically on the ballot paper, we would then have had to contest that in court. Even though we weren't in control of the NEC, there were still those elements on the NEC that recognised that to have a coup against the recently elected leader, and then to try and prevent him going on the ballot paper as well, was just unacceptable.

For Momentum this was both very good news – its hero was on the ballot – but very bad news because large numbers of its supporters might not be able to vote for him. Beth Foster-Ogg:

The one bit that really freaked everyone out was when they did the cut-off date for members being able to vote. Everyone panicked because we just thought, well we know we have the membership. But we don't know when they joined. We thought that most of them had joined after Jeremy's first election. And they suddenly weren't able to vote, and that was really scary. Loads of people on our team couldn't even vote.

However, although the electorate was more restricted now he was on the ballot the probability of winning a new leadership race was high. Jon Lansman:

As soon as they lost the core battle over Jeremy being on the ballot paper, Tom Watson knew he was going to fail because he knew that we had the numbers to win and the ability to win.

He knew that the only way they could do it was through a coup in which Jeremy was just kept off the ballot.

The NEC meeting was followed by Angela Eagle dropping out of the race to be replaced by Owen Smith. He had some support, but the leadership race was to be held over the summer culminating in a September contest. Jon Lansman was campaign director and Momentum was suddenly alive again, but the process led to two challenges in the courts that were to dominate proceedings until mid-August. Two days after the NEC, Michael Foster popped up to challenge the process in the High Court. He was a talent agent, donor to the Labour party and former parliamentary candidate. He was no fan of Corbyn's, especially over the issue of Israel. His legal challenge was whether Corbyn should have to be nominated to stand again. Two weeks later the High Court threw out his petition. From the other side, Labour was sued by five of its members, including one too young to be named, over its decision to freeze the votes of supporters who had joined after 12 January 2016. It was estimated that 130,000 people were affected. The case was made that these £3 supporters had joined on the premise that they could vote and this was in effect a contract. Crowdsourcing was used to fund this challenge and eventually raised over £90,000.

Jeremy Corbyn was in the odd position of agreeing a High Court action against the party of which he was leader. Tensions were growing. Online abuse of MPs and supporters of Owen Smith were growing. The NEC had suspended local party meetings except for the election nominations. Angela Eagle had a brick thrown through her constituency office window. In August, Tom Watson attacked Trotskyist entryism in Momentum naming the Alliance for Workers Liberty and the Socialist party (formerly Militant).

The legal challenge was supported by the High Court but then failed at the Court of Appeal on 4 August. By then the NEC had agreed to offer a window from 18 to 20 July when the £25 fee was extended to registered supporters. The relationship between Iain McNicol and the party leadership was not going to recover from this dispute. He was blamed for disenfranchising 130,000 members with the NEC ruling. The two-day window in July did see at least as many paying £25 for the privilege of voting.

Jeremy Corbyn was never going to lose this second election. Throughout August and early September, he did hustings with Owen Smith, whose principal election position was that he supported most of Corbyn's political positions but was better dressed and more likely to appeal to floating voters. By the election on 24 September, Corbyn was able to increase his number of votes to 313,000 compared to 250,000 the previous year. He won 62 per cent of the total compared to 59 per cent the year before. His lead in each of the three sections was higher than the year before. It was a triumph. The bigger issue was the impact the campaign had on the various groups within the Labour party itself. The victory had to be used to establish long-term power for the left.

29

The Importance of 2016

The strategic importance of this second leadership victory was greater than the surprise win in 2015. For the anti-Corbyn forces within the parliamentary party it was a disaster. Lucy Powell in 2018:

> I always said to colleagues at that time that there was no organisational fix around this. Jeremy actually needed to be beaten and kept off the ballot, but what would that do anyway? It was ridiculous. If that was all you had at that point, then you really had lost the argument. We lost the argument then and in so doing also absolutely toxified ourselves.

In Corbyn's reshuffle in October 2016, he had, for the first time, a shadow cabinet that reflected his political persona. The scars inflicted in June had not healed. Those who had gone were not invited back and a new generation were thrown into front-line politics. There were some older hands: John McDonnell as shadow chancellor, Emily Thornberry at foreign affairs, Diane Abbott as shadow home secretary and Jon Trickett as an all-purpose advisor and tactician. There were also younger faces: Angela Rayner at education, Kate Osamor at international development, Keir Starmer (who had resigned but was allowed back into the fold) in the key job as shadow Brexit secretary and Rebecca Long-Bailey as shadow chief secretary of the Treasury – later to replace Clive Lewis at shadow business. They could all settle into their roles against a new Conservative frontbench appointed by Theresa May and overshadowed by Brexit. The anti-Corbyn forces were unforgiving of those who stayed. Jonathan Ashworth reflecting on this period in August 2018:

> The amount of aggression, nastiness and so on, was extraordinary. The weekend after the conference, when he did his reshuffle, he offered me health secretary but said come off the NEC. They thought that because I was taken off the NEC, I should resign as the shadow health secretary. That showed how angry and upset the PLP were when they saw that Jeremy was re-elected with such a thumping majority in 2016.

Corbyn had his team at LOTO. Karie Murphy was now running the shop, with Simon Fletcher sidelined and Anna Midgley off to Unite. Andrew Murray of Straight Left, the Stop the War Coalition and Unite now also joined LOTO on a part-time basis. The leadership for the office was established and was determined to keep primacy over the wider left and the party.

Outside parliament, the impact of the summer of 2016 was immense. Momentum went from being Lansman and a few young activists with a membership of a few thousand to a mass movement in only three months. The campaign to get Jeremy Corbyn elected had seen a large overlap with Momentum. Lansman had a role in both. Emma Rees was national organiser of Momentum and James Schneider moved from Momentum to Corbyn's office after the campaign. Momentum was now far more visible and the national connection with Corbyn, and the more extreme views of the Trotskyists in the local groups, was explored in two undercover exposés of the organisation by the *Mail on Sunday* in July and then Channel 4's *Dispatches* in September. Beth Foster-Ogg:

> We had two undercover journalists, which, as a nineteen-year-old girl, was scary. For the first six months, and therefore at the

beginning of the leadership election, we didn't do any background checks, anyone who walked into the office was welcome.

The immediate impact was to push up its membership even more. One thousand two hundred members joined the day after *Dispatches* was aired, taking the organisation from 4,000 in April to 20,000 in September. The impact this had on finances and morale was immediate. Lansman and the movementists now were working toward a common goal. The problem was that the surge in membership also meant the fundamental goals of the organisation had to be defined. Jon Lansman:

> After the coup, everybody came back together again, and it was wonderful. We beat the bastards, we'd raised loads of money, we got loads of members, you know, it was all fantastic and then it all started again, and people started hating each other.

Lansman and Foster-Ogg went to the 2016 Labour party conference knowing they had won the leadership and were sitting on the membership spike but somehow it was not translating into action. Beth Foster-Ogg:

> We then had the party conference, which I think was a massive learning curve for Momentum. We had just won, but conference was still awful. Everyone was still in suits, nearly all the delegates were from the right, all the conversations were still completely unpolitical, and we lost nearly every rule change and debate on the floor. I was still Jon's PA at that point. He and I sat in conference, watching it, and he was getting increasingly frustrated at still not winning any of the actual changes to the Labour party. So that was a bit of an eye-opener for me because I thought, we need to take this whole 'transform the Labour party' thing seriously.

This was a turning point because the practical part of Jon Lansman, from the organised traditional left, was beginning to persuade his much-younger colleagues that they had to get real. Momentum had to have an organisational purpose within the Labour party. For that to happen, it had to identify those who were not going to agree. At the same time, it had to continue to appeal to a mass membership within the Labour party of 520,000 members. This meant combining a range of different skills and objectives and led to major shifts in the organisation between September 2016 and September 2017. It also led to an alternative conference where the young would be drawn into politics, The World Transformed (TWT). It created powerful roles for the young activists and a new constitution with Momentum, becoming a body committed to the Labour party and campaigning within it. Beth Foster-Ogg and Adam Klug had spotted that something had to be more appealing. Beth Foster-Ogg:

> The World Transformed was an idea initiated quite early on that year. Let's do a street festival of education and music and stuff because that's what Momentum was like at that point. Let's do a festival at Labour party conference.

The first TWT festival took place in Liverpool in September 2016 after Corbyn's second leadership victory. Sixty-five volunteers hosted a fringe festival with workshops, music and drinking. Emma Rees, Adam Klug and Beth Foster-Ogg all took part. Beth led some of the training sessions:

> I did a session on privilege where I made everyone stand, it's a really fun game. It's a combination of physical education, kind of like training workshops, and then art, music, theatre, dance. And then massive parties. It was great. Really fun.

Clearly one needed to be of a certain generation. The level of enthusiasm grew successively in 2016, 2017 and 2018. Every year, this became part of Momentum's appeal and political influence over the main conference. In 2017:

We had 7 per cent of the delegates. We didn't tell them what to wear, but everyone was wearing red and pink, Jeremy Corbyn t-shirts, and fabulous dresses. And there was such an energy, people were excited to be there. Most of them were first-time delegates who had joined because of Jeremy. They all wanted to speak, they had interesting speeches, there was actual debate. This was the first time in the year that anyone had questioned the finance report. Important members should be able to ask, 'What are you spending the money on?' It hadn't happened for twenty years. Really obvious stuff, but the conference hall had such an energy. It felt so much more like what we were trying to achieve.

At the same event in 2016, Jackie Walker, a vice-chair of Momentum, exposed the inherent problem of Momentum welcoming everyone into the organisation. She criticised Holocaust Memorial Day for only commemorating Jewish victims. Earlier she had blamed Jews for being financiers of the sugar and slave trades. The growing pains of the organisation were becoming very visible. Manuel Cortes threatened to disaffiliate from Momentum over Walker's comments. Now Momentum's internal issues needed to be sorted out, as the institutional control of the Labour party was still up for grabs. For the veterans of the left, the memory of 1982 was still powerful. In the three years from 1978, its influence had driven major constitutional changes and a powerful challenge by Tony Benn for the deputy leadership. Then it lost it all and within a year; the left's influence over the party had disappeared for a generation. In 2016, the leadership had been secured but the NEC was still vulnerable and the General Secretary Iain McNicol and the party staff were regarded as internal opponents. Over the summer, the left had created a slate of candidates for the constituency section of the NEC drawn from CLPD, the Grassroots Alliance and Momentum. It won all six seats including Ann Black and the perennials, Christine Shawcroft and Pete Willsman. Yet the NEC was still run by the centre-left. It was dominated by union delegates and when the leaders of the Scottish and Welsh Labour parties, Kezia Dugdale and Carwyn Jones, were given the right to nominate their own representatives, the left smelled a rat.

Despite confirming that any future leader would automatically be on the ballot (they weren't going to repeat that mistake again) the speeches from delegates at conference accused the NEC of a stitch up. 1982 had raised its head again. Overall, the conference felt like a hangover after the party of Corbyn's leadership campaign. The MPs who wanted him out were demoralised and the young activists felt alienated. The new Conservative prime minister Theresa May, was still riding high in the polls. Between September and December 2016, the Conservatives were never less than ten points ahead and after the party conferences, rose to 15 to 20 per cent ahead.

In October, Corbyn's reshuffled shadow cabinet had to adjust to taking on the resurgent Conservative party. May had appointed Boris Johnson as foreign secretary, David Davis as Brexit secretary and had fired both George Osborne and Michael Gove. She was enjoying dominance as a Remainer who had pledged to deliver Brexit. As the PLP was adjusting to this new reality, so Momentum was facing up to its inner demons. The initial clash between the institutionalists and movementists had gone; now Lansman's argument for control was backed by the established staff who were having to endure the problems that had been created by a lack of organisational structure. Emma Rees, Rachel Godfrey Wood, Harry Hayball, Beth Foster-Ogg and Max Lansman may have been young, but they had been through two leadership fights, two undercover media exposés and two years of induction in Labour party and internal machinations. The internal challenges now had to be met. Jon Lansman:

> When the coup happened, first of all, it reunited everybody. Once we had established the original structure, local groups elected people to regional groups, then the regional groups elected people to a national committee. But you also had the unions, and organisations like CLPD and the LRC nominating

people. Those were the basic methods of getting on the national committee. There were beginning to be arguments and there were also a lot more sectarians in all the local groups. The Trots did their usual thing, everybody got bored and people voted with their feet. The groups were getting smaller, more sectarian and more unpleasant.

The ultra-leftists were the same problem they had always been. Rachel Godfrey Wood, who was by now on the permanent staff:

I think they were less interested in the campaigning side, movement-building side, training up activists, and using digital communications – a lot of the things Momentum is quite well known for today. There were a lot of people who had an ability to impose themselves but didn't actually have an interest in that. What they wanted was to turn Momentum into the organisations they could never have built on their own. Because it already had a base of support that they could not have created on their own.

It was tough for the staff. Harry Hayball had been asked by Emma Rees to get involved in the social media campaign, which he ended up running:

Loads of us realised the importance of management structures in an organisation. It was just really inefficient and ineffective to have it that chaotic. Just having clear delineations of responsibility, ways to get sign-off. Because, on the second leadership campaign, that was really bad.

Hayball would go on to have a major impact on the 2017 general election campaign, but was learning on the job:

When I was working on the second leadership campaign, I was gradually learning more and trying to figure out what I didn't know. Social media was an important part of the Corbyn campaign as a way of gathering people and enthusing them. But it was done in a very amateurish way. There wasn't much strategy or thinking behind it, or understanding.

Lansman decided it was time to act. In late October he initiated a meeting of Momentum's steering committee, at which he advocated moving to one member one vote instead of the delegate system used since its inception. At the same time, symbolic parliamentary by-elections were taking place. On 20 October, Batley and Spen elected Tracy Brabin in a by-election uncontested by all the other major parties to honour the memory of Jo Cox. On the same day, David Cameron's seat was held by the Conservatives. He had finally left the chaos he had created. In November, Zac Goldsmith, having lost the London mayoral election to Sadiq Khan, resigned his Richmond Park seat to protest against government support for a new runway at Heathrow. In a by-election he ran as an independent but, without a conservative challenger, was beaten by the Lib Dems.

At the same time, British politics were to be given a new example of political upheaval from the US. On 8 November 2016, Donald Trump was elected President. 2016 was a contender for the year that killed both globalism and liberalism. It made Jeremy Corbyn's election even more unusual but reflected the same underlying causes: anger at elites, social media as the engine of change supplanting traditional communication outlets, and a sense of the impossible becoming the norm. Hillary Clinton's campaign was rooted in assumptions of 1990s certainties – liberalism, globalism and experience. She could afford to be lacklustre as she held all the cards, similar to the Remain campaign over Brexit that had cost Cameron and Osborne their jobs. Theresa May should have looked at the Clinton campaign and taken note. 2017 would see this lesson being tested again: strong, stable and experienced had not worked for Burnham or Cooper, Cameron or Clinton against the new chaotic forces in politics.

Momentum was attracting more members as the Labour party attracted new recruits and getting more attention. Emma Rees:

We were increasingly bringing the movement into the party and changing the party, making it more connected to the movement. Tory ministers over the previous two years had said things like, 'Momentum are thugs, they're hooligans, they're completely deluded, they're totally naïve, they're Trots,' you know, a whole host of names, and yet the membership number was going up and up and up and up. The adversity we faced as an organisation, as a movement, and the way that we responded to it was really important for our success.

In November, Laura Murray, Momentum's Women's officer, accused the Alliance for Workers Liberty of trying to force Lansman out and mount a coup. The Alliance for Workers Liberty attacked Lansman as being 'politically conservative'. His response was to take the OMOV proposal to Momentum's 21,000 members but this was defeated by one vote at a steering committee meeting in December. Jeremy Corbyn urged Momentum to unify.

Over Christmas, the plans were laid to create a new constitution. The company which owned the data that led to the creation of Momentum was still controlled by Jon Lansman; he had the power to close the whole thing down. Instead, plans were laid to appeal to the membership, rather than going through a delegate structure that was wanted by the AWL. Jon Lansman:

> They wanted to have it in an old-fashioned way; a delegate conference that constantly developed policy on what we should do. We recognised that that would be a disaster.

All the experience from the 1980's suggested that the real fight should not be about Momentum but about the wider struggles inside and outside the party, and if Momentum and the left were to succeed, they had to sort this out, fast. Jon Lansman again:

> Did we want to spend several months infighting within Momentum or did we want to spend it on the other things that we had to do? . . . We had to expect a general election at any

time. We had to both prepare to support Jeremy doing well in the general election, and the local elections. We had to prepare for the next year's Labour conference in order to keep and extend our control. Because we didn't control the bureaucracy, we still didn't control the NEC, and therefore what was going to happen in the selections, in the long run, we had to win selections in order to begin to change the complexion of the PLP.

What followed next was a masterclass in how to reform an organisation overnight. The messy way Momentum had been created now gave an opportunity.

> We recognised, based on the legal advice, that we didn't have a membership organisation at all. If we didn't have a membership organisation, we didn't have a constitution. Who could introduce it? The answer was, no one. So, we created the organisation. That was the principle. We had to do it suddenly because if anybody knew what we were up to, they'd find a way to stop it.

The best thing was to divert attention while drawing up plans for change. Let the Trotskyists focus on a delegate conference they wanted to control.

> We had to maintain the fiction of going ahead with this conference. Poor Emma had to go and act as secretary for this conference. Put up these awful people, these lunatic sectarians.

They rallied support through the fourteen-person steering group, the leader's office and the membership.

> We did have a majority on the steering group. We persuaded LOTO that we needed to do this. We did a survey of our members' opinions on the back of a Christmas message from Jeremy. So Jeremy was essentially endorsing the survey and that went out before Christmas. And we postponed the steering group until after Christmas.

Max Lansman, on preparing a new constitution in secret:

> That was quite demoralising for lots of people and it was very difficult, just from a purely administrative perspective. Everybody had to work until two in the morning over Christmas, and everyone was exhausted. We had to do it on the basis of a theory of what would happen afterwards. It was always inherently uncertain and so you could have done it all and then alienated loads of people and then still the whole organisation would collapse.

The team worked outside the main office. They were arguing about the detail until the final moment. Jon Lansman:

> We were still writing the constitution that day on a phone call and trying to get it all finalised. There were arguments going on between the staff because there were still tensions about what kind of organisation we were. Some of these were quite serious, but everybody was united about the principle. We were just arguing about the small print. We agreed the constitution. We got it ready to send out on the website with a link in the email. We sent the agenda out and asked people to respond as soon as possible. We'd lined people up, so actually, within about fifteen minutes, we had a majority. And I then sent the email out to everyone saying: 'Thank you very much. I've now got a majority.' And at the same time, Beth pressed the button to send the email out to everybody in the organisation.

A classic tactic of management control that was not exactly within the traditions of Labour party democracy. Yet because Momentum had never been properly constituted in the first place, it was allowed. This had the effect of making Momentum not only a fully legal entity for the first time but also pledging it to the Labour party. Lansman wrote to all members of the steering committee.

Dear Colleagues

I am writing to explain why, in consultation with a number of others in Momentum, the leader's office and trade unions that have supported Jeremy Corbyn, I have decided to propose today that we immediately act to put Momentum on the proper footing that those dependant on the success of Jeremy's leadership need it to be and our members want it to be.

Most of our members joined Momentum because they support Jeremy Corbyn and want to help him achieve what he is trying to do. We must put behind us the paralysis that has for months bedevilled all our national structures, and focus on our most urgent task – winning the general election that could come within months, by turning Labour into an effective force committed to that task, and to the transformative government that would follow.

I have also taken legal advice, based on a review of a substantial body of Momentum records, which is that in order to operate effectively as an organisation with members, Momentum needs written rules or a constitution with which all its members agree, and in our current circumstances, the only way of agreeing such a constitution which is binding on the relationship between the organisation and our members is to seek the individual consent of each of our members and affiliates.

It would commit to the Labour party, create an internal election and management structure and allow effective campaigning techniques. In short it would become an effective element within the Labour party and have it as its priority.

The response was, to put it mildly, outrage. The Communist party of Great Britain now working under the name Labour Party Marxists went berserk:

Neither Lansman nor Corbyn had any interest in Momentum becoming a vibrant, decision-making, member-led organisation that could fight for democracy and socialism. Any such organisation would undoubtedly embarrass the Labour leader sooner or later. A truly democratic conference would see motions criticising this or that particular attempt of Corbyn's to become a 'populist', which had, for example, seen him zig-zagging over the question of immigration, Trident and Brexit.

From that moment, Momentum became a different type of organisation and its politics were orientated entirely around the Labour party. Momentum was bigger and better than CLPD, with a clear agenda for taking power rather than only influencing those in power. It was relaunched in March 2017 with a new ruling body and conference. In April, members' representatives were elected for the regional seats on its new ruling body. It was now geared up for any future challenges.

On 23 February, by-elections were caused by Tristram Hunt leaving politics to become Director of the Victoria & Albert museum and the resignation of Jamie Read in Copeland. Both were seen as centrist opponents of the new regime within Labour. Momentum mobilised for both by-elections with activists and new apps designed to encourage carpooling and phone banking. It worked in Stoke but Copeland was lost. This was a serious blow to Labour and Momentum as it was the first time since 1982 that a governing party had won an opposition seat in a by-election. It was also the first time Momentum's campaigning had failed.

The Conservatives were riding high. The polling data in March and April 2017 was consistent and staggeringly one-sided. They were never less than 40% in the polls and reached 44% in May compared to Labour's average of 25%. This was 1983 all over again. Theresa May had promised not to hold an early general election, but who could ignore these figures against a divided Labour party? Like David Cameron, she could use a public vote to reinforce discipline within her own party. She could get a mandate to push forward her version of Brexit and then establish a government in her image. On 18 April she announced a general election for 8 June 2017.

PART EIGHT

The Four Summers of Jeremy Corbyn: The Summer of Fun

'Ohhh, Jeremy Corbyn'
Glastonbury Crowd, 2017

30

The Apotheosis; The 2017 General Election

Jeremy Corbyn had won every fight since 2015. The introduction of OMOV, the impact of social media and the disorganisation and failures of his opponents in the PLP had combined to give him an unassailable position as leader. In normal times he would be facing three years before a general election in which to develop a style and leadership qualities within the House of Commons. These were not normal times.

The upheavals in the Conservative party had created a new government under Theresa May who, having been home secretary for six years, was primarily known for her attacks on immigration and her fights with the police force. She had been overshadowed by the posh boys in No. 10 and No. 11 Downing Street and kept her own small group of advisors in the Home Office; just like Jeremy Corbyn in LOTO. Now she had an opportunity to overwhelm her own internal opposition of hard-line Brexiteers and establish a parliamentary majority greater than the twelve seat majority won by Cameron in 2015. She had got Article 50 through parliament; she had appointed Brexiteers to her cabinet, she had fired the most obnoxious of her enemies and she was leading by a margin of 15 per cent in the polls. What could possibly go wrong?

For Corbyn, the election had potential up and downsides. Local elections were held on 4 May, after the general election had been called but before the launch of manifestos. Seumas Milne and

others in this office had assumed that any general election might be
called for the same day but May's decision, eccentric in retrospect,
was to call a general election with a two-month campaign and still
have the local elections two weeks into it. This appeared to pay off
as the Conservatives enjoyed an 8 per cent swing at the expense of
UKIP who lost every council seat they were defending and gained
one at the expense of Labour. Labour's vote dropped by 4 per cent.
It lost seven councils against the Conservative gain of eleven and
lost mayoral elections in Tees Valley and the West Midlands which
it had been expected to win. Andy Burnham won the Manchester
mayoral race and announced he would stand down as an MP at the
same time. Like Sadiq Khan in London, he was careful to distance
himself from Corbyn during and after the campaign. The BBC
calculated that if these results were applied to the general election
to be held six weeks later, the Conservatives would win 38 per cent
to Labour's 27 per cent, 18 per cent for the Lib Dems and 5 per
cent for UKIP. Even in Scotland the Conservatives were gaining
against both Labour and the SNP.

Although this appeared bad news for Labour, it actually freed
up both major parties to follow their respective leader's instincts.
Theresa May and her advisors, Nick Timothy and Fiona Hill, were
so encouraged that they produced a presidential campaign rooted
around May as a 'strong and stable leader' and a manifesto assuming
such a large majority that radical changes would be advocated
without having been agreed by most of the cabinet. The campaign
was to be about her and giving her the mandate and majority to
govern without compromise after sorting out Brexit.

The local elections forced Jeremy Corbyn to do almost the
same thing. Unlike May, he could depend on his innate strength
as a campaigner and was used to having his back to the wall. For
thirty-five years Jeremy Corbyn and most of his inner office had
fought losing causes, but 2015 had shown that it was possible to
break through. His advisors, led by Andrew Fisher, were to create
a manifesto in their own image. There was no time to do anything
else. The New Labour credo, partially followed by Ed Miliband in
2015, had been to compromise and triangulate with the appearance

of being a 'responsible' putative government. For Corbyn and his supporters, this was pointless if they were already heading for a disaster and not what they wished to do anyway. They could be unfettered. Expectation management had already taken place at the start of the campaign. The only way was up, and for Theresa May, the opposite was true.

For forty years, the left had campaigned for an open process when writing the manifesto – it was the cause for which CLPD had been created in 1973. They had also wanted a more democratic process of selecting candidates to stand in parliamentary seats and so it was ironic that in 2017, for the first time, the leadership was of the left yet had neither the time nor the inclination to follow these precepts. The manifesto was written in LOTO by Andrew Fisher. On 21 April, the NEC announced it was invoking an emergency procedure to get constituencies to agree candidates in only twelve days. Where candidates had already been selected, in around 200 seats, they were automatically selected. In vacant seats without a sitting MP, the NEC and regional boards would select a candidate. Adverts appeared on Labour's website on 21 April and candidates had two days to apply. In twelve seats, Labour MPs were retiring and the NEC would place candidates. Three retiring MPs were women and they would be replaced by women.

All of this meant that the process was entirely undemocratic but quite efficient. The unions had a major place on regional boards and the NEC. In total, forty-seven new Labour MPs were elected in 2017 following the fifty-three in 2015. It was a generational shift caused by Labour's strong showing overall and the speed with which candidates had been selected and Momentum also had some influence over candidate selection. For the first time, the left was influencing the party's future MPs.

On 16 May Labour launched its manifesto in Bradford. *For the Many, Not the Few* was 128 pages that had been pulled together by Fisher over the previous three weeks. The draft had to be agreed under a Clause V meeting consisting of representatives from the shadow cabinet, Labour's senior staff from its HQ at Southside, the NEC and the Welsh and Scottish national parties. Unsurprisingly perhaps, it was leaked four days before its launch. However, the recriminations and blame for the leak did not detract from the debate around its main proposals, which continued until its real launch.

The manifesto was a clear repudiation of the politics of austerity. Everything was seen through the prism of the life in Britain after Brexit and the impact the severe cuts had made to life in Britain over the previous seven years. In its foreword it stated:

> Britain is the fifth richest country in the world. But that means little when many people don't share in that wealth. Many feel the system is rigged against them. And this manifesto sets out exactly what can be done about it. This election is about what sort of country we want to be after Brexit. Is it one where the majority are held back by the sheer struggle of getting by? That isn't the Britain Labour is determined to create. So, let's build a fairer Britain where everybody is able to get on in in life, to have security at work and at home, to be decently paid for the work they do, and to live their lives with the dignity they deserve.

Compare this to the Conservative's manifesto launched two days later in Halifax, which Labour had held in 2015 with a majority of only 428. With an introduction written in the first person by Theresa May, it stressed the need for a strong and stable government around the issue of Brexit.

> The next five years are the most challenging Britain has faced in my lifetime. Brexit will define us; our place in the world, our economic security and our future prosperity. So now more than ever Britain needs a strong and stable government to get the best Brexit deal for our country and its people. Now more than even, Britain needs a strong and stable leadership to make the most of the opportunities Brexit brings for hardworking families. Now more than ever Britain needs a clear plan.

The contrast could not have been greater. Even the layout and printing of the two documents was different. Labour's was well laid out, written in clear, declarative sentences with pictures. It was an easy read in a modern style. The Conservative manifesto read like a booklet from the 1960s and looked the same. Full of dense details and long sentences without any relief. It was a policy document, not a political call to arms.

Labour's manifesto took the risk in conventional terms of advocating a higher taxation rate of 45 per cent on those earning more than £80,000 per year and 50 per cent above £123,000 per year, increasing corporation tax from 21 per cent to 26 per cent, and setting the target of eliminating the deficit within five years. It promised infrastructure investment through a £250 billion National Transformation Fund. It would continue HS2 and superfast broadband development, it would create a National Education Service including a promise of thirty hours of free early years child care and it would remove £200 billion of cost by changing public-private sector procurement. The headline proposals were to renationalise rail, energy, water and Royal Mail companies. Fracking would be banned. Twelve billion pounds of welfare benefit cuts would be frozen, tuition fees would be abolished and free lunches for primary school pupils would be paid for by removing the exemption on VAT for public school fees. This was a very striking set of spending proposals that were to be paid by £48.6 billion of extra tax taken from higher tax payers, corporation tax and attacking tax avoidance schemes. If nothing else, it had the claim to be optimistic and aggressive in the need to end austerity and attack deprivation. It had a lot of similarities with the New Labour manifesto of 1997. Where it differed was in the raising of income tax. Gordon Brown had taxed in many ways but always avoided this direct confrontation over the rewards for the rich. John McDonnell was going against forty years of political theory that stated voters wanted lower taxation.

The Conservative manifesto focused on 'Five great challenges'. They were: the need for a strong economy, Brexit, creating meritocracy, an ageing society and fast-changing technology. This document pledged to get immigration down below 100,000. It pledged more money to the NHS and education but removed free school meals to replace them with free school breakfasts. A marginal saving for no purpose other than to give Labour a huge stick to beat them. It pledged to reduce corporation tax to 17 per cent, increase income tax allowance to £12,500 and the higher rate to £50,000 by 2020. It aimed for a balanced budget and talked of governing from the mainstream. It focused on constitutional issues, strong defence and the rule of law. It also had a section entitled 'A restored contract between the generations' which included lifting the ban of grammar schools but the most dramatic proposals were about the elderly. It removed the triple lock on pensions, taking away the automatic 2.5 per cent annual increase and advocated a dramatic shift on social care. Free state help would be withdrawn from those with over £100,000 of assets including the family home. This was based on four times the level of means testing and would be paid after death. The winter fuel allowance for better off pensioners would also be scrapped.

The author of the report on social care, Sir Andrew Dilnot, had proposed that individual contributions of social care costs would be capped at £35,000. The Conservative manifesto had ignored this with a much more radical plan. He slammed their proposals, as did Jeremy Corbyn, who immediately dubbed it 'a dementia tax'. Another further sign that the Conservatives were assuming a landslide victory and as a sop to her backbenches, Theresa May proposed a new free vote on repealing the ban on fox hunting. On Brexit, the two parties disagreed on every issue within the proposed Great Repeal bill – on immigration, on workers' rights and on trade.

The immediate reaction to Labour's manifesto was that it was accused of profligacy, yet it didn't really matter as it couldn't win. Even Len McCluskey who, as he had become more influential had decided that his role as general secretary of Unite was also to be a political commentator, declared that victory would be extraordinary and that winning 200 seats (a net loss of twenty-nine) would be a successful result. In the interview with *Politico* he also supported the manifesto, attacked Theresa May's hard Brexit and blamed the media for attacking and undermining Corbyn's appeal. McCluskey stated: 'I'm not optimistic'.

However, the stronger reaction was against May's manifesto. Attacking one of the Conservatives' main support groups, the elderly, was not such a great idea. The dementia tax attracted vast amounts of criticism. It was revealed that May's policy advisor Nick Timothy had dropped the proposal into the manifesto at the last minute against the advice of the No. 10 policy unit. As reaction grew, Tory ministers being sent out to debate the policy realised that it was unsustainable and, by Monday 22 May, it was suddenly announced that a cap would be placed on the amount people would have to pay. This was obviously a U-turn but Theresa May, in the tradition of politicians in a hole, just kept on digging. She denied that it was a bad policy included by an unelected advocate and subsequently dropped it. It could almost have been a Labour party cock-up. The Conservatives were normally much more professional than this.

Slowly the polls were changing. Three polls taken by three different polling companies on 20, 21 and 22 May showed that Labour had risen to 34 per cent whilst the Conservatives had dropped to 47 per cent in one poll and 42 per cent in another. Although the lead was still large, it meant that Corbyn would surpass Labour's result in both 2010 and 2015 and that he was making inroads. He also gave a speech to Chatham House in which he addressed the biggest criticisms of his political background by laying out his principles on foreign policy. This included the creation of a minister for peace. He was not a pacifist, but he would not use nuclear weapons as a deterrent and he would not slavishly follow the Americans:

My generation grew up under the shadow of the cold war. On television, through the 1960s and into the seventies, the news was dominated by Vietnam. I was haunted by images of civilians fleeing chemical weapons used by the United States. I didn't imagine then that nearly fifty years later we would see chemical weapons still being used against innocent civilians.

What an abject failure. How is it that history keeps repeating itself? . . . Today the world is more unstable than even at the height of the cold war. The approach to international security we have been using since the 1990s has simply not worked.

Regime change wars in Afghanistan, Iraq, Libya, and Syria – and western interventions in Afghanistan, Somalia and Yemen – have failed in their own terms and made the world a more dangerous place.

This is the fourth general election in a row to be held while Britain is at war and our armed forces are in action in the Middle East and beyond. The fact is that the 'war on terror' which has driven these interventions has failed. They have not increased our security at home – just the opposite. And they have caused destabilisation and devastation abroad.

A week later on 22 May, and for the second time in a year, an election campaign was interrupted by an act of violence. A terrorist set off a suicide bomb of explosives and homemade shrapnel at Ariana Grande's concert in the Manchester Arena. Twenty-three people were killed and 139 injured, many of them teenagers and children. It was the worst attack since the July 2005 bombings in London. The major parties agreed to an immediate suspension of campaigning for four days. This was a disastrous attack and showed the enormous pressure that security and police forces were under. From a political perspective, Theresa May, with all her background in security and policing, should have been able to be the strong and secure leader she promised.

On 26 May, in the shadow of Manchester, Corbyn gave a second speech written by Seumas Milne and Andrew Murray on terrorism and security. He praised the emergency services and stated 'terrorists and their atrocious acts of cruelty and depravity will never divide us and will never prevail.' He defended Muslims. He defended his record in speaking to terrorist groups in the past, 'That will almost mean talking to people you profoundly disagree with.' He presented himself as a seeker of peace and conflict resolution. He argued that the emergency services and police cannot do their job facing the cuts, 'We cannot be protected on the cheap.'

He then talked about foreign policy:

> Many experts, including professionals in our intelligence and security services, have pointed to the connections between wars our government has supported or fought in other countries and terrorism here at home . . . The responsibility of government is ensuring the police have the resources they need, that our foreign policy reduces rather than increases the threat to this country and at home we never surrender the freedoms we have won, and that terrorists are so determined to take away. Too often government has got it wrong on all three counts.

The speech was immediately and predictably condemned by the Conservatives, but the combination of both speeches was enough to give Corbyn a position on security that could be defended for the rest of the campaign. This became even more relevant when there was a second terrorist attack on 3 June in London, when a van was driven at pedestrians on London Bridge by three terrorists, who then stabbed people in Borough Market. Eight people were killed and forty-eight injured before armed police shot the attackers. Once again, the campaign was halted, this time for two days, and on its resumption the Labour accusation that cuts to the police force, 19,000 under Theresa May as home secretary, had contributed to the security failures began to undermine May's assertion that she was the better prepared for the dangers of the modern world.

As the campaigns progressed they became two different battlegrounds. The physical meetings, speeches and personal images and appearances on the mainstream media, and the battle for the social media landscape that opened communications with millions of potential voters, especially younger voters. From 26 May to election day, the Labour campaign gained traction. Rallies and crowds got bigger and bigger. Corbyn became more at ease on the campaign trail and May became increasingly tense. He was speaking at open meetings, she at closed meetings.

Jeremy Corbyn not only enjoyed doing it, he *looked* like he enjoyed doing it. Rally after rally, meeting after meeting, he was doing what he enjoyed and the numbers were growing. Theresa May simply was not as good or as warm a speaker, nor was she as comfortable in front of crowds that might be uninterested or hostile. The tight group around Corbyn in LOTO had the advantage of knowing him well and knowing what he enjoyed.

The difference between the campaigns was also evident on mainstream media. A succession of televised debates took place, featuring the leaders of seven political parties in the name of balance. The only two in which Corbyn and May were in the same studio (but not at the same time) were in front of invited audiences and subject to interview by Jeremy Paxman on Sky and Channel 4 on 29 May, and David Dimbleby on BBC Television on 2 June. Paxman tried to recreate his bullying of Miliband from 2015 but neither Corbyn nor May rose to it. Arms crossed, glowering, he looked like a tetchy schoolmaster accusing May of being a 'blowhard collapsing at first sign of gunfire'. He attacked her for calling the general election, interrupted and played to the audience who laughed at her. On 31 May, five party leaders, but not Theresa May or Nicola Sturgeon, took part in a seven-way debate. May was pilloried for not attending and her surrogate, Home Secretary Amber Rudd, came under constant attack from all the others. By the BBC debate on 2 June, both leaders were under pressure from the public audience. May was accused of being a liar, of regretting calling the election, and of not getting into a debate. Corbyn was asked about his record on Northern Ireland and his position on the use of nuclear weapons. What was the reality of him ever exercising their use? Would he allow Iran or North Korea to bomb us first?

The key soundbite was Theresa May under attack about falling living standards, from a nurse of twenty-six years' experience, living on the same salary as 2009. May produced the line 'there isn't a magic money tree' which both patronised the nurse and infantilised the answer. This was the latest in a series of appearances where Corbyn had surpassed expectations and May had under-performed.

What about the new battleground of social media? An analysis by Matt Walsh of the London School of Economics makes fascinating reading. From the 19 April to 8 June the 'likes' on Facebook went as follows:

Labour Party 543,241 to 956,915; an increase of 76 per cent
Jeremy Corbyn 839,332 to 1,138,239; an increase of 35 per cent
Theresa May 343,562 to 419,094; an increase of 22 per cent
The Conservatives 565,915 to 629,277; an increase of 11 per cent

The sheer volume of output was not only double that of Conservatives, it also had more traction and was seen by more people. The Momentum campaign sat separately from the official Labour campaign and this is where Harry Hayball and his video maker, Paul Nicholson, came into their own. Momentum's numbers tracking the impact of their videos were highly detailed and specialised. Hayball was thrown into the deep end by Emma Rees, who explained:

There are probably very few other people who could say they've had the same kind of level of personal impact that Harry had. He had to learn so quickly, because it wasn't just the skills, it was also the political judgement, the way of communicating with people and the understanding of all these different things that were going on.

Hayball and Nicholson were to produce the most powerful piece of media of the whole campaign. Once the election started, they produced videos and assessed their impact and reach. This was judged on viewing for 3 seconds, 10 seconds or the whole video at 75 or 90 seconds. Harry Hayball:

I was interested in passive learning. Even at that level of just appearing on your feed, if you just saw and swung past Corbyn, it was good. I think that did have some impact. The same way it does when you walk past a newspaper stand and look over at the headlines. With social media, you have a very direct contact with people. So, you direct all the message without mediation, but it came with social endorsement, usually. It was your friends sharing and liking stuff, and that's how it appeared in your feed.

Hayball and Nicolson produced a video, 'Tory Britain in 2030 – Daddy, why do you hate me?' which was a huge hit. It purported to feature a father in 2030 explaining to his daughter why free school meals, small school classes and cheaper universities were a thing of the past. 'Why,' she asked, 'can't I have all that stuff?'

'Because I voted for Theresa May' he answered. It ended on the message: 'Vote Theresa May, because your children deserve worse,' and when asked, 'Dad do you hate me?' he replied, 'Obviously.'

Harry Hayball:

That was our biggest in the election. That had a reach of 17 million, and then video views were 8 million. That's a three second view. Then, about two and a half million watched it to the end, and 100,000 people shared it.

The level of impact of Momentum compared to the official Labour party videos was calculated as follows:

- The official campaign produced fifty-five videos, Momentum fifty-eight
- The official compaign had 10.5 million views, Momentum 13.9 million
- On the 3 second count the official campaign had 3.4 million uniques, Momentum 8.4 million
- On 10 second count the official campaign 1.6 million, Momentum 4.9 million
- On 35 second count the official campaign 820,000 uniques, Momentum 2.5 million

The impact of this campaign among social media users was enormous. The level of overlap was not that great as they were reaching slightly different audiences and retaining different levels of support, and Hayball's analysis showed that of Momentum's 8.4 million uniques compared to Corbyn's 3.4 million, only 1.6 million were shared. The longer people watched the video the less overlap there was. Momentum also added to the official campaign by creating apps to direct people to different constituencies and training new recruits in canvassing techniques. The guru for this was Beth Foster-Ogg:

> During the general election, I brought in four Bernie Sanders organisers, and we did the persuasive conversations training. My job was to get it done in as many marginals as possible. So, I had to coordinate these four Americans, one of whom had never left the US before, going around the country. Every day we trained a different large group in a marginal, then came back, gave feedback and sent them out again. I even did some of the training myself. The reason we got them was because of the 'wow' factor.

By the end of the campaign, Foster-Ogg had created training programmes for 3,000 activists and Momentum's app 'My Nearest Marginal' had been used by 100,000 supporters to go to different constituencies. A WhatsApp group on election day contacted 400,000 young people to get them to vote. All of which was necessary because the divisions between LOTO and the party machine in Southside were becoming much more evident throughout the campaign.

As the polling got tighter, more money was given by the major unions, led by Unite. The internal battle for resources within an election campaign is always difficult, but the 2017 campaign saw a degree of fighting between LOTO and Southside that was exceptional. Southside appeared to agree with Len McCluskey's original prediction of 200 seats being a good result, and this logic led them to a highly defensive strategy. After the election, the *Independent* published a detailed report showing that the Labour campaign was less effective at turning votes into seats than at any time since the 1950s. It drew its data from an organisation called Labour Roadmap which described itself as a data analytical organisation devoted to helping Labour win power. It showed that, despite taking 40 per cent of the vote, the efforts of the party and its voting went not into marginals but into Labour seats. In Labour-held seats, the favourable swing was 10.4 per cent; in seats held by other parties that might be winnable only 8.4 per cent.

Despite a few remarkable successes in Kensington and Canterbury, the impact of Corbyn's campaign was to solidify the Labour vote, but still be fifty-five seats behind the Conservatives. The debate remains whether this was due to Labour's gains being not enough to win or whether the allocation of money, effort and party support was misallocated. This was the accusation levelled at the party campaign: that money and resources were directed into mainly winnable seats rather than marginals. The allegation of the left is that those seats had Labour MPs who were less likely to support the leadership in the future. The other side of the argument was that Labour had to reinforce its defences and only in the last stages of the campaign did it appear that the Conservatives were not heading for a landslide. Rachel Godfrey Wood:

> We were aware of the same polls that the Labour party based that defensive strategy on. The places we were encouraging people to go to was like a fifty-fifty mix of defensive and offensive, which to me was quite sensible. Not that radical, right? But it was very important to demonstrate to people that 'Yes, we are going to win and there are places we can win. We're on the advance and this is how to do it.'

The polling in the last eight days of the campaign showed Conservative leads of anything from 2 per cent to 12 per cent depending on the poll. On 7 June, eight polling companies published the last polls of the campaign. Labour's lowest share of the vote was 33 to 35 per cent. Its highest was 38 to 40 per cent. The Conservatives were never lower than 41 per cent and one poll had them at 46 per cent. Would a switch of resources and campaigning effort have gained more seats? It almost certainly would have had an impact, but to overcome a fifty-five seat margin with the Conservatives consistently over 40 per cent would be impossible. The more important factor was the collapse of the vote of all the other parties.

On election day the shock result was announced. The Conservatives had failed to win an overall majority. From a position of total dominance in the polls at the start of the campaign it had a net loss of thirteen seats to 317, despite gaining 42.4 per cent of the vote and a swing of 5.5 per cent. Sensationally, Labour had gained a net thirty seats on 40 per cent of the poll, a gain over 2015 of 10 per cent to 262. It was the closest result between the two major parties since February 1974 and their highest combined vote since 1970. Jeremy Corbyn had won the highest number of votes (12.9 million) for Labour since 1997. He had achieved the highest percentage since 2001. It was the highest gain percentage from one election to another (10 per cent) since the historic victory of 1945.

Both parties were astonished by the result, though it was not difficult to know who was more damaged. On the eve of the most complex negotiation for any government in living memory, Theresa May had gambled on enhancing her authority and command of the House of Commons by calling an election that looked like a shoo-in. Now she had to struggle on with a divided party, no overall majority and her reputation for being a safe pair of hands badly impacted. She quickly cobbled together a deal with the Democratic Unionist Party (DUP) in Northern Ireland that gave her a slim working majority over all the other parties. The SNP had retained thirty-five seats, losing twenty-one to the other parties. UKIP went from 12.6 per cent to 1.8 per cent. Its bubble had burst. The Lib Dems from 7.9 per cent to 7.4 per cent and only 12 seats. Corbyn's third success in under two years was the most unexpected result of all.

31

Consolidation

For the first time since he decided to run in 2015, Jeremy Corbyn could look at the Labour party as his domain. He had confirmed his position as leader, had a shadow cabinet that was about as supportive as he could make it, albeit with a far greater level of inexperience than some of those now on the backbenches, and the membership was 564,000 in December 2017, an increase of 20,000 over the twelve months. This compared to an estimated 124,000 membership of the Conservative party.

Momentum was growing and would eventually have a membership of 41,000. Its constitution now gave it the basis for organised activity within the Labour party at every level. The internal focus would now be on consolidating control of the NEC at the party conference in September. In comparison, Theresa May now had the unpalatable role of leading a minority government in the most difficult task of any government for decades. The magic money tree had been shaken to put an extra billion pounds into Northern Ireland, which was without a devolved government after a long-running dispute involving the DUP. The Conservatives had replaced UKIP as the party of Brexit and anti-immigration and it was now partnered up with the most right-wing and most difficult of the parties in Northern Ireland.

May's political position that summer was of a lame duck leader who was only kept in office because of the impossible task of Brexit. It was negative strength. Her party could remove her at any time but that would trigger another damaging election process and it was better to let her endure. For the country, her lack of impact on the campaign trail had contrasted poorly to Corbyn's evident personal warmth and pleasure of being on the stump.

The contrast was made even more obvious by the Grenfell Tower disaster. Owned by Kensington and Chelsea council, one of the richest boroughs in London with a duty of care to their predominantly council-housing tenants, the Grenfell Tower burst into flames on the night of 14 June. It caused seventy-two deaths, seventy injuries and 223 people were evacuated to watch their homes burn. Dealing with the fire took all night and the efforts of 250 firefighters, seventy fire engines and 100 ambulance crews as the building's cladding fed rather than impeded the fire. A public enquiry was set up, but the political impact was immediate. Corbyn visited the site the following day and met the homeless families who were shocked by the death and injuries to their loved ones, as they sat in the shadow of the building. He was described as 'one of us' as he publicly hugged and spoke to residents. On the same day, Theresa May visited the firefighters and other emergency services but failed to meet a single resident. The disparity between the pictures of the two leaders was utterly damaging to her, but even more so was the lack of empathy she showed. It went beyond normal politics. As did the event ten days later when Jeremy Corbyn went to Glastonbury and wowed the crowd with a speech from the main stage. He was suddenly hip. The crowd responded by singing 'Ohhh, Jeremy Corbyn' for several minutes.

Over the next six weeks leading up to the party conference season, as Labour was still polling 40 per cent, it was very hard for Corbyn's internal party critics to attack him after the election result. The time had come to leverage this new reality in a new attempt to control the NEC and sort out other constitutional issues. The new shadow cabinet was beginning to focus on policy and, within the NEC, a number of key constitutional changes were enacted. Constituency representation had been set at six places for years. This was now increased to nine with three new members to be elected by OMOV in the following three months. One more union place would also be added and went to USDAW – the centrist shopworkers union. The seats occupied by the Scottish and Welsh parties were also debated given the controversy the previous year.

The leadership rules were examined, again, and the 15 per cent bar for nominations dropped to 10 per cent. This would apply to anyone standing, including a sitting leader. The key debate was whether nominations could be by groups other than the PLP allowing constituencies and trade unions to have a say in the initial nominating process. This would represent the final erosion of the PLP's power. The status of much of this would be examined in a review led by Katy Clark, a former MP and political secretary to Corbyn, to be reported at the 2018 conference. It was seen as the potential engine of much greater change and consolidation for the left. However, in the interim, the election of three new CLP representatives in November would mean the left had a solid majority on the NEC and, assuming the Scottish and Welsh parties and a representative of Black, Asian and Minority Ethnic (BAME) candidates could be elected by OMOV, the left would be in control for years to come.

Following the conference, the elections for the three new NEC places took place. Jon Lansman and two other members of the left slate were elected. They each received over 60,000 votes. The next candidate, Eddie Izzard, received just under 40,000. The left's electoral machine drawn from Momentum, CLPD and the Grassroot Alliance was now a proven operation. All nine representatives from the constituencies had been on the left slate. They included Pete Willsman and Christine Shawcroft as the long-standing representatives of CLPD and the GRA, Ann Black who occupied the role of conscience of the NEC and now, Jon Lansman, forty years after he had first lobbied members of the NEC in the toilets in Brighton to get support for the forty/thirty/thirty version of the electoral college. It had been a long road to political respectability.

If this voting bloc was significant, so was the departure of Emma Rees as national coordinator of Momentum. She and Adam Klug finally got their long holiday that had been interrupted in 2015. Her replacement was the multilingual Laura Parker who, after working for the EU in Bulgaria and Romania for six years as director of child protection and then in a variety of NGO positions, spent nineteen months in Corbyn's office as his private secretary. Parker was less rooted in the Labour movement, yet she was to take Momentum to the next phase of its development.

2017 had started with Momentum's internal strife, the loss of the by-election in Copeland, the Article 50 rebellion and terrible polls. It ended with a revitalised party with growing membership, a successful election campaign and Labour leading the polls against a minority government. 2018 was to be the start of the real Corbyn Labour party. This confidence was displayed in March 2018 when the long-awaited plan to remove Iain McNicol as general secretary of the Labour party was achieved with his elevation to the House of Lords. The general secretaryship could now be added to the list of appointments controlled by the left. The immediate front runner was Jennie Formby, a Unite appointment on the NEC and former political director of the union, and close friend and ally of Len McCluskey. Along with Karie Murphy and Andrew Murray, Unite's influence was becoming all-powerful within the highest ranks of the Labour party and reinforced McCluskey's personal influence as he increasingly waded in on Labour party matters. With Murphy and Formby in two pivotal jobs, his influence would only grow.

This produced the first cracks in the unity of the left. For three years, balance among the left groupings in the unions, the parliamentary party and the activists had been kept as they fought together for unified objectives. The unions had put substantial funds into the general election campaign, they had supported Corbyn over the chicken coup and they wanted control of key posts when they impacted on union influence. Momentum was the prime vehicle for the new entrants in the constituency parties that had been fundamental to Corbyn's success. It had been reformed, fought the election with its social media and activist operations, influenced the selection of candidates in seats for the election itself and now had elected representatives on the NEC. The left caucus of the NEC had around twenty-one members of an NEC of thirty-nine. The slate of left activists, the centre-left Grassroots Alliance, now had nine seats of which six were drawn from Momentum. It was the biggest voting bloc on the NEC.

For forty years, Jon Lansman had argued and fought for greater democracy within the Labour party. For him, this meant the ordinary membership would have a greater say over the organs of the party and policy. It was the foundation of the CLPD. Over the years it hadn't really mattered because any victory driven by the left was a good victory; union support was critical to securing those victories. Now they had won and he was on the NEC. It was time for the objectives to be met. Lansman had been known to push this agenda before – at the end of the 2015 leadership election he had been frozen out after arguing for mandatory reselection on *Newsnight*. However, emboldened by Momentum's contribution to the general election campaign and his own elevation, he was prepared to stand up for his principles again despite the annoyance this might cause.

He now found that command and control under a left leadership was pretty similar to that under any leadership. Centralisation of power would always be the goal of LOTO as the leader's office always wanted more control no matter who the leader was. Karie Murphy's reputation for being extremely controlling was already growing within the Labour movement. It was LOTO that engineered the removal of McNicol, and LOTO with Unite that was pushing for Formby to take the general secretaryship. Lansman saw that LOTO and Unite were too close and becoming too controlling. He floated the idea of challenging Formby for the general secretaryship:

> I was concerned about the process by which the general secretary was appointed. We actually had on the agenda a proposal for the general secretary to be elected. I wanted to see a democratic party. We had a mass membership party. I think you need to listen to your members and be responsive to the view of your members and you need to empower your members if you want to continue to engage them and be able to mobilise them in support of your objectives.

I felt at the time that it was being stitched up in the traditional Labour way, with a union putting in its nominee. Wasn't that exactly how every general secretary of the Labour party has been appointed for years? It wasn't about Jenny the person. It wasn't about who she worked for. It was the fact that nobody was consulted. The NEC is responsible for the government of the party. I don't want Labour leaders to run the party. I want the NEC on behalf of the membership and the affiliates to run the party.

Most members of the NEC wanted a proper process. Smaller unions wanted a proper process. I believe that in making a stand in favour of a proper process, I think I was speaking for the majority, the mainstream of the Labour party, which Momentum now represents. If we replaced a right-wing command and control structure with a left-wing command and control structure, we would piss off and lose the membership.

Under pressure from Corbyn and McDonnell, Lansman pulled away from the fight, but the point was made. The arguments in March were about positioning between the grassroots and the union establishment. This would become more obvious at the party conference in September, but in March it would be overtaken by a much bigger set of issues that would occupy the NEC, LOTO and Jeremy Corbyn for the next six months. The challenge now came from Corbyn's own past.

PART NINE

The Four Summers of Jeremy Corbyn: The Long, Hot Summer

'Jeremy Corbyn; Labour is not a threat to Jewish
life in Britain'
Guardian, 2018

32

The Baggage of the Past

After three years of success, there was bound to be a rebound. From the euphoria of winning the leadership, beating off the 2016 attempt to remove him and the surprise of the 2017 general election, Jeremy Corbyn and his supporters could afford to focus on solidifying their position within the party and prepare their appeal to the wider electorate. With Brexit occupying Theresa May's minority government, there was a genuine opportunity to push a new domestic agenda that would focus on the effects of austerity (now in its eighth year) that were becoming increasingly evident. Throughout 2018, independent reports into the state of Britain were emphasising the levels of deprivation and poverty among the worst off in society and the lack of opportunity for those in their twenties and thirties who had graduated with high levels of debt and no chance of meeting the aspirations such as home ownership that their parents had achieved in the 1980s. In December 2017, a Joseph Rowntree Foundation report stated that 14 million people in Britain, more than a fifth of the population, lived in poverty and 400,000 more children and 300,000 more pensioners were living in poverty than five years earlier.

Throughout 2018, other organisations such as the Institute of Public Policy Research's commission (that included the Archbishop of Canterbury) and a United Nations report on UK poverty followed up with further reports on the deepening levels of poverty. The UN report in November accused the government of being in state of denial about the impact of universal credit and the reduction of services from local government to the needy. On the day Theresa May had risen to the role of prime minister, she had talked about discrimination and one-nation conservatism and the focus of her government to be families that were 'just managing'. Two years later, with the distraction of Brexit and the longer-term impact of austerity, this intention had been lost. The 2017 general election further weakened her ability to craft an agenda outside getting Brexit through.

For Labour this should have been a political godsend. Its 2017 manifesto had firmly established the principle of tax and spend, there was no need to triangulate to lower taxes as New Labour and even Ed Miliband had done. Jeremy Corbyn, John McDonnell and the shadow cabinet could unashamedly declare they would tax more to spend more. However, despite this, the two major parties remained neck and neck in the polls. The doubts about Corbyn's leadership among the wider electorate were not going away and most of 2018 was going to reinforce those doubts over issues that were nothing to do with domestic economic policy and everything to do with issues of his particular past, as well as those of his closest advisors.

The issues that were to dog Jeremy Corbyn were rooted in his previous focus on international affairs. His views on Palestine, Israel and Zionism were to crystallise into accusations of antisemitism in 2018. This was compounded by his and Seumas Milne's response to the role of Russia and its attack in Salisbury in March 2018. The great shadow cast by Brexit came into sharp relief in 2018. All of these were rooted in the essential mystery Jeremy Corbyn was to most electors. Prior to 2015 he had no real public profile and indeed had not wanted one. For decades, he was known even within the left as an internationalist whose priorities were as much about Mexico as Manchester. No one in the political establishment had really focused on his actions because he occupied a small space on the left of British politics. Not off the radar, just under it. After 2017, when it appeared that Labour could win power with Jeremy Corbyn as prime minister, the attention fell on his beliefs.

As a backbench MP he had focused on many causes. Between 1989 and December 2015 he had signed 19,485 early day motions and acted as proposer of nearly two thousand. Within a bewildering range of interests, they demonstrated his overwhelming focus on overseas rather than domestic issues. A snapshot shows the following range:

Human rights: 61 times
Middle East: 49 times
International politics and government: 38 times
Africa: 30 times
Arms control: 29 times
Higher education: 19 times
Asia: 18 times
Students: 16 times
Latin America: 15 times
Industrial relations: 13 times

Like a lot of people on the left in the wilderness years, he ploughed his own furrow. In the early 1980s he, alongside Tony Benn, John McDonnell and Ken Livingstone, got stuck into the issue of Northern Ireland and support for Sinn Féin. Unlike them he also focused on conflicts in the Middle East, Latin America and Asia. Over the next thirty years he met with 'terrorists' or 'men of violence' and argued by so doing it paved the way for a peaceful resolution of a conflict. When events led to peace in Northern Ireland and the end of apartheid in South Africa he claimed to be on the right side of history and it further reinforced his sense of mission. His role in the Stop the War Coalition in 2001 against the invasion of Afghanistan and in 2003 over Iraq was founded on his vehement opposition to every western intervention undertaken since the second world war. His view of any action, always applied to the US and its allies including NATO, the UK and Israel was that western interventionism was actually western imperialism. His credentials were as an anti-imperialist, an anti-capitalist and a unilateralist. During the New Labour years, no one in the Labour leadership really cared what Jeremy Corbyn was doing. Hilary Armstrong, a former chief whip under Tony Blair, revealed in 2017 that Corbyn's habit of voting against New Labour had led some members of Islington North to plan his deselection. Tony Blair had vetoed the idea as he was no threat to the established political order.

Despite this level of activism, he had never really penetrated mainstream media and found outlets elsewhere. Over the years he was a regular on *Russia Today* (RT) along with Nigel Farage, George Galloway, Alex Salmond and Ken Livingstone. He had also appeared on the Iranian Press TV for which he was reportedly paid £20,000 between 2009 and 2012. OFCOM, the broadcasting regulator, then banned it from broadcasting in the UK. He appeared after the reports of the assassination of Osama Bin Laden both disputing whether he had been killed and then describing it as a tragedy along with all other acts of aggression.

One place he could rely on similar views to his own was in the *Guardian* through its comment editor and columnist, Seumas Milne, whom Corbyn hired to be his personal think tank, strategist and communication representative in 2015. This was a controversial appointment given Milne's revisionist views in support of the Soviet Union – even after 1989 when the Soviet bloc collapsed. Milne had sought to redress the portrayal by western historians of the Soviet era under Stalin. In 2014, he had appeared on a platform with Vladimir Putin in Sochi during a Valdai Discussion Club meeting. In one of his last articles for the *Guardian* before joining Corbyn's office in March 2015, he wrote about how Putin was undervalued in the west and the incursion over Ukraine was the fault of NATO and western imperialism. This slant was to be seen again in 2018.

Both Jeremy Corbyn and Seumas Milne also had long-standing views on the Palestinian conflict with Israel and both had campaigned in support of the Palestinians since the 1970s. Milne had travelled there as early as 1975 and when he arrived at Oxford University was a committed exponent of the 1975 UN resolution declaring Zionism to be racism. This was rescinded in 1991 but for anyone involved in left student politics in the

1970s, it was a common accusation against the state of Israel with anti-Zionism becoming directly equated with Palestinian rights. This increasingly became an argument, not about the actions of the Israeli state, but of its fundamental right to exist. As the 'Zionism is Racism' campaign started in the 1970s, so it became conflated with the anti-racism campaigns of the 1980s. The belief was that being anti-Zionist was acceptable because if you were also an anti-racist you couldn't, by definition, be antisemitic. These distinctions began to get very thin. In universities it led to the banning of Jewish societies. In 2005 the Israeli Apartheid Week began in Toronto and spread to campuses around the world. It accused Israel of being an apartheid state and built the Boycott, Divestment and Sanctions (BDS) campaign against it.

The Jewish community had always been an active player within the Labour movement. It started in 1903 with the formation of Poale Zion, later renamed the Jewish Labour Movement. Since 1945 there had been a long list of Labour MPs – both Jewish and non-Jewish – and Labour party leaders from Attlee to Brown, who had supported the state of Israel. Ed Miliband was the first Jewish leader of the Labour party and son of two Jewish immigrants. In 2017, nine members of the PLP were Jewish.

Despite this history, in the 1980s and 1990s hostility to the Jewish community from the left began to build. This was partially from its perceived support of political leaders whom the left despised. Several prominent Jews had supported Margaret Thatcher as MP in Finchley in north London. In the 1990s, this support switched to Tony Blair and Gordon Brown who were both strong advocates of Israel. For the left this demonstrated a consistent pattern of supporting the wrong people. Being a Blairite was as bad as being a Tory, particularly after Iraq in 2003. From 2015, the accusations of antisemitism were countered by descriptions of being a Blairite plot.

Israel itself had become much harder to defend after the collapse of the Oslo Accords of 1993 and 1995 with the subsequent assassination of Prime Minister Yitzhak Rabin. The second intifada of 2000-2005 saw violence escalate. Actions against Israelis by

Hamas in Israel and by Hezbollah in Lebanon were met by heavy retribution by the Israel Defense Forces. Hamas eventually became the governing party of Gaza with Fatah controlling the West Bank. The population of the two enclaves was estimated to be 4.5 million living in terrible conditions, especially in Gaza. After years of intermittent clashes in 2009, Israel reacted to Hamas rockets fired from Gaza and used overwhelming force from land, air and sea. Hundreds were killed. The bloodshed led to a series of rallies, mainly organised by the Stop the War Coalition in support of Gaza and Hamas. The attacks on Gaza were condemned as 'a wanton act of aggression by Israel' by both Jeremy Corbyn and Seumas Milne who reiterated support for Hamas in a rally in Hyde Park:

> The media and politicians in this country and all over the western world would have you believe that the cause of this suffering and this carnage is the rockets of Hamas that are fired into Israel. That is to turn reality on its head. The Palestinian people have the right, as any occupied people under law and under all political and legal conventions, the right to resist. Israel, as an illegal occupying power, has one obligation, and that is to withdraw. Even now, despite the horrific casualties, Hamas is not broken and will not be broken, because of the spirit of resistance of the Palestinian people.

It is worth noting that the Covenant of Hamas states that 'Israel will exist and will continue to exist until Islam will obliterate it' and that 'There is no solution for the Palestinian problem except by Jihad.'

During the various rallies that month, representatives of Hamas and Hezbollah were invited to the House of Commons by Jeremy Corbyn and described as friends. This action in 2009 was entirely in keeping with his record as a backbench MP of appearing with people and on forms of social media that would later come back to haunt him. One example was 'Palestinian Live', a closed Facebook group that an undercover researcher penetrated and exposed. It included links to Holocaust deniers, allegations about

Israel being involved in 9/11 and supporting ISIS, and (a repeated theme) conspiracy theories involving the Rothschild family – a longstanding antisemitic trope dating back to the Nazis. Corbyn was in Palestinian Live, but later claimed without his knowledge. This would become a favoured line of defence.

After he became front runner in the Labour leadership race the first public clash between Jeremy Corbyn and the Jewish community came in August 2015 from the Jewish press – *The Jewish Chronicle* and *Jewish News*. The *JC* was edited by Stephen Pollard whose politics could not be more different from those of Jeremy Corbyn. On 12 August 2015, Pollard fired the first shots in this war by publishing a list of questions concerning Corbyn's past associations with accused anti-Semites ending with:

It is difficult not to see a pattern in Mr Corbyn's associations, and his refusal at any point to answer the fears of the Jewish community raised by these associations. In a nation where, thank heavens, racism and extremism are now regarded as beyond the pale, it is little short of astonishing that a man who chooses to associate with racists and extremists is about to become leader of one of our two main parties and could conceivably become prime minister.

At the same time, *Jewish News* published evidence that Corbyn supported BDS. Despite this, there was some hope that getting elected to the leadership would allow some flexibility to reach an accord and Corbyn agreed to address a hustings at the Jewish centre, JW3, in north London during the leadership campaign. One Jewish Labour member said:

I sat in front of him when he did the Jewish hustings at JW3 where he made no apologies for anything he said. It was very stark in terms of his views and what his position is. He has very little, if not zero, understanding or appreciation for what 21st century antisemitism looks like and that it's even an issue.

Over the six months after his victory, an uneasy truce held within the PLP. The membership had vastly increased, social media was an open forum for many views and gave the new entrants in Labour a voice. As new members joined from a variety of leftist political backgrounds, there was a slow but rising tide of antisemitic comments spewing out on social media: comparing Israeli actions to those of the Nazis and the treatment of the Palestinians to the holocaust; an obsession with the Rothschilds as 'a Frankenstein monster working with the US and Israel'; the image of the star of David, the Israeli flag and a rat captioned 'the real plague'; and the accusation that ISIS was a plant of Israel. A growing number of cases began to be referred to the Labour party's disciplinary process through its disputes panel and then the National Constitutional Committee. This poison was getting into the mainstream and, after two people were expelled for antisemitism, came to a head in March 2016 when the respected journalist Jonathan Freedland published an article in the *Guardian* entitled 'Labour and the left have an antisemitism problem' after two expulsions for antisemitic trolls:

> I suspect many in Labour and on the wider left dearly wish three things to be true of this problem. That these are just a few bad apples in an otherwise pristine barrel; that these incidents aren't actually about racism at all but concern only opposition to Israel; and that none of this reflects negatively on Jeremy Corbyn.

But this did not stand up to the overt antisemitism of some of the attacks, or the levels of abuse experienced by many in the party:

> Which brings us to Jeremy Corbyn. No one accuses him of being an anti-Semite. But many Jews do worry that his past instinct, when faced with potential allies whom he deemed sound on Palestine, was to overlook whatever nastiness they might have uttered about Jews, even when that extended to Holocaust denial or the blood libel – the medieval calumny that Jews baked bread using the blood of gentile children.

Thanks to Corbyn, the Labour party is expanding, attracting many leftists who would previously have rejected it or been rejected by it. Among those are people with hostile views of Jews, two of whom have been kicked out, but only after they had first been readmitted and once their cases had attracted unwelcome external scrutiny.

The question for Labour now is whether any of this matters. To those at the top, maybe it doesn't. But it feels like a painful loss to a small community that once looked to Labour as its natural home – and which is fast reaching the glum conclusion that Labour has become a cold house for Jews.

At the very least this article could be taken as a clarion call – Freedland was no right-wing supporter of Israel. Jeremy Corbyn's reaction was captured on camera by the *Vice* television crew that had been following him. He described the article as 'utterly disgusting subliminal nastiness'. He wasn't getting the message. This was then compounded by two incidents involving national figures. Naz Shah had defeated George Galloway in Bradford West. She was a representative of the New Left in the House of Commons and a member of the shadow Treasury team as well as the Home Office select committee. She wrote three Facebook posts arguing for Israel's population to be 'transported' out of the Middle East to the US, asking for an online poll to see if Israel had committed war crimes and comparing Israel to Nazi Germany. She resigned from the frontbench and was then suspended from the party. In an interview with the BBC's World at One she insisted that she 'wasn't antisemitic' but conceded 'what I put out was antisemitic', which was unusually honest. In 2017 she met representatives of the Board of Deputies in Bradford and tried to bridge the gap. This produced a response by one of them: 'Naz Shah is one of the only people involved in Labour's antisemitism crisis who has sought to make amends for her actions, and for this we commend her and now regard Naz as a sincere friend of our community.'

Ken Livingstone then decided to wade in. For years he had been in and out of the limelight, finally losing power in London in 2008 but still hanging onto some influence on the left. He had always been the leader of the pack and now he had to endure watching his former deputy John McDonnell and ally Jeremy Corbyn taking all the glory. However, he had taken a role as cheerleader for the new regime and was supposed to be running a review of defence policy. He went on his LBC radio show and alleged that Hitler supported sending Jews to Israel: 'He was supporting Zionism before he went mad and ended up killing six million Jews'. He repeated it in numerous interviews throughout the day and was then fired by LBC. The media captured Labour MP John Mann shouting at him in the street. The NEC decided to suspend rather than expel Livingstone. He refused to apologise and, when asked about this incident on camera, Jeremy Corbyn icily refused to answer whether he condemned the remarks. Instead, Labour set up an enquiry into antisemitism to be conducted by well-known barrister and director of Liberty, Shami Chakrabarti who promptly announced she was joining the Labour party and, in August, accepted a life peerage recommended by Corbyn. It was hoped her report might be enough to relieve the pressure of the issue within the party. It was the first serious public attempt to deal with the accusations of antisemitism. She was respected, it might work. Her report was published on 30 June 2016 in the middle of the chicken coup. She wrote:

> The Labour party is not overrun by antisemitism, Islamophobia or other forms of racism. Further, it is the party that initiated every single United Kingdom race equality law. However, as with wider society, there is too much clear evidence (going back some years) of minority hateful or ignorant attitudes and behaviours festering within a sometimes bitter incivility of discourse.

She went on to condemn the use of terms like 'Zio' which was being used on social media as an abusive slang word for 'Jew' and the stereotypes against Jewish people. She recommended better trained staff, a general counsel for the Labour party, a readily accessible complaints procedure, a greater role for the NCC and no lifetime bans – only two-year suspensions. It was seen as an attempt at compromise but also fairly feeble in addressing the problem. Events at the press conference to launch the report itself then demonstrated the size of the problem. At the launch, Corbyn appeared to compare the Israeli government of Netanyahu to Islamic extremists, which didn't quite sit with the report that had suggested resisting making comparisons of this type. Ruth Smeeth, a Jewish MP, walked out in tears after a row with Marc Wadsworth, a black anti-racist activist and Momentum supporter, about her receiving a press release from the *Daily Telegraph*, an action that he alleged was 'colluding with the media'. She called on Jeremy Corbyn to resign for his failure to intervene. Wadsworth was suspended from the Labour party (of which he had been a member for one month).

This incident reaffirmed the view of Corbyn's opponents that he was supportive of attacks on them by the left and reinforced the views of his supporters that he was under attack. It unleashed a full-scale social media assault on Smeeth that was becoming typical of the toxicity of the issue. In one particularly vicious piece in the *Electronic Intifada*, Tony Greenstein wrote 'UK Labour MP Ruth Smeeth was funded by Israel lobby' and spoke of her being 'a mistress of the house talking to her uppity black servant'. He went on: 'This tantrum and the orchestrated hysterics which followed were deliberately designed to destabilise the Report and focus attention on the false antisemitism narrative.' Greenstein, who described himself as a socialist, anti-Zionist and anti-racist was going to have a part in this saga again in the next two years when he was expelled. He was one of a number of Jewish anti-Zionist leftists who were to become increasingly vocal in defence of Corbyn.

For the rest of that summer, Jeremy Corbyn was engaged in fighting the second leadership election where the battle lines between the left and its opponents became even more divisive. By September, his victory was assured and most of his opponents had resigned. On social media, accusations of treachery were levelled against Blairites and any other perceived opponents. More and more members of the party were being referred to the disciplinary panel for antisemitism as they blamed 'Blairite' conspiracies for the accusations against Corbyn himself. The sheer volume of

It stated that Jeremy Corbyn was asked about his and Seumas Milne's past associations.

> In the face of questioning about his relationships with a number of individuals associated with antisemitism, Mr Corbyn defended himself on various grounds – in some cases, by denying that he was aware that those individuals had made antisemitic remarks. Mr Corbyn was specifically challenged about the views of his executive director of strategy and communications, Seumas Milne, who had been filmed at a demonstration in 2009 at which he said that Hamas 'will not be broken' due to the 'spirit of resistance of the Palestinian people.' Mr Corbyn told the committee that he did not think it 'appropriate' for him to be asked questions about the views of 'every single member of staff' he employs, and said that he had not seen the video concerned, but described Mr Milne as a man of 'immense intellect' and a 'scholar'.

On Shami Chakrabarti, the report was damning about her agreement to be the author of the report, accept a peerage and then join the shadow cabinet. It concluded that:

> While the Labour leader has a proud record of campaigning against many types of racism, based on the evidence we have received we are not persuaded that he fully appreciates the distinct nature of post-second world war antisemitism.

It noted that the attacks on his fellow Labour MPs were ignored.

> . . . including antisemitic death threats from individuals purporting to be supporters of Mr Corbyn. Clearly, the Labour leader is not directly responsible for abuse committed in his name, but we believe that his lack of consistent leadership on this issue, and his reluctance to separate antisemitism from other forms of racism, has created what some have referred to as a 'safe space' for those with vile attitudes towards Jewish

people. . . . The failure of the Labour party to deal consistently and effectively with antisemitic incidents in recent years risks lending force to allegations that elements of the Labour movement are institutionally antisemitic.

No one, after reading this, could be ignorant of the potential damage being done. One way to resolve it would be by fast and effective clearance of disciplinary cases concerned with racial abuse and antisemitism, but this did not happen. The 2017 Labour conference did offer one olive branch when it gave the Jewish Labour Movement (JLM) the Del Singh award for best practice as an affiliated organisation, and was presented by Jeremy Corbyn to Louise Ellman. It then agreed a rule change proposed by JLM to strengthen Labour's position on prejudicial behaviour and appeared to be some sort of rapprochement. Unfortunately, it was immediately undermined by the Jewish anti-Zionists who were the most vocal opponents of Israel. At the 2017 conference, they set up Jewish Voice for Labour to be both the anti-Zionist alternative to the JLM and fervent defenders of Jeremy Corbyn. In the side meeting, there was a call for Labour friends of Israel and the JLM to be expelled from the Labour party. The noise on this issue was going to get louder throughout the summer of 2018.

33

The Dialogue of the Deaf

If arguments about antisemitism were temporarily subdued in early 2018, another problem was about to emerge, one rooted in the history of the leader's office. On 4 March, two Russian intelligence officers arrived in Salisbury in Wiltshire to place Novichok, a virulent nerve agent, on the door handle of former Russian double agent and defector, Sergei Skripal. His daughter, Yulia, had arrived from Russia to visit him the previous day. By 4.15 p.m. the Skripals were found slumped on a park bench by a police officer who also became contaminated. In July, two people were additionally affected after finding the bottle in which the virus had been transported. One died, such was the virulence of the nerve agent and the seriousness of the attack.

On 12 March, Theresa May's statement to the House of Commons explained that the Novichok had been manufactured in the Soviet Union in the 1980s: the use of a nerve agent contravened almost every unwritten code of the intelligence agencies. She described it as a 'despicable and reckless act' and she was giving the Russian state, as opposed to rogue individuals, a deadline to explain its apparent actions. She stated that 'the government has concluded that it was highly likely that Russia was responsible.' May called on the international community to condemn Russia. This was a moment in the House of Commons when the government of the day and leading opposition parties would normally agree to condemn an attack on British citizens and mutually condemn the perpetrators. Instead, Jeremy Corbyn opened by condemning the attack but asking for a 'robust dialogue' with Russia and then associated the attack with Russian oligarchs living in London who had contributed £800,000 of donations to the Conservative party. No condemnation of Russia from the Labour leader, just an obfuscation.

As the parliamentary debate continued, Seumas Milne was briefing journalists and, like Corbyn, avoided any criticism of the Russian government. He benchmarked it against the false intelligence that led to the Iraq war in 2003 and the existence of Russian oligarchs in the UK. The Labour leader and LOTO were not going to condemn Russia. Labour MPs at Westminster including Chuka Umunna, Anna Turley and Mike Gapes took to Twitter to criticise both Corbyn and Milne. The national press piled in the following day. In the short term, the Conservatives moved ahead of the Labour in the polls and in an opinion poll on 13 March, Theresa May's personal ratings on who would make best prime minister moved to 34 per cent over Jeremy Corbyn's 26 per cent. Her handling of the Salisbury attack was approved by 41 per cent of those polled, compared to Corbyn's 16 per cent. Fifty-six per cent of those polled wanted Russian diplomats to be expelled and 49 per cent wanted *Russia Today* taken off air. Only months later did Corbyn and LOTO accept the fact that Russia was directly involved, despite in the days following the poisoning, both Emily Thornberry and John McDonnell accepting the case against it.

If that wasn't enough to undermine the public perception of Jeremy Corbyn, the same month the accusation of antisemitism raised its head again. In 2012, a decision had been made by Tower Hamlets council in London's East End to paint over a mural on a wall. This was an overtly antisemitic portrayal of a Monopoly board resting on the backs of naked workers whilst bankers, described by its painter as 'made up of Jewish and white Anglos', sat at the table. In 2012, the artist had complained on Facebook that his work was being removed. Jeremy Corbyn had responded with 'Why. You are in good company. Rockerfeller [sic] destroyed Diego Viera's mural because it included a picture of Lenin.'

Despite *The Jewish Chronicle* publishing it in 2015 the story remained dormant until 2018 when it was resurrected on Twitter. On Friday 23 March, Luciana Berger repeatedly tried to raise it with Jeremy Corbyn and his private office. LOTO went into its normal defensive position. By 2 p.m. she tweeted:

I asked the leader's office for an explanation about this Facebook post first thing this morning. I'm still waiting for a response.

Later that day a spokesman replied 'In 2012, Jeremy was responding to concerns about the removal of public arts on the grounds of freedom of speech. However, the mural was offensive, used antisemitic imagery which has no place in our society and it is right it was removed.' This occurred the same afternoon that Corbyn sacked Owen Smith, his rival in 2016 for the leadership, from the frontbench for daring to suggest another referendum on Brexit.

Over the weekend, fury grew, both over Corbyn's 2012 tweet and LOTO's failure in 2018 to answer Berger. The Jewish Board of Deputies and Jewish Leadership Council called a demonstration against antisemitism in Parliament Square at 5.30 p.m. on Monday in which they also intended to deliver a letter to the leader since the PLP had its regular meeting on a Monday. Over the weekend Tom Watson apologised on behalf of the party and Corbyn expressed sincere regret that he hadn't looked at the mural closely enough and that he opposed the production of antisemitic material of any kind.

This whole episode can be seen as a precursor of all the problems to come later that summer. The original calls to his office might have alerted Corbyn or his senior staff to the fact that there was a problem; they failed to respond in any adequate way. If you weren't an ally – and Luciana Berger was definitely not perceived as an ally – they would simply cut you off and fail to respond. The insulation of the leader was their priority and default position. It was a pattern to be repeated throughout the next six months.

On Monday 26 March, hundreds turned up for the demonstration. They included MPs such as David Lammy, John Woodcock, John Mann and Stella Creasy, who were not Jewish. Luciana Berger, Wes Streeting and John Mann all spoke in front of placards stating 'Dayenu #EnoughisEnough'. Across the square the new Jewish Voice for Labour tried to mount a rival demonstration, calling it all a smear against Corbyn.

Leaving the demonstration, Berger went to the PLP meeting in which she not only repeated her speech, but berated her fellow MPs by saying that it was no use people expressing private support for her, she wanted public support. This was greeted by a standing ovation from everyone except the frontbench who sat stony-faced. In a later interview, Jeremy Corbyn condemned the abuse that was being hurled at Labour MPs at the demonstration and rejected the argument that it had been about smearing him, but by now the bloggers in his defence were focused on the idea that accusations of antisemitism were a Blairite plot to challenge him.

The lack of clarity in Labour's disciplinary structures was being questioned. The party had a disputes panel selected from members of the NEC, with Christine Shawcroft as its chair for the previous six years. It was her role to refer cases for expulsion or suspension to the separately elected National Constitution Committee. This cumbersome process was not designed for dozens of referrals for antisemitism. She had also been caught up in a row about Tony Greenstein, who had attacked Ruth Smeeth in 2016, was expelled for antisemitism, readmitted and then resuspended. She had acted as his 'silent friend' in his most recent hearing despite being chair of the committee. Shawcroft was forced to step down after an email emerged showing she had questioned the suspension of a council candidate who had engaged in holocaust denial, despite not having seen the Facebook post in which he made the claim. She then wrote a post saying the antisemitism row was 'being stirred up to attack Jeremy'. Forty Labour MPs and peers signed a letter demanding she should leave the NEC itself. She was replaced as chair by Claudia Webbe, an Islington councillor and ally of Ken Livingstone and Jeremy Corbyn.

The division was now clear. The extreme levels of abuse overwhelmed any discussion about the rights or wrongs of the Palestine issue. Within the mainstream of the left this was a huge problem. Having worked for years to get the project off the ground, having built a political campaign around the candidacy of Jeremy Corbyn and having fought off challenges from the Blairite and centrist left, it was now faced with either defending the project's new army of supporters, or pretending that the abuse it wasn't really happening. Its main suggestion was that political education against antisemitism would guide people away from this form of abuse.

On 2 April, Momentum got ahead of the official party and issued its own statement: 'Momentum acknowledges the anger, upset and despair within the British Jewish community at the numerous cases of antisemitism in the Labour party.' It went on to condemn the party's:

> . . . failure to date to deal with them in a sufficiently decisive, swift and transparent manner. Current examples of antisemitism within the Labour party are not only a problem of a few, extreme 'bad apples', but also of unconscious bias, which manifests itself in varied, nuanced and subtle ways and is more widespread in the Labour party than many of us had understood even a few months ago.

Momentum also said that while Corbyn's opponents were 'opportunistically using this issue as a way to undermine his leadership', this did not reduce the need to challenge antisemitism. Laura Parker was by then the national Coordinator of Momentum:

> I think on antisemitism we took a very mature approach. Having Jon Lansman as our chair meant that he personally was in a very difficult position. He was getting antisemitic crap. He was getting people expecting him to defend the leadership, to attack the leadership, to have all sorts of opinions. A lot of it, because he's Jewish. And at one point I remember saying to him,

'This is unfair. You happen to be Jewish, that doesn't mean you're responsible for answering to all of this.'

We just took two breaths. We wanted to recognise that there was a problem, full stop. There was also a political manipulation. Full stop. You can acknowledge both of those things without denying the first. We would say something measured and balanced which we would attempt to position in a slightly different place, a better place. Because the party was handling it badly. Then we made a commitment to doing some awareness raising and training for our own membership.

On 17 April, the House of Commons held a debate on antisemitism in front of the deputy speaker and former Labour chief whip, Rosie Winterton. Luciana Berger and Ruth Smeeth delivered powerful speeches including the scale of abuse they had received. Accused of being agents of the CIA, Mossad, and MI5; vile Zionist bitches, threatened with abuse and violence; and that was only the material they felt could be revealed in public. In private, the scale of attacks against them and Louise Ellman were such that examples were referred to the police. The following week Jeremy Corbyn met with Jewish leaders but did not commit to helping to fight this form of extremism. One report of his meeting with the Jewish representatives said he simply shrugged when told that he was failing to sufficiently criticise the waves of abuse from his supporters. 'He has this habit of just staring and just shrugging,' one said.

The next morning Ruth Smeeth walked to the disciplinary hearing of Marc Wadsworth, escorted by fifty Labour MPs and peers. On arriving at the hearing, she was heckled by protesters and accused of being part of a witch-hunt. The ugliness was getting out of control. Wadsworth was expelled. Then Len McCluskey got involved. He wrote an article for the *New Statesman* on 25 April that widened the gulf even further.

After the usual declaration that the few people of antisemitic views should be expelled from the party he launched into an attack on 'the activity of a few dozen Labour MPs who appear to wake up each morning thinking "how can I undermine Jeremy Corbyn today?"' He linked the MPs who had voted against Corbyn over Syria in 2015 with 'those who work overtime in trying to present the Labour party as a morass of misogyny, antisemitism and bullying'. They were 'a dismal chorus whose every dirge make winning a Labour government more difficult.' He named various MPs but then attacked the leader of Israel's Labour party for severing relations with Corbyn's office. He called this a 'cynical and outrageous smear' and wrote 'I look with disgust at the behaviours of Corbyn-hater MPs who join forces with the most reactionary elements of the media establishment and I understand why there is a growing demand for mandatory reselection'. Given his close relationship with LOTO, this two-page article could be to be taken as a semi-official response to the protests about abuse aimed at Jewish MPs. The threat of mandatory reselection sprang off the page. Attack had become the best form of defence; calling it all a Blairite plot gave cover to those engaged in the abuse, which itself continued.

On 3 May 2018, local elections took place and resulted in Labour narrowly gaining in seats but saw the major parties get the same percentage vote – 35 per cent. The impact of antisemitism was displayed in Labour's failure to win Barnet council in north London. The Conservatives were in a quagmire over Brexit and May's failure to gain a majority in 2017 to retain a parliamentary majority yet Labour could not get a breakthrough.

In May, Ken Livingstone finally resigned from the party rather than be expelled. He claimed he was doing it to stop being a distraction, that he was loyal to Corbyn and was no anti-Semite. Corbyn in return made no comment. One of his most persistent followers, Chris Williamson MP, immediately called Livingstone a towering figure of the Labour movement. Williamson later announced he would be doing his own road trip to constituencies advocating mandatory reselection of sitting MPs whom he considered enemies of the Corbyn project. He also shared a Jewish Voice for Labour platform with the expelled Toby Greenstein at the 2018 Labour party conference.

It is difficult to image how things could have got much worse but, in July, a succession of different events combined to take the whole issue into the open and turned Corbyn's fourth summer into a disaster. The impact of the daily events moved from the dozens of disciplinary cases that were getting bogged down in Labour's arcane processes to a wider set of accusations about him. The NEC started to discuss whether the party should adopt the International Holocaust Remembrance Alliance (IHRA) code. This was to take on a symbolic importance quite beyond anything that was expected. The IHRA was first discussed on 3 July at the NEC's Organisational Committee. Adopting the code was an opportunity to rebuild trust. Its definition of antisemitism that had been adopted by thirty-one countries and numerous organisations. It states:

> Antisemitism is a certain perception of Jews, which may be expressed as hatred toward Jews. Rhetorical and physical manifestations of antisemitism are directed toward Jewish or non-Jewish individuals and/or their property, toward Jewish community institutions and religious facilities.

This was not disputed by the organisation committee, but the IHRA guidelines had also included eleven examples as guidelines. Labour decided to keep the first six and then start to remove and amend the rest. It could be argued that some of Labour's amended examples were an improvement – for instance it included examples of abuse such as 'yid', 'kike' and physical descriptions of Jews, talking about them as the ruling classes and references to 'Jewish bankers' etc. Where the changes are much more politically charged and ambiguous is in the treatment of Israel. The two key clauses of the IHRA were:

1. Denying the Jewish people their right to self-determination, e.g., by claiming that the existence of a State of Israel is a racist endeavour.
2. Applying double standards by requiring of it a behaviour not expected or demanded of any other.

These were replaced by the Labour party by much longer clauses that sought to allow more wiggle room about 'the nature of discourse' of the right to self-determination of the Jewish and other peoples. On the foundation of the State of Israel, the party wanted the clear assertion that it was not racist to assess:

> The circumstances of the foundation of the Israeli State (for example, in the context of its impact on the Palestinian people) including critical comment on – differential impact of Israeli laws or policies on different people within its population or that of neighbouring territories.

And on the term Zionist:

> The term 'Zionism' is intimately bound up in the history of Israel's foundation as a State and in its role in international relations more generally. It is inevitable that the expressions 'Zionism' and 'Zionist' will feature in political discourse about these topics. The meaning of these expressions is itself debated. It is not antisemitism to refer to 'Zionism' and 'Zionists' as part of a considered discussion about the Israeli State.

By adding more language and more complexity, the Labour party thought it was covering itself over anti-Zionism and attacking antisemitism. It didn't recognise the problems with this approach: the Jewish organisations and MPs who had been under sustained attack had no trust left. No rewrite was going to be acceptable without a lot of discussion and explanation beforehand. Jennie Formby as general secretary claimed she had consulted them. The NEC moved to approve this amended set of guidelines. The Jewish Labour Movement wrote to it threatening legal action and disputing it had read in full or agreed the amended definitions. No one was prepared to meet and discuss amending this new code. The Labour party was fixed into its processes and taking a fully defensive posture.

On 12 July, Jon Lansman wrote in the *Guardian* supporting the new guidelines with the headline 'Labour's antisemitism code is the gold standard for political parties'. Lansman was in a box. He was the creator of the 'project', he was as responsible as anyone for Corbyn's rise; he had created Momentum and he was on the NEC. He was also a lapsed but interested Jew, a visitor to Israel and had suffered antisemitism. He defended the new wording on the basis that the IHRA was not sufficiently clear; that legitimate criticism of Israel policies should not be silenced. He attacked the Jewish organisations who did not 'have the credibility to criticise a political party's robust, thorough and far-reaching code of conduct'. Which 'provides clarity, context and detail.' His last paragraph read:

> Conflating legitimate criticism of Israel with antisemitism is dangerous and undermines the fight against antisemitism. Clear and detailed guidelines are essential to ensure that antisemitism isn't tolerated, while protecting free speech on Israel's conduct within a respectful and civil environment. This is what Labour's code of conduct provides. We should be celebrating and replicating it.

The following week brought these conflicting positions into hard divisions. On Monday 16 July, the PLP met and voted overwhelmingly for the original IHRA code to be enacted. This was now supported by a wide range of MPs from the middle ground of the party such as Keir Starmer and Tom Watson. Neither Jeremy Corbyn nor Jennie Formby were at the meeting. Ed Miliband now spoke in support of the IHRA code. Richard Burden, the chair of the All-party group on Palestine, voted against adopting it on the basis it was against stifling legitimate debate over Israel and Palestine. The actual wording of the various codes had ceased to be relevant, it had become a far more symbolic issue.

That day more than sixty British Rabbis, from all sections of the Jewish community and who normally would not be agreeing with one another, wrote to the *Guardian* condemning the new code. At a three hour NEC meeting, a row broke out in which CLPD's Pete Willsman asked for a show of hands for those who had ever witnessed antisemitism in the Labour party and accused some Jewish people of being Trump fanatics making up evidence since 'social media can be falsified very easily'. Despite attempts to close him down, he continued to rant on. He was on the disputes panel that had been monitoring all the disciplinary cases. It was recorded and later leaked from the NEC meeting. Jon Lansman and Tom Watson both opposed him and Watson tweeted 'For the avoidance of doubt, Willsman has always been a loudmouth bully. He disgusts me.' When the recording was released, Corbyn and others were criticised for not stopping him. In fact, they were all so used to his behaviour that they had just ignored him.

The NEC approved the new code without a vote, but it opened up the idea of new consultations with Jewish groups. It also agreed to consider more than fifty disciplinary cases in September to try to speed up its internal processes. The lack of understanding implicit in agreeing the code, yet still holding it open for further discussion as a sop, showed that the NEC simply did not understand how bad the situation had become. Wes Streeting, the chair of the All-party parliamentary group of British Jews, called it an 'utterly contemptible decision'.

That night, parliament was engaged in a series of knife-edge votes on Brexit. The central lobby was packed with MPs, visitors, and journalists as MPs trooped in and out of the chamber. During a lull in the voting, Jeremy Corbyn was approached by Margaret Hodge who accused him of being a racist and anti-Semite. Afterwards, she repeatedly denied swearing at him and declared she was frustrated by his habit of failing to engage on the issue, 'I chose to confront Jeremy directly and personally to express my anger and outrage. I stand by my actions and my words'. She was referred to the general secretary on a disciplinary charge which, of all the misplaced actions that summer, was about the most ill-conceived. Margaret

Hodge was not only up for a fight, she also had extremely good legal representation. She wrote:

> I joined the Labour party to fight racism. In the 1960s the Labour party was the natural home for Jews. To find myself fifty years later, in 2018, confronting antisemitism in my own party is completely and utterly awful. How have we got here? Under Jeremy's leadership, the Palestinian/Israeli conflict has been allowed to infect the party's approach to growing antisemitism. It appears to have become a legitimate price that the leadership is willing to pay for pursuing the longstanding cause of Palestinians in the Middle East. Because of that, antisemitism has become a real problem in the Labour party. In the last year, my colleagues and I have been subjected to a growing number of antisemitic attacks on Facebook, Twitter and in the post.

A second Labour MP, Ian Austin, the adopted son of Jewish holocaust survivors, was also referred for having a row with the Labour party chair, Ian Lavery. The following week, on the day before parliament rose, the PLP discussed the IHRA code. Ruth Smeeth and Louise Ellman had proposed absorbing the original code into the standing orders and as this required a ballot, it had to be deferred to September. Outside LOTO's bunker the wider left was beginning to realise that this needed to be sorted out. On 23 July the three newspapers of the Jewish community published a common front page. *The Jewish Chronicle, Jewish News* and *Jewish Telegraph* jointly declared 'United we stand'. Their joint editorial read: 'We do so because of the existential threat to Jewish life in this country that would be posed by a Jeremy Corbyn-led government.'

The Israeli government also played its part in the growing bitterness. In July it passed a bill that stated that only Jewish people had the right to self-determination in the State of Israel. Liberal Jews around the world condemned this as a clear act of prejudice and accused Israel of acting as an apartheid state.

On the same day as the three Jewish newspapers condemned Corbyn, Daniel Barenboim, the conductor and pianist, condemned Israel for:

> A law that confirms the Arab population as second-class citizens. It follows that this is a very clear form of apartheid. I don't think the Jewish people lived for 20 centuries, mostly through persecution and enduring endless cruelties, in order to become the oppressors, inflicting cruelty on others. This new law does exactly that. Therefore, I am ashamed of being an Israeli today.

The country was divided over Brexit, the government was weak and vulnerable, and Labour was plunged into a dispute that was spreading into hundreds of disciplinary cases, an NEC at odds with the PLP, with a leader accused of being a racist anti-Semite by a highly respected veteran MP and of posing an existential threat to Jewish people. It was now impossible to describe this purely as a Blairite plot.

The more attuned members of the left project were recognising that this was an impossible situation and, despite defending the Labour version of the code as Lansman had done in July, were hoping for a respite. In the first week of August, as *The Jewish Chronicle* published the audio clip of Pete Willsman's rant at the NEC, Momentum decided to drop him from its slate for the NEC. This was the first split within the left groups on the slate. CLPD, now a rump under Willsman's chairmanship, decided to go on supporting him. Voting for the slate had already started and no one knew whether he would get on when the votes were declared in September.

Behind the scenes, peace overtures were being made. John McDonnell was beginning to publicly move away from LOTO by engaging on the issue. *The Times* reported on 31 July that he met Jeremy Corbyn to suggest dropping the fight with Margaret Hodge. Other shadow cabinet members and leaders of the left were highly uncomfortable about the problem. Andrew Murray, the old campaigner from the Stop the War Coalition was reported to advise Corbyn to go back to the IHRA code and, on 1 August, Ian Austin MP wrote a blistering attack in the *Evening Standard* citing the numerous examples of antisemitism within the party. Even LOTO in the bunker realised that it had to do something and tried to respond with a statement by Jeremy Corbyn on 3 August published at 5.30 p.m. He started by responding to the three Jewish newspapers:

> I do not for one moment accept that a Labour government would represent any kind of threat, let alone an 'existential threat', to Jewish life in Britain, as three Jewish newspapers recently claimed. That is the kind of overheated rhetoric that can surface during emotional political debates. But I do acknowledge there is a real problem that Labour is working to overcome.

He accepted the Labour party had been too slow in dealing with disciplinary cases and needed to address the issues and finally stated:

> People who dish out antisemitic poison need to understand: you do not do it in my name. You are not my supporters and have no place in our movement.

But he failed to pull back from Labour's new version of the IHRA code while accepting that it should have been more widely consulted. This was his first attempt to address the Jewish community on its specific concerns, but it was already a problem. The response was published on Friday evening at precisely 5:30 p.m. when most practising Jews would not be reading the *Guardian* website. It was also spotted that some of it was lifted from an earlier piece in the *Evening Standard* in April; a cut and paste version of a statement of contrition posted on Friday night. This was not great. His defence of the new Labour party version of IHRA was the key point in the article. The *Guardian* summed it up in an extraordinary headline: 'Jeremy Corbyn: Labour is not a threat to Jewish life in Britain'.

In the background, Labour meetings such as 'Arise – a festival of the Labour left' were holding meetings in which the Palestinian cause was getting more and more support and groups like the Jewish Voice for Labour claimed that Corbyn was being smeared. A Blairite plot was still being alleged and anyone arguing with the narrative was under attack from the social media. Tom Watson gave an interview in which he stated that the Labour party would face eternal shame over antisemitism and the attacks on Margaret Hodge and Ian Austin should be dropped. This resulted in 50,000 tweets calling on him to quit under the twitter hashtag #ResignWatson.

It was clear that the IHRA code would be adopted within the PLP but unclear what the NEC would do in September. Would anyone back down? The plot thickened once more and two stories from Jeremy Corbyn's past rose up. On 10 August, the *Daily Mail* revisited the story printed in the *Sunday Times* during the 2017 general election and published pictures from 2014 of Jeremy Corbyn at the Hammam al Chatt cemetery in Tunis. He had been attending a conference hosted by the Palestine National Authority which, while it had representatives from many Palestinian groups who were recognised by the UN as legitimate representatives, it also included members of known terrorist organisations. The organisers invited him to lay a wreath at the cemetery that had the graves of those whom the Palestine Liberation Organisation (PLO) regarded as martyrs. In 2014 he declared he was laying a wreath to commemorate forty-seven people killed in an Israeli raid on the PLO in 1985. In 2018 the *Daily Mail* alleged he was actually at a memorial of the three men from the group Black September who killed eleven Israeli athletes in Munich at the Olympics in 1972, an act or terror condemned by the world.

Corbyn was attacked by the Israeli Prime Minister and first defended himself by saying he was present but not involved with the wreath laying. The problem was that the picture showed him holding the wreath itself. Later that week *The Times* revealed that the man standing directly behind him was Maher al-Taher, the leader-in-exile of the Popular Front for the Liberation of Palestine (PFLP) who, a month after the photo was taken, claimed responsibility for an axe and knife attack at a synagogue in Jerusalem in which four rabbis, one of whom was British, were killed during morning prayers. The PFLP was a known terrorist organisation and had been declared as such by the EU two years before Corbyn stood a few feet from its leader-in-exile.

As the condemnations flew in and LOTO struggled with its leader's response, the fundamental fact had to be recognised that Corbyn's ability to ignore unpleasant facts about websites, online supporters, attendees at conferences and other places where his name had been freely used was no longer being accepted as pure naivety. The harsher judgement was that he just did not care and, since he was irrelevant in mainstream politics before 2015, no one had noticed. They certainly cared in the summer of 2018. He was pilloried in the mainstream media and the search was now on for other examples of his past associations.

Two weeks later a video was released showing him at a meeting in 2013. He was speaking at the Palestine Centre in which earlier there had been an altercation between two British Zionists and the Palestinian National Authority's official representative, Manuel Hassassian. In the video Corbyn said of the two Zionists who had challenged the ambassador:

> They clearly have two problems. One is that they don't want to study history, and secondly, having lived in this country for a very long time, probably all their lives, don't understand English irony either. Manuel does understand English irony and uses it very effectively. So I think they needed two lessons, which we can perhaps help them with.

On the face of it, he couldn't have pressed the antisemitic button any harder. If by Zionists he meant Jews, he was engaging in a classic attack on Jews not being truly British – the perennial outsiders who could never be accepted. It was ripe for condemnation. One of the two men stated his family had been in Britain for over one hundred years. MPs rushed to condemn the remarks. In yet another statement issued on a Friday night, he said that he did not use the term 'Zionist' as a euphemism for 'Jewish' and he was simply defending the Palestinian ambassador from attack.

The challenges to him were not just over the issue of antisemitism. It was an emotive issue and caused the greatest response from both sides, but the wider scope of objection was over his whole international focus. Stephen Kinnock, who was elected a new MP in 2015 characterises the wilder aspects of Corbyn's supporters on social media:

The big conspiracy theories that drive the section of the party that supports Jeremy are around the EU being a Neo-liberal plot and around the shady cabal of Jewish financiers. Some of that is connected to Palestine and Israel but I actually think it's more about an anti-capitalist narrative, in the way in which the capitalist system is run.

Kinnock was not going to leave the Labour party but the suspicion in the summer of 2018 was that a group of Labour MPs were looking at antisemitism, Brexit and the threat of mandatory reselection and saw four more years before a general election in which they would suffer at the hands of the left and be a battered minority. This was reminiscent of 1980 when the gang of four left to create the SDP. The difference was that there was no substantial leadership of this group of potential defectors. MPs such as Chuka Umunna and Chris Leslie were rumoured to be holding meetings, but they were not Roy Jenkins or Shirley Williams. Umunna also accused the Labour party of being an institutionally racist party. It was enough to conflate the row about antisemitism with accusations of treachery and a Blairite plot.

Margaret Hodge's lawyers fired letters to Jennie Formby that were published on Twitter. LOTO took the strategy of ignoring the row about the Tunis picture and the 2013 video, and the issue of the IHRA code was still hanging over the NEC and PLP. Finally, moves were made to solve the problems by figures outside the leader's office. John McDonnell, Jon Lansman and the leaders of the three largest unions – GMB, Unite and Unison – were all giving advice. The accusations against Hodge, which had never been clearly defined, were dropped. It took until November for the charges against Ian Austin to be dropped. The union leaders stated that the original IHRA code should be adopted at the next NEC meeting. This did not stop Len McCluskey from again attacking the leaders of the Jewish organisations for 'truculent' hostility against Corbyn. In the same article he attacked Chuka Umunna for using the antisemitism row to ferment a new political party and denied the accusation of racism against Labour.

Corbyn himself tried to move on by giving a speech on media policy at the Edinburgh television festival. Of course, none of this would change opinions about Jeremy Corbyn himself. At the end of the month the former Chief Rabbi, Jonathan Sacks, used the *New Statesman* to up the rhetoric. He attacked Corbyn as being antisemitic and compared his comments on the video from 2013 to Enoch Powell's 'rivers of blood' speech of 1968 in that it 'undermines the existence of an entire group of British citizens by depicting them as essentially alien.' For anyone old enough to remember Powell's speech, this was an attack of real potency. It had been levelled against new waves of Commonwealth immigrants from the West Indies and Indian subcontinent and had provoked years of racial conflict. It was a unique example of a mainstream politician, as Powell then was, engaging in incitement to violence against groups based on the colour of their skin. The attack by Sacks was quite specific and extreme. It produced a backlash in Corbyn's favour. It also demonstrated that the rhetoric over Palestine, Israel and antisemitism were not just confined to the wilder shores of social media. Everyone was out of rhetorical control and there was no obvious way to go back.

By the first week of September it was clear that the NEC would have to change its stance on the IHRA. The Jewish Labour Movement met on 2 September. In a series of sessions Jon Lansman attended and used the 'unconscious bias' explanation to argue that education could address some level of antisemitism. The audience were not having it. Luciana Berger, Louise Ellman and other Jewish politicians talked about their experiences of the last month. Margaret Hodge gave an extraordinary interview describing her row (without swearing) with Corbyn and its aftermath. The most dramatic intervention came from Gordon Brown who made a rare public speech in which he demanded the party adopted the whole IHRA code, talked about his own and his father's commitment to Israel, the lack of consultation with the Jewish community over the code, and about the attacks through social media. It was, he declared, about the soul of the Labour party. Jeremy Corbyn had to get a grip on it.

Two days later the NEC met and, just to show how remote Corbyn was on this issue, there was one final act of defiance from him. By now everyone wanted to move on from the row over the IHRA code. There was unity except from the leader himself. He produced a statement trying to mitigate it. It agreed the full original code but then added the attachment that it shouldn't be regarded as antisemitic to describe Israel, its policies and the circumstances around its foundation as racist. This not only went directly against the IHRA illustration it reopened all the arguments of the summer and it appeared to act as a justification of the views of Corbyn and Milne over the previous twenty years. It was a sign that he had not accepted any of the criticisms, even from his own side.

Members of the NEC were reported as telling him to withdraw. These included Jon Lansman and Rhea Wolfson, both Jewish and both of the Momentum slate. They were joined by Tom Watson, Ann Black and Eddie Izzard. This was enough to get a compromise that the NEC would not accept the amendment but would welcome further consultation over the code after conference. Furthermore, that any legitimate criticism of Israel and the Palestinian question was still welcome.

No vote to accept the IHRA code into the Labour party code of conduct was actually taken. Like Tom Watson at the start of August, Jon Lansman now came under sustained attack on social media for betrayal, both for dropping Pete Willsman from the Momentum slate and for this latest lack of support for Corbyn. The following week the PLP voted in a secret ballot to adopt the code. There were eight votes against. On 19 September the NEC met again and agreed to speed up handling of antisemitism cases. This would mean doubling the size of the National Constitutional Committee by adding fourteen places that would be elected in the autumn.

The whole episode over antisemitism could be regarded as a storm in a teacup involving relatively few people and not politically significant against other issues of the day, such as Brexit. Yet it was a telling insight into the character and problems around Jeremy Corbyn and his new movement. The sheer weight of social media was a phenomenon over which no one had any control. Throughout 2018, attacks on anyone perceived to be outside the Corbyn project were fair game. This even extended to Tom Watson and Jon Lansman when they fell foul of the modern day sans-culottes.

Jeremy Corbyn showed that at the age of sixty-nine, he was not prepared to explain his past. No one had paid any attention before he became leader. To explain his past connections by saying he didn't know was much more difficult when under the public spotlight. He and his close staff also showed that they were unused to public exposure and playing defence. The sheer lack of intelligent response to criticism, the Friday night statements and the lack of transparency were the fault of his office and himself. They were born of the traditional response of small groups on the left and right to ignore all criticism. If you ignore critics, they will go away. A refusal to respond was the default position of many of these groups, and in the world of the left, ignoring and deflecting attacks was a normal position. This was combined with Corbyn's personal default position since becoming leader, which was to be charming in private but silent in public, especially when it came to his army of social media supporters and their more extreme behaviour. One example that stood out was when Rosie Duffield, the Labour MP for Canterbury where the Conservatives lost the seat for the first time since 1885, came under attack from six Momentum supporters who had passed a motion of no confidence in her for attending a rally against antisemitism. Her colleagues in the House of Commons and Momentum stopped it. Corbyn wrote to her privately to offer support but when it came to a public show of support, he was not prepared to do it. As she said in an interview in the *Guardian*:

> It would be really nice if Jeremy could help each MP going through this with a personal statement, to make it clear that people – even those who do it without knowing it – don't do it in his name. I am not an anti-Corbyn MP just because I am standing up to antisemitism. That is a really clear line we could adopt.

Corbyn's failure in 2018 was one of leadership. To see him among supporters is to show that he loved the adulation. The failure to lead those supporters away from the attacks on his political enemies was an aspect of being in the wilderness for so long. He didn't want to give an inch, which had the effect of making him an enabler for those attacks; silence in public merely exacerbated the problem. His speech when elected leader in 2015 talked about a different type of politics. No matter how difficult he found Luciana Berger, she had to have a police escort to Labour party conference in 2018 as a Labour MP. He gave the impression that he simply didn't know it was happening. One MP said:

> The kind and gentle politics is just words and it's absolutely meaningless because, in my seventeen years in the Labour party, I've never seen it this bad. It's toxic, so toxic. It's really unpleasant. It's also physically present in meetings. It comes through in every

single form, it's not just Twitter, we get it in the post as well and people call our offices. Someone's been arrested for the abuse that they've directed at my staff, let alone at me.

For the left it was a problem of perception and action. Laura Parker, even in September 2018, was holding to the theory that the attacks on Corbyn were part of a wider agenda:

> I think someone else's grid was antisemitism, unconscious bias and an internal opposition that would exploit any weakness such as antisemitism or Brexit. It was not thought through by the leadership. 'Not in my name' should have been much more decisive. . . . We have hard line activists some of whom are Jewish using Zionism as an attack.

One of the differences between Momentum and the Labour party was Momentum's ability to challenge the online abuse head-on. If the Labour party was to take this issue seriously it needed online community engagement officers who can police it. Harry Hayball:

> Momentum as the grassroots movement can take a more proactive role, call out anti-Semites and exclude them from online communities and oppose them. We can call out anti-Semites unlike the Labour party which hasn't taken social media seriously enough.

For Jon Lansman, this had been a wake-up call.

> The number of disciplinary cases of abuse had been a dozen a year and it was now hundreds and women got the worst of it. One of the things that troubled me was whether this was something just lurking unseen or created by the process. We sent people on courses to recognise prejudices and overcome 'unconscious bias' against Jews that people didn't seem to recognise. I think everybody was guilty of doing too little too late. I didn't realise

that it was as big a problem as it is. We have to own up to antisemitism, deal with it, wake up and recognise it. The Jewish anti-Zionist left was deeply damaged in this because they denied the existence of the problem. There was clearly a problem of perception in the Jewish community.

The issue of antisemitism had dominated Jeremy Corbyn's fourth summer. Now, the party conference of 2018 would seek to redress the political balance back towards Labour's policies, internal fights over the democracy review and Brexit.

34

The Wheel Turns

After the summer dominated by antisemitism, the Labour party conference in Liverpool acted as a decompression chamber. There were big issues to debate and resolve and one, Labour's response to Brexit, would be critical in determining events throughout the Autumn. However, the conference itself encompassed other issues that had arisen since 2015. It included policy announcements from John McDonnell and other frontbench speakers focusing on the programme for a future Labour government; it had the results of the democracy review that was supposed to be the culmination of the battle for Labour party democracy started forty years earlier; it had demonstrations supporting Palestine and the alternative conference in TWT. It was the necessary resetting of Labour's appeal to its members and the wider electorate.

Before the conference started, the NEC considered Katy Clark's proposals for constitutional change. In 1982, the trade union barons had stopped the advance of the left, and thirty-five years of political wilderness had followed. In the run-up to the 2018 conference, the world was a very different place. Jeremy Corbyn was leader, Momentum was established with 42,000 members and 180,000 supporters and the Labour party membership had a membership of 550,000. The left had triumphed. Even in the NEC elections, despite being dropped from the 'JC9' slate of the left, Pete Willsman was re-elected over both Eddie Izzard and the capable and long-serving Ann Black. A left candidate could win even if the slate didn't want him to.

The democracy review was a link between CLPD's campaign in the 1970s and Momentum in 2018. Laura Parker saw it:

> Rebalancing power in the party so individual members have a greater say on the NEC and in constituencies. The promise of Corbynism was that we would do politics differently.

For months, the review had been gathering data and it was expected that on the two great issues of the 1970s and 1980s – mandatory reselection and election of the leader – the final acts in the drama would be enacted. CLPD had won mandatory reselection of MPs in 1979 but as part of the Kinnock era this had been watered down in 1990. After 2015 it had come up again with the re-emergence of the left. Momentum had campaigned extensively for open reselection; described by Laura Parker as a 'rebranding of mandatory reselection' which meant every MP would have to face a challenge in every parliament; just like CLPD had wanted in 1974. It would be hard for the left to complain too much about the election of the leader after the Collins report of 2014 and two subsequent elections of Jeremy Corbyn. However, it also wanted the rules changed so that any part of the Labour movement, the constituencies and unions as well as MPs, could nominate a leadership candidate and with 10 per cent of the nomination, a candidate could stand. The challenge, as in 1982, was the great culture clash at the heart of the left, between the grassroots and the union establishment. In 2015, the party was opened up to a flood of new members who used social media as a form of communication in which they all had an individual voice. Momentum, as a grassroots organisation, had to accommodate, manage and reflect many disparate opinions. It would be difficult to find a culture more at odds with the traditional unions. As Laura Parker put it:

> It's two different cultures. In Momentum, where you don't have to be in a group to participate and you can make your voice heard,

and in the unions where you have collective decision making, a line and discipline. That's their bedrock. It's a contradiction in the way you do politics. Not right or wrong but different positions that have to be accommodated.

Jon Lansman's challenge to Unite in March over the Labour party general secretaryship was an example of the grassroots challenging the control of the unions over a key post. Momentum's desire for more change was not necessarily going to sit well with the unions or even LOTO.

In the run-up to conference, the democracy review was delivered very late to the NEC. Most of the recommendations were, in time-honoured Labour party tradition, too complex to be decided and were pushed on to the 2019 conference. Some rule changes reinforced the power of the left, including the decision to allow a new election for any vacancy that appeared in the NEC itself. The traditional rule had been that in the case of any resignation, such as Christine Shawcroft's in March, the first-placed loser would automatically step up – as Eddie Izzard had done. Changing the rule to allow for a new election would mean the left could win. This was the result of the lessons learned in the early 1980s when the left had lost power; when you have the machine do not allow any loss of your grip on it. This now exceeded anything that New Labour had attempted. Pete Willsman and Christine Shawcroft had been elected as token leftists in the 1990s and now it would be impossible for anyone to get elected against the dominant group in the party.

The NEC also finally approved the IHRA with all eleven examples, and the National Constitution Committee would be increased from eleven to twenty-five members to handle the rising tide of disciplinary cases. This was a sign that the five big unions were taking control. They would have fourteen seats on the NCC. There was also a discussion about creating a second deputy leadership post for only women candidates, although this was hastily dropped during the conference.

The reassertion of union weight was also seen when the demands for open reselection were substantially watered down. The NEC agreed that a selection process would only be triggered if a third of local party members, or a third of trade union branches voted to have a contest. Although this theoretically reduced the threshold from 50 per cent to 33 per cent for a reselection to happen it made it much more complicated and was not what Momentum wanted at all. The left representatives ended up accepting it without a vote.

On the election of leader, Momentum had flooded out the NEC with its calls for an equal threshold of 10 per cent from any part of the party to nominate a candidate. MPs would theoretically have no say at all in who might be chosen. This was now changed to a candidate needing 10 per cent of MPs plus 5 per cent of constituency parties or trade unions, which actually raised the bar. The unions had flexed their muscle with the leader's support. In the conference itself, Unite was attacked at by outraged delegates and even Jon Lansman at TWT had to lay down the law to his own grassroots. There were shouts of betrayal from the floor of conference and at the TWT, just like in the good old days.

Despite these apparent defeats, the dominance of the left was reflected throughout the conference. It had a slew of policy statements by the new generation of Labour leaders: Angela Rayner, Rebecca Long-Bailey and Jonathan Ashworth, who all staked their claims for the future. However the main statement was inevitably by John McDonnell, as the principle agent of the leadership's strategy. Almost all his commitments on nationalisation and tax had been made in the 2017 manifesto, he denounced the levels of poverty and destitution that had been revealed in the recent Institute of Public Policy Research report. In a speech that was reminiscent of the days of Tony Benn and the left's economic plan of the 1970s he proposed giving workers in public companies of over 250 staff a 10 per cent stake that would give them a dividend of £500 per annum after shares were transferred into an 'Inclusive Ownership Fund'. He proposed that the balance of value after the dividends were taken would be used by government in public services. In other words, it would be new tax. This was a radical plan. It was one thing for workers to have seats and a vote on the boards of public companies, but it was quite another for a new tax to be levied on those public companies. It was the first sign that McDonnell's previous charm offensive to business might come under strain.

Aside from economic policy, the other major event in the hall was when Emily Thornbury gave her speech as shadow foreign secretary, although it wasn't her speech that attracted the headlines. Outside the hall, the Labour Party Marxists handed out a newspaper with the banner headline, 'Why Israel is a racist state' and pro-Palestine protestors handed out hundreds of Palestinian flags. Thornberry's speech was interrupted by hundreds of flags being waved in the hall.

TWT also had its fair share of the ranting and excesses that were very much a feature of the fringe meetings of yesteryear. The inevitable Chris Williamson recreated the 1980s 'Labour against the Witch-Hunts' which used to be about defending Militant but now saw him defending Jackie Walker and Tony Greenstein after their expulsions. And Laura Smith, a new, young MP, decided to call for a general strike for the first time in ninety years if a general election was not called. This was greeted by a standing ovation from Richard Burgon, Labour's justice spokesman. They were swiftly denied by the Labour leadership.

Jeremy Corbyn's leader's speech summed all this up. He proclaimed labour as a mass party that was now funded properly by its members. He attacked the media and finally accepted the need to fight antisemitism head-on, whilst also proclaiming that Labour would recognise a Palestinian state on getting into office. He focused on his real appeal: attacking poverty and deprivation. On Europe, all options were on the table but he offered to support the government if a deal was reached that included a customs deal and a soft border for Northern Ireland. In short, he was not the Jeremy Corbyn of three years earlier. The journey from 2015 through the election of 2017 had empowered him. The confidence of the conference was sky high. The political agenda was set for the next six months, when the only certainty would be uncertainty over Brexit, which would dominate everything.

PART TEN

Brexit and Beyond

35

The Shadow of Brexit

Overshadowing all of this was Europe – the issue that had been toxic within the Conservative party since 1971, but within Labour had lain relatively dormant up to 2015. That was about to change.

For the Conservatives, Brexit kept demonstrating the burden of unexpected consequences. In 2010, David Cameron wanted the Fixed-Term Parliaments Act to bind the Lib Dems into the coalition. No one imagined that eight years later it would mean a minority Conservative government losing a key vote by a historic margin, yet still managing to stay in office. On succeeding Cameron in July 2016, Theresa May would repeatedly commit to actions that backfired on her. From appointing Brexit supporters David Davis and Boris Johnson to the jobs of Brexit secretary and foreign secretary, through calling the 2017 general election and failing to win a majority, May spent the years 2017 to 2019 in office, yet barely in power. Brexit eclipsed everything for her and, despite his best efforts to avoid it, for Jeremy Corbyn.

May's basic assumption from the start was that the executive should unilaterally control as much as possible to force Brexit through; an approach that was challenged almost immediately by a businesswoman, Gina Miller, who won her case in the Supreme Court that parliament must approve the triggering of Article 50. This coincided with May laying out her core objectives and principles of negotiation with the EU in her Lancaster House speech on 17 January 2017. It included twelve objectives for the smooth transition out of the EU. The first was 'certainty' and crucially this included the confirmation that 'the government will put the final deal that is agreed between the UK and the EU to a vote in both Houses of Parliament, before it comes into force'. On 15 January 2019, almost two years to the day, this 'meaningful vote' was overwhelmingly lost.

Theresa May's other stated objectives included three issues that were to return repeatedly over the following two years. First, the challenge of the Irish border – the common travel area with Ireland. Second, control of immigration – she had a long-standing fixation with this subject from her days as home secretary. Finally, free trade with European markets, which she qualified by saying 'what I'm proposing cannot mean membership of the single market'. These red lines would become her red barriers with both European and UK politicians as the Brexit process unfolded.

For the Labour leadership, Europe was primarily an issue to be left as much as possible to the Conservatives. In Ed Miliband's 2015 manifesto, he argued the need to reform Europe from within, but held out no real prospect for a referendum. Harriet Harman, as Labour's acting leader, supported Cameron's referendum bill. The 2016 referendum campaign showed the new leadership's reluctance to campaign in support of Remain alongside David Cameron and their Blairite opponents within the party. Jeremy Corbyn, Seumas Milne and some of the members of the shadow cabinet such as Jon Trickett, who were old enough to have supported the left's anti-EEC campaign in 1975, were always at odds with those drawn from the New Labour cabinets of yesteryear who were in favour of Remain.

The principal and official campaign to stay in the EU in 2016 was 'Britain Stronger in Europe'. This was the latest manifestation of the big tent of centrist politics stretching back to Roy Jenkins in 1971, 1975 and through the New Labour years. It was run by Will Straw and had a cross-party board including Lib Dems such as Sir Danny Alexander, New Labour potentates such as Peter

Mandelson and pro-European Conservatives such as Damian Green MP. It was chaired by Sir Stuart Rose. Campaigning alongside David Cameron and George Osborne, it would have made a great coalition government twenty years earlier. When the referendum was lost, it became 'Open Britain' and featured Peter Mandelson, Roland Rudd (a city PR millionaire and brother of Conservative cabinet member Amber Rudd), James McGrory, a former Lib Dem spin doctor, Nick Clegg and Nicky Morgan, a former Conservative education secretary who had been fired by Theresa May. This group pledged to campaign to remain in the single market and for a final parliamentary vote on any deal. In 2017, up to twenty people would regularly gather to discuss two issues: how to mitigate Brexit and, for the New Labour members, how to fight Jeremy Corbyn.

A fledging left organisation in favour of staying in Europe had a small role in the referendum campaign as an alternative. Another Europe is Possible (AEIP) came from the left in 2015, and its founding statement described it as an organisation 'across the spectrum of the progressive left, working across party political lines to campaign for democracy, human rights and social justice'. It had a few committed activists who had sprung from the student and anti-austerity movements in 2010 and joined the Labour party as part of the great influx of 2015. Michael Chessum was a student activist who had become part of the early Momentum steering group in late 2015 and simultaneously helped create AEIP. As it became clear that there would be a referendum, Chessum and a few allies decided that there had to be an independent left campaign to focus on the moral issue of free movement challenging the mainstream narrative. Michael Chessum:

> The idea started immediately after the 2015 general election when a few people decided that the mainstream Remain campaigns were going to be terrible. David Cameron was going to call a referendum at some point. It wasn't clear when. We thought we had a couple of years to get our act together. It turned out, no. The referendum was going to happen very quickly indeed.

Which put him at odds with the official Remain campaign.

> If free movement's your moral issue, who's got the best record on that? The answer is not the old New Labour establishment. We watched them sell migrants down the river.

This push from the left had only four full- and part-time staff and no real funding or structure.

> We organised the biggest event of the Remain campaign. A big conference with John McDonnell and all the rest of it. And we organised a speaker tour with the likes of Owen Jones, Caroline Lucas and Clive Lewis. Our two big core groups were Momentum, which affiliated to us in the course of the campaign, and we ended up being based in Momentum's offices, and the Green party.

When the referendum was lost and the result accepted by Jeremy Corbyn, attention moved away from Brexit to the chicken coup and second leadership election. Within Momentum, Jon Lansman's successful launch of a new constitution in January 2017 led to a split with Chessum who opposed it and would go on to focus on AEIP rather than Momentum.

Gina Miller's legal victory provoked Theresa May to activate Article 50 as fast as possible. Once approved by parliament, the departure deadline would be established in law. It was never considered that preparing the negotiating ground before enacting Article 50 might be a better approach and that if a deal failed to be negotiated in good time, it would place huge pressure at the end of the process against a hard deadline. May and Brexit Secretary David Davis' negotiating strategy was to threaten the possibility of the chaos of no deal whilst trying to find allies among twenty-seven governments who could be used to put pressure on the EU Commission's negotiators. This fallacy continued for the next two years as the EU held remarkably firm to a collective and consistent approach on all the key issues, especially the Irish border.

Article 50 exposed Labour's fault line. On the first vote of the bill on 1 February 2017, 114 MPs voted against it, including forty-seven from Labour who defied a three-line whip. The House of Lords passed two amendments that would have guaranteed the rights of EU nationals living in the UK and allow parliament a veto over the outcome of the Brexit talks. Both of these were voted down when the bill went back to the House of Commons. Theresa May now had her Brexit with two years to negotiate a deal. The deadline, which looked a long way away, was 29 March 2019. Jeremy Corbyn stated in the House of Commons:

> Article 50 is being triggered because of the result of the EU referendum. But it is only the start of the process. Labour, at every stage, will challenge the government's plans for a bargain-basement Brexit with Labour's alternative of a Brexit that puts jobs, living standards and rights first.

This was Corbyn's tacit acceptance of Brexit. It was reinforced by the creation of six tests for Labour to support any Brexit deal, which were formulated by Sir Keir Starmer. Although only elected to parliament in 2015, he had a distinguished career as a barrister, a Queen's Counsel and, for five years, as director of public prosecutions. He was not a natural supporter of the Corbynista left but was given the challenge of shadowing David Davis and the newly-formed Department for Exiting the European Union. He also had the unenviable job of evolving Labour's position in face of the scepticism of Jeremy Corbyn, LOTO and John McDonnell on one side, and Remainers such as Chuka Umunna and Andrew Adonis on the other.

In March 2017, he laid out Labour's six tests. They included a deal having 'the exact same benefits' as under a customs union; protections on the future relationship with the EU with respect to migration, national security, regional policy; and preventing 'a race to the bottom.' They were to become the security blanket of Labour's Brexit strategy until 2019. When in doubt, voice the six tests that allowed a broad level of obfuscation through 2017 and most of 2018.

When the general election was called in April 2017 the official Labour position was spelled out in its manifesto as a party committed to leave the EU.

> Labour accepts the referendum result and a Labour government will put the national interest first. We will prioritise jobs and living standards, build a close new relationship with the EU, protect workers' rights and environmental standards, provide certainty to EU nationals and give a meaningful role to parliament throughout negotiations.

Despite this official support for Brexit there were three anti-Brexit groups now operating within the party. Like everyone else at the start of the general election campaign, they all assumed that the Conservatives would win a big majority and they were really fighting for as soft a Brexit as they could get.

Open Britain had a fundamental problem. It was the last group of people who the Labour leadership under Jeremy Corbyn and John McDonnell would listen to. The scars between New Labour veterans (with their younger allies Chuka Umunna and Chris Leslie) and the left were just too deep. After the failure of the chicken coup in 2016, everything that was seen as challenging the leadership was regarded as a Blairite plot. This was already apparent in the antisemitism row. The more Open Britain appeared to be a regrouping of the Blairite centre aligned with other parties, the less traction it had with Labour's leadership.

On the other wing was AEIP. Michael Chessum:

> Before the general election in 2017, Another Europe is Possible wasn't necessarily pursuing a 'stop Brexit' strategy. It was our formal position to demand a referendum with an option to Remain on the final deal. But we weren't really talking so much about that because saw that that wasn't really going anywhere. We were mainly focused around free movement. That was the big one.

Then, a new group appeared, that was to act as the catalyst between these two wings by bringing in funding and organisation for a resolutely anti-Brexit campaign. In deep frustration, David Lammy, the pro-Remain MP for Tottenham, thought there needed to be an organisation to mobilise a pro-EU grassroots campaign. This became 'Best for Britain' run by Eloise Todd. She was a highly experienced executive who had worked within the EU parliament for five years and then Bono's 'ONE' campaign for nine years as a lobbyist. Like Laura Parker from Momentum, she was from Yorkshire, a committed Remainer and unmarked by years of in-fighting within the Labour movement. Todd was also a close friend of Jo Cox, whose murder had overshadowed everything in the 2016 referendum. By January 2017, she was ready to take a leadership role in a new type of campaign. She advocated a clear strategy that would focus not on getting a soft Brexit but on *stopping* Brexit. She hired a team with an eighteen-month campaign plan 'Time to talk, time to listen, time to decide'. It was due to launch on 1 April 2017 but was delayed until 19 April when everything was thrown into confusion by Theresa May. Eloise Todd:

> On 18 April I was on the phone with this guy from a small social agency and he said, 'She's called a bloody election, what are we going to do?' And I said, 'Well there's only one thing to do. Let's do tactical voting, and I'm afraid all that peace, love, and cross-parties' stuff has to fly out the window, because if they get a massive majority, we're screwed. And not only will we have Brexit, they can do what the hell they want. The only thing we've got to do is try to limit their majority.'

Todd switched the focus of a campaign that had not yet been launched.

> I gave my team an instruction and set up a crowdfunder and said, 'We're going to do two things. We're going to promise a tactical vote dashboard to make recommendations in England

and Wales, and we're going to promote champions that are going
to speak up independently against Brexit.'

Coincidently, she had a meeting planned with Tony Blair on the
day the election was called and presented her idea for tactical voting
which was reminiscent of his victories in 1997 and 2001. Todd
then had a launch press conference with Gina Miller:

> The world's press came because they thought she was going
> to announce that she was standing against Theresa May in
> Maidenhead. I'm sure it was quite disappointing for them to hear
> about our campaign plans for a tactical dashboard! We kicked off
> the campaign and we built the tactical vote dashboard. We did
> the crowdfunder for over £400,000, which was biggest political
> crowdfunder in UK history, at the time. And we committed to
> spend it all during the election.

Kensington was an example of the potential impact. It was won
by Labour by only twenty votes after 3,000 people had checked
Best for Britain's tactical dashboard about the candidates in the
constituency. This was replicated in other marginal constituencies
including support for pro-Remain Conservatives such as Anna
Soubry and Nicky Morgan. On election night, the result shook the
anti-Brexit world. Now there was a hung parliament and all to play
for. Eloise Todd had proven the value of a targeted digital campaign
and Best for Britain was suddenly having an influence. The primary
focus now had to be the Labour party and persuading its leadership
that being anti-Brexit was an acceptable position from the left and
not just the centre. Eloise Todd:

> The fact that this agenda was owned by the political centre was
> a massive problem in getting those people on board. We had an
> independent position that recognised the importance of getting
> Corbyn on board through genuinely trying to approach it as
> an independent group which helped to reduce the Conservative
> majority.

Another Europe is Possible also saw the new opportunity. Michael Chessum:

> It became clear to us that the whole game had changed. No majority in parliament for the Tories. We had a strong Corbyn opposition which was on the offensive. So we took a turn after the elections towards being more anti-Brexit, straight out anti-Brexit.

The Labour leadership now had to face Brexit much more seriously. With twenty months to the Brexit deadline, it had to face May's damaged government on one side and an energised anti-Brexit base on the other.

By August 2017, after weeks of negotiations with John McDonnell, Keir Starmer started to push for a time-limited transitional period after the departure date. The 2017 Labour party conference was an opportunity to open the debate further but LOTO and Momentum did not add Brexit to the agenda. Despite this, Starmer made a speech in which he advocated for a deal that retained the benefits of a customs union. There was already muted criticism of Momentum and the Labour leadership for the passivity of the party's stance. The insurgents of 2015 were now the establishment accused of preventing debate. Michael Chessum:

> We were one of the big stories of conference, but it was the left going for free movement and the right going for single market and neither quite going for an anti-Brexit position. They were coming from the economics angle. We were coming from the free movement angle. But, of course, it got deprioritized by Momentum. As far as I understand it, that decision was taken pretty poorly in a back room and under heavy pressure from LOTO.

The left campaign for a second referendum was increasingly frustrated. As *Guardian* journalist Zoe Williams said, 'it was perilous to the soul to throw in with Open Britain'. Williams and other supporters from the left focused on AEIP, the media, academia, NGOs and the TSSA union run by Manuel Cortes, who had always been a committed European.

At a Labour shadow cabinet awayday in February 2018, Corbyn and McDonnell made a move, or 'an evolution' as McDonnell put it, towards support for a customs union itself. Hard Brexit would no longer work and especially not on the issue of the Northern Ireland border and its impact on the Good Friday agreement. On 26 February, Jeremy Corbyn gave a speech. He said that any deal must be about jobs and living standards, security and, crucially, 'during the transition period, Labour would seek to remain in a customs union with the EU and within the single market.' Given Corbyn's long history on the anti-European wing of the party, this was significant. Labour was still accepting the referendum result, but in a much softer way than the government.

The pressure was reinforced by yet more anti-Brexit organisations such as Our Future Our Choice (OFOC) and For Our Future's Sake (FFS), aimed at younger supporters. Then in April 2018, 'People's Vote' was launched in the Electric Ballroom in Camden, North London. Its public faces included MPs such as Chuka Umunna for Labour, his co-chair the Conservative Anna Soubry and Lyla Moran of the Lib Dems. It attracted a wide range of support from comedians, television celebrities, actors and additional funders as well as organisations that feared the impact of Brexit such as the Royal Colleges of Midwives and Nursing and the British Medical Association. Its leadership included advisors from the eras of New Labour and Ed Miliband; Tom Baldwin and Alastair Campbell. Its wide base of political supporters grew to include Caroline Lucas from the Green party, Jo Swinson of the Lib Dems and others from the SNP and Plaid Cymru. The founder of Superdry, Julian Dunkerton, donated £1 million to the campaign.

Over the next six months People's Vote gained traction, but the battle in parliament was still about a soft or hard Brexit. In May 2018, the House of Lords held a series of votes on matters relating to the EU Withdrawal Agreement bill (WA). For the last vote on whether to keep the UK in the Europe Economic Area (EEA) post-Brexit known as the 'Norway Option', Labour instructed its peers to abstain, but eighty-three Labour peers, including Lords Kinnock, Mandelson and most of the big beasts of New Labour, voted for the amendment. When this came back to the House of Commons in June, Labour again asked its MPs to abstain, but seventy-four rebelled to vote in favour of the EEA and fifteen abstained to vote against. It was a three-way split. Keir Starmer now came under fire from both the EEA advocates and the representatives of the Leave constituencies who wanted a clear declaration that Labour understood the result of the referendum. He tried to balance the aims and objectives of the competing tendencies within Labour's ranks. Although the Remainers were making a lot of noise, the more dominant wing within the leadership were the Leavers, who were in favour of Brexit as official party policy for a variety of ideological and pragmatic reasons – the so-called 'Lexiteers'.

The Lexiteers included the old Stalinists of the Communist party tradition who had always opposed European integration as a threat to the Soviet Union. There were others from an ultra-left background who also opposed it as capitalist conspiracy and wanted left internationalism to rule. These two groups had always opposed the EU and the recent events in Greece had confirmed their view of its failings. Seumas Milne and Jeremy Corbyn could be said to have represented these factions.

In LOTO, there was concern expressed that that the EU was a threat to a future Labour government by its rules of state aid preventing the nationalisation that was at the heart of Labour's 2017 manifesto. There was also the less public view that no matter how bad things became under Brexit, as long as the Conservatives owned the problem, Labour would benefit electorally. This partially explained LOTO's lack of enthusiasm for a second referendum.

The wider group of Labour Leavers were less ideological but looked at the referendum result and saw a huge threat if Labour reneged on the original vote. The analysis of the result of the referendum almost passed by without notice in June 2016. Although It was clear that there was a national 52 to 48 per cent majority in favour of Leave, it took much longer for the political map to be defined by constituency breakdown. Research shown in 2018 by Professor Chris Hanretty of Royal Holloway University for BBC Data estimated the proportion of Leave and Remain votes in every constituency and showed a much larger number of parliamentary seats voted to Leave than to Remain. His study showed that of the seats won by Labour in the general election of 2017, 61 per cent had voted to leave the EU. This reinforced the belief that support for a People's Vote would result in Labour losing seats in the north and the Midlands. It was not just an ideological concern of the leadership; it was heartfelt by many Labour MPs who feared for their seats. The calculation was that Labour had to be seen to support Brexit and should triangulate leave voters from 2016 with its core vote in the 2017 general election. This became a dominant argument within the leadership throughout 2018 despite the increasing pressure from the membership for a second referendum.

AEIP was still pushing, although Michael Chessum was the only member of staff until June 2018.

> We ran a nationwide speaker tour over that summer called The Left Against Brexit. For those of us who operate at a grassroots level, you could just sense the base of the Labour party and the Labour left, there was just this kick that was looking at the way the Brexit negotiations were going.

The frustration with being blocked at the 2017 conference was rebounding.

> There was this feeling that we needed to push this debate. The left needed skin in this game. My attitude towards this was, 'Look, if it's me versus the forces of darkness in the leader's office, in a smoky back room where no one's looking, they're going to win every time. If it's us versus Lexit or Brexit triangulation in front of a membership that is overwhelmingly on our side, we've got a chance.' So our strategy was to throw open the doors and shine as much light onto this debate as possible. We wanted this

happening in public view. We wanted this to happen in front of the membership and that's where party democracy came in.

The most visible sign was Labour Live in June, an attempt to create a mini-Glastonbury by the Labour party that had to be bailed out by Unite when it failed to sell enough tickets. For the first time since his election, Jeremy Corbyn saw internal opposition from the left with banners and stickers proclaiming 'Bollocks to Brexit' and 'Love Corbyn Hate Brexit'.

Best for Britain was now channelling funds to groups such as AEIP and Hope Not Hate and developing the strategy with them to get to Labour constituency parties and activists. It was working behind the scenes to push the agenda through the more public-facing groups. It also had 300,000 supporters who were used to lobbying MPs and who helped distribute the data commissioned to show support for a second referendum. This reflected Eloise Todd's lobbying experience, while Michael Chessum was beginning to resemble Jon Lansman in CLPD's heyday. Model motions were sent to every CLP in support for a second referendum. The funding allowed for regional organisers and committed protests.

On 23 June 2018, the second anniversary of the first referendum, People's Vote organised a rally calling for a second referendum. Not a single member of the shadow cabinet was on the platform. Momentum made a move to poll its members, which was discouraged by LOTO and put off until after the Labour party conference. The pressure was coming from the grassroots and membership of the party, exactly those people Jeremy Corbyn and the left had worked forty-five years to represent. He was the first leader to spring from CLPD and claim to take his policy from the membership. Yet he faced pressure for a position with which he did not agree and did not support.

If this was bad for Labour, it was nothing compared to the fight within the Conservative party. The discontent within government bubbled as the Cabinet met at Chequers on 6 July 2018 to agree a collective position for future negotiations with the EU. May announced the negotiating position with the EU. This included a 'common rulebook' on goods but not services, continued reference to the Europe Court of Justice over EU law, and critically a 'combined customs territory' between the UK and EU to avoid a hard border in Ireland and remove the 'backstop arrangement through frictionless trade'. Free movement would end. It was a 100-page document that tried to unify the Conservative party but it came under immediate attack from the Conservative's right-wing version of the Militant Tendency, the European Research Group (ERG). ERG was now working as a party within a party with its own whipping operation in the House of Commons, who condemned it as a sell-out and effective acceptance of a single market. The EU also rejected it as unworkable for good measure. The thin veneer of collective agreement lasted a grand total of three days when David Davis resigned as Brexit secretary, followed a few hours later by Boris Johnson as foreign secretary. It was an opposition's dream.

Polling data among Labour members and in Labour Leave seats was showing stronger support for a new referendum. In August, the *Observer* reported two YouGov polls of more than 15,000 people which showed that 112 seats that had supported Leave would now vote Remain, 341 seats in all. It appeared to show that the biggest switch was in the north of England and Wales, key Labour areas. If this was accurate, the argument against a second referendum on pragmatic grounds looked much weaker.

By the time the Labour conference gathered in Liverpool in September, 151 motions had been submitted to get Brexit on the agenda. The newspapers were full of articles by Labour politicians such as Tom Watson pushing for a People's Vote. For the leadership there were two problems with this. Throughout the summer Labour had argued, not for a second referendum, but for a general election. In private meetings and public interviews it argued that only an election would satisfy the electorate and Labour would commit to a renegotiation with the EU if it won. The second issue was what question a referendum would actually ask. Len McCluskey and John McDonnell had taken the position that reviewing any proposed deal was one thing but repeating the question of whether Britain should remain would alienate support from Leave voters.

On the Sunday night, union and constituency delegates gathered for five hours to composite or combine all their various proposals into one under Keir Starmer's watchful eye. Michael Chessum was outside the hall. Of the 151 motions, 120 were anti-Brexit. Of those, seventy to eighty reflected the model motion that AEIP had lobbied for over the summer. AEIP had galvanised CLPs to send their motions to conference and now had its seven regional organisers identify delegates who would be in attendance and could be briefed by Chessum to get the right result. It was exactly what had happened in 1980 and 1981 when the electoral college was won by the left, with Chessum recreating the role of Jon Lansman nearly forty years before but with rather different tools at his disposal.

> We hired a room in the Liverpool Hilton, across the road from the main conference centre. We must have briefed almost 100 delegates. I had them on a Whatsapp announce list and they all went into that room with the brief. We had a group of about eight to ten more closely briefed delegates who were all on a Whatsapp chat in the room as well. I couldn't get into the room so I was huddled outside on a laptop on Whatsapp going 'Fight! Fight! Fight!'

The five-hour meeting included drafting about having a radical agenda and free movement but the key debate was on the mandate that would be handed to the leadership about Labour's future actions. Should the push to have a general election take precedence over a People's Vote? And would a vote include Labour committing to Remain? AEIP had worked out language with delegates from the GMB and TSSA unions. It was agreed to have an open-ended commitment to the second referendum that would not specifically mention that Labour would campaign for Remain. That would be too provocative. Getting a motion passed within the compositing meeting that would commit the party to a referendum would itself be a big step forward.

The GMB, TSSA and AEIP knew that they would face all sorts of different agendas in the room. There were pro-Brexit unions such as the Bakers, there were delegates who were pro-referendum but anti-free movement and there were those who had their own specific objectives around many other issues that they wanted included. All of this had to be agreed by debate in which any resolution might appear. The longer the debate, the more exhausted delegates became, the greater the danger of being ground down – exactly as was intended by the New Labour inventors of this process twenty years earlier. The power would be in united action by allies such as the GMB and TSSA union delegations and the AEIP's constituency representatives. They could keep their delegates focused on the end result. The backing of the Unison bloc vote for the motion would also ensure that the pro-referendum forces would ultimately have the numbers to carry the day on the conference floor, giving them strong leverage in the room.

Then the traditional power politics of Labour conferences kicked in. The GMB suddenly told Chessum that they were dropping out. The leadership had told Unison to withdraw support and the GMB felt it had to drop out as well. The TSSA, led by Manuel Cortes, ended up proposing GMB's draft as Chessum sat outside the room drafting and redrafting on a laptop. This finally produced a composite motion that would push first for a general election and then keep 'all options remaining on the table, including campaigning for a public vote'. The final composite did not say whether that public vote would advocate Remain. It was deliberately left out to keep the peace with the leadership. Given the history of confused messages between Starmer and McDonnell, it was inevitable that the morning after the compositing session, when both were asked what a vote would mean, Starmer said if Remain was not on the ballot it would be a choice between 'catastrophic and less catastrophic'. At the same time, McDonnell was saying it would not be on the ballot as a question. At times like these, a return to

New Labour's media messaging tactics would not go amiss; they were flatly contradicting one another in public.

On the Tuesday, Starmer made an unusually upbeat and confident speech to conference. He sent his speech to the leader's office for Seamus Milne to edit and send to journalists. He advocated a general election as the best option, followed by a People's Vote. So far so normal, but he then he went off script and said 'No one is ruling out Remain as an option'. The hall went berserk; a standing ovation and cheers.

The euphoria lasted about an hour when Len McCluskey's deputy at Unite, Steve Turner, led the attacks. The conference was happy, Unite and the leadership were not. Turner said that if Labour were to have a second referendum it would only be on the terms of departure; to endorse a deal negotiated by the government of the day or no deal, 'despite what Keir Starmer may have said.' The importance of this composite was that it gave everyone wiggle room to avoid committing to a course of action. The term 'constructive ambiguity' became prominent.

Throughout the autumn, as the debate on Brexit and Labour's position was to become more fraught, the composite became a reference point for all views. Its sequencing of judging Theresa May's deal against the six tests, rejection of no deal, calling for a general election and then 'all options on the table' allowed obfuscation as the Conservatives struggled with their internal divisions. Sooner or later this compromise would run out of road, but by then the Conservatives might be in even deeper trouble than Labour. For now it was enough to allow his supporters to give Jeremy Corbyn the benefit of the doubt.

36

The Fault Lines Exposed

There were eight weeks between the Labour conference and Theresa May bringing her deal to parliament on 17 November 2018. May faced constant attacks from her own ranks. As she battled to get a deal with the EU, rumours abounded of a leadership challenge that would need forty-eight letters to be sent to the chairman of the Conservative's backbench committee, the 1922 Committee. The ERG and those who had resigned her government were determined to fight any compromise and the DUP found itself in a position of huge power as its ten votes became the critical swing element in the House of Commons. Jeremy Corbyn was able to use the conference resolution to avoid trouble, but as the clock counted down, he was under pressure to choose between the Leave and Remain wings of the Labour movement. In both cases, the leaders of the two major parties had to choose between prioritising their internal party management or finding solutions that would appeal beyond their natural constituencies.

These divisions were soon on open display. On 20 October, People's Vote organised another rally in London in which hundreds of thousands marched (some estimates were up to 700,000) for a new referendum. It was the biggest march since the campaign against the Iraq war in 2003. Speakers and attendees included celebrities, actors and comedians including Steve Coogan, Dominic West, Delia Smith and Gary Lineker. The political class was represented by Alastair Campbell, Sadiq Khan, Chuka Umunna, David Lammy,

Caroline Lucas and Anna Soubry. As in the summer, not a single member of Labour's leadership in parliament attended or spoke.

Five days later, Theresa May was due to make a statement to the House of Commons and meet with the 1922 Committee. A series of anonymous Tory MPs were quoted in the Sunday press that she was 'entering the killing zone', she should 'bring her own noose' and she 'would be assassinated'.

In November, a series of polls showed support for a People's Vote. Within the Labour party the most significant was the long-awaited poll on 5 November of Momentum members. The results were:

- 92 per cent of members wanted all Labour MPs to vote down Theresa May's Brexit deal if it did not meet Labour's six tests
- 89 per cent believed a no-deal Brexit should be rejected as a viable option
- 92 per cent prioritised a general election.

In the event of no general election:

- 41 per cent of members supported a public vote in all circumstances
- 28 per cent supported a public vote as an option if no general election
- 12 per cent supported it *only* if there is no general election.

Overall, there was a clear majority for a second referendum if a general election was not called. It all depended on whether the Labour leadership would eventually move to supporting a second vote if all other options failed, which would be the true fight within the movement. Everyone was waiting for Theresa May to bring back her deal and see how Labour's leadership would react.

On 14 November 2018, the British government and the EU published an agreement that was to form the basis of Theresa May's strategy until the end of January 2019. It was signed on 25

November by the UK and the twenty-seven EU member states. The 589-page Withdrawal Agreement (WA) set out the details of the divorce arrangement that included an implementation or transitional period to take place between 29 March 2019 and 31 December 2020. The UK would be treated as part of the EU during this period but would not take part in the European Parliament elections in May 2019. New trade agreements with third parties could be signed during the transitional period to come into force from 1 January 2021. It was a legally binding agreement. Alongside the WA was the Political Declaration that set out the basis for the long-term relationship between the UK outside the EU and the member states. It was only twenty-six pages long. It was not detailed or legally binding. All the focus was on the WA.

In her Lancaster House speech in January 2017, Theresa May had made certainty the key objective. Twenty months after enacting Article 50, the WA produced huge levels of uncertainty. It included an agreement that £35 to £39 billion would be paid to the EU whilst the UK remained in the Union and resolved issues such as security, citizens' rights, Cyprus and Gibraltar. The biggest problem was over the Irish border.

'Best endeavours' would be used to complete the trade negotiations before July 2020, only eighteen months after March 2019. That was a huge aspiration given the complexity of the potential deal. The Good Friday agreement and an open border with Ireland would still have to be guaranteed irrespective of when a future trade deal was concluded. A backstop was thus included that guaranteed an open border until a further trade agreement was mutually agreed. The government's argument was that the backstop would never have to be used, as a deal would be reached before the deadline. This required a leap of faith that May's critics in the DUP and the ERG were not prepared to grant her. The backstop could exist in perpetuity under this agreement.

The reaction within the government was explosive. On 15 November, the day after it was released, Dominic Raab, the Brexit secretary who had replaced David Davis, now resigned. He was joined by seven minsters including cabinet minister Esther McVey.

Between the 2017 general election and 15 January 2019, Theresa May's government suffered thirty-two resignations, twenty-two of which were over Brexit. On 16 November, it was rumoured that Michael Gove, who had recently returned to the cabinet, would also resign, but he chose to stay in office, albeit not as the latest Brexit secretary. That role went to the unknown minister Stephen Barclay. In a piece of political theatre that backfired, Jacob Rees-Mogg, the chairman of the ERG, gave a press conference on the pavement outside parliament where he called for a vote of no confidence in Theresa May. The world waited for it to happen . . . and waited. Like the plotters in the chicken coup, Rees-Mogg had neither a plan nor the votes.

For Labour, the weeks of November 2018 were full of constructive ambiguity; Jeremy Corbyn did interviews and speeches in which he held tightly to the process of winning a motion of no confidence and triggering a general election. He told Sophy Ridge of *Sky News* on 18 November a second referendum was 'not an option for today' and when asked how he would vote if it happened, he stated 'I don't know how I would vote, it would depend on what the options would be at the time'. He told *Der Speigel* that 'we can't stop Brexit'. This elicited a strong reaction from his supporters on the left. Manuel Cortes in *Huffington Post* called for an emergency Labour conference to back a fresh referendum. Thirty CLP delegates who had been part of the compositing meeting called for Corbyn to support a second referendum. In a letter to Corbyn published in *Labour List* they stated his answers were 'not aligned with party policy' and did not show commitment 'to party democracy'.

Although Jeremy Corbyn condemned the WA, when would he move to the next step, a motion of no confidence that might trigger a possible general election? In advance of the promised meaningful vote on the proposals, Theresa May offered him a live television debate. The BBC suggested that it would be in front of a live audience, ITV suggested that it would be just the two of them and a moderator. Both May and Corbyn refused to countenance having representatives of either People's Vote or the hard Brexit positions. The Conservatives wanted it on BBC; Labour wanted ITV. In the end, they couldn't agree to a TV debate at all. If ever there was a sign of dysfunction, it was politicians refusing to appear on prime time television to explain their position.

On 4 December, the first of five days of debate began in parliament. They opened in a state of unparalleled chaos. The government suffered three defeats in the course of a few hours. When it repeatedly tried to avoid publishing the attorney general's advice to the cabinet on the WA, the House of Commons passed a motion by eighteen votes holding the government in contempt of parliament. In the history of the UK's parliament, no government had ever been held in contempt. It was a unique slap in the government's face. Dominic Grieve, a pro-Remain Conservative MP then proposed that if the WA was rejected – which looked like a certainty – then May should have twenty-one days to come back with new proposals that could be amended by MPs. Parliament could seize control. This, too, passed.

On day two, as the debate continued, the Attorney General's advice was published. At this point, Len McCluskey got involved, just as he had during the antisemitism debate in the summer. He called a meeting with Unite's sponsored Labour MPs in the House of Commons and told them not to support the idea of a People's Vote. Claiming that immigration undermined workers' wage levels, he wanted the MPs to support Labour's six tests and a no confidence motion when it eventually came. Although it was estimated that at least sixty-two Labour MPs supported a second referendum along with the minority parties and a few Conservative supporters, this would not be enough to win a vote in parliament without the Labour party calling a three-line whip.

On Monday 10 December, the Court of Justice of the European Union issued its judgement on a case brought by several Scottish MPs and MEPs that the UK could rejoin the EU by simply withdrawing the Article 50 notice. It did not need approval from the twenty-seven countries simply to rejoin the club. Good news for Remainers, if they could get a second referendum.

On Tuesday 11 December the sheer weight of negative speeches in the House of Commons led May to pull the meaningful vote that had been promised for two years. To general uproar, she declared she would go back to European leaders at an EU Council meeting three days later to ask for more reassurance on the backstop. She was attacked from all sides as she continued to declare that the UK would still leave on 29 March 2019. She was now trying to buy time to win over the votes she needed by playing as long a game as she could. No deal suddenly looked like a real possibility.

The ERG pushed ahead with trying to remove May and forty-eight letters were finally sent to the chairman of the 1922 Committee. It held its leadership ballot the following night. May won by 200 to 117. She could not be challenged within the Conservative party for at least another twelve months. In return she promised not to fight the next election. On Thursday 13 December, she went to the European Council to ask for assurances on the backstop and was, inevitably, rebuffed.

Where was Labour throughout this chaos? Pulling the vote also put pressure on Jeremy Corbyn. The SNP, Plaid Cymru and the Lib Dems all demanded Corbyn call his motion of no confidence; he refused by saying the time was not right and it could not win. The strong suspicion now was that he did not want a motion of no confidence because it would lose, and he would then have to face the prospect of choosing a People's Vote. Instead, Labour and the other opposition parties had emergency debates with no outcome attached.

The 2018 conference motion had been clear. There would be a motion of no confidence put down to get a general election. If that failed, all other options would be examined. Remainers and second referendum advocates believed Labour must now take this option. Polls showed over 80 per cent of Labour members wanted a People's Vote and there were mounting demands for a special conference. Yet Corbyn did not act and despite a state of almost total governmental paralysis, the opinion polling throughout December 2018 showed the two parties neck and neck with the Conservatives on 38 per cent and Labour on 37 to 39 per cent. As 2018 drew to a close, there was no government vote, no motion of no confidence and no resolution. Everyone waited for January. Meanwhile, the clock was ticking down to 29 March 2019.

When parliament returned after Christmas it was announced that the five-day debate would resume and the meaningful vote would finally take place on 15 January. On the first day of the debate, Dominic Grieve proposed that if the vote was lost, the government would have to present a Plan B within only three working days. This was passed by 308 votes to 297. Backbenchers appeared to be gaining control over the executive. On day five, the meaningful vote finally took place, almost two years to the day from when Theresa May had made her Lancaster House speech and laid out her twelve objectives. She had been reaffirmed as leader of the party and prime minister only two weeks before, but the vote was the biggest government defeat in history. Only 202 MPs voted for her deal with 432 voting against. Under any other circumstances, the government would have resigned, and a general election called. Yet David Cameron's Fixed-Term Parliaments Act saved his successor; the only way she could be removed was by losing a motion of no confidence. Finally, on the night of 15 January, Jeremy Corbyn ran out of time and called it. The following day he lost it. May won by 325 to 306. The DUP's ten votes had backed her. If the DUP had voted with Corbyn, the government would have lost by one vote.

UK politics now had a government that could not get its primary legislation through, a prime minister who could not be removed by her party, an opposition that could not win a motion of no confidence, and a deal that was in stasis with no other governing activity taking place. Even Theresa May knew she had to do something and for the first time, she reached out beyond her party to try to get cross-party discussions. The minority parties all agreed to meet her, as did prominent Labour backbench MPs such as Yvette Cooper and Hilary Benn. Jeremy Corbyn, whose relationship with May in the House of Commons was glacial (among other things he had appeared to call her a 'stupid woman' in a debate in December), refused a meeting unless no deal was taken off the table. While the government was reaching out to other prospective Labour Leavers,

Corbyn made speeches in Wakefield and Hastings repeating his position that May's red line against the single market had to be dropped. He stuck to his own six tests. For Corbyn, Brexit was a bad smell that just would not go away. Why was he so desperate to avoid committing to a second referendum when his membership seemed so much in favour?

For months, LOTO's position was not to alienate any potential voter in a general election. The strategy of triangulation assumed that Labour's voters in 2017 would naturally vote for it again and the centre ground on Brexit sat with Leavers, so Labour must appeal to them. One last heave could attract Leave voters in those marginal seats who thought Labour was with them. This strategy also appealed to the natural Leavers in the shadow cabinet and LOTO. It was also deliberately lacking in clear leadership; by being passive, the Conservatives would take all the pressure. If Theresa May somehow pulled off her deal, it would split the Conservative party. If no deal happened and was as disastrous as was being predicted by every expert, then the electorate would blame the Conservatives in the next election. It was not based on an ideological view of Brexit itself. The prism was of electoral calculation.

Over the course of January, a succession of frontbenchers attacked the idea of a second referendum. Angela Rayner:

> I don't think that people want to see a delay in Article 50, I don't think that people want to see a second referendum. They want to see parliamentarians working together to carry out what happened as a result of the referendum.

Ian Lavery, Labour's Chairman, wrote an article in the *Guardian* on 25 January. It referred to decades of neglect, economic misery, lack of investment and that Labour would put down an amendment to look at all options, including if all else failed, the possibility of a People's Vote. He continued:

> A radical, redistributive Labour government is the answer to the woes of our country and for our communities, not rerunning

a divisive campaign that seems likely to deliver the same result again and do nothing to answer the demand of a country crying out for real change.

This strategy was completely at odds with those campaigners within Labour who had pushed against Brexit as a matter of principle and who were reading polls in a different way. In a YouGov poll taken on 23 to 24 January 2019, the dangers of the leadership's stance were becoming more apparent. The results were compared to polls taken in May and June 2017. The overall sample results showed a marked drop in Corbyn's personal ratings among some key demographics. Triangulation and a lack of leadership were damaging him personally. When asked whether Corbyn was:

Competent?
• 25 per cent said yes compared to 34 per cent in 2017
Incompetent?
• 54 per cent said yes compared to 46 per cent in 2017
In touch?
• 25 per cent said yes compared to 40 per cent in 2017
Out of touch?
• 60 per cent said yes compared to 44 per cent in 2017
Honest?
• 31 per cent said yes compared to 49 per cent in 2017
Dishonest?
• 41 per cent said yes; compared to 23 per cent in 2017.

If these figures weren't bad enough, the detail among key groups was at least as bad. There was still support among the youngest age group, but the figures were narrowing:

18-24 years olds
• 42 per cent found him competent; 29 per cent incompetent
• 42 per cent found him in touch; 37 per cent out of touch
• 39 per cent found him honest; 30 per cent dishonest.

If the leadership wanted to avoid alienation from its membership, it needed to show a clear path and strategy and at least some connection to its campaigning roots. It was banking on older Leave voters and running the risk of annoying everyone else. It had to show cohesion where the Conservatives were not. A perfect opportunity arose when Home Secretary Sajid Javid published his white paper on immigration for a debate on 28 January, the day before the Brexit debate. The issue of immigration was one that tore at the fabric of the Labour soul. Free movement was a key issue for AEIP and one that divided it from the older view of union leaders like Len McCluskey. For the Labour left, including Jeremy Corbyn and Diane Abbott, it was a moral issue and one in which they had a long history of defending immigrants' rights and welfare. The white paper set out conditions for EU citizens to stay in the UK. It reflected Theresa May's previous role at the Home Office where she had been aggressively against immigrants. This Act established a benchmark value of £30,000 as a salary for those immigrants wishing to stay in the UK. For those 'lower-skilled workers', which on this criterion would include a vast range of people working in the NHS and other vital services, they would be allowed a temporary twelve-month stay in the UK and would not be allowed to bring in dependents or claim benefits. There was an emphasis on those staying learning English, having 'British values' and being financially independent. It pledged in one short clause to improve the current immigration systems that were generally regarded as failing.

These values could not be much further way from free movement or the Labour party's values. It seemed obvious that as shadow home secretary, Diane Abbott would oppose this legislation. Instead, in a scene reminiscent of the welfare row in 2015 that had so damaged Andy Burnham's leadership chances, Labour decided that it would not vote against this bill, despite condemning it. Diane Abbott referred to the 2017 manifesto agreeing that free movement would end and, on that basis, Labour could not resist the bill. It would abstain. Social media and backbench MPs such as Chris Leslie and Angela Smith went ballistic. Only ninety minutes later, Labour announced it would vote against the bill, but only with a one-line whip which meant many of its MPs missed the vote. It was passed by 297 votes to 234 with only 178 Labour MPs present for the vote. It was a failure to oppose a key piece of legislation which an earlier version of Jeremy Corbyn or Diane Abbott would have fought to the end.

The following day, parliament voted on seven amendments to Theresa May's deal. There was the opportunity to vote for a Labour amendment that included a vague reference to a second referendum as well as two other amendments that were designed to act against the possibility of no deal. As yet another deadline crept closer, it was obvious that Theresa May was not going to amend her deal. Under pressure from her party chairman, chief whip and, it was reported, her husband, she moved back into her safe zone of trying to appease the ERG and DUP. This led to an outcome that no one could have predicted even a week earlier.

As parliament voted for each of the seven amendments, the fundamental splits became more apparent. Labour's motion lost by 296 to 327 with two Labour MPs voting against it. Labour also backed a motion from Yvette Cooper that would ensure that if no conclusive deal had been voted through by the end of February 2019, Article 50 would be extended and the possibility of crashing out of the EU with no deal would be made impossible. This was voted down 298 to 321. Seventeen Conservatives voted for it, but among those voting against were fourteen Labour MPs with another eleven abstentions, including eight shadow ministers. A second motion against no deal was passed but it was not binding for the government.

The most remarkable vote was by the Conservatives who were whipped by the government to vote in favour of an amendment by Sir Graham Brady. Theresa May voted down her own deal with the EU and now sought new ways of solving the Northern Ireland question including removing the backstop. After two years of negotiation and an absolute refusal to go back on her own deal, Theresa May was now going back to the EU to reopen the negotiation. The vote was 317 to 301 with seven Labour MPs voting for it.

This vote gave May her best night as prime minister and reinforced her view that only by keeping the bulk of the Conservative party behind her would she stand a chance of winning her deal. She had two weeks until 14 February to go back to Brussels and either win a concession on the backstop or show that she had tried, failed and with only five weeks to 29 March, that her deal was the only option or there would be a no deal Brexit. For this to get through the House of Commons, she would need some Labour MPs to back her. The question was how to get them.

Having spent two weeks refusing to meet her, Jeremy Corbyn finally gave in. May deployed members of her cabinet to meet those Labour MPs who had voted against Yvette Cooper's motion and the seven who had voted for Sir Graham Brady. One of these, John Mann, was openly quoted about the fact that there may be access for his constituency to a £50 billion investment fund set aside by the government. The MPs who were approached were anti-Corbyn, represented constituencies that were in economic distress, had voted Leave and were in highly marginal seats. Even Len McCluskey went in to see what might be on offer. John McDonnell described this as 'pork barrel politics', the same magic money tree that had been shaken for the DUP in 2017.

The parliamentary Labour party was now split into a number of factions. There was the frontbench and its loyalists which kept pushing for a customs union and maintained the need for a general election. It paid lip service to a People's Vote as a last option. There were the twenty-five Labour MPs who had voted against or abstained on Cooper's amendment. There was a group of 70-100 Labour MPs who wanted a People's Vote. There were the die-hard Brexiteers. There were the MPs such as Stephen Kinnock and Lucy Powell who advocated a Norway solution that included a customs union and single market but also free movement.

The government's mad scramble for a position in the two weeks from 29 January to 14 February showed its desperation, but it also showed something about Labour, its leadership and the future of the Labour party. Although the left had won almost total control of the internal machine, it was facing the biggest issue in British politics for three generations and it was being tested. Within the leadership – the NEC, the frontbench, Momentum and Unite – there was an older generation who regarded Brexit as a painful distraction. The left project had to be protected at all costs. Brexit was exposing too many internal rifts.

Those Labour members who had joined in 2015 and 2016 saw the 2017 general election campaign as the springboard to a new type of politics. Jeremy Corbyn's personal position was of vital importance to sustaining this view. They had been sustained in 2018 by the belief that he was open to persuasion, that he could be persuaded to see a second referendum not as a Blairite plot but as a policy overwhelmingly supported by the membership. This hope was now being exposed as naivety. In the Brexit debate of 29 January, he had repeatedly and ostentatiously refused to accept a question from Labour backbencher Angela Smith about a People's Vote and refused to listen to calls for a special conference to even discuss it. These were not the actions of a life-long supporter of party democracy. Repeated off the record attacks on Corbyn were coming from the left, based on confusion about his true motives. Rachel Shabi, an activist of the left and Momentum, wrote in the *Guardian* on 30 January, the day after the immigration bill:

> We're here, then. The point at which a Labour leadership that won support for being different ends up being the same. The stage that jaded observers warned was an inevitability of politics, no matter who was in charge. The day that a political project with impeccably pro-migration credentials triangulated into abstention on a miserable, destructive Conservative immigration bill.

She expressed a view that was being voiced by many from the left who were looking to the future.

> Only a leadership that has grown detached from its support base could produce such a failure of judgment in the first place. It doesn't bode well because, put simply, without letting in the lifeblood of its grassroots, this Labour leadership will atrophy.

If the natural supporters of the left project were getting confused, those who had always opposed the Corbyn leadership found the party increasingly intolerable. There had been a truce of sorts between the various factions of the party from the party conference to end of 2018, but now antisemitism and threats of the deselection of Corbyn critics returned as a series of no confidence motions were passed in the constituency parties. Rumours of a breakaway party being formed involved at least six but possibly far more Labour MPs including Luciana Berger, John Mann, Angela Smith, Chris Leslie, Gavin Shuker and Chuka Umunna. Of course, their leaving would make the left's position even stronger in both selections and future leadership contests. This was compounded by accusations of antisemitism. Luciana Berger, as Chair of the Jewish Labour movement, raised the issue of the backlog of disciplinary cases still unresolved in the party. Labour MPs voted unanimously for the party to answer eleven questions about the handling of the issue. Jennie Formby, the general secretary, told them that she answered to the NEC, not them, and that she would not respond. Two days later Berger refused to answer whether or not she was supporting the launch of a new party. Her local party then moved two motions of no confidence in her. One of the sponsors stated on Facebook, 'she should be exposed for the disruptive Zionist she is'. Berger, a leading Jewish MP, under police guard for months and heavily pregnant, was defended by a host of MPs including Ed Miliband, Jonathan Ashworth and Yvette Cooper. Tom Watson spoke up in the House of Commons:

> As the deputy leader of my party let me say to the honourable colleagues facing that abuse, and in particular my friend and comrade the member for Liverpool Wavertree, that she has our solidarity, our support, as she battles the bullying and hatred from members of her own local party. They bring disgrace to the party that I love.

Under this pressure the local party withdrew its no confidence motions.

The manoeuvring on Brexit now engulfed the competing factions. The TSSA was given research from Hope Not Hate and Best for Britain that showed Labour would lose forty-five seats in a snap election if it supported a Brexit position, including five of its seven MPs in Scotland. It would only lose eleven seats if it supported Remain. It could suffer a collapse of support equal to that in 1983. The report said that Labour's supporters overwhelmingly viewed Brexit as a Tory project. It also said that 17 per cent of Labour's 2017 supporters would be very likely to support a new party to fight Brexit while 27 per cent would be 'fairly likely to'. This report was delivered by Sam Tarry of the TSSA to a meeting including John McDonnell, Jon Lansman and Laura Parker of Momentum. Given its dramatic findings, it was agreed to keep it confidential. Two days later it was leaked. Most of the shadow cabinet and Tom Watson, Labour's deputy leader, had not seen it.

At the same time, rumours abounded about the depth of contact that the government was having with Len McCluskey. Forty members of Unite wrote an open letter to the *Guardian* citing their concern that their general secretary was 'entering into direct negotiations with Theresa May over the Tory Brexit deal'. Given McCluskey's role as an ally of Jeremy Corbyn and the LOTO coterie of Karie Murphy and Seamus Milne, it was seen as a prelude to the leadership supporting a soft Brexit. On Thursday 7 February this suddenly crystallised. Theresa May was in Brussels in fruitless talks with EU leaders. There seemed to be no way she could get the backstop removed as the ERG wanted, however, there might be support from another source. Jeremy Corbyn wrote her a public letter that focused not on the WA but on the Political Declaration:

Labour has long argued that the government should change its negotiating red lines and seek significant changes to the political declaration to provide clarity on our future relationship and deliver a closer economic relationship with the EU. That would also ensure that any backstop would be far less likely to be invoked. The changes we would need to see include:

- A permanent and comprehensive UK-wide customs union. This would include alignment with the union customs code, a common external tariff and an agreement on commercial policy that includes a UK say on future EU trade deals. We believe that a customs union is necessary to deliver the frictionless trade that our businesses, workers and consumers need, and is the only viable way to ensure there is no hard border on the island of Ireland. As you are aware, a customs union is supported by most businesses and trade unions.
- Close alignment with the single market. This should be underpinned by shared institutions and obligations, with clear arrangements for dispute resolution.
- Dynamic alignment on rights and protections so that UK standards keep pace with evolving standards across Europe as a minimum, allowing the UK to lead the way.
- Clear commitments on participation in EU agencies and funding programmes, including in areas such as the environment, education, and industrial regulation.
- Unambiguous agreements on the detail of future security arrangements, including access to the European Arrest Warrant and vital shared databases.

We believe these negotiating objectives need to be enshrined in law before the UK leaves the EU to provide certainty for businesses and a clear framework for our future relationship.

This letter could be judged depending on the recipient. It potentially gave Theresa May her deal on the WA against commitments to be made on the longer-term political declaration, but she would have to drop her own red lines to agree it and divide her own party. Would the national interest supersede the party interest? For Corbyn and the Labour leadership, the five new conditions allowed them to claim credit for supporting a soft Brexit. It was perfect positioning; if May rejected them, the blame could be shifted to the Conservatives for allowing no deal to happen. It might be a future electoral card that allowed Labour to claim its hands were clean. For the supporters of a soft Brexit within Labour – a Norway-type deal or Common Market 2.0 – such as Lucy Powell and Stephen Kinnock, this looked like a possible solution. One estimate was that forty to fifty Labour MPs would support a deal if it included the correct level of protection for workers' rights. Which was exactly what Len McCluskey claimed to be negotiating. For Remainers it was a body blow – it confirmed for them that Corbyn was a Brexiteer. Chuka Umunna immediately disowned it. Owen Smith said he might leave the party. It was clearly a last resort, but Brexit was full of last resorts. However, the positive spin they could put on it was that if May failed to agree, then the only option left for Corbyn would be to support a People's Vote. The left supporters of Remain were stunned.

A YouGov poll in *The Times* showed that the Conservatives had a seven-point lead over Labour at 41 to 34 per cent. Theresa May had a twenty-one point lead over Jeremy Corbyn as prime minister. It also showed that only 60 per cent of Labour voters wanted Corbyn to be leader and that support for Leave had dropped to 39 per cent. Brexit had turned out to be as toxic for Labour as it had for the Conservatives. Jeremy Corbyn's letter was worthy of Harold Wilson at his best. It appealed to the centre ground of the PLP, smacking of pragmatism. It managed to alienate Remain supporters from both the left and the Blairite wings of the party whilst appealing to the soft Brexiteers. While all political attention remained on Brexit, Labour could not move the debate onto other issues that were much more important to it. On 18 February, rumours became reality as Chuka Umunna, Luciana Berger, Chris Leslie, Angela Smith, Mike Gapes, Gavin Shuker and Ann Coffey left the Labour party. The pressures of Brexit and antisemitism were just too much. Was this 1981 all over again? They had no party and no leader but it was the first crack in Labour's façade. Brexit had now caused Jeremy Corbyn to face up to the challenge of leadership. Only time will tell if it will keep his supporters behind him for the challenges ahead.

37

Epilogue

There is a huge opportunity for a dynamic and radical party of the left in Britain in the second decade of the 21st century. Poverty levels are rising, economic growth slowing and the government of Theresa May is consumed and exhausted by Brexit. Across wide swathes of policy – transport, immigration, universal credit, housing and foreign policy – the government is paralysed. Change is needed, and the question for the left leadership of the Labour party is whether it is able to meet the challenge to deliver it.

For Labour's supporters and voters of the last forty years, it has been a long road; the equivalent of supporting a once great football club that has failed to win a serious trophy for decades. Labour's three title winners were Atlee in 1945, still revered; Wilson in 1964, almost forgotten; Blair in 1997, now rejected. It seemed in 2018 that Jeremy Corbyn would never have a better chance to emulate them and win power from a sitting Conservative government.

This book has chronicled the dramatic sweeps, changes and false dawns in Labour's fortunes since the early 1970s. One defining feature is how different its history has been to that of the Conservatives. In the forty years between 1979 and 2019, the Conservatives have almost always been able to bury ideological differences under the promise of power. Only three times did it allow this focus to waver: from 1979 to 1982 when Margaret Thatcher was under attack by her own cabinet but was saved by the Falklands War and the creation of the SDP; from 1992 to 1997 when divisions over Europe damaged John Major's leadership and led to thirteen years of New Labour rule, and from 2013 to 2019 where, once again, disagreements over Europe created the widest possible divisions and the ERG acted as a party within a party.

Labour's history is quite the reverse. The different elements of the Labour movement in the mid-seventies; the big tent centrists, the pragmatic centre-right, the Tribunite soft-left and the New Left have never really gone away, they have just taken different forms over the decades. Every generation has won internal power by defining themselves by what they were *not* and by repudiating the previous leadership. The New Left was defined by its attacks on the Labour governments of Wilson and Callaghan. Kinnock, Smith and Blair defined their need for control against the perceived chaos of the Bennite years. Brown defined his leadership by not being Blair. Miliband won by running against the record of New Labour. The left in 2015 won by running against everyone else.

When Vladimir Derer created the CLPD in 1973, his tactical genius was to recognise that the obscure mechanisms of the Labour party – its conference resolutions, its compositing meetings, its power wielded through union delegations and the block vote – could all be utilised. If the membership controlled the manifesto, the selection of MPs and had a say in the election of leader, then power would flow up from the membership, not down from the leadership. The left won two out of three. The creation of the manifesto always remained firmly in the grip of the leader's office, but within ten years, mandatory reselection and the electoral college had become irrelevant as Neil Kinnock, John Smith and Tony Blair took control of the party. The use of influence and party mechanics were only effective if the leadership was weak or indecisive. If it was determined to rule, it would. This lesson was learned and absorbed by the left in its wilderness years.

The management exercised by New Labour was regarded as a necessary trade-off against winning power. From 1994, it was able to prepare for government by ruthlessly dominating the party. It was a small, single-minded group of people on a mission, able to influence the whole party by its ability to win elections. Its fall from grace and its failure to lock itself into the soul of the Labour movement happened after 2001 when it became convinced that its economic success allowed it to take huge risks with the party's support as a given. Iraq, constant tinkering with public service reforms, control freakery and alienation of the union movement all weakened the substance of that support. Yet still it kept winning. Ultimately there was only one force that could end New Labour – itself.

Ed Miliband's leadership tried to bridge some of these gaps, but in order to win he had to repudiate the New Labour leadership, including his brother. He remains the only Labour leader to have been elected as an MP in the 21st century. The transitional nature of his leadership will be most remembered for the unexpected consequence of Falkirk, with the first signs of the future impact of Len McCluskey, Karie Murphy and the Collins report. Although created in direct response to Falkirk, it ended up producing the conditions that fundamentally changed the party. The end of union control over financing has been replaced by a mass party of over 500,000 members. The unexpected consequence of dropping the bar of parliamentary nominations from 25 to 20 to 15 per cent made a change of leadership possible.

Although Tony Benn and Vladimir Derer both died in 2014, they would have recognised patterns in a lot of what has happened since from earlier years of the battle for the Labour party. New Labour's control freakery on NEC membership and candidate selection has been at least equalled by the left since it has taken power. Just as attacks on the leadership by the left in the 1980s and 1990s were ruthlessly quashed, so attacks on the leadership by the centre and right of the Labour party in 2016 to 2019 have been condemned, usually as 'Blairite plots'. In neither era could either side accept the need for unity; power has always meant domination. This has been exercised in exactly the same way by each generation through the leader's office, at conference and in the NEC.

In policy terms, where Tony Blair, Gordon Brown and Peter Mandelson fashioned something different in the Labour party by appealing to a centre ground that married market economics to social change, Labour's economic leadership under John McDonnell focused on economic policies that would be recognisable to Benn and Derer from the high days of the left on the NEC in the 1970s. The 2017 election manifesto reflected many of the tax and investment proposals from the earlier era.

Where they would have been more surprised was by the rebirth of the left through the engine of social media. Labour's membership went from 200,000 to 550,000 in two years. It led to a new leadership, to the creation of Momentum with over 40,000 members and to a financially secure Labour party that did not depend on union financing. This is a unique event in Labour history. CLPD's few volunteers with their leaflets, copying machines and envelope-stuffing barely registered. It is probable that neither Benn nor Derer would have accepted the downside of social media with the level of extreme attacks that are now a regular part of politics.

In one regard, they would recognise today's left. For three years the left's leadership has papered over its cracks. The fear of blowing it and the memory of 1983 when Neil Kinnock led the counter-revolution has kept them together. As John McDonnell said of the 2015 leadership win, the left had to:

> Get ready, start preparing now because what happens then is you realise after all those years in opposition on the left, all those years of defeat and failure, the responsibility is on your shoulders, absolutely on your shoulders. And if you don't get this right, the left will be out for another generation.

Yet it was perhaps inevitable that traditional disagreements would emerge. They always do.

Jeremy Corbyn was elected from nowhere as a new style of politician based on the promise of a new style of politics. It was brilliant marketing for a 66-year-old who was largely unknown. It depended on a cult of personality that attracted vast numbers of new members who renounced Labour's past and wanted something different and new. It created a level of expectation that no one could reasonably meet. His first two years in office were all positive as he enjoyed unalloyed success, but the seeds of trouble were always there. His private office with Seumas Milne and Karie Murphy was increasingly devoted to an agenda that was based on control and a very narrow view of the wider politics of the movement. This was reinforced by the interventions and support of Len McCluskey. The shadow cabinet and NEC were made compliant. LOTO ruled. Fault lines appeared and revealed that the coalition of 2015 and 2016 built around Jeremy Corbyn as a leader was not fully unified. By early 2019 the battle for the Labour party was not as much left against right, but old-style machine politics against the new membership and Leavers against Remainers. These fault lines can become significant chasms, as the left discovered in 1983.

As antisemitism became a stain on the Labour party, it clearly lacked the management and willpower necessary to tackle it. This says something about the leadership. The default position against any criticism was to attack Blairites, but this started to lose its impact. As LOTO's bunker became deeper, so doubts about Jeremy Corbyn's leadership grew; Brexit exposed this. Attacks now came not from the centre-right, but from the New Left activists who believed in Remain.

It is tempting to think that the power of the left today is unassailable, that its veteran architects have learned the lessons of 1983 and can control events. Jon Lansman has been a recurring figure in this book and a link with the past. He learned a painful lesson in the 1980s by failing to keep an alliance with the soft-left. As he said in 2019, unity is important:

We will only win by having the centre of the party with us and the left in 1983 allowed a massive split to appear between the soft-left and the Bennite left. Momentum positioned itself as unifying force in the 2017 general election. We want to unite people behind the programme we stand for. Jeremy won a broad section of the party. We mustn't lose that. We are here to stay as an agent of change.

At the same time, Lansman never forgot the alienation that he experienced from being on the wrong side of the power struggle in the wilderness years:

> The wilderness was horrible. I was treated as non-person with no contribution to make and a relic from the past. Over time, people would privately talk but eventually we were totally marginalised. You had to keep going and if we hadn't it would have got worse. We preserved the movement to come back and it's very satisfying that we managed to do that.

Since 2015:

> Much of it has been fun. Winning has been fun. I always wanted to win and although it was a massive buzz in 1979 to 1981 and it seemed like we were on the verge of winning, it didn't happen.

For those MPs and supporters of New Labour, the degree of alienation must be similar to that suffered by Lansman. For those subjected to abuse on social media for being 'Blairites', 'Tories', 'Zionists' and 'Traitors' the degree of attack is as hard. Len McCluskey's repeated attacks on anyone who disagrees with LOTO and Jeremy Corbyn are designed to force people out; not keep them in. The danger of Brexit is that two entirely different groups could be alienated. The centrists, who may form their own grouping within parliament, and the new movementists who may feel Jeremy Corbyn is not the leader they were promised. The risks are there. If Jeremy Corbyn suddenly appears to be an old-style Labour leader by failing to listen to the membership, taking advice from a small coterie of advisers and using the power politics of yesteryear, the danger is that the wide support he gathered in 2015 and 2016 from new, young members of the party will suddenly disappear. All the evidence suggests that much of the Labour membership wants a second referendum. LOTO's electoral pragmatism focusing on leavers may be the first step to disillusionment. The decline of membership suffered in 2000 may happen again and once again, it will be the natural supporters of the left who will leave.

Much depends on the leader. When Tony Benn lost his parliamentary seat in 1983, the year Jeremy Corbyn was first elected, the left lost its leader and influence. It regained neither until 2015. Jon Lansman compares the two figures:

> There is no doubt that Tony Benn was more charismatic, more inspiring and he had the experience which gave people a lot of reassurance, but Jeremy has hit the right note at the right time. His time has come, whereas Tony's politics were probably ten years too late . . . Jeremy has grown at every stage. He didn't want the job, he didn't want to be on the ballot paper and he's ended up as leader and potential prime minister. He has risen to the occasion at every stage.

In 1983 Neil Kinnock was waiting in the wings to unite the soft-left and pragmatic right who had stayed after the SDP rebellion. There was no leader from the left to fight him on equal terms. The next leader of the Labour party will either inherit a party that has been elected to power and to whom Jeremy Corbyn hands over the role of prime minister, or a party that has been consigned to five more years of opposition. If that were to happen, the danger for the left is that it has no new leader to replace Corbyn. There is a generational hole left by the wilderness years. The chances of a new Neil Kinnock uniting the party from the centre-left would look much more likely. 2023 would be 1983 all over again. Where will Momentum and the next generation of the left go?

In 2019, Labour will remain a party of protest, or find a formula to defeat a government that is deeply vulnerable? Can Labour set aside the internal divisions to become a party of power again? The battle for the Labour party is still wide open.

18 February 2019

Acknowledgements

This book is a sequel to *The Battle for the Labour Party* that, as a 24-year-old journalist, I co-authored with my uncle, Maurice Kogan, in 1981. The first three chapters of *Protest and Power* are based on that book, which was the first to look at the groups of the left that changed the Labour party in the 1970s. It has taken forty years to return to this subject. I'd like to thank my aunt Ulla and cousins Peter and Tom for agreeing to the reissue of the first book by Bloomsbury and its use in this latest work. Just to keep it in the family, I'd also like to thank my sister Helen and my father, Philip, from Kogan Page Ltd, my first publisher, for releasing the rights to Bloomsbury in the original book.

Aside from all this nepotism I have been incredibly lucky to have a coterie of well-connected people to help find interviewees and give me guidance. It was always my intention to talk to as wide a group as possible from all sides of the Labour movement and from the different elements of its history. I could not have reached them without a small group of friends from different wings of the party vouching for me and using their extensive contacts. I owe Rachel Kinnock, Scarlett MccGwire, Jon Lansman and David Triesman a huge vote of thanks. Nico Doherty was my researcher who did a great job of fact-checking and pointing out what I'd missed. My business partner Sara Munds was, as always, a rock and critic.

A group of astute readers kindly gave their time to read various iterations of the manuscript, including Sara, Rachel and Scarlett who I asked to judge the writing, and Mark Thompson, Sue Bishop, Bill Turnbull, Roger Mosey, Leah Schmidt and Rebecca Kogan who all gave helpful feedback from their different perspectives. The final result and any errors are mine alone. I owe them all thanks for their efforts to make me a competent writer and historian.

When I conceived of this book, I sent Richard Charkin a short treatment which was then taken up by the redoubtable Stephanie Duncan at Bloomsbury. The manuscript was researched, written, edited and produced in a few months, with the late addition of the final chapters in February 2019 as we waited to see what would happen in the rapidly changing world of British politics in the run-up to Brexit. Stephanie and all the team at Bloomsbury, particularly Claire Browne, Kealey Rigden and Rachel Murphy, handled this difficult author with great skill and (mostly) patience. It's been a pleasure working with them.

Finally, my wife Leah and daughters Rebecca and Emma who have had to endure nine months of my latest obsession. The words 'Labour', 'Party' and 'Book' have now been banned from the house. As always, I am grateful for their love, tolerance and support.

Index